W9-AVN-234

WHO, WHAT, WHERE, WHEN, AND *WOW!*

Enter at
your own risk!
MAKES CHILDREN AND ADULTS AS FAT AS PIGS.
GROVE'S TASTELESS CHILL TONIC
ON THE MARKET OVER 20 YEARS
MILLION BOTTLES SOLD LAST YEAR
Uncle John's
BATHROOM READER
BATHROOM READERS' INSTITUTE

Uncle John's WEIRD WEIRD WORLD

WHO, WHAT, WHERE, WHEN, AND *WOW!*

PORTABLE PRESS

Ashland, OR

UNCLE JOHN'S WEIRD, WEIRD WORLD

THANK YOU!
The Bathroom Readers' Institute would like to thank the people
whose advice and assistance made this book possible.

Gordon Javna	Michael Brunsfeld
Jay Newman	Peter Norton
John Dollison	Melinda Allman
Brian Boone	Sean Moore
Thom Little	Aaron Guzman
Kim T. Griswell	Blake Mitchum
Trina Janssen	Rusty Von Dyl
Emma Borghesi	John Javna
Sam Schuna	Thomas Crapper

Cover design by Sam Schuna
Interior layout and design by Moseley Road

For information, write:
The Bathroom Readers' Institute,
P.O. Box 1117, Ashland, OR 97520
www.bathroomreader.com
e-mail: mail@bathroomreader.com

ISBN-13: 978-1-62686-173-2 / ISBN-10: 1-62686-173-0

Library of Congress Cataloging-in-Publication Data

Uncle John's weird, weird world.
pages cm
ISBN 978-1-62686-173-2 (hardcover)
1. American wit and humor. 2. Curiosities and wonders. I. Bathroom Readers' Institute (Ashland, Or.)
PN6165.U5368 2014
428.6--dc23

2013044048

Printed in Shenzhen, China
First Printing
1 2 3 4 5   18 17 16 15 14

Table of Contents

SPORTS AND GAMES

MONEY AND POWER

OOPS!

FORGOTTEN HISTORY

CREATURE FEATURES

WEIRD SCIENCE

Introduction

You are about to enter Uncle John's Weird, Weird World!

For those of you who may be unfamiliar with the *Uncle John's Bathroom Reader*, we've been amassing incredible information and sharing it with our loyal fans for nearly 30 years. Our mission: To search the ethosphere for surprising facts, obscure information, forgotten history, little-known origins, odd news, head-scratching science, crazy quotes, wordplay, and whatever else we can find that we think you'll enjoy (in whatever room you choose to enjoy it). Our credo: "A *Bathroom Reader* is like life. Turn to any page—you never know what you're gonna get."

So who is this Uncle John character? I'm just a regular guy who happens to have an obsession for trivia and a brain like a sponge. I love to share my knowledge with others whenever I can, which also makes me very lucky…because I get to share it with you.

Accompanying me on this crazy journey is my ragtag band of fellow knowledge hounds, collectively known as the Bathroom Readers' Institute. We spend our days scouring books, newspapers, magazines, the Internet, and even bathroom walls to find

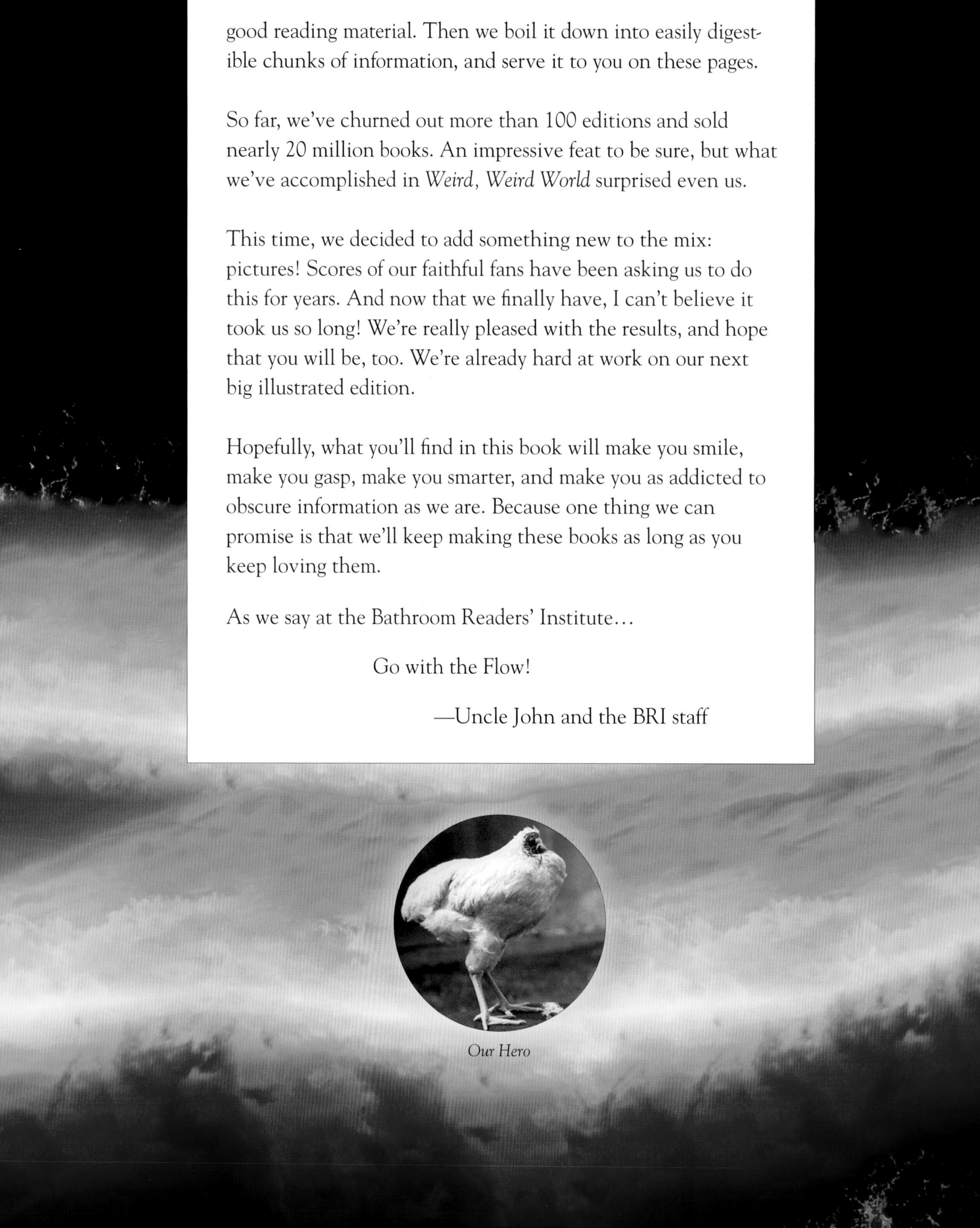

good reading material. Then we boil it down into easily digestible chunks of information, and serve it to you on these pages.

So far, we've churned out more than 100 editions and sold nearly 20 million books. An impressive feat to be sure, but what we've accomplished in *Weird, Weird World* surprised even us.

This time, we decided to add something new to the mix: pictures! Scores of our faithful fans have been asking us to do this for years. And now that we finally have, I can't believe it took us so long! We're really pleased with the results, and hope that you will be, too. We're already hard at work on our next big illustrated edition.

Hopefully, what you'll find in this book will make you smile, make you gasp, make you smarter, and make you as addicted to obscure information as we are. Because one thing we can promise is that we'll keep making these books as long as you keep loving them.

As we say at the Bathroom Readers' Institute...

Go with the Flow!

—Uncle John and the BRI staff

Our Hero

You're My Inspiration

It's always interesting to find out where the architects of pop culture get their ideas. These may surprise you.

Charlie and the Chocolate Factory

In the 1920s, England's two biggest chocolate makers, Cadbury and Rowntree, tried to steal trade secrets by sending spies into each others' factories, posed as employees. Result: Both companies became highly protective of their chocolate-making process. When Roald Dahl was 13, he worked as a taste-tester at Cadbury. The secretive policies and the giant, elaborate machines inspired the future author to write his book about chocolatier Willy Wonka.

The Marlboro Man

Using a cowboy to pitch the cigarette brand was inspired when ad execs saw a 1949 *Life* magazine photo—a close-up of a weather-worn Texas rancher named Clarence Hailey Long, who wore a cowboy hat and had a cigarette in his mouth.

Napoleon Dynamite

Elvis Costello used it as a pseudonym on his 1986 album *Blood and Chocolate*. Scriptwriter Jeremy Coon met a street person in New York who said his name was Napoleon Dynamite. Coon liked the name, and unaware of the Costello connection, used it for the lead character in his movie.

The Odd Couple

In 1962 TV writer Danny Simon got divorced and moved in with another divorced man. Simon was a neat freak, while his friend was a slob. Simon's brother, playwright Neil Simon, turned the situation into *The Odd Couple*. (Neil says Danny inspired at least nine other characters in his plays.)

Charlie the Tuna

The Leo Burnett Agency created Charlie for StarKist Tuna in 1961. Ad writer Tom Rogers based him on a beatnik friend of his (that's why he wears a beret) who wanted to be respected for his "good taste."

"I Don't Get No Respect"

After seeing *The Godfather* in 1972, comedian Rodney Dangerfield noticed that all the characters did the bidding of Don Corleone out of respect. Dangerfield just flipped the concept.

The highly respected Rodney Dangerfield

Missed It by One Letter

pOops!

It's a good thing that we at the BRI never make any typos, or it would be really embarrassing to call out these folks for getting one little letter rong.

- **Michigan election officials** missed it by one letter in 2006 when they printed 180,000 mail-in ballots that used the word "pubic" where "public" should have been. By the time the error was caught (by an election clerk after a professional proofreader missed it), 10,000 ballots had already been mailed out. The remaining 170,000 ballots were reprinted at taxpayers' expense. Total cost: $40,000. A similar—and possibly worse—error occurred on a billboard in Southbend, Indiana (below).

15 best things about our pubic schools.
SOUTHBENDON.COM

- **Pedro Urzua Lizana** missed it by one letter when he chiseled a new design for Chile's 50-peso coin in 2008. In his rush to finish on time, he accidentally left off the bottom stroke of the "L" in "CHILE." Result: 1.5 million coins—all in circulation—are inscribed with "REPUBLIC DE CHIIE." Lizana was fired.

How would I know how she spells her name?

- **David Beckham** missed it by one letter when he gave the Hindi translation of his wife's name to a tattoo artist. It was supposed to be "Victoria," but instead it said "Vihctoria," which is what ended up (in huge letters) on the soccer star's left forearm.

- **Eric Schmidt** missed it by one letter on his business card when he called himself "Chariman of the Executive Committee." (If you missed it, read that first word again.) If only there were some Internet search engine that he could have used to find a good spell-checking program. (Schmidt was the CEO of Google.)

The misspelled tattoo

- **The Georgia Department of Labor** missed it by one letter when a clerk sent a business license application to a carpet-cleaning company called Rug Suckers. But the package wasn't addressed to "Rug Suckers"—it was… something very naughty. The company's owner, Pepper Powell, called the Labor Department to complain, only to be told by the clerk, "I understood you to say that the company's name was Rug *uckers. I asked you twice and you replied, 'Yes, it was.'" Powell told the clerk that he would never dream of giving his company such a foul name. "What would be the point?" Georgia Labor officials agreed. They issued an apology and reprimanded the worker.
- **Stratford Hall**, a personalized holiday card company, missed it by one letter on the cover of its 2007 catalog: "Reliability: always upholding the highest standards for every detal."
- **The Victoria, B.C., Parks and Rec Department** missed it by one letter when it unveiled a statue of Emily Carr (1871–1945), an influential post-impressionist landscape painter and a hometown hero. Apparently nobody proofread the plaque that accompanies the $400,000 statue, which is cast with this inscription: "Dedicated to honour Victoria's best know citizen."
- **KTXL-FOX40 Sacramento** missed it by one letter in 2011 when it ran a graphic during a breaking news story that read "Obama Bin Laden Dead."
- **The *Torrance Press***, a newspaper in Southern California, missed it by one letter on a two-page advertisement: "Sleeping on a Sealy Is Like Sleeping on a Clod." Sealy terminated their contract. (That was the ad department's second chance with its potentially lucrative new client. A day earlier, the *Torrance Press* ran an ad that read, "Sleeping on a Sealy Is Like Slipping on a Cloud.")
- **E.S. Gaffney** missed it by one letter while working at the U.S. Department of Energy. She submitted a proposal to an official whose last name is Prono, but Microsoft Word's auto-correct feature changed it to "Porno." Gaffney's proposal was rejected.
- **The *Moscow–Pullman Daily News*** in Idaho missed it by one letter when it printed a recipe for a "Bowel Full of Brownies." (Does that make it a "typoo"?)

A bowel full of brownies

Misnomers

- The rare **red** coral of the Mediterranean is actually **blue**.
- The **gray** whale is actually **black**.
- Whale**bone** is actually made of **baleen**, a material from the whales' upper jaws.
- The Atlantic **salmon** is actually a member of the **trout** family.
- A **steel**-jacketed bullet is actually made of **brass**.
- **Heart**burn is actually pyrosis, caused by the presence of gastric secretions, called reflux, in the lower **esophagus**.
- The Caspian **Sea** and the Dead **Sea** are both actually **lakes**.
- The horseshoe **crab** is more closely related to **spiders** and **scorpions** than crabs.
- The Douglas **fir** is actually a **pine** tree.
- Rip**tides** are actually **currents**.

Lava Lampology

It oozes, it undulates, it never stops...and it never goes away. Most people thought Lava Lamps had died and joined Nehru jackets in pop culture heaven. But no—they're still around. Here's a quick course on the history and science of lava lamps.

Egg-straordinary History

Shortly after leaving the Royal Air Force at the end of World War II, an Englishman named Edward Craven-Walker walked into a pub in Hampshire, England, and noticed an odd item sitting on the counter behind the bar. It was a glass cocktail shaker that contained some kind of mucous-like blob floating in liquid. The bartender told him it was an egg-timer.

Actually, the "blob" was a clump of solid wax in a clear liquid. You put the cocktail shaker in the boiling water with your egg, the bartender explained, and as the boiling water cooked the egg, it also melted the wax, turning it into an amorphous blob of goo. When the wax floated to the top of the jar, your egg was done.

Light Duty

Craven-Walker saw a money-making opportunity floating in front of him—he could turn the egg timer into a lamp and sell it to the public. He tracked down its inventor, a man known today only by his last name, Dunnet, only to find he had died—without patenting his invention. So Craven-Walker was able to patent it himself.

Craven-Walker spent the next 15 years perfecting the lamp so it could be mass-produced. In the meantime, he supported himself by making "art-house" films about his other passion: nudity. (In those days, pornography was illegal in many places, and the only way around the law was by making "documentaries" about nudism. Whether he was a genuine nudist or just a pornographer in disguise is open to interpretation.)

The essence of the lava lamp: "a motion for every emotion"

Coming to America

In 1964 Craven-Walker finished work on his lamp—a cylindrical vase he called the *Astrolight*—and introduced it at a novelty convention in Hamburg, West Germany, in 1965. Two Americans, Adolph Wertheimer and Hy Spector, saw it and bought the American rights. They renamed it the Lava Lite and introduced it in the U.S., just in time for the psychedelic '60s. "Lava Lite sales peaked in the late sixties," Jane and Michael Stern write in *The Encyclopedia of Bad Taste*, "when the slow-swirling colored wax happened to coincide perfectly with the undulating aesthetics of psychedelia....They were advertised as head trips that offered 'a motion for every emotion.' "

Floating Up...and Down...and Up...

At their peak, more than seven million Lava Lites (the English version was called a Lava Lamp) were sold around the world each year, but by the

Whoa! Horses can kick backward, forward, and sideways.

Austin Powers, international man of mystery and lover of the lava lamp (Mike Myers | New Line Cinema | Warner Bros)

early 1970s, the fad had run its course and sales fell dramatically. By 1976 sales were down to 200 lamps a week, a fraction of what they had been a few years before. By the late 1980s, however, sales began to rebound. "As style makers began to ransack the sixties for inspiration, Lava Lites came back," Jane and Michael Stern write. "Formerly dollar-apiece fleamarket pickings, original Lava Lites—particularly those with paisley, pop art, or homemade trippy motifs on their bases—became real collectibles in the late eighties, selling in chic boutiques for more than a brand new one." Not that brand-new ones were hurting for business—by 1998 manufacturers in England and the U.S. were selling more than 2 million a year.

Lava Light Science

Only the companies that make lava lights know precisely what chemicals are in the lamp, and in what combination—the recipe is a trade secret. But the principles at work are pretty easy to understand:

- When the lamp is turned off and at room temperature, the waxy "lava" substance is slightly heavier than the liquid it's in. That's why the wax is slumped in a heap at the bottom.
- When you switch on the bulb and it begins to heat the fluid, the wax melts and expands to the point where it is slightly lighter than the fluid. That's what causes the "lava" to rise.
- As the wax rises, it moves farther away from the bulb, and cools just enough to make it heavier than the fluid again. This causes the lava to fall back toward the bulb, where it starts to heat up again, and the process repeats itself.
- The lava also contains chemicals called "surfactants" that make it easier for the wax to break into blobs and squish back together."
- It is this precise chemical balancing act that makes manufacturing the lamps such a challenge. "Every batch has to be individually matched and tested," says company chemist John Mundy. "Then we have to balance it so the wax won't stick. Otherwise, it just runs up the side or disperses into tiny bubbles."

Lava, up close and personal

Troubleshooting

What if you have a vintage lava lamp, but can't get it to work right? No problem. The Internet is full of lava light lovers. Here are sample queries we found on the website *www.OozingGoo.com*:

Q: *I have an older style lamp that I bought in the late '70s. It was in storage, but I came across it last year, and I've been using it from time to time. It was working fine, until it was knocked over (darned cats). Nothing broke, but now, the liquid has gone cloudy. Is there anything I can do? I don't want to get rid of it, but it's not as enjoyable any more.*

A: Sorry. I'm afraid you can't fix it, but you can buy a replacement bottle in a range of colors. (Order through the website.)

Q: *My son went to college, and his lava lamp was turned off for a year. Now it won't work. The red lava is lying at the base like a can of worms, and there seems to be some metallic substance/rings in the lava. There is also one-half inch of fluid missing from the lamp. Can this lamp be fixed?*

A: STOP! DON'T MESS WITH IT! You may not even have a problem. The liquid is supposed to be about one-half inch down—it gives room for expansion due to heat. Are you sure you have the right bulb? 40 watt frosted appliance. Leave the lamp on for long periods—4 hours each day for a week—sometimes they come back. Good luck!

Bathroom News

Flush Before You Fly

China Southern Airlines was losing money, so they found a new way to save fuel—but it depended entirely on their customers' cooperation. At the airport, customers are asked to go to the bathroom before they board the plane. Why? Because every time an airplane toilet flushes, it uses up to a liter of fuel. "The energy used in one flush is enough for an economical car to run at least 10 kilometers," says pilot Liu Zhiyuan, who always does his business on the ground before doing it in the air.

A flush in time...

Splish Splash I Was Taking a Bath

A Russian couple were relaxing in the living room of their apartment after dinner one evening. At the same time, in the apartment directly above, a woman was relaxing in her bathtub, soaking in the warm water, her head back, eyes closed, thoughts meandering, starting to doze offffff...creeeak... CRACK! (crumble crumble) CRASH! "EEEEE-Ahhhhggh!" THUD! After the tub and ceiling plaster landed on the floor below, the woman looked up out of the tub to see the couple staring at her in bewilderment. She later told reporters, "They seemed as shocked as I was when they saw me lying there. Naked. In the bath. In the middle of their living room."

Finland is rated the cleanest country in the world.

Snap, Crackle...Flop

Wheaties and Rice Krispies have taken up permanent residency in America's breakfast bowls—these forgotten cereals, not so much.

Fruit Brute: General Mills debuted a line of five monster cereals in the 1970s: Franken Berry, Yummy Mummy, Count Chocula, Boo Berry, and Fruit Brute. The biggest flop of the bunch: Fruit Brute. But it has a cool factor—filmmaker Quentin Tarantino collects old cereals, and his personal box of Fruit Brute has appeared in his movies *Reservoir Dogs* and *Pulp Fiction*.

Graham Crackos: Kellogg's released this graham-cracker-flavored cereal in the late 1970s, a few years before the crack-cocaine epidemic that hit American cities. In light of this, old commercials for Crackos become unsettling. In one, a character named George arrives at a suburban house to deliver a box of Crackos to a family. In the background, a cheery balladeer sings, "Something new is comin' to town, George the Milkman is bringin' it 'round." After the mother takes a bite, she asks George if the cereal will help slow her kids down. "Long enough for them to eat," he replies.

Mr. T Cereal: Based on the fool-pitying strong-man's animated self in *Mister T*, his early-1980s cartoon show, it was made up of crispy corn chunks shaped like the letter T. Essentially, Mr. T Cereal was a clone of Alpha-Bits, but with just one letter.

Ice Cream Jones

Ice Cream Cones: Available in two flavors, chocolate-chip or vanilla, this cereal consisted of crunchy puffs and sugary cones. The brand—which featured a smiling cartoon character named Ice Cream Jones who delivered the cereal to kids on a bicycle—disappeared within a year of its 1987 debut, possibly because parents didn't fall for the claim that the ice cream-flavored cereal contained "four wholesome grains and eight essential vitamins!"

Prince of Thieves: This cash-in on the 1991 film *Robin Hood: Prince of Thieves* had a couple of problems: 1) Manufacturer Ralston-Purina couldn't get the rights to *Thieves* star Kevin Costner's likeness, so they had to put a generic Robin Hood image on the box, and 2) the cereal was supposed to look like little arrows...but came out resembling a certain part of the male anatomy.

Strange Animal Lawsuits

In the Middle Ages, it was not unusual for animals to be put on trial as if they could understand human laws. These lawsuits were serious affairs.

The Plaintiffs: Vineyard growers in St.-Julien, France

The Defendants: Weevils

The Lawsuit: In 1545 angry growers testified to a judge that the weevils were eating and destroying their crops. According to reports: "Legal indictments were drawn, and the insects were actually defended in court."

The Verdict: Since the weevils were obviously eating the crops, they were found guilty. In 1546 a proclamation was issued by the judge demanding that the weevils desist…and amazingly, they did. The farmers weren't bothered by weevils again until 1587. Once more, the insects were put on trial; however, the outcome is unknown.

The Plaintiffs: The people of Mayenne, France

The Defendants: Mosquitoes

The Lawsuit: In the 1200s, a swarm of mosquitoes were indicted as a public nuisance by the people of the town. When the bugs failed to answer the summons, the court appointed a lawyer to act on their behalf.

The Verdict: The lawyer did such a good job pleading their case that the court took pity. The judge banished them, but gave them a patch of real estate outside town where they would be allowed to swarm in peace "forever."

The Plaintiffs: Barley growers in Autun, France

The Defendants: Rats

The Lawsuit: In 1510 the rodents were charged with burglary, having eaten and destroyed the barley crop. A young lawyer named Bartholomew de Chassenee was appointed to defend them. When the rats failed to appear in court, Chassenee successfully argued that since the case involved all the rats of the diocese (the area under jurisdiction of one bishop), all of them should be summoned.

A French tapestry from the early 1500s shows noblemen and women treading and pressing grapes to make wine.

Somebody call my lawyer!

Weevil

Kids as young as seven can join the Society of American Magicians.

When the rats failed to appear again, Chassenee argued that it was because they were scared by "evilly disposed cats which were in constant watch along the highways." Since, by law, the rats were entitled to protection to and from court, the plaintiffs "should be required to post a bond" that would be forfeited if the cats attacked the rats on their way to court.

The Verdict: Unknown, but the publicity gave Chassenee the reputation as one of France's greatest lawyers.

What a load of cock-and-bull!

The Plaintiff: The city of Basel, Switzerland

The Defendant: A rooster

The Lawsuit: In 1474 the rooster was accused of being (or helping) a sorcerer. The reason, according to the prosecutor: It had laid eggs... and as everyone knows, an egg laid by a rooster is prized by sorcerers. On top of that, it was shown "that Satan employed witches to hatch such eggs, from which proceeded winged serpents most dangerous to mankind." The rooster's lawyer admitted it had laid an egg, but contended that "no injury to man or beast had resulted." And besides, laying an egg is an involuntary act, he said, so the law shouldn't punish it.

The Verdict: The judge refused to allow the lawyer's argument and declared the rooster guilty of sorcery. Both the unfortunate fowl and the egg it had allegedly laid were burned at the stake.

The Plaintiffs: The Grand Vicar of Valence, France

The Defendants: Caterpillars inhabiting his diocese

The Lawsuit: In 1584 the Grand Vicar excommunicated the insects for causing destruction to crops, and ordered them to appear before him. When they didn't appear, a lawyer was appointed to defend them.

The Verdict: The lawyer argued his case, but lost. The caterpillars were banished from the diocese. When the caterpillars failed to leave, the trial continued until the short-lived caterpillars died off. The Vicar was then credited with having miraculously exterminated them.

Bizarre Beasties

Short-Order Cook

Kanzi is a 31-year-old bonobo (a pygmy chimpanzee) who lives at the Great Ape Trust in Des Moines, Iowa. Under the tutelage of Dr. Sue Savage-Rumbaugh, the primate can understand 3,000 words and "say" 500 words by pointing at symbols. But Kanzi's most amazing ability is that he cooks his own food. It started when he was young. Said Savage-Rumbaugh, "Kanzi used to watch the film *Quest for Fire*...about early man struggling to control fire. He watched it spellbound over and over." Then she taught the bonobo how to light a match. Now (with human supervision) Kanzi can pan-fry his own hamburgers and roast marshmallows on a stick.

Beauties on the Quack Walk

The Duck Fashion Show is exactly what it sounds like: Ducks wear fancy outfits, including little hats, and waddle up and down a catwalk to the delight of onlookers. Duck handler Brian Harrington has been dressing up his "Pied Piper Ducks" since the 1980s. He takes them to agricultural fairs throughout Australia, where the not-so-ugly ducklings show off the latest quack fashions—including "evening wear," "bridal wear," and "off to the races." They're always a big hit.

Earth's Greatest Hits

Every so often a hunk of rock hurtles out of the sky and slams into our planet, creating a gigantic hole and wreaking havoc. Here are some of the more impressive cosmic splats.

Chicxulub, Yucatán

About 65 million years ago, a giant meteor six miles wide splashed down in the Caribbean region of Mexico. It probably split in two shortly before impact. The result: two craters that are a combined 102 miles in diameter. The meteors fell in a sulfur-rich area of the Yucatán Peninsula, kicking up billions of tons of poisonous dust. The sky all over the world was dark for six months, making global temperatures drop below freezing. That climate change, according to most scientists, caused the extinction of half the Earth's existing species... including the dinosaurs.

Grand Tetons, Wyoming

In 1972 a 1,000-ton meteor entered the Earth's atmosphere high above the Grand Tetons at a very shallow angle and then skipped back out into space like a stone skipping off the surface of a lake (but not before being recorded by Air Force and tourist photographers). If it had gone all the way through the atmosphere, it would have hit Canada and the impact would have rocked the area with a blast the size of the Hiroshima A-bomb.

Tunguska, Siberia

On June 30, 1908, Russian settlers north of Lake Baikal saw a giant fireball streak across the sky. Moments later a blinding flash lit up the sky, followed by a shock wave that knocked people off their feet 40 miles away. The blast was estimated to be more than 10 megatons, toppling 60 million trees over an area of 830 square miles. What was startling about the Tunguska blast was that there was no crater, which led to speculation about the blast: A black hole passing through the Earth? The annihilation of a chunk of antimatter falling from space? An exploding alien spaceship? Research ultimately revealed that the devastation was caused by a meteor about 450 feet in diameter that exploded four to six miles above the ground. If it had landed on a city, no one would have survived.

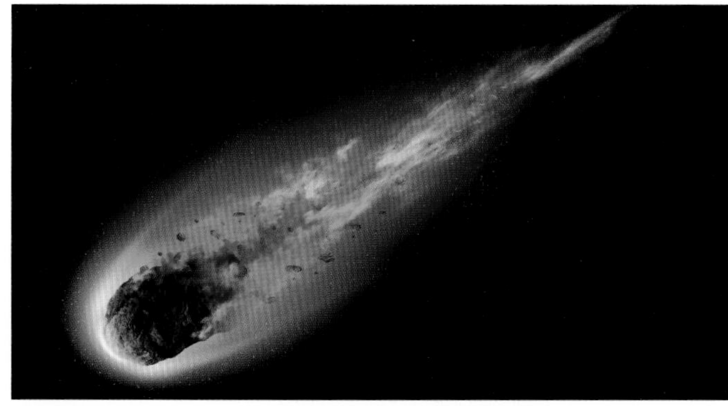

Look out below! A meteor hurtling through the upper atmosphere.

Barringer Meteor Crater, Arizona

Located in the middle of the desert, this crater is important because it was the first one on Earth positively identified as the result of a falling meteor. The meteorite that made the crater was about 150 feet in diameter, weighed about 300,000 tons, and was traveling at a speed of 40,000 mph when it landed. The crater is three quarters of a mile wide and was named for D. M. Barringer, the mining engineer who correctly identified it. He also believed that the actual meteorite was still lodged below the Earth's surface and could be mined for its iron content. (He died before studies revealed that it had vaporized on impact.) Scientists say a meteor of this size can be expected to hit the Earth every 50,000 years. Since this one fell to Earth about 49,000 years ago, we could be due for another one soon.

Meteor Facts

- So far 150 impact craters have been identified on the Earth's surface.
- Oldest crater on Earth: Vredefort Crater in South Africa. It's two billion years old.
- Meteors the size of a basketball hit Earth once a month.
- More than 25,000 meteors bigger than 3.5 ounces hit every year.
- Meteors as large as the one that hit Tunguska impact the Earth every 100 years or so. Bigger explosions, the size of the largest H-bombs, take place about once every 1,000 years.
- Terminology: In space it's a meteor; on the ground, it's a meteorite.
- A large meteorite is always cold to the touch. The outer layers are burned off from its trip through the atmosphere; the inner layers retain the cold of deep space.
- In 1994 the comet Shoemaker-Levy 9 slammed into the atmosphere of Jupiter, generating an explosion the equivalent of 300 trillion tons of TNT. The comet was estimated to be three miles in diameter; the hole it made was larger than Earth. If it had hit our planet instead of Jupiter...well, you do the math.

Barringer meteor crater

But That's Not What He Said!

Because quoting what other people say is often like playing a game of "telephone," what ends up in our collective memory often isn't exactly what the speaker said.

Karl Marx

He supposedly said: "Religion is the opiate of the masses."

But actually: "Religion is the sigh of the oppressed creature, the heart of a heartless world and the soul of soulless conditions. It is the opium of the people," is what Marx really said. The misquote implies that Marx believed religion "drugs" people. The full quote suggests that Marx had a better understanding of why many people flock to religion.

Karl Marx

The Tarzan family calling Cheeta to come for dinner

Tarzan

He supposedly said: "Me Tarzan, you Jane."

But actually: This line was never uttered in any Tarzan film, nor in the original Edgar Rice Burroughs novel.The quote stems from an interview in which Tarzan actor Johnny Weissmuller made up the line as a comment on the films' simplistic dialogue.

John Kerry

He supposedly said: "Who among us doesn't like NASCAR?"

But actually: This quote was well circulated during the 2004 presidential election, often characterizing Senator Kerry as awkward, out of touch, and pandering to blue-collar voters. Turns out that when *New York Times* columnist Maureen Dowd mocked Kerry for the quote in a March 2004 column, it was the first time the quote had ever appeared. Dowd had just made it up.

Sgt. Joe Friday (Jack Webb)

He supposedly said: "Just the facts, ma'am."

But actually: On the TV show *Dragnet*, the no-nonsense cop said, "All we want are the facts, ma'am." Satirist Stan Freberg spoofed the show on the 1953 hit record "St. George and the Dragonet," in which he says, "I just want to get the facts, ma'am." It was Freberg's line, not Webb's, that became synonymous with the show.

Jimi Hendrix played a comb and wax paper "kazoo" on his 1968 recording of "Crosstown Traffic."

William Congreve

He supposedly said: "Hell hath no fury like a woman scorned."

But actually: Close, but not quite. In his 1697 poem "The Mourning Bride," Congreve wrote: "Heaven has no rage like love to hatred turned/ Nor hell a fury like a woman scorned."

Adm. David Farragut

He supposedly said: "Damn the torpedoes! Full speed ahead!"

But actually: According to *The Yale Book of Quotations*, the Civil War admiral never uttered this famous rallying cry at the Battle of Mobile Bay in 1864. It appeared in print in 1878, but news reports and accounts of the battle make no mention of the phrase.

The King James Bible

He supposedly said: "Money is the root of all evil."

But actually: Money is not evil; loving it is. The full quote, misheard over the years, is: "For the love of money is the root of all evil" (1 Timothy 6–7).

Marie Antoinette

She supposedly said: "Let them eat cake."

But actually: The queen was said to have made this sarcastic remark when told that many people in France had no bread to eat. In reality, French revolutionaries spread the rumor to stir up hatred for the monarch and support for overthrowing the crown.

Marie Antoinette (sans cake)

James Cagney

He supposedly said: "You dirty rat!"

But actually: It's commonly assumed to be a line from Cagney's film *Public Enemy Number One*, but the line isn't in that movie…nor in any others. Where the misquote originated is unknown.

James Cagney

Warhol (left) with Tennessee Williams

Warhol the Enigma

"I'd prefer to remain a mystery. I never like to give my background and, anyway, I make it all up different every time I'm asked. It's not just that it's part of my image not to tell everything, it's just that I forget what I said the day before, and I have to make it all up over again."

—Andy Warhol

Lemons

Just about everyone has owned an unreliable car. Uncle John's was a 1979 Triumph Spitfire that caught fire one time when he drove it home from the mechanic. But that piece of junk was nothing compared to these losers.

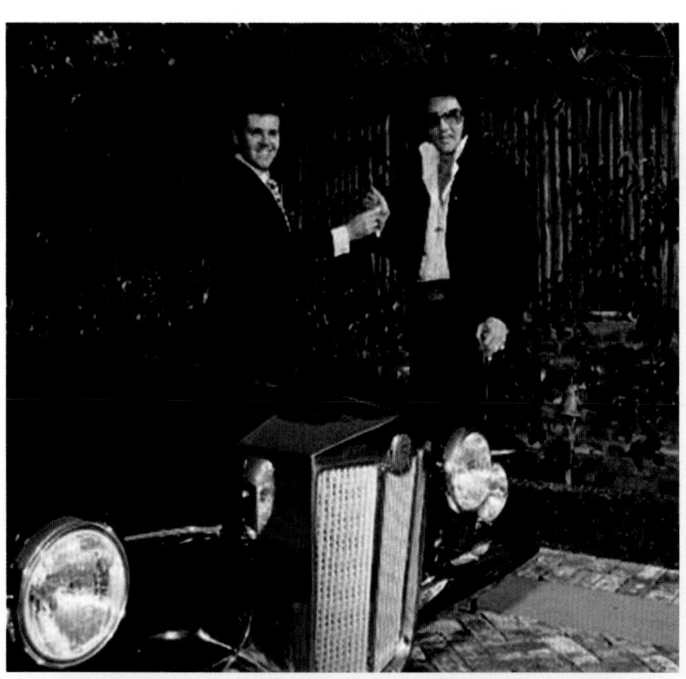

Jules Meyers hands Elvis the keys to his Stutz Blackhawk.

The Stutz Blackhawk (1972–87)

From 1911 through the early 1930s, the Stutz Motor Car company was one of the most exclusive automakers in the United States, but by 1935 it was bankrupt. In the late 1960s, an investment banker named James O'Donnell resurrected the Blackhawk name and began converting Pontiac Grand Prixs into ultraluxury two-door coupes. It had running boards, fake chrome exhaust pipes along both sides of the car, and a spare tire sunk into the trunk lid. Leather luggage that matched the leather seats came standard; mink carpets and a mink-lined trunk were optional. The company also offered to build limousines, convertibles, and four-door sedans based on the same design. The Blackhawk debuted at $23,000 in 1972 and nearly doubled in price to $43,000 for 1973, when the average new car cost about $5,000.

Fatal Flaw: The Blackhawk looked like a pimp-mobile designed by Liberace and was probably the ugliest ultra-luxury car ever made. Besides, how many people were dumb enough to pay Rolls Royce prices for a Pontiac Grand Prix, even if the trunk was lined with mink? Elvis Presley was: He bought the first production model (and later bought four more). Evel Knievel bought a Blackhawk; so did Robert Goulet, Dean Martin, and Sammy Davis, Jr. With its goofy looks and customers like these, the Blackhawk was doomed to be ridiculed as a plaything of celebrities with more money than taste. Still, O'Donnell managed to build more than 500 cars before finally going out of business in 1987.

The Chrysler TC Maserati (1989–91)

In the mid-1980s, Chrysler was looking for a car that would help improve its stodgy image. So it bought part of the Italian auto manufacturer

TC Maserati

Maserati. The two companies then worked on a joint venture: the turbocharged TC Maserati convertible.

Fatal Flaws: Timing was one problem—Chrysler announced the car in 1986, but production snafus kept it off the market for nearly three years, during which time many potential customers bought other cars. Image was another problem—the TC was touted as something new and different, but it was built on Chrysler's K-car platform and was virtually indistinguishable from a regular Chrysler LeBaron convertible, even though it was hand-assembled in Milan and cost a lot more. About the only difference was that the TC had a faulty engine that blew its oil seals when it overheated. And it did that a lot, warping the poorly designed cylinder heads that were one of Maserati's few contributions to the car. Faulty oil pressure gauges kept the problem from being detected until the engine had already been destroyed. Even if the engine hadn't been such a dud, customers balked at the idea of paying Maserati prices for a car that looked just like a LeBaron. Chrysler sold only about 7,300 of the cars before it pulled the plug in 1991.

The Jaguar XJ40 (1986–94)

Jaguar began designing a replacement for its aging four-door XJ6 sedan way back in 1972, but the financial troubles of parent company British Leyland kept it from coming to market for 14 long years. Finally in 1986, the XJ40 hit the showroom floor. It was billed as the most advanced car in the world, complete with electronic self-leveling suspension, a dashboard computer that detected and diagnosed mechanical faults, and nearly two miles of wiring to support these and numerous other fancy electronic gadgets.

Fatal Flaw: The fault dete
supposed to alert owners to m
before they became serious (and
system was the faultiest equipment
few trips to the dealership to service p
turned out to be nothing, most owners ig
the system even when it detected real faults
Result: Repair costs went up instead of down.
XJ40 was supposed to address Jaguar's notorious reputation for unreliability, but all it did was make it worse. It wasn't until Ford bought Jaguar in 1990 that the company's image began to improve.

Alfasud

The Alfa Romeo Alfasud (1872–83)

In the late 1960s, Alfa Romeo announced that instead of building its new mini car, the Alfasud, in Milan, where it had always built its cars, it was shifting production southward to Naples (*sud* is Italian for "south"). And they would manufacture Alfasuds at a rate of 1,000 cars a day, faster than the company had ever made cars before.

Fatal Flaw: Alfa Romeos didn't have a great reputation for quality to begin with, and when production moved south things got much worse. Few workers in Naples had ever built cars before, and they had trouble keeping up with the fast production pace. Even worse, they were building the cars using poor-quality recycled steel from the Soviet Union and sabotaged components made in Milan by workers upset about losing jobs to the south. Door

Jaguar XJ40

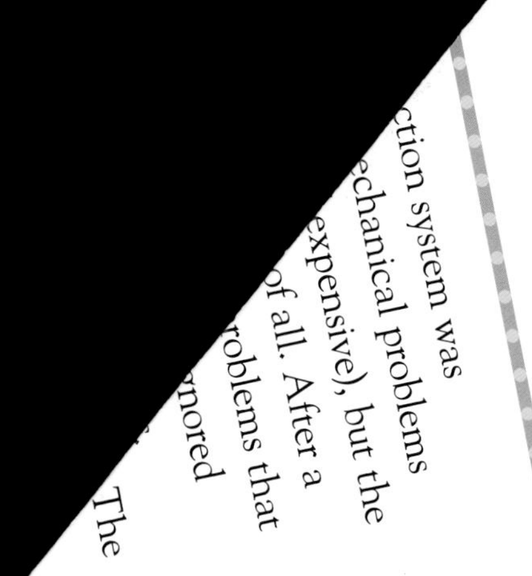

...oke off in owners' ...und them; ... driven too hard. ... few are still ... cheap, little ...d is actually

...1976–89)

... making James Bond's ... close to going under in the mid-1970s when the makers decided that building a four-door sedan—the company's first—would be a good way to raise cash. Aston Martin didn't have the money to engineer the new model from scratch, so the company just extended the chassis of one of its two-door sports cars and built a big sedan onto it. The Lagonda sold for nearly $50,000 when it was introduced in 1976; a decade later it sold for nearly $150,000. For a time it was marketed as the "World's Most Expensive Sedan."

Fatal Flaws: The Lagonda was emblematic of everything that was wrong with automotive design in the 1970s. It was ugly—it had a long, pointy snout that was as angular as a piece of paper folded in half. And it was unreliable—the "futuristic" red LED instrument panels failed so often that they were eventually replaced with little cathode ray TV screens, which failed even more often. The wiring was buggy, the pop-up headlights didn't pop up, the handling was squishy, and the paint job was so bad that the car became known as a rust bucket. That was a lot to put up with in the "World's Most Expensive Sedan," and although the company spent 15 years and untold millions of dollars trying to work out all the bugs, the Lagonda never did catch on with Aston Martin purists. Only about 600 Lagondas had been manufactured by the time the company ended production in 1989.

Aston Martin Lagonda

ODDs and ENDs: Ticker Shock

... eaking news ... ... the crawls and graphics you see on news channels ... ... sometimes get goofed

- "Breaking News: Fire destroyed by home" (Fox 5)
- "Bernanke on the Housing Market: BLAH blah BLAH blah BLAH blah BLAH blah BLAH" (CNN)
- "Space Shuttle traveling nearly 18 times speed of light" (CNN)
- "Will high gas prices cost your kids their eductaion?" (Fox News)
- "Tiger Woods Takes Leave From the Game of Golg" (CNN)
- "Authorities are reminding everyone to now allow impaired drivers to get behind the wheel" (CNN)
- "Breaking News: Many words should fit on this sentence bar. Do not try to type in a paragraph to tell story" (KDKA 2)
- "Norah O'Donnell—The White Ho" (MSNBC)
- "Memorial Day Weekend: Buckle up, Slow down & Drink & Drive" (KARE 11 News)
- "Fight over N.Y. Mosque Shits to D.C." (CNN)
- "dsfgdfgfsfgdf sdfgsdfgsdfgsdfg" (Fox News)

In Australia you can buy emu jerky from vending machines.

What Price Beauty?

Some people will do almost anything to themselves in the pursuit of looking younger and more attractive.

Lips

In 2010 more than a million American women underwent lip augmentation surgery. In addition to older treatments to plump up lips, such as silicone, paraffin wax, and cow-collagen injections, some women have opted to enhance their lips with purified tissue taken from research cadavers or compounds made from their own skin. Cost: $1,500–$3,000

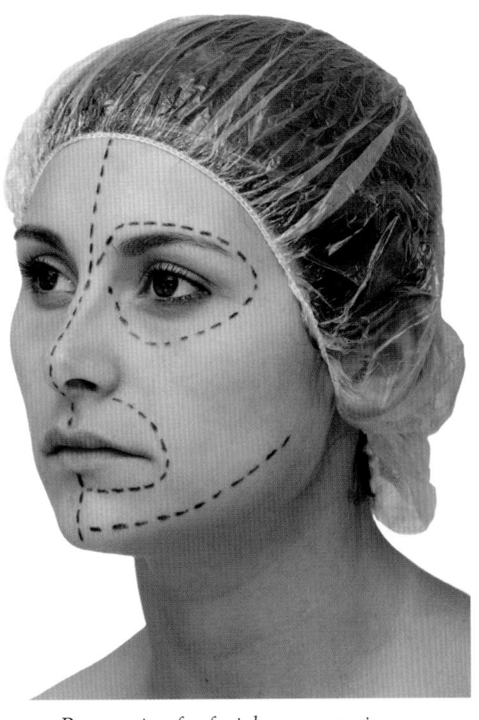

Preparation for facial augmentation surgery

Eyes

A new fad emerged in 2002 in the Netherlands. Ocular surgeons there developed a technique for implanting tiny bits of jewelry into a patient's eyeballs. (It's legal in the Netherlands, but not elsewhere.) Most popular styles of the platinum mini-jewel: a heart, star, or half moon, which is then dropped into a small incision in the eye's clear outer membrane. Cost: €700 ($860)

Feet

The problem with expensive designer shoes—they're often too narrow to fit the average foot. Solution: Some surgeons in Los Angeles and New York are reportedly offering "pinky toe tucks," in which the bones of a woman's pinky toes are surgically shaved to make their toes straighter and their feet narrower. Cost: $1,000 per toe

Abs

The fastest-spreading trend in male cosmetic surgery is "abdominal etching," also known as precision liposuction. Men can have a plastic surgeon suck out only the fat between their stomach muscles. Result: instant "six-pack." Cost: $5,000–$10,000

Butt

Responding to fears of leaking silicone butt implants, some plastic surgeons now offer "Brazilian butt lift" surgery. They liposuction fat from chubby parts of the patient's body, then inject it into their flat buttocks. Cost: $7,000

Tongue

Body-modification enthusiasts use their bodies like a canvas—they favor tattoos, piercings...and, since it first appeared in 1996, tongue splitting. Surgeons use lasers, a scalpel, or even fishing line to split the tongue from tip to center. Cost: $750

"What? Is there something on my face?"

Random Origins

Once again Uncle John answers the question: Where does all this stuff come from?

Kitty Litter

How about a little privacy, please?

In January 1948, in Cassopolis, Michigan, a woman named Kay Draper ran into trouble: The sandpile she used to fill her cat's litter box was frozen solid. She tried ashes, but wound up with paw prints all over the house. Sawdust didn't work, either. As it happened, her neighbors, the Lowes, sold a product called Fuller's Earth, a kiln-dried clay that was used to soak up oil and grease spills in factories. Ed Lowe, their 27-year-old son, had been looking for a new market for the stuff—he'd tried unsuccessfully to sell it to local farmers as nesting material for chickens. On the spur of the moment, he convinced Draper that this stuff would make great cat litter. He put some Fuller's Earth in paper bags and labeled it "Kitty Litter" with a grease pen. Then he drove around trying to sell it. (Actually, he gave it away at first to get people to try it.) Once people tried it, they came back for more.

The Aerosol Can

In 1943 the U.S. Agriculture Department came up with an aerosol bug bomb. It used liquid gas inside steel cans to help World War II soldiers fight malaria-causing insects (malaria was taking a heavy toll on the troops). By 1947 civilians could buy bug bombs, too, but they were heavy "grenadelike" things. Two years later, an inventor named Robert H. Abplanalp developed a special "seven-part leak-proof" valve that allowed him to use lightweight aluminum instead of heavy steel, creating the modern spray can.

License Plates

The first license plates for automobiles appeared in France in 1893. In the United States, the first state to require them was New York in 1901. Two years later, Massachusetts became the first state to issue them. But these early plates were inconsistent. Some were issued by towns or states, others were homemade, and they could be made of wood, clay, porcelain, or metal. More inconsistencies: Some plates displayed the owner's initials, some displayed the owner's registration number, and others were numbered sequentially according to when the cars were purchased. How long did it take for license plates become the 6 x 12-inch metal rectangles we know today? Half a century. In 1957 Congress finally passed national standards for what are technically called "vehicle registration plates."

We're Under Attack!

Many Bathroom Readers *ago, we wrote about the 1938 radio broadcast of* The War of the Worlds. *Here's what happened when a radio station in Ecuador performed its own version of the drama 11 years later.*

Special Reports

left: Orson Welles delivering the infamous broadcast
below: Men Hunting, *a scene from* War of the Worlds

The story of the *War of the Worlds* radio broadcast is well known: In 1938 Orson Welles adapted H. G. Wells's classic science fiction novel into a radio drama told in the form of emergency news broadcasts describing the invasion of Earth by hostile aliens from Mars. Despite the fact that the show was a regularly scheduled installment of *Welles's Mercury Theater On the Air*, and that it was introduced as fiction, many listeners mistakenly believed that Martians had actually landed in New Jersey. Welles later apologized, insisting that he hadn't intended to fool anyone—it had all been an unfortunate misunderstanding.

Six years later, in Santiago, Chile, the radio drama was restaged with similar results. Although the radio station in Santiago advertised the program for a full week before it aired, and made several announcements during the show intended to prevent listeners from becoming alarmed, the broadcast still resulted in mass confusion and was blamed for causing at least one fatal heart attack.

We Interrupt this Program...

Just a few years later, in 1949, a radio station in Quito, Ecuador, decided to produce a new version of *War of the Worlds*, but this one was different: Radio Quito pulled out all the stops in an effort to convince everyone within broadcast range that Ecuador was actually being attacked by invaders from outer space.

Here's how they did it: Weeks before the show was to air, the station began planting fake UFO-sighting stories in the local newspaper. That, producers hoped, would soften up the audience, making them more vulnerable to the suggestion that they were under alien attack. Then they swore all the actors and production staff to complete secrecy and, amazingly, no one leaked the real story to the press. Finally, they began the show by actually interrupting regularly scheduled programming to bring citizens of Quito—a city of 250,000 people—the "breaking news" that the town of Latacunga, just 20 miles south, was under attack.

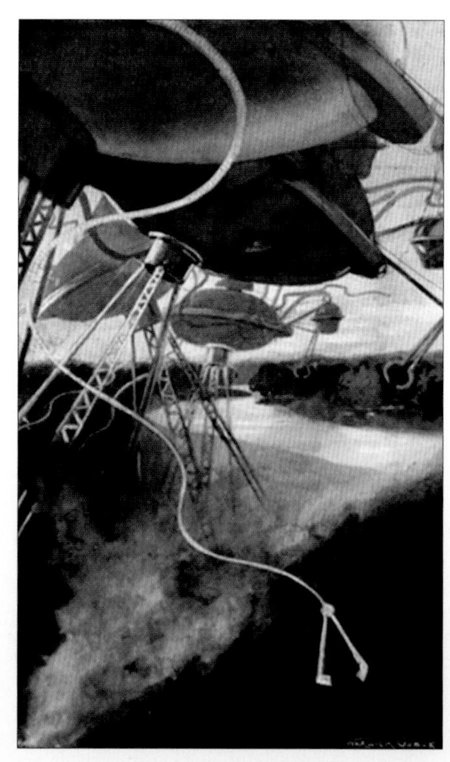

An illustration from Welles's original novel

At that moment, the only people in Quito who knew it was just a radio play were inside the studio. Simply refusing to let on in any way that the story was fake would have been bad enough, but Radio Quito went a step further,

below: Thunderchild, *a scene from* War of the Worlds

and had one of the actors imitate the voice of Quito's mayor. Women and children, the fake mayor instructed, should run into the jungle and hide. All ablebodied men, meanwhile, were to arm themselves in preparation to mount a defense of the city.

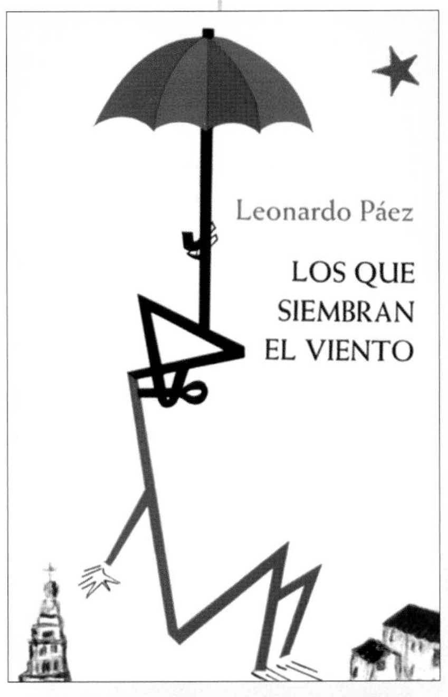

The book written by Leonardo Páez explaining his role in the Quito War of the Worlds *broadcast*

The Show Must Go Off

Listeners, meanwhile, had no way of knowing that what they were hearing wasn't real. Skeptics had only to look out their windows to see that something was going on. Interviewed a half-century later, one witness to that night's events in Quito recalled his family piling into their car to flee the city. He described complete chaos on the roads, where thousands of residents believed they were fleeing for their lives.

The chaos found its way to the radio station, prompting the actors to stop the performance. That's when things got really ugly: Upon learning that the "invasion" had been a hoax, the frightened crowd transformed into an angry mob—they attacked the building that housed the radio station and burned it to the ground.

By the time the Ecuadorian army managed to break up the riot, six people had died in the fire and several more had been injured by jumping out of third-floor windows to escape the flames. In the aftermath, the station's artistic director, Leonardo Paez, was deemed responsible for creating the panic. His misguided sense of "entertainment" brought such an angry backlash from the citizens of Quito that Paez was forced to change his name and flee the country. He never returned.

Random Origin: The Stradivarius

Antonio Stradivari was born in Cremona, Italy, in 1644. As a young man he came under the tutelage of a famous violin maker named Nicolo Amati. He proved a gifted student and, before his training was even completed, began putting his own labels on the violins he made, using the Latin form of his name, Stradivarius. He soon realized that violins could sound even better, so he started experimenting with different kinds of woods and different shapes. That process gave the violin its modern form—shallower in construction, less arched in the belly and back, with an improved bridge and a new varnish, deeper and darker than the yellower varnish Amati had used. In the 19th century, a few more changes were made to the design of violins so that they could be heard more easily in large auditoriums. But for the most part, all modern violins follow the style established by Stradivari more than 300 years ago.

A Stradivarius made in 1703, on display in the Musikinstrumenten Museum, Berlin

Naturally Weird

Fascinating phenomena brought to you free of charge by Mother Earth.

Petrified objects strung above the Knaresborough Well

The Petrifying Well

Do you have a teddy bear that you'd like to turn to stone? (Who doesn't?) Just stuff it in a suitcase and take it to the town of Knaresborough in North Yorkshire, England. There, on the banks of the river Nidd, you'll find a huge, barrel-shaped, smooth, and oddly sculpted rock, from the top of which spring water flows continuously. Hanging from ropes across the rock's face, in the path of the falling water, are a bunch of items, including hats, shoes, and teddy bears, and they've all been turned to, or are in the process of turning into, stone. That's because the water has an especially high mineral content—so high, in fact, that the giant rock itself was created by the dripping water over thousands of years. Anything that's hung on the rock and exposed to the rush of the water gets slowly covered in the minerals and becomes petrified. (Small, soft toys like teddy bears take three to five months to petrify, the site's owners say, while larger, nonporous items can take up to 18 months.) The Knaresborough Petrifying Well has been a tourist attraction in England since 1630, when the grounds were sold by the English crown to a local lord. Petrified items that once belonged to famous people are on display at the site's museum. They include a purse left there by author Agatha Christie and a cowboy hat brought by John Wayne.

John Wayne's hard hat

A roll cloud over Uruguay

(Similar wells can be found in other locations around the world, but Knaresborough's is by far the most famous.)

Penitentes in South America

Penitentes

If you were high in South America's Andes Mountains on a summer day, you might come across a shocking sight: What looks like forest of hard, icy spikes—hundreds of them—all standing close to one another, many up to 15 feet high. They're a rare snow formation known as *penitentes*, Spanish for "penitent ones," and are so named because a field of them resembles a procession of monks in white robes. Scientists say the phenomenon is caused by a combination of the very cold, dry, and windy conditions along with bright summer sunlight, which causes snow to melt in the strange, penitente-forming way.

Roll Clouds

Also known as "morning glory clouds," roll clouds are long, tube-shaped clouds that look like they're rolling across the sky. They're usually low to the ground—just a few hundred feet up—and enormous: The tubes can be several hundred feet across and more than a mile long. They've been known to move at speeds of up to 35 miles per hour, so it's like looking up at a giant rolling pin moving across the sky. And sometimes they travel in crowds of clouds: You might see more than one, moving along in succession. Meteorologists still aren't sure what causes them. They're rare—the only place where they appear regularly is in the sky above the Gulf of Carpentaria in Australia's far north, where they're seen every year in the early morning from September to mid-November.

A Seganku by Any Other Name

Was Shakespeare right when he wrote that a rose by any other name wouldn't smell as sweet? And if so, would a skunk smell the same if we still called it a seganku*?*

Skunk: The Algonquian natives used the word *seganku*, which means "one who squirts." Colonial settlers spelled it "squunck," which eventually became "skunk."

Moose: Another Algonquian name comes from the Narragansetts of Rhode Island, who called the big beast a *moosu*, which means "he strips off," referring to the moose's ability to remove bark from a tree while foraging for food.

Elephant: The Masai people of Africa call the elephant an *olenkaina*, which roughly means "he with hand," referring to the elephant's trunk, which it uses to prepare food, feed itself, pick up objects—and as a portable shower head.

Kangaroo: A long-standing legend said that when explorer James Cook asked the aboriginals of Australia for the name of "that jumping animal," they answered, "*kanguru*," which meant "I don't understand you." Cute, but not true. The tale was debunked in the 1970s. *Kanguru* was, in fact, the aboriginal name for the gray kangaroo, which eventually became the general English name for all kangaroos.

Giraffe: The Arabic people—who probably got the name from an African language—called

giraffes *zarafa*, which means "one who walks swiftly," because the animals can really move when they need to. Afrikaaners called it a *kameelperd* ("cameleopard" in English) from "camel" and "leopard," referring to the giraffe's camellike body and leopardlike spots.

Rhino: It's easy to see how the rhinoceros got its name: *Rhino* is Latin for "nose," and *ceros* is Latin for "horn." Though it's commonly thought that the white rhino is called "white" based on the corruption of a Dutch word for "wide" (referring to the animal's mouth, which is wider than the hooked lip of the black rhino), that is a fallacy. The truth is that etymologists aren't sure exactly why the white rhinoceros is so named. One theory suggests the animal's name comes from its appearance during a favorite pastime: wallowing in wet, chalky soil.

Hippo: The term *hippopotamus*, meaning "river horse," comes from the ancient Greek. However, the semiaquatic hippo's closest relatives aren't horses—or even pigs, which some say they resemble—but cetaceans, like whales and porpoises.

Koala: Ancient aboriginals called koalas *gula*, which loosely means "no drink." The reason: The koala gets most of its liquids from the eucalyptus plants it eats.

Why are you ignoring me?

Just Plane Rude

In February 2008, as a JetBlue red-eye flight from San Diego to New York was boarding, a standby passenger named Gokhan Mutlu was informed that the plane was full. But a flight attendant offered to let him sit in her assigned seat; she would sit in the "jump seat," which folds down from the inside wall of the plane. So Mutlu settled into seat 2E and was happily on his way. But about 90 minutes in, the pilot called the dozing passenger to the front and informed him that the flight attendant was uncomfortable in the jump seat. She needed 2E. And because it was against regulations for a passenger to sit in the jump seat, Mutlu would have to sit in the bathroom…for the rest of the flight. Mutlu protested, but (according to him) the captain said, "This is my plane, under my command, and you should be grateful for being on board." (Mutlu also claimed that while they argued, the flight attendant sat in his seat pretending to be asleep.) So what could Mutlu do? He spent the remaining three hours in the bathroom, with no way to strap himself in during turbulence. As he was deplaning, he says the pilot told him, "I don't think you appreciate what I did for you." Mutlu replied, "You locked me in the bathroom." To which the pilot said, "I brought you home." At last report, Mutlu was suing JetBlue for $2 million.

Year the first *X-Men* comic book was published: 1963.

Stalls of Terror

Going to the bathroom is usually a pleasant experience…
unless you happen to go in one of these bathrooms.

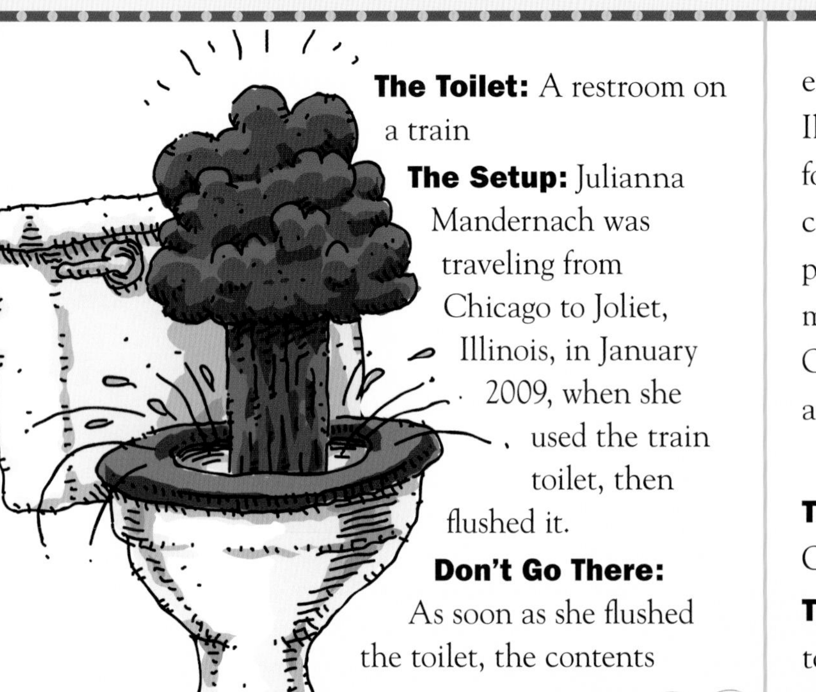

The Toilet: A restroom on a train

The Setup: Julianna Mandernach was traveling from Chicago to Joliet, Illinois, in January 2009, when she used the train toilet, then flushed it.

Don't Go There: As soon as she flushed the toilet, the contents exploded all over her. She sued the Northeast Illinois Regional Commuter Railroad Corporation for an undisclosed amount, saying the exploding commode left her with injuries of a "personal and pecuniary nature." (If we didn't know better, we might think "pecuniary" was legalese for "stinky.") Oddly, the suit wasn't filed until January 2010—almost a year later. The case is still pending.

The Toilet: A portable toilet in the city of Gomel, Belarus

The Setup: A 45-year-old man popped into the toilet to do his business in June 2004.

The Apollo 11 astronaut who didn't walk on the Moon: Michael Collins.

Don't Go There: While the man was still inside the toilet, thieves wrapped a rope around it, loaded it onto a flatbed truck, and drove away. They had not only stolen a porta-potti—they had stolen an *occupied* porta-potti. The man was unable to escape until the bouncing truck jostled the rope loose enough for him to open the door slightly, after which he jumped off the moving truck and broke his collarbone. He was taken to the hospital and later reported the incident to police, who tracked down the stolen toilet to a home in the area...and arrested the poopetrators.

The Toilet: The downstairs bathroom in the home of the Bueller family of Rechlinghausen, Germany

The Setup: In November 2008, Dennis Bueller, 13, had just sprayed the bathroom with a can of aerosol air freshener. Then, being a 13-year-old, he started playing with his dad's lighter.

Don't Go There: The can ignited—and blew Dennis through the bathroom window and out into the yard. "I sprayed the toilet because it smelled," he later told Britain's *Daily Mail.* "Then I began fiddling with a lighter my dad left in there and suddenly there was this big orange *whoosh!* of flame. I woke up outside with my clothes burned off me and smelling like a barbecue." Dennis suffered burns over much of his upper body, but he recovered. "He realizes he was a bit dim," said his father.

The Toilet: A home in Iowa City, Iowa

The Setup: Nitasha Johnson, 20, was in the bathroom with her sister one evening in March 2010. They were arguing.

Don't Go There: The argument escalated. Johnson grabbed the lid off the toilet tank and bashed her sister with it. The sister was taken to the hospital, where she was treated for injuries to her foot and finger. Nitasha Johnson was arrested on charges of domestic assault...and thrown in the can.

The Toilet: The great outdoors, Croatia

The Setup: Ante Djindjic, 29, was riding his motorcycle on a rural road in September 2007 when he had to pee. So he stopped to take care of business by the side of the road. The next thing he knew, he was waking up in a Zagreb hospital.

Don't Go There: Djindjic had been struck by lightning. Doctors think the lightning bolt must have grounded itself through his urine stream. "I don't remember what happened," he said later. "One minute I was taking a leak and the next thing I knew I was in hospital." Luckily, all Djindjic suffered were minor burns on his chest and arms.

Pop Music Anagram Quiz

Unscramble each of these anagrams to find the name of a pop star or band. *(Answers on p. 287)*

1. Yea armchair!
2. Very bolo!
3. Multi-bearskin jet
4. Lard-fed pep
5. Ai! S.O.S!
6. Eat new sky
7. Hairy camera!
8. Be girly jam
9. Spoon god
10. Miking eel, you
11. Is so merry
12. These bleat
13. Fish, toe, frog
14. Silver spy eel
15. O, pant lordly!

Odd fact: The average female opossum has 13 nipples.

Symbolic Origins

They're on flags, packages, street signs, trash cans, and even bathroom doors. Where did they come from?

Biohazard

Story: In 1966 Dow Chemical engineer Charles Baldwin was developing medical-hazard containers for the National Institutes of Health's cancer division. Scientists at all of the different medical facilities he visited dealt with dozens of biological hazards, such as used needles, viruses, and blood, urine, and stool samples. There was no one universal way of telling at a glance which substances were especially dangerous (or "biohazardous"). With the help of the Dow package design team, Baldwin developed several "warning" symbols—all bold, universal, and easy to were presented with the different designs. But the one most remembered was a "blaze orange" circular symbol with sharp points. Today it's one of the world's most recognizable symbols. Even people who don't know what "biohazard" means quickly grasp that it's saying "beware."

Star and Crescent

Story: Non-Muslims strongly associate this symbol with Islam. But Islam doesn't officially recognize it, and it didn't even start out as a Muslim symbol. Around 342 B.C., Philip of Macedon (Alexander the Great's father) was laying siege to Perinthus, a city in Byzantium. According to legend, after months of direct attacks, the Macedonians had decided to tunnel under the city walls when a meteor suddenly ripped through the sky. The omen terrified them, and they retreated. The meteor and the crescent moon—the symbol of the Byzantines' protector god, Hecate the Torch Bearer—became the symbols of the city of Byzantium (now Istanbul). The Ottoman Turks, who conquered the city in the 14th century, put the symbol on their flags. After the Turks adopted Islam, the symbol came to be associated with the religion as well.

The Ankh

Story: The ankh is an ancient Egyptian symbol that was adopted by other ancient cultures too. There are many theories on how this shape came to be associated with the idea of "life": a mirror used for self-contemplation, a phallic symbol, or a double-bladed axe representing life and death, for example. A recent theory by bio-Egyptologists Andrew Gordon and Calvin Schwabe suggests that the ankh is a representation of a bull's thoracic vertebra, which, when viewed in cross-section, does look like an ankh. The bone sits between the bull's shoulders, just above the forelimbs, which Egyptians believed held the animal's vital life-force.

Hockey great Wayne Gretzky once paid $125,000 to play a game of tennis against Andre Agassi.

Male and Female

Story: The conventional explanation is that the "male" symbol represents the shield and spear of the ancient Roman god Mars, a symbol of masculinity, and the "female" symbol is the mirror held by Venus, an icon of femininity. But taxonomist William Stearn says those symbols are actually corruptions of the ancient Greek letters used to spell out the names of those Roman gods. The Greek name for Mars was *Thouros*, which starts with the letter theta, or θ. Venus was called *Phosphoros*, which starts with the letter *phi*, or Φ. Stearn claims that over time Greek writers shortened the words *Thorous* and *Phosphoros* into just *theta* and *phi*, which evolved into the symbols we're familiar with today.

Mr. Yuk

Story: The Pittsburgh Poison Control Center created this symbol in 1971 to coincide with the introduction of their 24-hour accidental-poisoning hotline. It was designed to replace the common skull-and-crossbones symbol on poisonous materials because children equated that one with pirates, adventure, and fun, instead of danger. Among the symbols tested, children responded most negatively to a neon green, grimacing face with a protruding tongue that looks like it just swallowed something horrible. One child called it "yucky," leading to the name Mr. Yuk. Regional poison control centers around the United States distribute over 40 million black-and-green Mr. Yuk stickers every year.

The Body Eclectic

"You start out happy that you have no hips or boobs. All of a sudden you get them, and it feels sloppy. Then just when you start liking them, they start drooping."

—Cindy Crawford

"My mother told me I was dancing before I was born. She could feel my toes tapping wildly inside her for months."

—Ginger Rogers

"The only things I really love about myself physically are my ankles and my hair."

—Valerie Bertinelli

"Although the whole mind seems to be united to the whole body, I recognize that if a foot or arm is cut off, nothing has thereby been taken away from the mind."

—René Descartes

"Your body is not the real you, it's just the meat you live in. I like that: it means that the real me doesn't really have a humongous butt."

—Jessica Zafra, author

"If you ever need a helping hand, you'll find one at the end of your arm."

—Yiddish Proverb

If your body was a used car, you wouldn't buy it.

Jerry Seinfeld

"Yeah, some kids called me fish lips because I had these really full lips. Now I'm sure all those same girls are getting collagen injections, so I'm having the last laugh."

—Denise Richards

"You can only hold your stomach in for so many years."

—Burt Reynolds

Snow Big Deal

Think you know about snow? Well, there's a winter storm watch...starting on this page.

- Snowflakes get their start when water vapor in the atmosphere condenses and becomes ice. In the middle of the flake is usually a teensy bit of dust that collected the vapor, which in turn collected more moisture and froze into a water crystal.
- The shape of snow crystals is determined by atmospheric moisture and temperature—the warmer the air, the bigger the crystals. The shapes of the flakes also depend on air temperature.
- Most snowflakes are six-sided, but if you took a microscope outside during a snowstorm, you might see rod-shaped flakes, cup-shaped flakes, and eight- or twelve-pointed stars.
- The best snowmen are made when the air temperature is closer to the freezing point. That's because snow that's slightly melted will stick together better than the dry, fluffy stuff.
- According to one report, the largest snowflakes ever fell near Fort Keogh, Montana, in January 1887. People claimed the monster flakes were "larger than milk pans." Some scientists say that might have been possible, noting that snowflakes measuring 6 inches across are real (though rare) occurrences.
- Although it can vary greatly depending on the wetness or dryness of the snow, the general rule of thumb is that 10 inches of snow equals an inch of rain. If the snow is dry and fluffy, the amount of snow is higher. If the snow is wet and heavy, the ratio can be as low as 3 inches of snow to an inch of rain.
- In 1941 New Hampshire became the first state to create an official policy for using salt on snow and icy roads. Salt lowers the melting point of snow, making roads more wet than icy.
- The U.S. record for the most snow came in the 1998–99 season in Washington State when the Mt. Baker Ski Area received 1,140 inches... which made a snowbank about the height of a nine-story building.

Staying cool.

Huh?

From a letter to the editor in the Arkansas Democrat*:*

"As you know, Daylight Saving Time started a month earlier this year. You would think that members of Congress would have considered the warming effect that an extra hour of daylight would have on our climate. Or did they?"

The sun's surface is transparent.

Just Plane Facts

"If God had really intended man to fly, he'd make it easier to get to the airport," wrote George Winters. With that in mind, here are a few facts to contemplate as you fly the friendly skies.

Duty free? No, the Unclaimed Baggage Center in Scottsboro, Alabama

- The Unclaimed Baggage Center in Scottsboro, Alabama, sells 10 million items of lost luggage every year.
- Air travel is the second-safest mode of transportation. The elevator/escalator is first.
- Airlines update the fares in their computers 250,000 times a day.
- The first airplane toilet was a hole in the fuselage through which a passenger could see the countryside passing below.
- Only 25% of the passengers in First Class pay full fare. The rest are upgrades, frequent fliers, and airline employees.

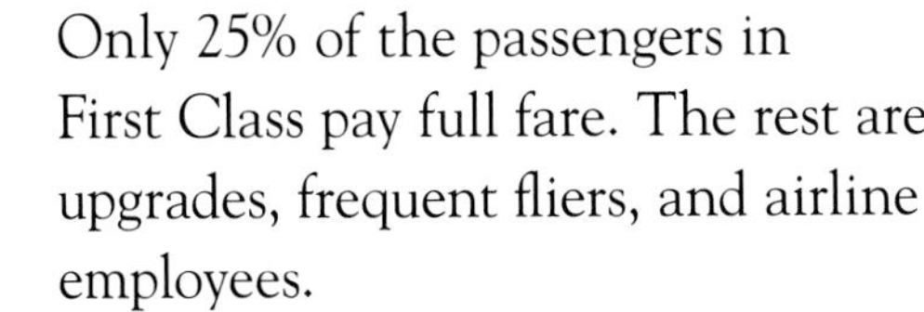

Airbus 380

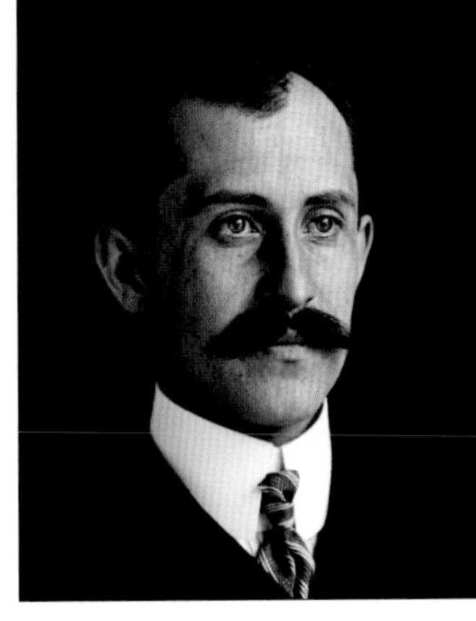

If you have a bad flight, blame these guys: Wilbur and Orville Wright.

- Tolerance for alcohol drops by 30% at 30,000 feet—which explains the number of staggerers disembarking from flights.
- In 2009 the Civil Air Authority reported 3,520 cases of "air rage." The average perpetrator is 30 to 39 years old. A disproportionate number are seated in Business or First Class. Alcohol is usually involved.

Traveler displaying symptoms of reduced alcohol tolerance

- Between 1916 and 2000, more than 3,500 sightings of Unidentified Aerial Phenomena (UAP) were reported and documented by military, civilian, and commercial pilots and their flight crews.
- The biggest passenger plane in the world is the Airbus 380 superjumbo jet. It can carry 853 passengers and, if set upright, would rise 23 stories.
- A Boeing 747's wingspan (120 feet) is longer than the Wright brothers' first flight (112 feet).
- The longest commercial flight is the nonstop from New York to Hong Kong, traveling 8,439 miles over the North Pole in 15 hours, 40 minutes.

Your ride is here.

Some prehistoric dragonflies had wingspans as big as a hawk's.

40 Uses for WD-40

More than 60 years after its invention in 1953, WD-40 can be found in four out of five American homes. Here's what it can do. (Warning: We haven't tried all of these.)

The List

1. Removes grime from book covers.
2. Prevents mud and clay from sticking to shovels and boots.
3. Removes grease and oil stains on clothes.
4. Softens new baseball gloves.
5. Cleans chrome fixtures in bathrooms.
6. Makes puck slide faster on a hockey table.
7. Cleans and softens paint brushes.
8. Cleans and protects cowboy boots.
9. Removes crayon from walls, carpet, wall-paper, plastics, shoes, toys, chalkboard, monitors, screen doors, and rock walls.
10. Eases arthritis pain (spray the painful joint.)
11. Cleans piano keys.
12. Removes super strong glue from fingers.
13. Keeps wicker chairs from squeaking.
14. Removes scuff marks from ceramic floors.
15. Cleans and protects copper pots and pans.
16. Polishes and shines sea shells.
17. Removes water spots from mirrors.
18. Removes tea stains from counter tops.
19. Keeps pigeons off window ledges (they hate the smell).
20. Removes ink from carpet.
21. Keeps metal wind chimes rust free.
22. Prevents mildew growth on outdoor fountains.
23. Removes gunk from plastic dish drainers.
24. Cleans dog doo from tennis shoes.
25. Removes tomato stains from clothing.
26. Gets ink stains out of leather.
27. Removes roller-skate marks from kitchen floor.
28. Unkinks gold chains.
29. Penetrates frozen mailbox doors.
30. Removes tar from shoes.
31. Cleans silver plates and trays.
32. Removes soap scum in the bathroom
33. Polishes wood.
34. Takes the squeak out of shoes.
35. Removes a stuck ring from a finger.
36. Wipes off graffiti.
37. Removes Silly Putty from carpet.
38. Loosens burrs, thistles, and stickers from dogs and horses.
39. Removes bumper stickers from cars.
40. Removes duct tape.

And Three Really Odd Uses

- When John Glenn circled the earth in 1962, his spacecraft, *Friendship VII*, was slathered in WD-40 from top to bottom. NASA engineers hoped it would reduce friction upon reentry.
- In 2001 a burglar in Medford, Oregon, broke into an apartment wielding a can of WD-40. He sprayed the occupant with the lubricant and demanded money, then escaped with the man's wallet and car keys (but was later apprehended).
- Responding to inquiries from the Pike Anglers Committee of Great Britain, the British Environment Agency states that they "do not recommend the use of WD-40 as fish bait."

Ready for action!

The World's Most Dangerous Races

Any race—whether by foot, car, or dogsled—has its risks. But some are a lot riskier than others.

Isle of Man Tourist Trophy Race

Since 1907 this island in the Irish Sea has hosted what many consider to be the most prestigious motorcycle race in the world—and one of the deadliest. The route, called the Snaefell Mountain Course, takes 200 twists and turns through 37 miles of narrow streets and rural roads lined with stone walls, pushing the limits of the drivers and motorcycles. (The course was originally designed for bicycles.) In 1914 the race claimed one of its first casualties when a rider named Frank Walker, who had been in the lead, blew a tire. He kept riding, in spite of falling twice, and in a desperate attempt to catch the leaders, he shot past the finish line and crashed into a wooden barrier. He was posthumously awarded third place. Since then, the average speed has risen to almost 130 mph, causing more fatalities. To date, 225 racers have lost their lives.

Isle of Man Tourist Trophy Race

Big Pardubice (*Velka Pardubicka*)

The course of this venerable steeplechase lies in the quiet university town of Pardubice, 65 miles east of Prague in the Czech Republic. Every October since 1874, about a dozen riders and their horses gallop off from the starting line for a 10-minute cross-country race over a 4¼-mile course littered with 31 different jumps, ditches, hedges, and other obstacles. Collisions are commonplace, along with spectacular falls. The fourth jump, known as the Taxis, is considered the most treacherous steeplechase jump in the world. Clearing its 5½-foot-high hedge jump is one thing; navigating the 8-foot descent and the 16-foot water ditch that follows is next to impossible. At the 1984 event, two horses crashed into a third as they fell at the Taxis jump, creating a flailing mass of hooves and riders. More horses fell into the quagmire, and by the end of the race, only 4 of the 12 starters crossed the finish line. No riders were killed, but one horse was injured so badly that it was euthanized on the spot. The high frequency of limb-crushing injuries to both horses and riders has made Big Pardubice the object of numerous animal-rights protests—as well as one of the most-watched races in Europe.

Baja 1000

This sprint across 1,000 miles of treacherous desert is an automotive clash of dune buggies, motorcycles, and ATVs. Drivers battle brutal terrain while

5 most popular fruits worldwide: bananas, apples, oranges, watermelons, and plantains.

clockwise, from left: The Big Pardubice; The Iditarod; Baja 1000

navigating blind turns, washouts, and silt-choked gullies. To make it even more interesting, spectators dig potholes and place homemade jumps on the course, a practice so common—and so dangerous—that drivers alert each other to the makeshift hazards via radio. Over the 40-year history of the event, there have been dozens of crashes and hundreds of injuries but relatively few fatalities. Most of those have involved spectators (and one cow) rather than drivers. Indy 500 legend and Baja 1000 competitor Parnelli Jones once called racing the Baja "a 24-hour plane crash."

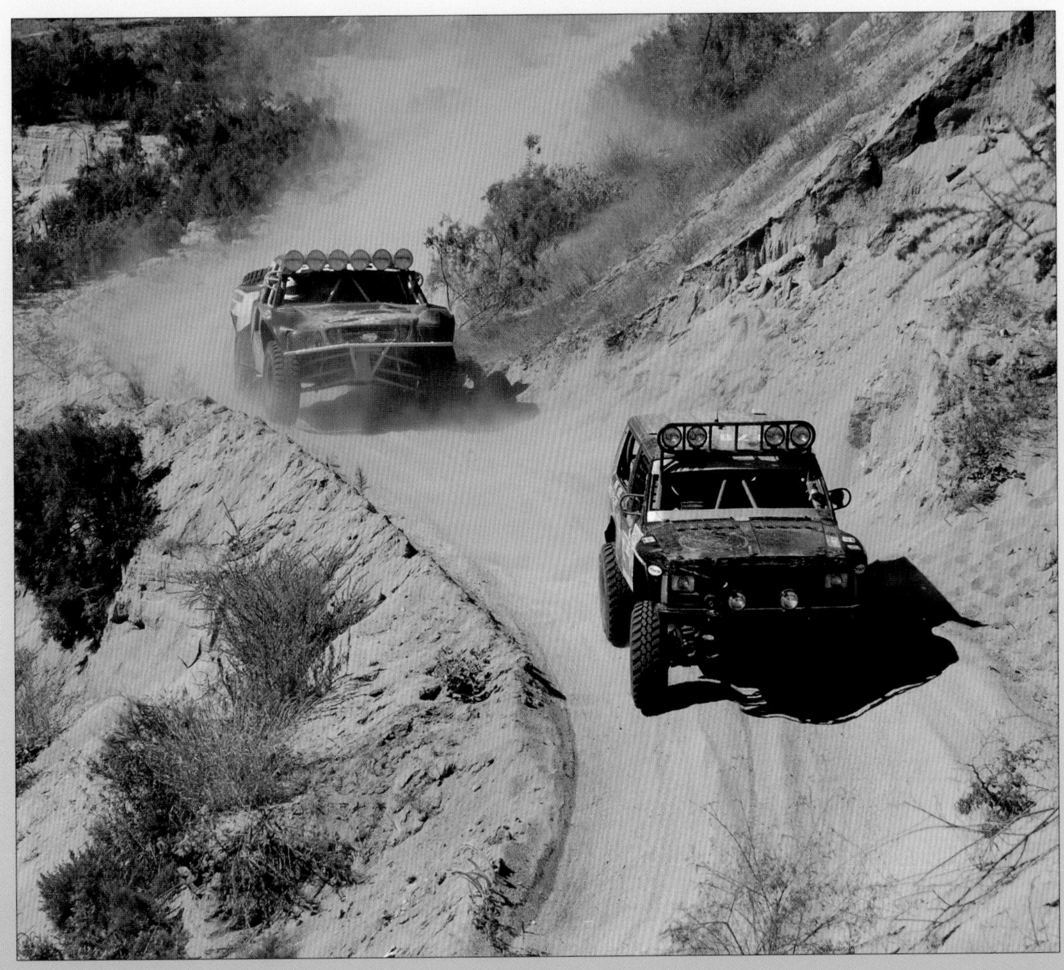

The Iditarod

In the world's most famous dogsled race, 50 mushers and as many as 800 dogs brave 1,150 miles of rugged Alaskan backcountry in temperatures that can reach –50°F. This so-called

The best powder snow for skiing is made of "stellar dendrite" snowflakes.

"Last Great Race on Earth" is extremely difficult to finish—more people have climbed to the top of Mt. Everest than have crossed the Iditarod finish line. Depending on the severity of the weather, the course can take 10 to 17 days to complete. Human fatalities are rare—the most common injuries are bruised ribs, broken wrists, and concussions from falls off the sled. But the dogs aren't so lucky. The average sled dog burns about 11,000 calories per day during the race—roughly eight times as much as a Tour de France cyclist burns. Each year about one dog out of three is unable to finish the race due to injury or fatigue and has to be flown out. And since 1973, at least 142 dogs have died during the Iditarod.

Dakar Rally

Dakar Rally

In 1977 French racecar driver Thierry Sabine got lost in the Sahara desert during a road race from France to the Ivory Coast in West Africa. The experience convinced him that the North African desert was a perfect location for an off-road endurance car race. A year later, the first Paris–Dakar rally took place, a grinding 5,000-mile marathon that usually begins in Paris, winds its way south to the Mediterranean Sea (where the cars are ferried across to Africa), and then zigzags across the Sahara through some of the world's most inhospitable terrain before it ends in Dakar, Senegal. Over the years, 45 drivers and crewmembers have been killed by every conceivable kind of hazard—crashes due to blown engines and tires, sandstorms, flash floods, and even raids by hostile Tuareg nomads. In 2008 the race was canceled due to threats from Mauritanian rebels. The competition has three classes—cars, motorcycles, and trucks—and teams will do almost anything to win, including sabotage. Each year fewer than half of the racers finish the course. The level of personal risk is so high that every vehicle displays a sign listing its riders' blood types. In 1986 founder Sabine became a victim himself when the helicopter he was riding in crashed into a dune in Mali during a sandstorm.

Marathon Des Sables

Marathon Des Sables

Runners have their choice of grueling events: marathons, biathlons, and triathlons. And then there's the granddaddy of all footraces: the Marathon des Sables

Sleep tight: There are over 6 billion dust mites in your bed.

(Marathon of the Sands), a week-long 150-mile race across the scorching desert of southern Morocco. It's the equivalent of running 5½ marathons…in 120°F heat. And you have to carry all your own food—enough to last you the whole week. Each year about 700 runners start the race; barely half reach the end. Not surprisingly, dehydration is the single biggest reason runners drop out (a medical team following the racers provides intravenous saline drips). And even the failures can be spectacular.

The race's most celebrated washout was an Italian runner named Mauro Prosperi, who was about halfway through the race in 1994 when he got lost in a sandstorm. He wandered off course by several hundred miles, ran out of food and water, and was forced to eat bats and drink his own urine to stay alive. In despair, he tried to commit suicide by slashing his wrists…but he was so dehydrated that his blood clotted too quickly for him to bleed to death. Nomads eventually found him in an abandoned mosque, babbling incoherently. Prosperi recovered and came back to compete in three more Marathons des Sables. He never won.

Mauro Prosperi tries to stay on track.

"Pasteur Cured Rabbis"

…and other real answers given on real tests by real students, collected by their poor, poor teachers and passed along to us.

- "Sir Francis Drake circumcised the world with a 100-foot clipper."
- "Ancient Egypt was inhabited by mummies and they all wrote in hydraulics."
- "The Magna Carta provided that no man should be hanged twice for the same offense."
- "The Civil War was between China and Pakistan."
- "A myth is a female moth."
- "Miguel de Cervantes wrote *Donkey Hote*."
- "The colonists won the War and no longer had to pay for taxis."
- "Benjamin Franklin discovered electricity by rubbing two cats backward and declared, 'A horse divided against itself cannot stand.'"
- "To change centimeters to meters you take out centi."
- "Lincoln's mother died in infancy, and he was born in a log cabin which he built with his own hands."
- "In the Olympic games, Greeks ran races, jumped, hurled the biscuits, and threw the java."
- "The sun never set on the British Empire because the British Empire is in the East and the sun sets in the West."
- "Louis Pasteur discovered a cure for rabbis."
- "Lincoln went to the theater and got shot in his seat by one of the actors in a moving picture show."
- "The French Revolution was accomplished before it happened and catapulted into Napoleon."
- "*Homer* was not written by Homer but by another man of that name."

Hindu holy days begin at sunrise, Jewish holy days at sunset, and Christian holy days at midnight.

Evacuate Now!

No, it isn't an article on Ex-Lax. These are the stories of some of the most famous and infamous mass evacuations of people in history.

Dunkirk, France

Trapped! In May 1940, nine months into World War II, several German Panzer divisions tore into France, then swooped north, and in just days reached the English Channel. In the mayhem, hundreds of thousands of British, French, and Belgian troops were trapped in a pocket around the harbor town of Dunkirk, France, surrounded by a much larger and better-equipped German army. If they were killed or captured, said British Prime Minister Winston Churchill, "the whole root, core, and brain of the British Army" would be lost, setting the stage for a Nazi invasion of Great Britain.

Winston Churchill

Evacuate! British leaders decided to evacuate as many soldiers as possible. They put out a call to all English citizens for private vessels—and more than 700 responded. On the night of May 26, an armada of 200 destroyers, along with the 700 fishing boats, yachts, barges, sloops, and private ships of every kind, poured across the English Channel. Those "little boats of Dunkirk," as they were later called, motored up to the shoreline, loaded soldiers aboard, and ferried them to the waiting destroyers. This went on for nine days, all amidst the din (and danger) of artillery fire from land and strafing bullets and bombs from Luftwaffe airplanes. When it was over, an astounding 338,226 soldiers had been carried safely back to England. The evacuation of Dunkirk was hailed as a "miracle," proved to be a huge morale-booster for the British, and may have thwarted the German invasion of Britain.

Troops being evacuated from Dunkirk on a destroyer about to berth at Dover, May 31, 1940

Mississauga, Ontario

Trapped! Minutes before midnight on November 10, 1979, an axle on a 106-car freight train in Mississauga, just outside Toronto,

Which part of a map is the ideo locator? The part that says "YOU ARE HERE."

Emergency work underway on the derailed Canadian Pacific freight train in Mississauga, Ontario, in 1979

broke, derailing 23 cars. Their cargo: explosive and toxic chemicals. The derailment immediately caused several propane tanker cars to explode and spilled the contents of several more—caustic soda, styrene, and toluene—onto the tracks. The fire from the propane tanks ignited vapors from the chemicals, causing a massive explosion with a fireball nearly 5,000 feet high. (People 50 miles away saw it.) Among the derailed cars, officials found a tanker carrying 81 tons of chlorine. And it was leaking. If it blew up, it could create a cloud of chlorine gas that could wipe out the entire city.

Evacuate! The entire city—including six nursing homes and three large hospitals—would have to be evacuated. Thousands of police, firefighters, emergency medical technicians, doctors, nurses, bus drivers, and other volunteers worked around the clock driving people to makeshift evacuation centers outside of town.

When it was over, more than 218,000 people were moved in less than 48 hours, and not a single life was lost. Until the much less successful post-Hurricane Katrina operation, it was the largest peacetime evacuation in North American history. (It took five days to get the site under control and, thankfully, the chlorine tank never blew.)

The *Republic*

Trapped! On the morning of January 24, 1909, the RMS *Republic,* a 570-foot luxury ocean liner, was heading from New York toward the Mediterranean with 742 passengers and crew aboard. At the same time, the SS *Florida,* a smaller ship, was headed into New York with more than 800 Italian immigrants aboard. In deep fog about 50 miles off Nantucket, Massachusetts, the two ships collided, killing three people on each ship. The *Republic* lost all power and was taking on water; the *Florida* was seriously damaged but still had power and wasn't sinking. Luckily for all involved, the *Republic* had a wireless radio onboard, and the operator sent out a distress signal. (It was the first time in history that a wireless radio had been used for a large disaster.) Another luxury liner in the area, the *Baltic,* got the signal and set out for the scene.

Illustration showing the damage to the bow of the SS Florida

Evacuate! The *Florida* quickly came about and was able to get alongside the sinking *Republic,* a feat in itself, considering the condition of both ships and the fact that they were in thick fog. Over the next several hours, everyone on the *Republic* was evacuated. When the *Baltic* arrived twelve hours later, they did it again, transferring passengers and crew from both ships—more than 1,500 people. And in eight-foot swells. It took eight hours, but they managed both evacuations without a single injury or death. The *Republic* went down while the rescue was still under way; the *Baltic* and the *Florida* made it safely back to New York.

Extra: The *Republic* was part of the White Star Line fleet and in its day called "unsinkable." Three years later, another White Star "unsinkable" went down in the North Atlantic: the *Titanic.*

There are about 10,000,000,000,000 ways to play the first 10 moves in a game of chess.

Eerie scenes from the town of Pripyat, abandoned after the Chernobyl nuclear plant explosion in 1986. left: A rusted and blackened ferris wheel; right: scores of gas masks strewn across a floor.

Extra Extra: Among the items purported to have been on the *Republic* when she went down: $265,000 in cash belonging to the U.S. Navy; several hundred thousand dollars in silver ingots; passengers' jewelry worth hundreds of thousands of dollars; and a secret five-ton shipment of American Gold Eagle coins straight from the mint and meant for the Czar of Russia. The ship was located in 1981. Two salvage trips have so far found no treasure…but future trips are planned, so stay tuned.

Pripyat, Ukraine

Trapped! You've heard of this town's more famous neighbor: Chernobyl, the city of 14,000 located about 10 miles southeast of the infamous nuclear power plant that experienced a massive meltdown on April 26, 1986. Pripyat was much closer to the plant, just two miles away, and it was the home of nearly 50,000 people. Even worse, the prevailing winds at the time of the accident shifted, blowing the radiation straight into Pripyat. Within hours the entire city was contaminated with radioactive fallout. The people in the city were told nothing. The next day, 1,100 buses arrived from the Ukrainian capital of Kiev, about 70 miles away, but the drivers had to wait for an official order to do anything.

Evacuate! The order didn't come until midnight. When it finally did, those buses left with every man, woman, and child from every home, nursing home, and hospital—all 50,000 people—and in less than three hours the city was completely empty. Despite all the waiting and unnecessary exposure to radiation, the evacuation was an extraordinary success and without question saved many lives.

Extra: Today, there is still an "exclusion zone" with a radius of about nine miles around the plant where people are not allowed to live. The city of Pripyat still stands outside the zone, but more than two decades later, it's still a ghost town.

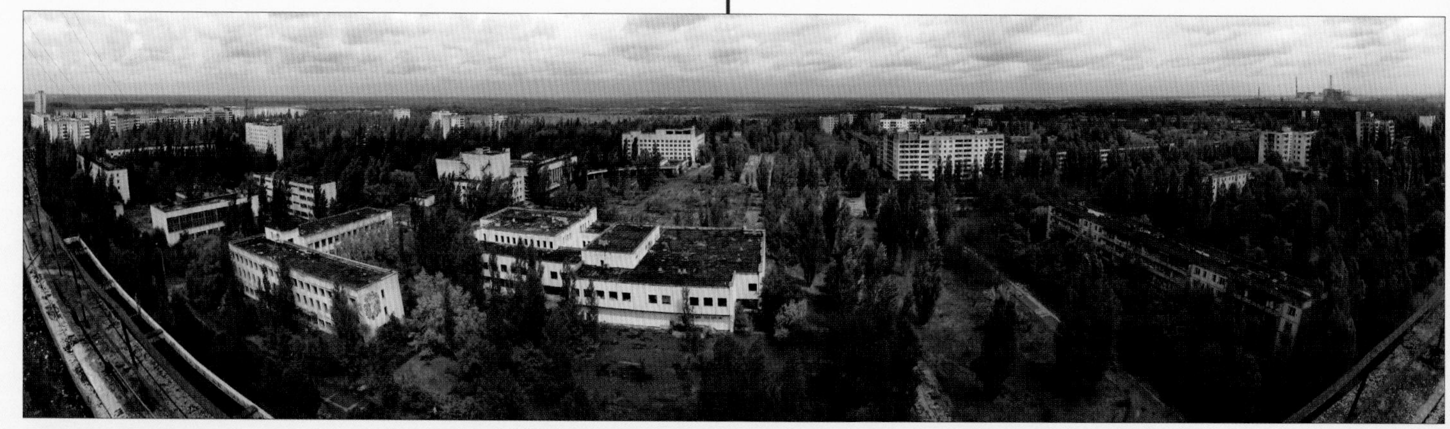

The abandoned town of Pripyat. The Chernobyl nuclear power plant reactor no. 4 can be seen on the horizon at far right.

Q: "Little Briar-Rose" is the original title of what fairy tale? A: "Sleeping Beauty."

Freaky Fish Tales

Sometimes we wonder if fish are actually aliens.

Fish Out of Water

Ginger the goldfish lives in a bowl on top of a cabinet in the home of Barbara and Alan Woodward. In late 2008, Barbara awoke to discover that Ginger had jumped out of his bowl and was lying on the floor behind the cabinet. The cabinet was too heavy for Barbara to move, she was late for work, and Alan wasn't there. So she left. When Barbara returned 13 hours later, she expected to find a dead fish, but there was Ginger, flopping around in the middle of the floor. "It's a Christmas miracle!" Barbara told reporters. (Biologists have been unable to explain how the fish survived for so long without water.) Ginger doesn't swim as well as he used to, but there is now a cover over his bowl just to be safe.

My, What a Pretty Eye You Have

When the "Cyclops Shark" showed up on the Internet in 2011, most people dismissed it as a Photoshopped hoax. But it turns out that the picture is real. The dead fetal shark was removed from the belly of a pregnant female caught by an angler in the Gulf of California. Like an actual cyclops, it has one large eye located in the center of its face. The strange shark was sent to Mexican biologist Felipe Galván-Magaña, who confirmed that the lone eye had all its optic nerves, so had the animal been born, it most likely would have been able to see. However, it was too malformed to survive for long. Calling the find "extremely rare," Galván-Magaña said such genetic mutations are not unheard of—there have been a few other documented cases of cyclops animals.

Weird catch of the day: an albino cyclops shark

Where the Sun Don't Shine

"The key thing for fish living on coral reefs is to find somewhere to hide and not get eaten," said Martin Attrill, a marine biologist from England's Plymouth University. He's talking about pearlfish, found along Australia's Great Barrier Reef. They will take up residence in any "hole" they find suitable, even an oyster (hence the name). But the pearlfish's preferred home is actually inside the butt of a sea cucumber (known as the "ocean's slug"). "The pearlfish are essentially living in a burrow," said Attrill. "They come out at night to feed from the sea cucumber's colonic cavity. It is moist and safe in there, and quite often, the pearlfish live in there in pairs."

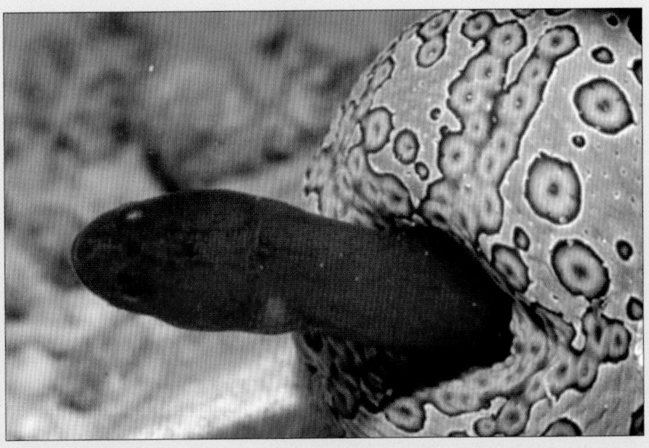

A pearlfish emerging from a sea cucumber's butt

Cotton swabs cause more injuries than razor blades.

The Greenspan Effect

To lighten things up, here's a silly wordplay game that Uncle John used to play when he was a kid. Take a boring quotation and give it fun new nouns, verbs, and other parts of speech. The resulting quote won't make sense, but it certainly won't be boring.

Alan Greenspan

Mad-Libs (and Cons)

Trying to understand the blathering babble of a government technocrat can be frustrating. Former federal Reserve chairman Alan Greenspan was a prime example. A newspaper article that started with "Alan Greenspan said today…" would easily generate the numbing sensation of your brain being dropped into a bucket of custard. But wait! Don't despair! The BRI has come up with a way for any ordinary person to actually enjoy quotes from any bloviated official.

Directions

1. Take any quote of Mr. Greenspan's, like this one: "Spreading globalization has fostered a degree of international flexibility that has raised the possibility of a benign resolution to the U.S. current account imbalance."
2. Make a list of the nouns in the quote:
   - globalization
   - degree
   - flexibility
   - possibility
   - resolution
   - account imbalance
3. Replace them with some more interesting nouns:
   - globalization—poodles
   - degree—trousers
   - flexibility—funkiness
   - possibility—exoskeleton
   - resolution—Keith Richards
   - account imbalance—banana cream pie
4. Now, fixing the grammar as necessary, the quotation becomes: "Spreading poodles have fostered trousers of international funkiness that have raised the exoskeleton of a benign Keith Richards to the current U.S. banana cream pie." Isn't that better?
5. But wait—you can keep going. Make a list of the verbs in the quote and replace them with your own:
   - spread—yodel
   - foster—mutate
   - raise—ooze
6. Now you have: "Yodeling poodles have mutated trousers of international funkiness that have oozed the exoskeleton of a benign Keith Richards to the current U.S. banana cream pie."
7. Now, the adjectives:
   - international—yellow
   - benign—moldy
   - current—charbroiled
   - U.S.—aboriginal

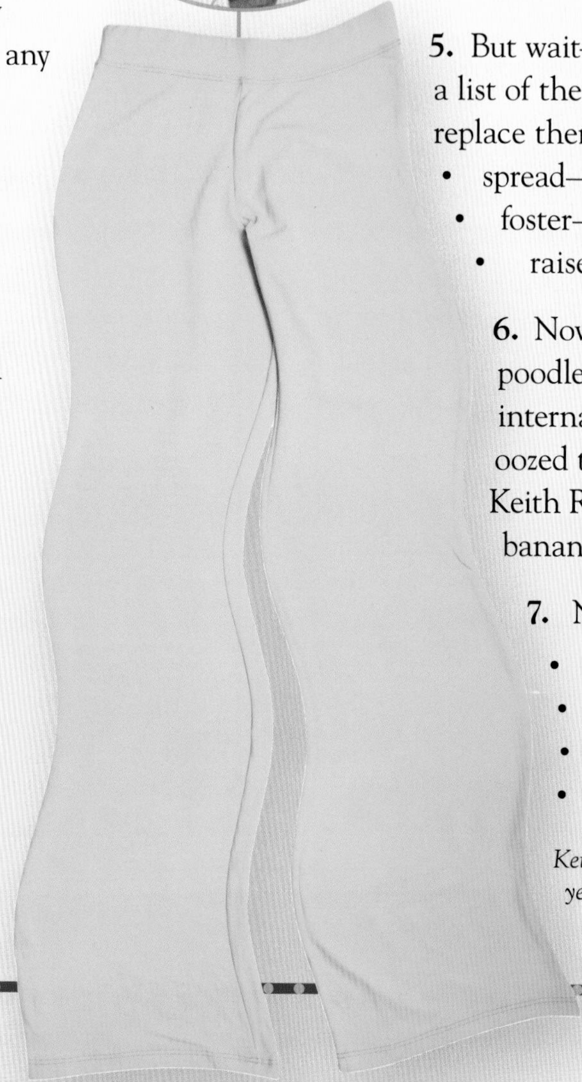

Keith Richards in funky yellow trousers

8. And we get: "Yodeling poodles have mutated trousers of yellow funkiness that have oozed the exoskeleton of a moldy Keith Richards to the charbroiled aboriginal banana cream pie."

Your Turn

Here are two more quotes that you can plug your own silly words into:

> "The risk exists that, with aggregate demand exhibiting considerable momentum, output could overshoot its sustainable path, leading ultimately in the absence of countervailing monetary policy action to further upward pressure on inflation."
>
> **—Ben Bernanke, former Federal Reserve chairman**

> "The hours of non-hours work worked by a worker in a pay reference period shall be the total of the number of hours spent by him during the pay reference period in carrying out the duties required of him under his contract to do non-hours work."
>
> **—Department of Trade and Industry's draft law for minimum wage**

All the Latest from the News Scream

Weird Ways to Die

Eight Arms to Kill You

One of the most popular snacks in South Korea: small octopuses, eaten alive. In 2002, a Seoul man was eating one at home and choked to death on it. Doctors removed the octopus, which was still alive and clinging to the man's throat. Statistics show that as many as six people a year in South Korea die that way.

By the Book

Early-20th-century Ethiopian emperor Menelik II had an unusual habit: When he felt sick or uneasy, he'd eat a few pages out of a Bible. He was feeling especially sick after suffering a stroke in 1913, so he ate the entire Book of Kings. A few days later he died of an intestinal blockage caused by the paper.

Good Luck, Bad Luck

Boonchai Lotharakphong, 43, ran a sportswear factory in Thailand. Facing money problems, he bought a flag from a fortuneteller who foretold good luck if Lotharakphong flew it from the roof of his factory. As Lotharakphong was carrying the flag to the roof, he slipped and fell to his death.

Cart-astrophe

Eighty-year-old Dennis Wiltshire of Neath, South Wales, liked to race grocery carts in his local supermarket. In August 2005, he hopped on a cart and rode it down a loading ramp, yelling "Wheeeee!" The cart spun out of control and Wiltshire fell off, fracturing his skull on the parking lot pavement. According to reports, he died instantly.

Candy Bits

The sweetest page in this book.

- Thanks to Halloween, the top five U.S. candy-selling days are all in October. Number one: the 28th.
- In ancient India, the Sanskrit word for a piece of crystallized sugar was *khanda*, which was later Anglicized to candy.
- One out of every five peanuts on Earth ends up in a chocolate bar.
- In 1925 Massachusetts chocolate salesman Robert Welch made a caramel lollipop on a stick, which he called the Papa Sucker. In 1932 the name was changed to Sugar Daddy.

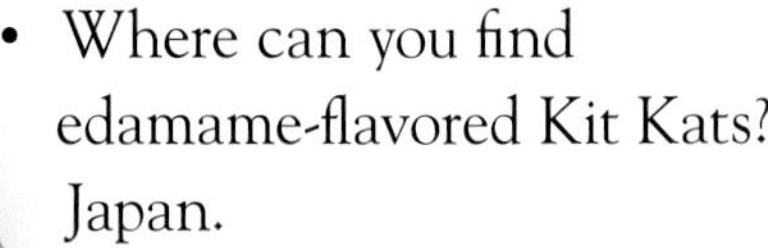

- Where can you find edamame-flavored Kit Kats? Japan.
- In 2001, a chocolate bar from Robert Scott's 1901 journey to the Antarctic was sold at auction. Price: $687.
- Every two and a half days, one billion M&M's are made.
- Candy Corn was once marketed under the name "Chicken Feed."

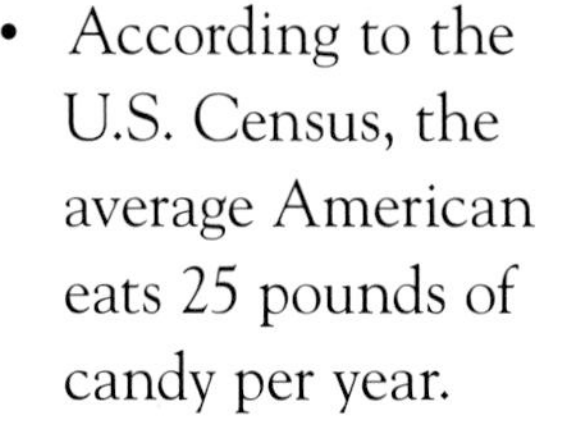

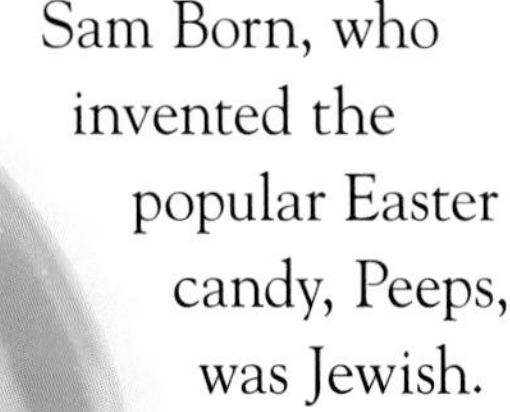

- Sam Born, who invented the popular Easter candy, Peeps, was Jewish.
- In the two weeks leading up to Christmas, two billion candy canes will be sold.
- The world's hottest sweet: Vertigo Pepper Candy, made with Bhut Jolokia, also known as the ghost pepper. It ranks at 2 million Scoville units on the hotness scale. (Atomic Fireballs rank at 3,500.)

- According to the U.S. Census, the average American eats 25 pounds of candy per year.
- Hershey's Kisses were introduced in 1907, but the company was unable to trademark the name "Kiss" for decades because the courts ruled that "kiss" was a generic term for a small candy. Hershey's finally got the word trademarked in 2001.
- The world's oldest person, Jeanne Calment of France, lived to be 122 years old. Until she was 119, she ate nearly two pounds of chocolate every week. (Results not typical.)

Tsunamis can travel as fast as jet planes.

Cooking with Roadkill

Most of us simply keep on driving when we see a splattered 'possum on the side of the highway, but a peculiar few ask, "Why let all that free meat go to waste?"

Clear and Pheasant Danger

One day in the 1950s, a 15-year-old British kid named Arthur Boyt found a dead pheasant on the ground while bicycling through a park near Windsor Castle. The creature piqued his curiosity, and he brought it home to show his mother. Mrs. Boyt responded in a way that might prompt a visit from a social worker today: She cooked the bird and told Arthur to eat it—not to teach him a lesson about the dangers of bringing home dead things, but because pheasants are game birds and good to eat.

Young Arthur happily ate the bird. Now in his seventies, he remembers the experience fondly. Boyt never lost his sense of wonder regarding the natural world: He became an entomologist, someone who studies bugs. And he never lost his taste for eating dead critters hit by cars, either. As he grew older and became philosophically opposed to hunting (cruel) and farm-raised meats (cruel and unhealthy), he obtained more and more of his meat on the road. The last time he purchased a piece of store-bought meat: 1976. All the creatures he's eaten since then—more than 5,000 animals in all—have been roadkill. Roast deer, spaghetti in hedgehog sauce, breast of barn owl, pheasant stew, pigeon pot pie, badger sandwiches (his favorite), you name it—if a car can hit it, Boyt has probably eaten it. He even eats rats, which he insists are delicious stewed. "People say rats carry disease, but I'd sooner eat a country rat than any raw meat you get served in restaurants," he told *The Times* of London in 2003.

Meat the Pressed

Boyt isn't alone. In the United States, more than a dozen states allow the collecting of roadkill for food, and the number is growing. In 2011, Illinois Governor Pat Quinn vetoed a bill legalizing the collecting of roadkill from the state's highways, fearing that people might themselves become roadkill while trying to drag critters off the asphalt. But the bill was so popular that the state legislature voted 87–28 to override the veto, and the bill is now law.

Pheasant with Potato and Grapes

The rules regarding collecting roadkill vary. In some states, a permit is required; in others, carcasses may be collected only during hunting season. Reason: Officials want to discourage "bumper hunting"—deliberately running down game animals at times of the year when shooting them would be illegal. In Alaska, food banks, homeless shelters, and other charities get first dibs on meat from the more than 800 moose killed by cars and trains each year. (One adult moose yields as much as 700 pounds of meat.)

Kids, Don't Fry This at Home

If you're thinking about taking the plunge, it's important to know that handling and eating roadkill can kill you if you don't know what you're doing. Just because that tasty-looking raccoon died when it was hit by a car doesn't mean it didn't have rabies. If you're not experienced at handling wild game meat, it's not worth the risk. That being said, here are some safety tips from the pros:

- Know the animal and the parasites and diseases it suffers from. Know the visible signs of these maladies, so that you can distinguish healthy animals from sick ones.
- Wear goggles and thick rubber gloves when handling roadkill and preparing the meat for cooking. This is necessary to prevent blood (which may be disease-infected) from getting into your eyes and cuts in your skin. After working with the animal, thoroughly wash your hands and any blood-stained clothing immediately.
- Best time to look for roadkill: early in the morning. Many nocturnal animals are hit by cars when they come out at night, and road crews are unlikely to pick them up until the next day. Cooler temperatures after dark help prevent the meat from spoiling.
- Refrigerate raw meat immediately. Be sure to cook the meat to an internal temperature of at least 170° to kill bacteria.
- Only undamaged meat is edible, so look for animals killed by "clean hits," i.e., critters that were struck once, thrown to the side of the road by the impact, and not hit again. Animals that have been run over and squashed flat ("road pizza") are inedible.
- Select only "fresh" roadkill—animals that have been hit by cars very recently. Evaluate them like fresh fish at the market. Is the animal's nose still moist? Are its eyes full and clear? Does it bleed bright red blood freely when you cut into its skin? These are signs of freshness. If it smells bad or rigor mortis has set in, leave it be.
- That's one school of thought, anyway. "I have consumed meat that was blown up, like horses on the Western Front (World War I)," Arthur Boyt told *The Times*. "If bodies are swollen, gasified, and green, they do taste different, but if you cook them thoroughly, you can still eat them. I have done it and had no repercussions."

Chew the Fat

So what do roadkill animals taste like? Here's a sampling:

Fox: Mild and salty, with little or no fat and a nice texture. (But it can make you burp.)

Rabbit: Bland.

Buffalo: High in protein, low in cholesterol, and half the calories and fat of beef, with a similar taste. Use in any beef recipe.

Swan: Unpleasant and muddy-tasting.

Ostrich: Tastes like venison and should be prepared as such. Best sautéed or grilled medium rare.

Pheasant: A rich flavor similar to chicken, which is improved if the bird is refrigerated, unplucked, for three days.

Rat: A salty taste like ham or pork. Good in stir-fries.

Frog: Flavor and texture similar to chicken. Also good stir-fried.

Bear: A strong taste that can be improved by refrigerating the meat for 24 hours. Good in pot roasts and stews; prepare like beef.

Goose: Dark meat that tastes like roast beef.

Pigeon: Meat that's "dark, rich, tender, and succulent," and good roasted, broiled, braised (fried, then stewed), grilled or sautéed. Serve medium-rare, or the meat will taste like liver.

Hedgehog: Fatty, with an unpleasant taste.

Boar: Flavor ranges from mild to pungent.

Roadkill tip: If your meat tries to hop away, it isn't dead.

The average American mom spends an hour a day behind the wheel of a car.

The Proper Stance

Success in any physical activity begins with knowing the proper way to stand. Here's how the experts say to do it.

Dart-Thrower's stance: The big toe of your dominant foot should be just behind the throwing line. Most of your weight should be placed on that leg; the back leg provides balance. Position yourself so your eye, the dart, and the target are in one line. Your shoulders should be as close to perpendicular with the throwing line as possible, but can be angled a bit so you're not wobbly. Your front toe should match that angle. Stand straight up. If you lean forward, you'll throw off your balance, and the dart could end up in the wall…or worse.

Chef's stance: If you have to swivel your body in order to stir or cut something, you're doing it incorrectly. Get directly in front of your work. Multitasking chefs who forget this rule can suffer from chronic back problems. Also, when your spine is twisted, you lack balance and need the counter to steady yourself. A poor stance can put you off balance, and lead to cut fingers, so make sure your weight is firmly planted on the back of your feet (and wear comfortable shoes).

Irish step-dancer's stance: Before the dance begins, place your arms at your sides, keeping your elbows straight (and don't plan to move them). Keep your back straight and your chin up. Then rotate your right foot outward, and put the toes of your left foot against your right heel (kind of like a ballet dancer). Then, if you haven't fallen to the floor, you're ready to dance a jig.

Tennis ball-boy's stance: It is imperative that ball boys (and girls) working the net stand straight up with their hands behind their backs and not move a muscle until the ball hits the net and play stops. Then they have to pounce on the ball and return to their stance as quickly as possible.

Wide-receiver's stance: In the old days, football receivers lined up like sprinters, with one hand on the ground. Today, the stance is between crouching and standing straight up. Lean forward with your non-dominant foot on the line. Your chin, chest, and knee should be directly over your front foot. Your other leg is bent behind you with the heel slightly off the ground. Your weight should be on your front toe. When the ball is snapped, you'll use your rear foot to propel you forward, and then your front foot to get you up to full speed in one step.

Photographer's stance: Whether you're using a point-and-shoot or a DSLR, stability is the key to preventing blurry images. Keep your feet planted on the ground with most of your weight on your upper legs. One foot can be slightly in front for more stability. Keep your elbows close to your body as you hold the camera up to your eye with both hands. Before you shoot, take a breath and let it out so you're relaxed. Now that you're stable, you don't have to continually adjust your balance.

Handgun-shooter's stance:
There are two main stances:

- The Weaver, invented by Jack Weaver in the 1950s, is the one most commonly used by cops because it makes you a smaller target. Place your feet shoulder-width apart with your dominant leg slightly back. Angle your support arm's shoulder toward the target, and bend your knees while keeping your body weight slightly forward. Then grasp the gun with both hands, keeping your elbows bent with the support elbow pointing downward.
- The Isosceles stance allows you to rotate like a tank turret. Face the target, keeping your feet shoulder-width apart, and bend your knees slightly. Extend your arms straight in front of you, locking at the elbows. When you square your shoulders, your arms will form an isosceles triangle (two equal sides).

Supermodel's stance: Drama! Emotion! Those are key for a successful fashion shoot. The way to create that look is by creating angles: Never stand straight toward the camera. Swivel your hips so your head is turned, accentuating your long neck (if you have one). Put your hands on your hips or over your head to create even more angles. According to fashion model Josie Maran, "The weirder the shape you make, the better." To create this drama, briskly walk to your mark, stop, swivel toward the camera, and strike a pose. You may feel foolish, but your photos will be stunning.

Golf-Putter's stance: Most pros say your toes should be two putter-head lengths from the inside edge of the ball, but everyone is sized a little

Medical term for the ring finger: annulary.

differently. The general rule is to stand so that your eyes are directly over the ball and to keep your shoulders square to the target line, so your spine isn't twisted. However, pros also say that if you sweat the technical stuff when putting, you'll usually miss. The key: Just "feel it."

U.S. Army's stance (at attention): "Both feet are flat and firm on the ground with the heels together and the toes parted at an angle of 30 degrees to the front-center of the body. The knees are braced by pushing them back slightly. The body is upright with the stomach pulled in and the chest pushed out; the back is straight. The arms are at the side of the body with the hands clenched fistlike, thumb pushing downward to help lock the arm at the elbow; the thumb is in line with the seams of the trousers."

Pee-er's stance (males only): The proper peeing stance is crucial when using a public men's room. If you have neighbors on either side, keep your elbows in. Stand far enough back that you avoid splash-back, but not so far back that you're hitting the floor. (And keep the vocalizations to a minimum.)

ODDs and ENDs

It's Just Batwash

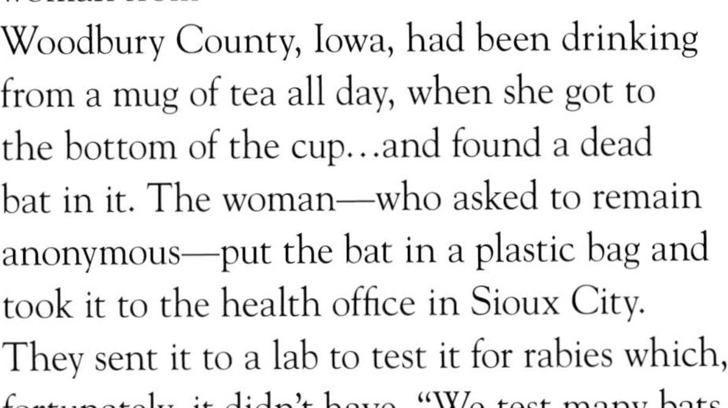

A 60-year-old woman from Woodbury County, Iowa, had been drinking from a mug of tea all day, when she got to the bottom of the cup...and found a dead bat in it. The woman—who asked to remain anonymous—put the bat in a plastic bag and took it to the health office in Sioux City. They sent it to a lab to test it for rabies which, fortunately, it didn't have. "We test many bats," said lab manager Mike Pentella, "but none that have drowned in a cup of tea before." The woman was said to be "recovering from shock."

Stand and deliver!

Speedy Delivery

Barbara and Johann Meyer were speeding down a street in their hometown of Wachtberg, Germany, in 2006 when police officers pulled them over: A surveillance camera had taken an image of them speeding through an intersection. The Meyers explained that they were on their way to the hospital, where Barbara was about to give birth. Not only did the officers cancel the ticket, they gave the couple a baby present—a plastic toy policeman with a speed gun in its hand. They also gave the couple the photo from the surveillance camera, suggesting they put it in the baby's first photo album.

Calorie counting as a means of losing weight first became popular in 1918.

Phreaky Phenomena

Hold on to your hats! These powerful and mysterious forces of nature are rare…but real.

The Perfect Firestorm

A fire tornado results when a fire is whipped into a burning frenzy by intense winds. Here's how this rare phenomenon works: First, a strong updraft of hot air hits a wildfire. As the hot air rises, it makes room for outside air to flow in. As that air whips in, it can form a whirlwind that picks up the flames and becomes a swirling column of fire nicknamed a "fire devil" or a "whirl." Fire devils often range from 30 to 200 feet high and usually last a few minutes. Like regular tornadoes, though, they can reach more than half a mile high with winds of 100 miles per hour…and they can be just as deadly. The worst fire devil occurred in Tokyo in 1923, when 38,000 people were killed in 15 minutes.

Where Ocean Meets Sky

Atmospheric gravity waves re-create the motion of the ocean, but in the sky. Waves of air move up and down as they roll through the atmosphere, fueled by buoyancy (the force that makes air rise) and gravity (which makes it fall). Climatologist Tim Coleman explains: "Gravity is what keeps them going. If you push water up and then it plops back down, it creates waves. It's the same with air." Gravity waves begin when a stable layer of air is displaced by a draft (from a storm, for instance), causing air to ripple across the sky. It's similar to the rings that emanate outward when a stone is thrown into stagnant water. Clouds develop high on the crest of each gravity wave and dissipate near the trough. So, to a person on the ground, gravity waves look like rows of clouds with clear sky between them. Their actual movement across the sky can really only be seen in time-lapse video.

UFO Landing Pads?

In 1985 astronauts made a fascinating discovery: A giant ring of ice had formed on Siberia's Lake Baikal, the deepest freshwater lake on the planet. The ice circle was perfectly round, rotated slowly, and was so huge that it couldn't even be seen from the highest mountaintop. It was only visible from space. Since then, other twisting ice structures, which one scientist calls "very, very rare," have been found on lakes and rivers in Russia, Scandinavia, and Canada. One, nearly three miles in diameter, was spotted from the International Space Station in 2009. It took more than 20 years, but researchers think they've finally figured out what causes the ice rings: methane gas rising from the bottom of cold bodies of water. Water warmed by the gas hits the ice at the top of the lake and begins to melt it. Then the earth's rotation causes the ice to turn.

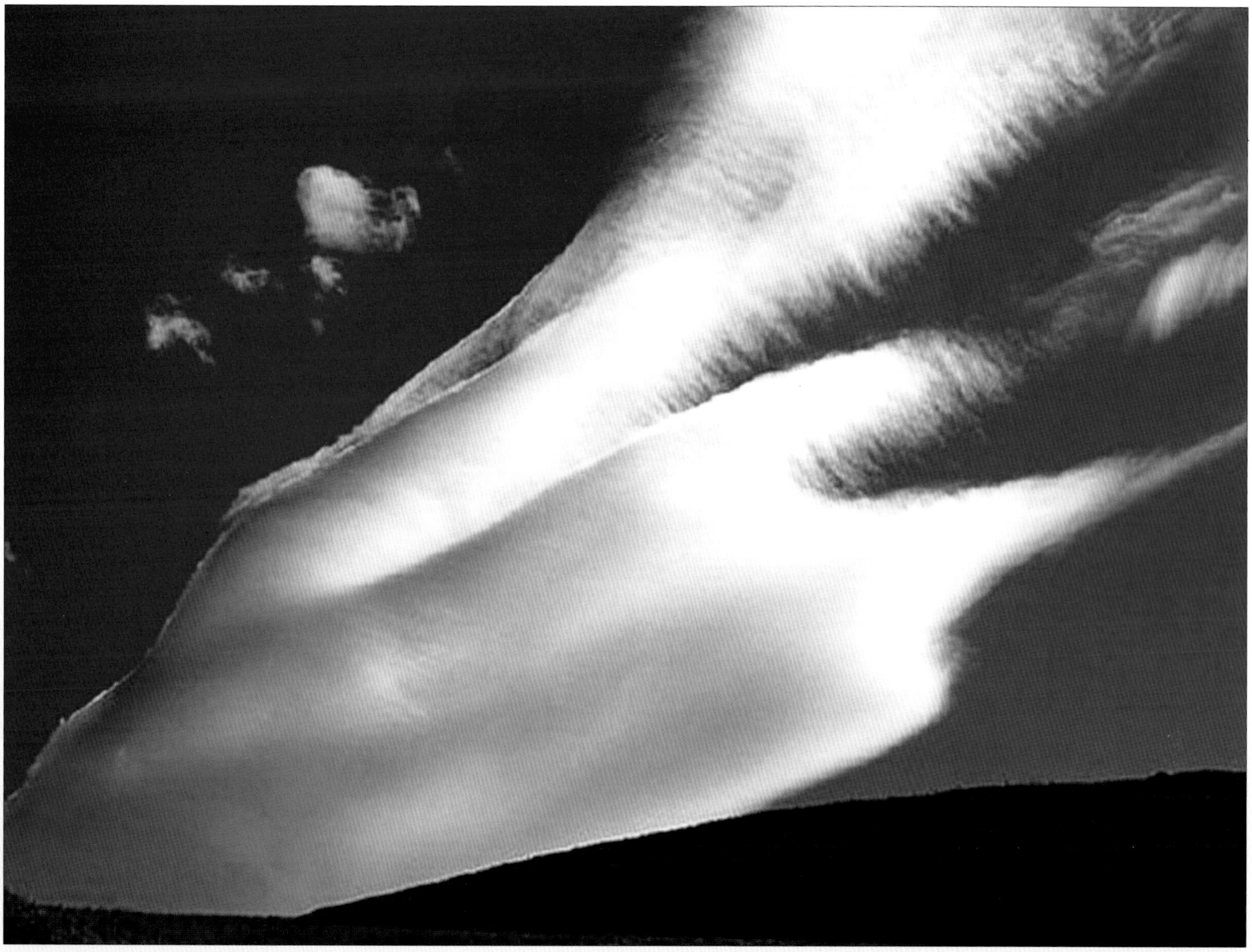

Wave cloud near St Abbs, Berwickshire, Scotland

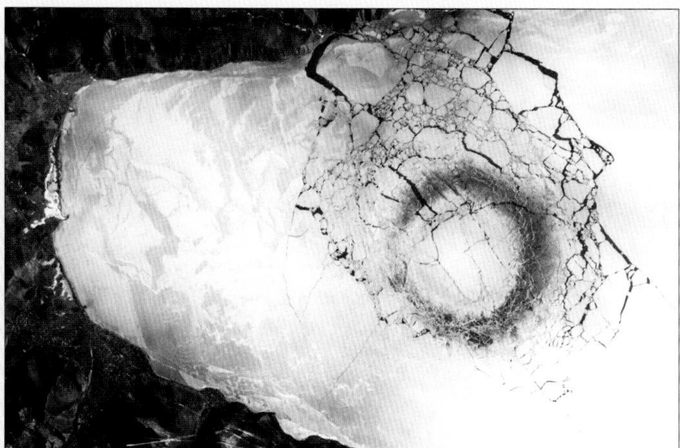

Ice rings on Lake Baikal

It's the Bloomin' Algae!

A fascinating spectacle sometimes seen in oceans and rivers is a red tide, or more accurately an "algal bloom." The water is tinted a brilliant red color by the overgrowth of an algae species that is normally microscopic. At night, red tide water turns an amazing bioluminescent blue. Why? When waves or boats disturb them, red algal blooms give off a brief flash of blue light. Algal blooms form when too many nutrients like nitrogen and phosphorus collect in water, causing the algae to reproduce so quickly that the ecosystem is overtaken. When these blooms coat the water's surface, they block sunlight, hog the oxygen, and kill off underwater plants and animals. Some red algal blooms also produce toxins that harm aquatic life and humans. Mammals can become ill or die if they swim in the water or eat shellfish harvested there. Algal blooms may hang around for months, wreaking havoc on the environment and the area's tourism trade.

Who's the Rarest of Them All?

A *circumhorizontal arc* (aka, "fire rainbow") is the world's least common natural atmospheric condition, but it's actually neither a rainbow nor a fire.

Artist Paul Cézanne taught his parrot to say "Cézanne is a great painter."

Although the phenomenon appears as rainbow-colored clouds sporting wisps that look like flames, it is produced by ice crystals, not warmth, and conditions have to be perfect for one to form. Start with cirrus clouds more than 20,000 feet high. Then add the sun also high in the sky, at least 58 degrees above the horizon. The clouds must contain hexagonal ice crystals just the right thickness and aligned horizontally with a flat face pointed at the ground. Similar to a prism, light enters through the vertical side face and exits through the flat bottom, producing an arc of colors that lights up the cloud. Some of these anomalies cover hundreds of square miles and last for more than an hour. However, due to the specific conditions they require, the arcs are impossible to view in latitudes below 55 degrees south or above 55 degrees north. Sorry, Canada!

Frog rain

It's Raining Amphibians

Once in a great while, people are forced to seek cover from a storm that drops not just rain, but…live animals. It happened in England in the 1800s, when jellyfish fell from the clouds; then, in the 1930s, frogs followed suit. In 2010 a remote town in Australia experienced showers of hundreds of spangled perch two days in a row. The kicker? The town was more than 200 miles from the nearest body of water. This phenomenon is truly a mystery. Some scientists theorize that massive evaporation, a strong updraft, or a tornado picks up aquatic life along with water, blows it

Red algae covering a lake water surface in Rotorua, New Zealand

Only U.S. state with a one-syllable name: Maine.

70,000 feet high, and carries it many miles before the winds die down and the animals fall with the rain. However, this doesn't explain the situations in which only a single species rains at once (like the perch in Australia), instead of a mixture of different animals. People in Honduras have a legend to explain this phenomena. Every summer

above and above right: Fish rain in Honduras

in Yoro, Honduras, fish rain down during thunderstorms. The Hondurans believe it's an answered prayer. Long ago, a Catholic priest prayed for food for the starving natives. Supposedly, that's when the fish rains began. Today, some of the fish fall into waterways and swim off. What do villagers do with the rest? Cook and eat them, of course. Waste not, want not.

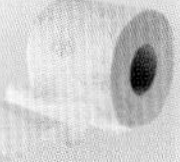

ODDs & ENDs

Virtual Folding

Conventional wisdom says that it's physically impossible to fold a piece of paper in half more than seven times. However, according to *The Economist* magazine, if you were able to keep folding it (and doubling its thickness), math principles theorize that the concentrated piece of paper would grow to astronomic heights:

- 10 folds = Width of a hand
- 12 folds = Height of a stool
- 14 folds = Average adult height
- 20 folds = Quarter of the Sears Tower
- 25 folds = Height of the Matterhorn
- 30 folds = Outer atmosphere of Earth
- 50 folds = Distance to sun
- 70 folds = 11 light years from Earth
- 100 folds = Radius of the known universe

Five Real Places to Spend Your Next Holiday

1. Christmas Valley, Oregon
2. Easter, Texas
3. Passover, Missouri
4. New Years Lake, Idaho
5. Valentine, Texas

Overshadowed

Literary giants Aldous Huxley and C. S. Lewis both died on the same day, but their passings didn't receive much press. Why? It was November 22, 1963, the day John F. Kennedy was assassinated.

10–4, Good Buddy

CBs, short for "Citizens Band" radios, dominated American highways in the 1970s...mainly for speedy truck drivers to stay one step ahead of the law. Here's some of their colorful lingo.

Convoy: a group of trucks traveling together for safety (from state troopers), often exceeding the speed limit.

Front door: the lead truck in a convoy. Its job is to "shake the trees"—spot any state troopers up ahead and warn the other trucks in the convoy to slow down.

Back door: the last truck in a convoy "rakes the leaves"—keeps an eye out for troopers sneaking up from behind.

A classic CB radio

Rocking chair/easy chair: a truck in the middle of the convoy. (They can relax, since they're not at the beginning or the end.)

Hitting the jackpot: getting pulled over for speeding. (The flashing lights on a patrol car look like a slot machine.)

Feeding the bears: after hitting the jackpot, a trucker has to pull over to the side of the highway to feed the bears, i.e., receive a speeding ticket.

Brush your teeth and comb your hair: slow down to 55 mph—a state trooper with a radar gun is "taking pictures" up ahead.

Plain brown wrapper: an unmarked patrol car.

Tijuana taxi: a marked police car.

Bear in the air: state trooper in a helicopter or airplane.

Someone spilled honey on the road: The bears are everywhere!

All clean: no bears in sight.

Bear in the bushes: a state trooper hidden from view.

Christmas card: speeding ticket.

One foot on the floor, one hanging out the door, and she won't do no more: driving as fast as you can.

In the pokey with Smokey: in jail.

Play Ball

Here are the tales of two baseballers—one who spent 16 grueling years getting into the records book, and another who did it in just one at-bat.

A League of Her Own

On July 31, 1935, the Cincinnati Reds oversold tickets for their night game. To avoid a potential riot, they allowed the extra fans—8,000 in all—to stand along the foul lines. It was so packed that the players had to muscle their way through the crowd to get to the field. When Reds batter Babe Herman was trying to make his way to the plate in the bottom of the eighth, a nightclub singer named Kitty Burke grabbed the bat from the surprised player and told her friends, "Hang on to him, boys, I'm going to take his turn at bat." Sure enough, she went to the plate against Cardinal Paul "Daffy" Dean. The bewildered pitcher shrugged and lobbed a ball to the blonde bombshell. Burke swung ferociously but only hit a slow roller toward first base.

Cal Ripken Jr.

Dean scooped up the ball and tagged her out (to a round of boos from the crowd). Although the at-bat didn't officially count, it was—and still is—the only time a woman has hit in a major-league game.

Kitty Burke

By the Numbers

The Baltimore Orioles' Cal Ripken Jr. played in a record 2,632 consecutive major-league games from 1982 to 1998. During Ripken's streak:

- 3,695 major leaguers went on the disabled list.
- 522 shortstops started for the other 27 teams.
- 33 second basemen played second base next to Ripken at shortstop (including his younger brother Billy Ripken).

Ripken also holds the record for the most consecutive innings played, with 8,243. He didn't miss a single inning from June 5, 1982, to September 14, 1987. His potential wasn't recognized early on, though—47 players were selected ahead of Ripken in the June 1978 draft.

Do Try This at Home

We were saving this article about home science experiments for our next Bathroom Reader For Kids Only, *but then we thought, why should the kids have all the fun?*

Potato-powered Clock

What You Need:

- 2 fresh, raw potatoes
- 2 shiny pennies
- 2 galvanized nails
- 3 short pieces of insulated wire with small alligator clips at each end
- 1 battery-operated LED clock (with battery removed)
- 1 black Magic Marker

What You Do:

Use the Magic Marker to mark the potatoes "1" and "2." Push the pennies edgewise into each potato, leaving some of each penny exposed. Stick the nails partway into each potato.

Using the first wire, attach one alligator clip to the penny in potato #1 and the other to the positive (+) terminal in the clock.

Using the second wire, connect one clip to the nail in potato #2 and the other to the negative (–) terminal in the clock. Take the third wire and clip one end to the nail in potato #1, and the other end to the penny in potato #2.

Result:

Look at your clock. It's running on potato power!

Explanation:

This is an *electrochemical reaction*, or a chemical reaction that produces electricity. In this case, the zinc coating on the galvanized nails and the copper in the pennies are reacting with chemicals in the potato, resulting in the movement of electrons—that's electricity!—through the potato, the wires, and the clock.

Bonus:

You don't need potatoes. Try lemons, apples, or bananas.

Egg in a Bottle

What You Need:

- 1 hard-boiled egg
- 1 glass bottle that's dry on the inside and has a fairly wide opening, but not wide enough to let the hard-boiled egg fall into it
- a little vegetable oil
- a small piece of paper (3 inches square)
- a match or lighter

What You Do:

Rub a little bit of oil around the inside of the lip of the bottle. Fold the piece of paper into a strip that can be easily dropped into the bottle's opening.

Ignite one end of the strip of paper and drop it into the bottle. Set the egg on the opening of the bottle while the paper is still burning.

Result:

You'll be amazed...as the egg starts to wiggle...then squish...and squeeze through the opening, falling into the bottle.

Explanation:

What you're seeing is a demonstration of how temperature affects air pressure. Before you drop the burning paper into the bottle, the temperature in the bottle and in the surrounding air are the same—so the pressure is the same, too.

But when you drop the burning paper in, the heat from the fire causes the air in the bottle to expand—or increase

About 2,000 people are injured every year from trying to pry frozen foods apart.

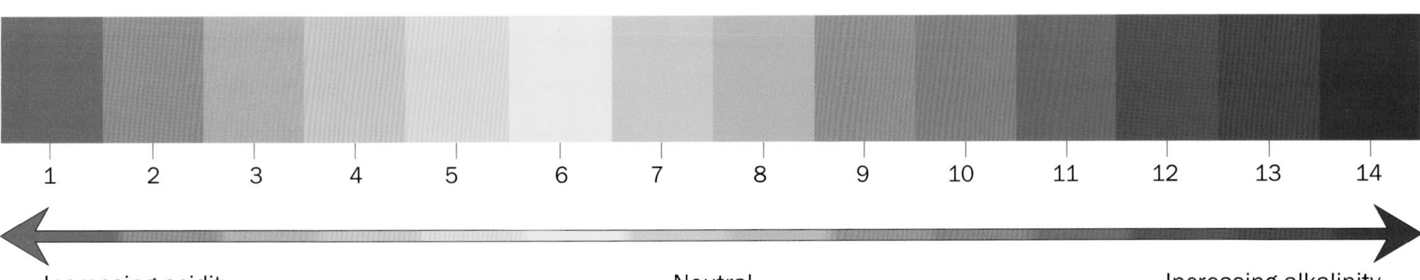

in pressure. (That's why the egg wiggles: air was escaping.) After the fire goes out (because the egg blocked oxygen from getting in), the air in the bottle cools down and contracts—or decreases in pressure. The air outside the bottle is now more highly pressurized than the air inside. High pressure naturally flows toward low pressure, so the air outside the bottle is drawn into it, and squishes the egg into the bottle in doing so. Once the egg is out of the way, the air pressure in and out of the bottle are equal again.

Cabbage-Juice pH Tester

Warning: If you're not allowed to use the stove by yourself, find someone to supervise.

What You Need:

- stove
- medium-sized pot
- measuring cup
- a head of red cabbage
- white vinegar
- baking soda
- pencil and paper
- assorted things from around the house

What You Do:

Chop up the cabbage and boil it in a pot of water for 20 minutes. Drain off the purple-blue cabbage water and pour it into the measuring cup. Allow it to cool.

Use a spoon and put a little bit of the purple-blue cabbage juice on a white surface, or in a white cup. Now add a tiny bit of vinegar to it. Now start over, but this time add some baking soda to the cabbage juice instead.

Results:

Vinegar added to the cabbage juice turns it bright red. Baking soda turns it green.

Explanation:

The reactions that you are witnessing are the result of the substances' pH level, or how acidic or how basic (or alkaline) they are. PH is measured from 0 to 14: Water is neutral, with a pH of 7. Anything less than 7 is an acid; the lower the number, the more acidic the substance is. Anything above 7 is a base; the higher the number, the more basic it is. Acids cause the cabbage juice to change toward purple, pink, and red; bases make it change toward blue, green, and yellow. And you can now determine, pretty accurately, the pH level of anything you can dissolve in water, using the chart above, with the approximate pH level on the top, and color on the bottom.

Go ahead, test some other things: beer, yogurt, maple syrup, shampoo—whatever you like. Any colors you get, just try to place them where you think they belong on the chart. You now have a simple, homemade pH-level testing system, useful for a variety of purposes. Extremely acidic or alkaline foods, for example, will be very sour or bitter, respectively.

And, more importantly, the water in your hot tub should have a pH level of between 7.2 and 7.8.

Bonus:

Cut some white paper into strips (coffee filters work well), soak them in cabbage juice for a few hours, take them out, and let them dry. You now have pH-level testing strips that work just as well as the ones you can buy in the store—and they'll last for months.

Try it: You can't hum if you're holding your nose closed.

How the Ballpoint Pen Got Rolling

Look carefully at the point of a ballpoint pen. There's a tiny little ball there, of course, which transports the ink from the reservoir onto the paper. It looks simple. But actually, developing a workable ballpoint pen wasn't easy. Here's the story of how it became a "Bic" part of our lives.

Making a Point

On October 30, 1888, John J. Loud of Massachusetts patented a "rolling-pointed fountain marker." It used a tiny, rotating ball bearing that was constantly bathed on one side in ink. That was the original ballpoint pen. Over the next thirty years, 350 similar ballpoint patents were issued by the U.S. Patent Office—but none of the products ever appeared on the market.

The main problem was getting the ink right. If it was too thin, the pens blotched on paper and leaked in pockets. If it was too thick, the pens clogged. Under controlled circumstances, it was sometimes possible to mix up a batch of ink that did what it was supposed to do until the temperature changed. For decades, the state-of-the-art ball point would (usually) work fine at 70° F, but would clog at temperatures below 64° and leak and smear at temperatures above 77°.

Our Heroes

That's how it was until the Biro brothers came along. In 1935 Ladislas Biro was editing a small newspaper in Hungary. He constantly found himself cursing his fountain pen; the ink soaked into newsprint like a sponge and the pen's tip shredded it. Eventually, he recruited his brother Georg, a chemist, to help him design a new pen. After trying dozens of new designs and ink formulations, the brothers—unaware that it had already been done at least 351 times before—"invented" the ballpoint pen.

Ladislas Biro's Birome

A few months later, while they were vacationing at a Mediterranean resort, the brothers began chatting with an older gentleman about their new invention. They showed him a working model, and he was impressed. It turned out that the gentleman was Augustine Justo, the president of Argentina. He suggested that the Biros open a pen factory in his country. They declined...but when World War II began a few years later, they left Hungary and headed to South America. The Biros arrived in Buenos Aires with $10 between them.

Surprisingly, Justo remembered them and helped them find investors. In 1943 they set up a manufacturing plant. The results were spectacular—a spectacular failure, that is. They'd made the mistake everyone else had made—depending on gravity to move the ink onto the ball. That meant the pens had to be held straight up and down at all times. Even then, the ink flow was irregular and globby.

A Pen Saved Is a Pen Earned

Ladislas and Georg returned to the lab and came up with a new design. The ink was now siphoned toward the point no matter what position the pen was in. The Biros proudly introduced their new improved model in Argentina—but the pens still didn't sell. They ran out of money and stopped production.

That's when the U.S. Air Force came to the rescue. American flyers, sent to Argentina during the war, discovered that Biro ballpoints

Actual therapy animals: Sadie the "bipolar assistance parrot" and Richard the "agoraphobia monkey."

worked upside down and at high altitudes. So the wartime U.S. State Department asked American manufacturers to make a similar pen. The Eberhard Faber Company paid $500,000 for the American rights in 1944, yielding the Biro brothers their first profitable year ever.

Esther Williams's promotions for the Reynolds Pen Company went swimmingly.

Ripoff City

About this time, a Chicagoan named Milton Reynolds saw a Biro pen in Argentina. When he returned to the U.S., he discovered that similar pens had been patented years earlier. Since the patents had expired, he figured he could get away with copying the Biro design. He began stamping out pens and selling them for $12.50 each through Gimbels department store in New York City. They were such a novelty that Gimbel's entire stock—a total of 10,000 pens—sold out the first day. Other manufacturers jumped on the bandwagon.

The Reynolds Pen Company hired swimming star Esther Williams to show that the pen would write underwater. Other manufacturers showed their pens writing upside down or through stacks of a dozen pieces of carbon paper. But despite the hoopla, ballpoint pens still weren't dependable. They plugged up or leaked, ruining many documents and good shirts. People bought one, tried it, and—frustrated—vowed never to buy another ballpoint as long as they lived. Sales plummeted.

Marcel Bich

Ladislas Biro

La Plum de Marcel

Meanwhile, Marcel Bich, a French manufacturer of penholders and cases, watched with professional interest as the ballpoint industry took off and then crashed. He was impressed by the ballpoint pen's innovative design, but appalled by the high cost and low quality. He realized that if he could come up with a dependable, reasonably priced pen, he could take over the market. So he licensed the Biro brothers' patents, and began experimenting.

For two years, he bought every ballpoint pen on the market and systematically tested them, looking for their strengths and weaknesses. Then in 1949, Bich unveiled his triumph: an inexpensive ballpoint with a six-sided, clear plastic case. It wrote smoothly and didn't leak or jam. They were a huge hit in Europe.

Looking ahead, he knew that his name would eventually be a problem in America. Rather than risk having his product referred to as a "Bitch Pen," he simplified his name so it would be pronounced correctly no matter where it was sold "Bic."

Tip of a modern ballpoint pen

Conquering America

In 1958 Bic set up shop in the U.S. As it turned out, it wasn't his name that proved a problem—it was those shoddy pens people had bought a decade earlier. The American public had come to trust expensive pens, but refused to believe a 29¢ pen would really work.

So Bic launched an ad campaign to demonstrate that his pens would work the "first time, every time." He flooded the airwaves with TV commercials—many live—showing that Bic pens still worked after "being shot from guns, drilled through wallboard, fire-blasted, and strapped to the feet of ice-skaters and flamenco dancers." He also began selling them in grocery stores, and little shops near schools, where he knew students would see them.

The result: By 1967, Bic was selling 500 million pens—60% of the U.S. market. His competitors also began selling cheap, high-quality pens...and ballpoints were changed forever. As *Time* magazine said in 1972: "Baron Bich has done for ballpoints what Henry Ford did for cars."

7 Weird Names for Underwear

1. **Singlet:** British term for sleeveless underwear; the word refers to the fact that the item is made of only one thickness of cloth. ("Doublet" refers to a lined jacket—or two thicknesses of cloth.)
2. **Union Suit:** Comes from the fact that the upper shirt and lower drawers were "united" in one garment.
3. **Knickers:** British term for underwear. It comes from "knickerbockers"—short knee britches worn by New York's early Dutch settlers. The Dutch came to be known as Knickerbockers, and eventually that became shorthand for New Yorkers. (Later, it would be shortened to Knicks for the city's basketball team.)
4. **Cutty Sark:** "Cutty" used to mean "short"; a "sark" was a shirt—hence a short shirt became a skimpy nightgown.
5. **Pretties:** This term used for dainty lingerie dates back to the 1700s.
6. **Tap Pants:** Named after the loose, boxerlike pants worn by tap dancers.
7. **Merry Widow:** Inspired by a strapless corset worn by actress Lana Turner in the 1952 musical of the same name.

Lana Turner in The Merry Widow

What do groundhogs, woodchucks, and marmots have in common? They're all the same critter.

Code Brown

Some colorful shorthand from emergency room workers. Stat!

TMB: Too Many Birthdays (suffering from old age)

FORD: Found On Road Dead

House Red: Blood

TRO: Time Ran Out

Frequent Flier: Someone who is regularly taken to the hospital in an ambulance, even though they aren't sick (because it's something to do)

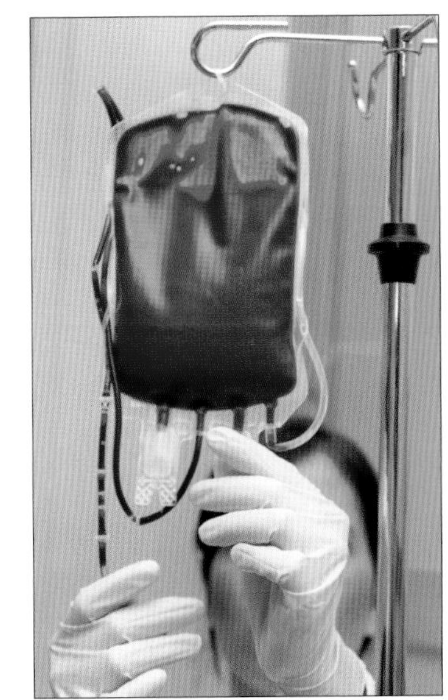

Flask of house red

Help! It's an ALP!

MGM Syndrome: A "patient" who is faking illness and putting on a really good show

WNL: Will Not Listen

SYB: Save Your Breath, as in, "SYB, he WNL"

Insurance Pain: An inordinate amount of neck pain following a minor auto collision with a wealthy driver

Code Zero: Another name for a "Frequent Flyer." The real radio codes range from Code 1 (not serious) to Code 4 (emergency)

Code Yellow: A patient who has wet the bed

Code Brown: You can guess this one yourself.

FOOSH: Fell Onto Outstretched Hand (a broken wrist)

T&T Sign: Tattoos-and-teeth. (Strange but true: Patients with a lot of tattoos and missing teeth are more likely to survive major injuries.)

DFO: Done Fell Out (of bed)

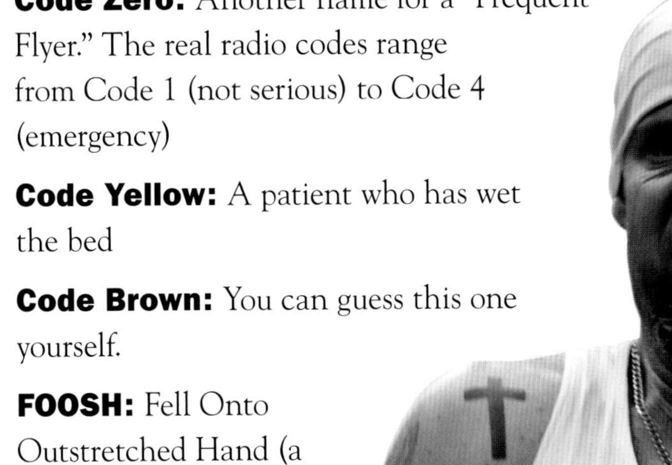

T&T sign

ALP: Acute Lead Poisoning—a gunshot wound

ALP (A/C): Acute Lead Poisoning (Air Conditioning)—multiple gunshot wounds

Flower Sign: Lots of flowers at a patient's bedside (may indicate the patient is a good candidate for early discharge, since they have friends and family who can care for them)

ART: Assuming Room Temperature (deceased)

Bagged and Tagged: A body that is ready to be taken to the hospital morgue (it's in a body bag and has a toe tag)

AMF Yo Yo: Adios, Motherf@#*!, You're On Your Own

My Yacht's Bigger than Yours

Already own a 10,000-square-foot mansion? Drive a $2 million Bugatti? Fly to Aspen and Martha's Vineyard for the weekend? It may be time to consider buying the ultimate status symbol—a megayacht.

Too Much Is Never Enough

Nothing says, "I have an obscene amount of money" quite like an opulent, oversized boat. In 1985 there were only 300 private yachts that were more than 100 feet in length. Today any one of those would be shorter than any of the top 100 largest yachts in the world. *El Horriya* (478 feet) is one of the largest and is the oldest megayacht. Built in London in 1865 for the King of Egypt, it is now a training ship for the Egyptian navy. The 408-foot *Savarona* (named for a type of African swan) ruled the seas for decades. Built in 1931 for

Ismail the Magnificent, king of Egypt from 1863 to 1879

American heiress Emily Roebling Cadwallader, this yacht features a 282-foot gold-trimmed staircase and movie theater. The ship's library takes up an entire deck. Since 2003, however, seven yachts have eclipsed the *Savarona* in size:

- The monstrous 538-foot *Eclipse* was built in 2010 for Russian oligarch Roman Abramovich for $1 billion, give or take a couple of hundred million. *Eclipse* has 24 guest cabins, a disco hall, multiple hot tubs, two helicopter pads, a mini "escape" submarine, a missile defense system, a laser-controlled anti-paparazzi "shield," a pair of swimming pools, and a crew of 70. It is one of four yachts the investment tycoon owns.
- The 531-foot *Dubai* was originally commissioned by Prince Jefri of Brunei in 1996 and later picked up for $300 million by the ruler of Dubai, Sheikh Mohammed bin Rashid Al Maktoum.
- Measuring 508 feet, *Al Said* is currently owned by Sultan Qaboos of Oman. Its six decks include a concert hall that can hold a 50-piece orchestra.
- The 482-foot *Prince Abdelaziz* was built in Denmark in 1984 for King Abdullah of Saudi Arabia.
- *Al Salamah* (456 feet), owned by Saudi Defense Minister Prince Sultan bin Abdul Aziz, was built in 1999 and has 60 state rooms and a glass-roofed indoor swimming pool.
- *Rising Sun* (454 feet), built in 2004 and owned by media tycoon David Geffen.

above: Roman Abramovich
below: the Eclipse

above: Interior of Andrey Melnichenko's motor yacht A
below: Melnichenko

- *Serene* (439 feet), the largest yacht ever built in Italy, was built in 2010 and features two helipads, a submarine, and an indoor saltwater pool that can double as a moorage for the ship's tender.
- *Al Mirqab* (436 feet), owned by the Emir of Qatar and constructed in 2008, has five electrodiesel motors, each with a power output of 28,000 kw. (A Porsche 911 Turbo has an output of 353 kw.)

Lessons in Excess

Not everyone can own the biggest yacht, so when a person is trying to keep up with the Joneses (or, in this case, the Rothschilds), sometimes it's not size alone that makes the person. For example, when Russian banker Andrey Melnichenko was outfitting his $300 million, 394-foot, 23,600-square-foot megayacht, the A, he focused on the little things—like bath knobs that cost $40,000 each, a spiral staircase with a $60,000 banister, and a lounge decorated with white stingray-hide wallpaper and chairs made of alligator skins and kudu horns. A veritable floating fortress, it is outfitted to match, with 44 security cameras with motion detection and infrared nightvision, fingerprint-only access to the 2,583-square-foot master bedroom, and 44-mm bombproof glass throughout.

Some people prefer the more traditional sailing yacht to the diesel-power found on most of today's floating mansions. Compared to the *Dubai*—which has four 9,625-hp MTU engines, a 277,410-gallon fuel tank, and a top speed of 26 knots (30 mph)—hedge-fund manager Elena Ambrosiadou's *Maltese Falcon* is a quaint little sailboat. The 289-foot yacht's DynaRig sailing system features 25,791 square feet of computer-operated sails for optimum efficiency. The *Maltese Falcon* can cross the Atlantic in only 10 days on wind power alone. Other touches include three decks with transparent floors and a saloon featuring a life-size Bugatti made of porcelain.

Why Buy?

Owning a megayacht isn't for everyone. Besides the high purchase price, the costs of maintaining and

In Japan, apple farmers use turkeys to guard their orchards against monkeys.

outfitting it can run into six figures per month. However, budget-conscious celebrities and socialites can still have all of the perks of an ocean-going palace without breaking the bank: by chartering one. There is a megayacht- for-hire to fit nearly every lifestyle and personality. For example, rapper/producer Sean "P. Diddy" Combs recently chartered *Solemates*, a 197-foot luxury yacht loaded with the latest in touch screen technology. Passengers control entertainment, climate systems, lighting, and blinds from 14 iPads installed around the boat.

Other amenities include a gym that converts into a disco with an $80,000 light-and-sound system, an inflatable floating trampoline, and three remote-control racing sloops. Rental: $850,000 per week. Other celebrities who rent instead of buy: the Jonas Brothers, Jon Bon Jovi, Mariah Carey, Robert DeNiro, John Travolta, and Russell Crowe, who chose the 110-foot yacht *Mustique* for a honeymoon cruise in 2003. Megayachting is a life fit for a king—or a queen: Just ask Queen Latifah, another frequent megayachter.

Eight Vital Elvis Presley Statistics

1. Driver's license number (Tennessee): 2571459
2. Waistline, 1950s: 32 inches; Waistline, 1970s: 44 inches
3. Blood type: O
4. Shoe size: 11D (he wore size-12 combat boots)
5. Social Security Number: 409-52-2002
6. U.S. Army draft number: 53310761
7. Checking account number: 011-143875
8. Length of his wedding to Priscilla Beaulieu: 8 minutes

below: Solemates

Oops!

It's always fun to read about other people's blunders. So go ahead and feel superior for a moment.

The Long and the Short of Things

Due to a birth defect, a Swedish police officer's right leg was slightly longer than his left leg. So in 2008, he found a surgeon who agreed to shorten the right one so that his legs would be equal. But the surgery was botched: The knee joint was put back in the wrong position, and one of the screws they used to hold the joint together came loose. During a second surgery, the doctor discovered another problem with the first surgery, which required a third one. That one was slightly botched, too, requiring a fourth. Each time, the surgeon had to take a little more off of the patient's right leg—which had been two and a half centimeters longer than the left. Now it's five centimeters shorter than the left.

Staying on Track

A Toronto police officer reporting to a robbery in January 2008 parked his squad car next to a convenience store, which was adjacent to some train tracks. While investigating the crime, a train rumbled past the store and demolished his squad car. "Maybe it was a little bit on the tracks," the officer admitted.

Fire Safety 101

While firefighters in Honolulu, Hawaii, were at the scene of a traffic accident in 2009, they received a call about a fire…back at their firehouse. The cause: They'd been cooking food on the stove and had forgotten to turn it off when the emergency call came in for the traffic accident. The firehouse fire caused $25,000 in damage.

CSI: Oops

Police in southern Germany feared that a female serial killer was running loose. After comparing evidence gathered over a period of 15 years, they noticed the same woman's DNA was present at 40

You said you like hot food.

RESCUE

RESCUE

crime scenes, linking her to dozens of robberies and three murders. It wasn't until 2009 that police made a major breakthrough in the case: The matching DNA samples didn't come from the evidence, they came from the cotton swabs that had been used to collect it. They concluded that a batch of cotton had been accidentally contaminated by a female worker at the factory many years earlier. The crimes remain unsolved.

Lower Education

At the end of the 2008–09 school year, a fifth-grade teacher in California (her name was not released to the press) decided to make a present for her students: a DVD featuring the year's best class moments. When some of the kids (and their parents) watched it at home, they were shocked when footage of a class field trip suddenly cut to a very naughty scene featuring the teacher and a man in one of their best moments. The teacher was mortified when she found out; she apologized profusely and got all of the DVDs back. Because the teacher is otherwise well respected, school officials called it an "honest mistake" and let her keep her job.

Man vs. Dryer

In 2009, 42-year-old Dave Chapman was doing a load of laundry at a friend's house in Waipopo, New Zealand. That evening, thinking his friend had put his laundry in the dryer earlier, Chapman went to the laundry room to change. "By then, I'd had a fair bit to drink," he later said. Chapman removed all his clothes except his T-shirt, and then looked inside the front-loading dryer for a clean pair of underwear. He couldn't find any, so he stuck his head inside. Still no underwear. So he climbed in even farther, past his shoulders...and got stuck. And the dryer was still hot.

Chapman started thrashing about but couldn't get out. He did manage to dislodge the dryer from on top of the washer, however, and dryer and drunken man crashed down onto the floor.

His friends rushed in but were unable to free him (or stop laughing). So they called for help. A few minutes later, rescue personnel arrived to free the half-naked man, whom they described as "agitated." It took two firefighters to hold onto the dryer and two more to pull Chapman out by his legs. He was bruised and had mild burns, but was otherwise okay. Only then did he find out that his underwear was still in the washing machine.

Superheroes' Religious Affiliations

Based on actual references in comic books.

- **Superman:** Methodist
- **Batman:** Episcopalian
- **The Hulk:** Catholic
- **The Human Torch (Fantastic Four):** Episcopalian
- **Wonder Twins:** Mormon
- **The Thing (Fantastic Four):** Jewish
- **Wolverine:** Buddhist
- **Ghost Rider:** Baptist
- **Thor:** Norse pantheon (of which he is a member)

Wolverine, at one with the universe (David Finch | Marvel Characters, Inc.)

Dads are less likely than moms to recognize that their child is overweight.

Wooden You Know?

Uncle John may never see...a thing as splendid as a tree—except for this article full of tree facts.

- In 2002 Luis H. Carrasco of Santiago, Chile, produced the world's only five-fruited tree after grafting different species onto a single tree. The fruits: apricots, cherries, nectarines, plums, and peaches.
- In memory of his wife Rachel, President Andrew Jackson planted a sapling on the White House lawn, grown from a seed from her favorite magnolia tree. Look on the back of an old $20 bill: It's the tree covering the left side of the White House.
- The slowest-growing tree in the world: a white cedar in the Canadian Great Lakes region. It grew to a height of four inches and weighed only 17 grams (0.6 oz.) after 155 years.
- Studies have shown that viewing scenery of trees can speed up the recovery time of hospital patients, reduce stress levels in the workplace, and increase employee productivity.
- More than a million acres of land worldwide (and 100,000 people) are used for growing Christmas trees.
- Native to Malaysia, the cauliflorous jackfruit yields the largest fruit grown on a tree—almost three feet long and 75 pounds (and it's edible).
- In one day, a tree can transpire 100 gallons of water through its leaves, creating a cooling process equivalent to five window air conditioners running 20 hours a day.
- The desert baobab tree can store up to 35,000 gallons of water in its trunk.
- Have you ever come across an old pecan tree that bends down to the ground and then turns upward? The Comanche were nomadic Plains Indians who marked their campsites by bending a pecan sapling and tying it to the ground. The last known specimen died in 2003, but there may be more, undiscovered.
- Because they constantly produce new wood to thwart decay, yew trees can live to be 4,000 years old. With such an amazing regenerative ability, scientists theorize that there is no reason for yew to die.

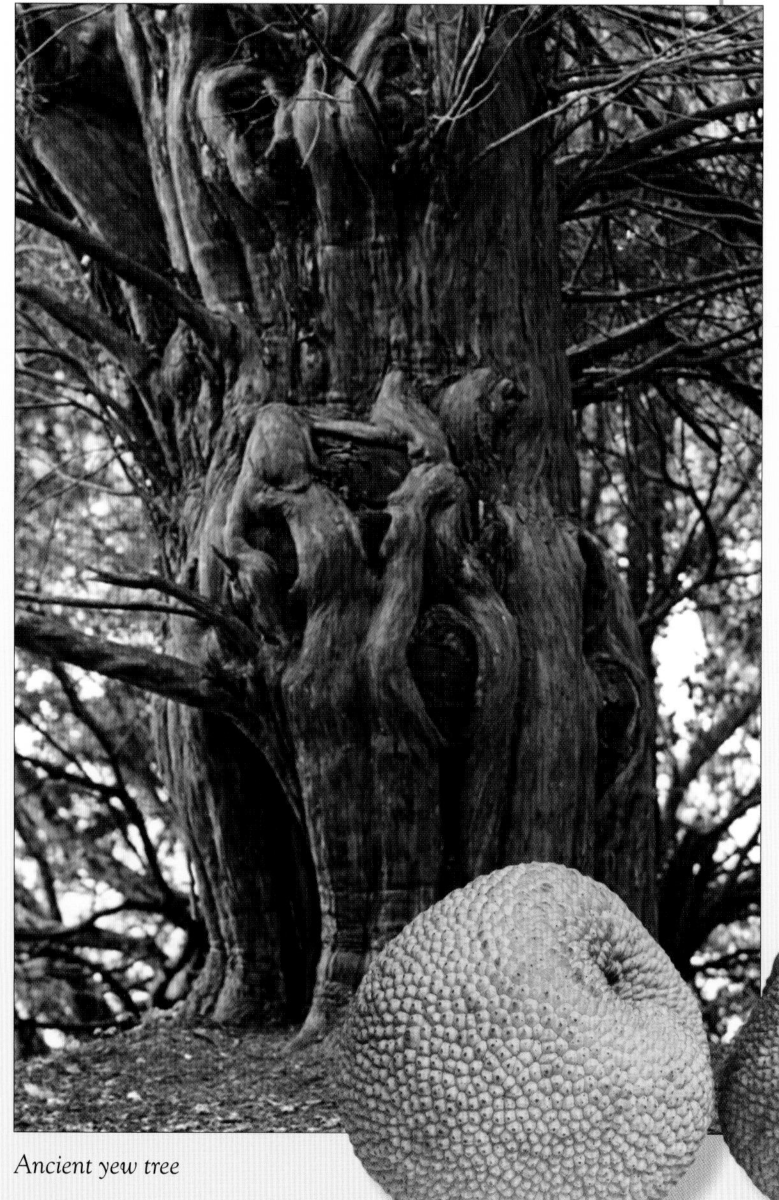

Ancient yew tree

left: Young jackfuit
facing page: A baobab tree in Botswana

The Atlantic Ocean grows an inch wider each year. The Pacific shrinks an inch.

Attack of the B Movie

Get ready to be THRILLED and TERRIFIED by the saga of the B Movie—from the MYSTERIOUS origins to its DIRECT-TO-VIDEO present! You will never be the same AGAIN!

How Depressing

The B movie's tale begins in the Great Depression of the early 1930s, when the number of people going to movie theaters began to decline. When film producers cast about looking for ways to entice cash-strapped audiences back into theaters, they discovered that people still liked movies, they just wanted more movie for their money. Thus was born the double feature, offering two movies—plus cartoon shorts, newsreels, and coming attractions—for the same admission price. It wouldn't do for a movie studio to offer two of its best current releases on the same bill. So studios came up with an alternative: the B movie.

Bottom Lines

B movies differed from main features in two ways—first, in their production standards. While main features were lavish affairs with big-name stars, top-flight directors, big budgets, and all the other bells and whistles, B movies were designed to be shot cheaply and quickly, using lesser-known actors and journeymen film crews. B movies also tended to be shorter than main attractions. Formulaic was not an insult to a B movie; that's just what the movie studios were aiming for.

Second, movie studios made money from B movies differently than they did from main features. Studios earned money from the main features by taking a cut of the box office profits collected by the theater owners (just like they do with films today). B movies, however, were offered to theaters for a flat fee. For movie studios, this meant there was only so much money that could be made from B movies. On the other hand, it also meant studios would make money no matter how these pictures did. "Small but safe" was the B-movie slogan.

B+ Movies

Although B movies were designed to be made quickly and cheaply, originally they weren't all bad. A number of horror and film noir classics (like 1942's *Cat People* and 1949's *Criss Cross*) were shot as B

False advertising: There's no mercury on Mercury—most of it is solid iron.

Roger Corman

movies yet became influential later. However, the reputation of the B movie began to fall in the late 1940s when the major film studios, which had previously had their own B-movie divisions (called B units), got out of the business. This left the lower-card part of the double bill to Poverty Row studios, like Republic Pictures (famous for its cheap Westerns), whose production standards were lower than those of the major studios.

By the 1950s, movies were no longer always formally bundled as double features. But there were quite a few quickie movie studios banging out cheap flicks for second-rate theaters; these exploitative and often shoddy (but also fun) flicks inherited the B-movie title from their predecessors. Some people even became famous for working in the genre. Director and producer Roger Corman, for example, rather notoriously banged out 1960's *The Little Shop of Horrors* in just two days; he has produced (to date) more than 360 films, none notably expensive. He also directly influenced A-list Hollywood by giving some of its most famous directors and stars their earliest breaks: Oscar-winning directors Francis Ford Coppola, Martin Scorsese, Jonathan Demme, Ron Howard, and James Cameron all got their start working for Corman.

In the 1980s and 1990s, B movies largely disappeared from U.S. movie screens. Producers began pumping their films directly into video stores, offering endless sequels to marginal horror films and cheaply produced action films.

B to the Future

Nowadays, the B movie is having something of a televised renaissance, as audiences intentionally go for the camp ridiculousness. Cable TV offers the SyFy Channel's Original Movie series, which unashamedly apes the "quick and dirty" B-movie production experience, cheaply cranking out titles like *Alien Lockdown*, *Mansquito*, *Sharknado*, and *The Man with the Screaming Brain*. These films get surprisingly high ratings for the network and have even been written up in *Wired* magazine and *The New York Times*. Which goes to show, you might be able to take the B movie out of the movie theaters, but not out of the hearts of audiences.

A large tree can have as many as 400,000 leaves.

The and the

The origins of two party animals.

First Came the Donkey

Andrew Jackson was a jackass. The slave-owning, Indian-displacing Democrat embraced that image—even though his Republican opponents were using it to deride him in the 1828 presidential election. Out of spite, Jackson added a jackass to his campaign posters. The image stuck with Old Hickory until his death in 1837. That year, a political cartoon called "A Modern Baalim and His Ass" (by a cartoonist whose name has been lost to history) was the first one to use a donkey to represent the entire Democratic Party. Then it faded from use.

Thomas Nast

The donkey symbol would have most likely died out completely had it not been resurrected 30 years later by Thomas Nast, an influential political cartoonist for *Harper's Weekly*. A liberal Republican (before the parties switched ideologies), Nast used a menagerie of animals in his cartoons. For instance, Democrats also became foxes and two-headed tigers, but it was the donkey that the party would eventually adopt as its mascot… even though it was originally meant as an insult.

The cartoon that started it all

Then Came the Elephant

Although an elephant was first used in a cartoon to describe Republicans in 1860, it was Nast who popularized that symbol as well. In 1874 he took issue with *New York Herald* editors who were running alarmist editorials that charged Republican president Ulysses S. Grant with "Caesarism." Rumors abounded that Grant would run for a third term in 1876, which, even though it was legal at the time, was severely frowned upon. (And the rumors were false.) Nast was a close friend of Grant's, so in the cartoon he depicted the *Herald* as an ass in lion's clothing who "roamed about in the forest and amused himself by frightening all the foolish animals." One of the frightened animals was an elephant, which Nash labeled "the Republican Vote." Nast and his contemporaries kept that image alive, as well as the Democrats' donkey. By 1900 both animals were firmly entrenched in American politics.

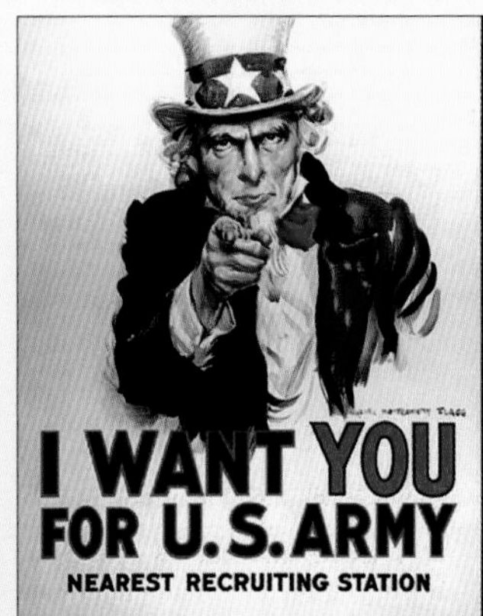

Nast-y Fact: Thomas Nast was also responsible for two other pieces of Americana—Uncle Sam's goatee and Santa Claus's plump belly.

Folk remedy for hiccups: suck on a lemon.

Sagan Says

Carl Sagan (1934–1996) was an outspoken astronomer and author whose life's mission was to explain the unexplainable.

"In order to make an apple pie from scratch, you must first create the universe."

"The fact that some geniuses were laughed at does not imply that all who are laughed at are geniuses. They laughed at Columbus, they laughed at Fulton, they laughed at the Wright brothers. But they also laughed at Bozo the Clown."

"It is of interest to note that while some dolphins are reported to have learned English—up to 50 words used in correct context—no human being has been reported to have learned dolphinese."

"The universe is neither benign nor hostile—merely indifferent."

"We live in a society exquisitely dependent on science and technology, in which hardly anyone knows anything about science and technology."

"We are like butterflies who flutter for a day and think it's forever."

"If we long to believe that the stars rise and set for us, that we are the reason there is a universe, does science do us a disservice in deflating our conceits?"

"All of the books in the world contain no more information than is broadcast as video in a single large American city in a single year. Not all bits have equal value."

"In science it often happens that scientists say, 'You know, that's a really good argument; my position is mistaken,' and then they actually change their minds and you never hear that old view from them again. It happens every day, but I cannot recall the last time something like that happened in politics or religion."

"Who are we? We find that we live on an insignificant planet of a humdrum star lost in a galaxy tucked away in some forgotten corner of a universe in which there are far more galaxies than people."

Wide World of Weird Sports

Tired of baseball, basketball, and football? Your worries are over—we've found some unusual alternatives for you.

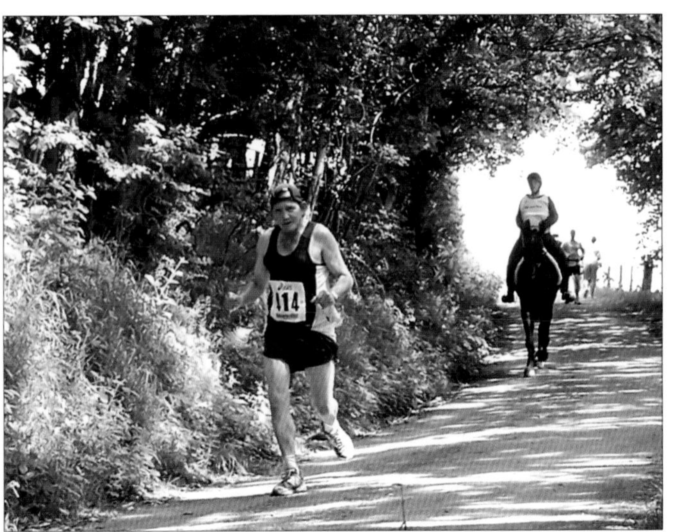

Man Versus Horse Marathon

Where They Do It: Llanwrtyd Wells, Wales

How It's Played: Just like it sounds: People and horses run a cross-country race, on the theory that given enough distance over twisting, uneven terrain, a man can run as fast as a horse. The 21.7-mile race (real marathons are 26.22 miles), which has been run each June for more than 25 years, grew out of a bar bet. Who won the bet? The guy who bet on the horses…at least until 2004, when a man named Huw Lobb beat 40 horses and 500 other runners to win first prize. (His time: 2 hours, 5 minutes, 19 seconds.)

Father Christmas Olympics

Where They Do It: In Gallivare, Sweden, 60 miles north of the Arctic Circle. (Not to be confused with the Santa Olympics held in—you guessed it—Llanwrtyd Wells, Wales.)

How It's Played: Fifty or more contestants dressed as Father Christmas come from all over Europe to compete in several different Santa-related categories, including sled riding, reindeer riding, chimney climbing, and gift wrapping (with points for speed and beauty). Contestants are also rated on generosity, jolliness, and their ability to Ho-Ho-Ho. Any Santa caught smoking or drinking in front of children is automatically disqualified.

Santa Clauses from around the world compete in Sweden.

If you're average, you'll have about 1,400 dreams this year.

Real Ale Wobble

Where They Do It: Wales

How It's Played: It's a grueling 35-mile mountain bike race in the rugged terrain around Llanwrtyd Wells, with three checkpoint/watering stations along the route. The only difference between this race and a regular bike race is that the checkpoints put out cups of beer for the riders instead of water. (Bikers may consume no more than 1½ quarts of beer during the race, and if you're under 18 you need a parent's permission to enter.) "Beer gets down to the parts that you don't get down to with water," says race organizer Gordon Green. "It fortifies the cyclists."

Human Tower Building

Where They Do It: Barcelona, Spain, during the Festa de la Merce each September

How It's Played: Large groups climb one another to form human towers as tall as nine people high. Then, when they've stacked themselves as high as they can, a small child climbs all the way to the top to make it just a little bit taller. According to one account, "horrific collapses are common and many participants have ended up in the hospital."

Underwater Hockey

Where They Do It: All over the United States

How It's Played: Teams of six players wearing fins, masks, snorkels, gloves, and helmets use 12-inch-long hockey sticks to push a puck across the bottom of a swimming pool. Most players can

The elevator was broken.

stay under water for about 20 seconds before they have to surface to breathe. The secret to winning is timing your snorkeling with your teammates so that you don't all swim to the surface at once, leaving the playing field wide open to the opposing team. Twenty-one teams competed in the 2014 U.S. Nationals in Minneapolis, Minnesota.

The fine art of cricket spitting

Cricket Spitting

Where They Do It: At the Bug Bowl festival, held every April at Purdue University in West Lafayette, Indiana

How It's Played: Thousands of contestants compete to see who can spit a dead, intact cricket the farthest. If the cricket loses its legs, wings, or antennae, the spit doesn't count. The world champion is Dan Capps, a mechanic at a meat-packing factory, who spit his cricket 32 feet in 1998. "It's just a matter of blowing hard," he says. "Crickets aren't very aerodynamic."

Where Alcohol Comes From

Ethyl alcohol (the kind you can drink) is created by a process known as fermentation. Yeast is added to fruit juice or a "mash" (a cooked mixture of grain and water), and the yeast consumes the sugars, creating two by-products: carbon dioxide and alcohol. But there's a natural limit to this process. When the alcohol content of the mixture reaches about 15 percent, the yeast loses its ability to convert any more sugars into alcohol. If you want alcohol with a stronger kick than that, you have to continue on to a second process: distillation.

Distilled spirits are made in a device called a still, which consists of a boiler, a condenser, and a collector. The fermented liquid is heated in the boiler to at least 173°F, the boiling point for alcohol. All the alcohol (and some of the water) boils off in the form of vapor. The vapor flows into the condenser, where it cools back to liquid form and is collected in the collector. The process can be repeated to increase the alcohol content even further. All distilled liquor is colorless when it is first made, but it can darken during the aging process, especially when aged in wooden barrels or casks. Some manufacturers use caramel or artificial coloring to darken their spirits.

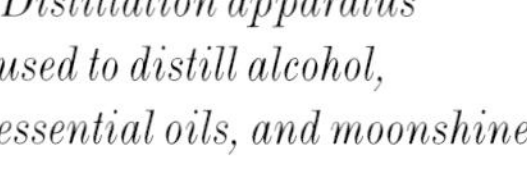

Distillation apparatus used to distill alcohol, essential oils, and moonshine

One in five Americans cannot say which president is on the $1 bill without looking.

Gross Cocktails

Culled from bartenders and bar guides from around the world, most of these drinks had to have been created—and consumed—on a dare.

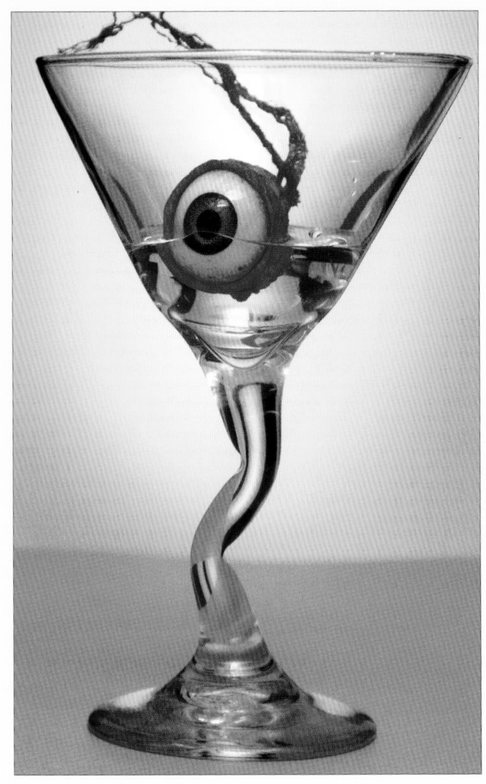

Beergasm

- 1 part beer
- 1 part whole milk

Black Death

- 1 part vodka
- 1 part soy sauce

Ranchero

- 2 parts tequila
- 1 part Tabasco
- 1 part ranch dressing

Relishious

- 1.5 oz Jägermeister
- A spoonful of pickle relish

Buffalo Sweat

- 3 parts bourbon
- 1 part Tabasco

Liquid Steak

- 1.5 oz rum
- Drizzle of Worcestershire sauce (The end result supposedly tastes like grilled meat.)

Smoker's Cough

- 1.5 oz Jägermeister
- A dollop of mayonnaise

Hot Sauce

- 1.5 oz pepper- flavored vodka
- 1 oz olive juice
- 1 oz tomato juice
- 3 oz Guinness
- Dash of Worcestershire sauce
- Dash of Tabasco (Garnish with blue-cheese-stuffed olives.)

Prairie Oyster

- 1.5 oz bourbon
- Dash of Tabasco
- 1 raw egg

Cement Mixer

1.5 oz Irish cream
A lime wedge
(The drinker sucks the wedge and holds the juice in their mouth while consuming the Irish cream. The acidity of the lime juice makes the creamy liqueur instantly curdle.)

Green Eggermeister

- 1.5 oz Jägermeister (or licorice-flavored liqueur)
- 1 pickled egg (Drink the booze while chewing the egg.)

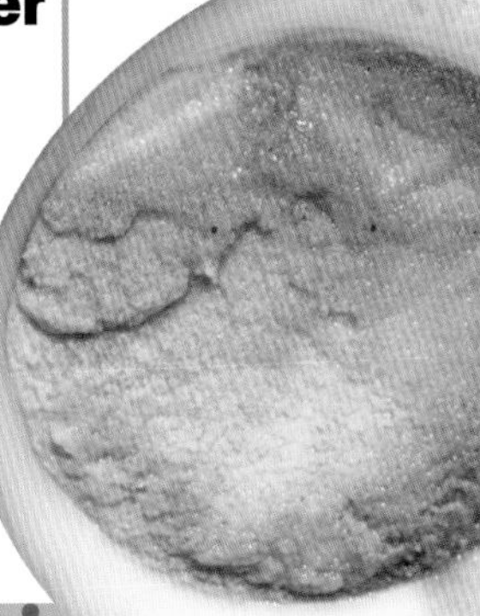

There are at least 33 species of sharks in the Gulf of Mexico.

How the Pilgrims Almost Missed America

Historical fact: The Pilgrims never called themselves "Pilgrims." In fact, they weren't known by that name until the 1840s. Here's how they made it from the Old World to the New World.

The Mayflower *carrying the Pilgrim Fathers across the Atlantic to America in 1620 (Marshall Johnson)*

Cramped Conditions

Seeking religious freedom, the Pilgrims set off from Plymouth, England, on September 6, 1620, more than a month behind their scheduled departure date, which meant they wouldn't reach their destination until winter. Historians can only guess as to the *Mayflower*'s exact size and shape (no pictures of her were ever painted), although most agree that she had two decks and three masts. "Considering the proportions of a number of known merchant vessels of the era," writes William Baker in *Colonial Vessels*, "the *Mayflower* might have had a keel length ranging from 52 to 73 feet, a breadth of 24 to 27 feet and a depth of 10 to 13 feet." Other historians say she may have been as long as 90 feet. Even so, that's roughly the size of a two-story, three-bedroom house. And that's what 102 passengers, 25 crew members, two dogs, many cats, and even more rats squeezed into for 66 days on rough and often stormy seas.

The *Mayflower* was designed to carry cargo, not people, so there were few cots or hammocks to sleep on. Some of the wealthier families paid the ship's carpenter to build cots, but most of the passengers slept on hard wooden floors on a constantly rocking boat. Seasickness was common. Because these people were heading to a

***Jurassic Park* briefly held the all-time box office record, until it was overtaken by *Titanic*.**

William Bradford

new life in an unknown land, they brought along as many of their possessions and rations as they could pack in… which made the living quarters below decks extremely cramped. A few of the passengers even slept in the shallop, a surveying boat that was stowed on the gun deck.

Smooth Start

The first few weeks of the voyage saw relatively calm weather, and the mood among the Pilgrims was good. It is commonly believed that the Pilgrims were a bunch of staid old men who wore black clothes and black hats with buckles. That's a myth. In reality, there was only one man over 60; the average age was 32; and there were 30 children on board. The Pilgrims even wore colorful clothes; For example, their leader William Bradford owned a "green gown, violet cloak, lead colored suit with silver buttons, and a red waistcoat." And unlike the stricter Puritans, the Pilgrims liked to sing and play games.

Rough Seas and Rougher Sailors

But after those first couple of weeks, the fun came to a stormy end. The sky grew dark and the ocean swelled. Then the rain began pouring and the wind blew—and hardly let up for the rest of the journey. The foul weather forced the Pilgrims to huddle in the crowded holds. The rain leaked in through the creaky deck boards, making their lives cold and damp. The children suffered the most—from both sickness and boredom. On the few nice days, kids were permitted to climb up on deck and run around. But Master Jones and the *Mayflower*'s crew of roughnecks weren't interested in cavorting with or entertaining their devoutly religious passengers. One of the sailors especially despised the Pilgrims, telling them that his only wish was "to throw your dead bodies into the sea and claim your treasures for myself." Luckily for the Pilgrims, he never got the chance. Bradford wrote:

> It pleased God before they came half seas over, to smite this young man with a grievous disease, of which he died in a desperate manner, and so was himself the first that was thrown overboard.

Bradford and Master Jones also had more than a few heated discussions, arguing about the route, the crew's attitude, and whether the creaky old ship was seaworthy. Jones made it very clear that even though Bradford was the leader of the Pilgrims, he was in charge of the *Mayflower*. Besides, in addition to the Pilgrims and the ship's crew, there were other paying passengers on board, about 30 regular folks booking passage to America. (Little is known about who these people were or where they ended up.)

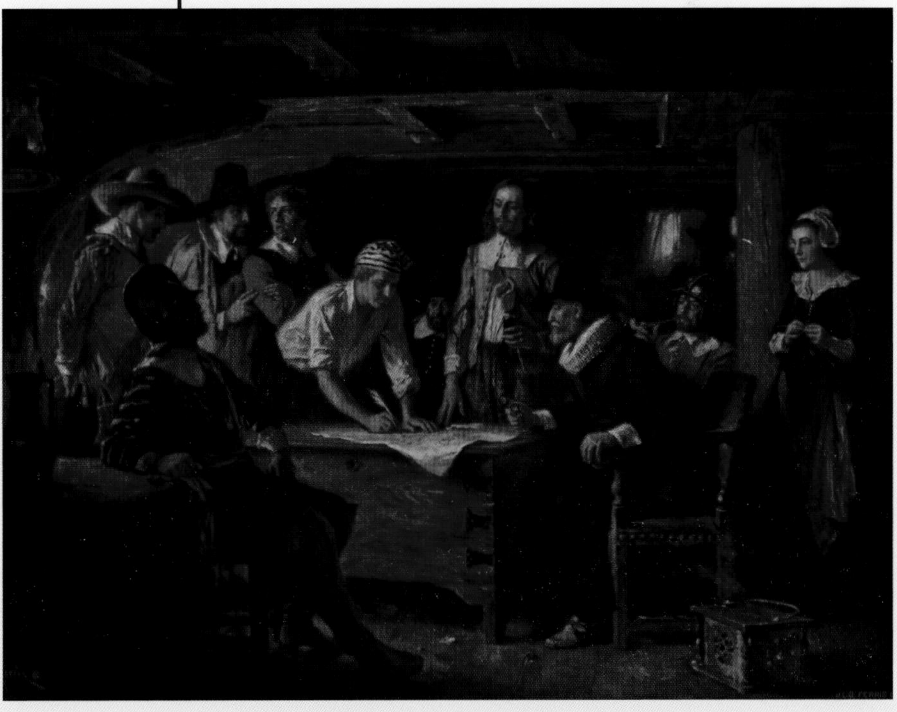

Passengers of the Mayflower *signing the "Mayflower Compact"*
(Jean Leon Gerome Ferris)

Around 1 in 14,000 people is born with dwarfism.

More Trials and Tribulations

For the most part, the Pilgrims kept to themselves and stuck together, spending their days and nights below decks praying, reading the Bible, singing songs, and sleeping. In the mornings and evenings, the 20 women prepared the meals, which consisted of salted meats, peas, beans, hard cheese, water, and beer.

During a particularly rough storm, one of the *Mayflower*'s main support beams cracked and splintered. This beam had been holding the ship together, and for a brief time it looked and felt like the old wooden ship might break apart. Luckily, one of the passengers had brought a "great iron screw," which was used to repair the beam and bind it back together.

During yet another storm, a 25-year-old Pilgrim named John Howland went up on deck to try to assist the crew, but when the *Mayflower* listed heavily, he fell overboard and was nearly lost in the North Atlantic. Howland was able to grab a rope hanging down from one of the masts…right before the current pulled him under.

If Howland had been a little slower, or if the crew had not been on hand to haul him in, America might be different today, because two of Howland's descendants would become president of his future homeland: George H. W. Bush and George W. Bush. (Other presidents whose ancestors came over on the *Mayflower*: John Adams, John Quincy Adams, Zachary Taylor, Theodore Roosevelt, and Franklin D. Roosevelt.)

Life and Death

Two of the Pilgrim women had especially rough voyages. Elizabeth Hopkins and Susanna White were each seven months pregnant when the *Mayflower* left England.

The constant rain and the ship's incessant tossing and heaving during six straight weeks of storms made their pregnancies that much more difficult. And the Pilgrims all wondered which would happen first: landfall or childbirth?

Hopkins gave birth to a baby boy while at sea. He was called Oceanus. White didn't give birth until shortly after they landed, when she delivered a boy named Peregrine. Oceanus's birth did little to liven the mood—the Pilgrims were cold and weary, and many were sick. A 12-year-old boy named William Butten fell ill early in the voyage and, despite the best efforts of the Pilgrims, died only two days before the Mayflower reached land.

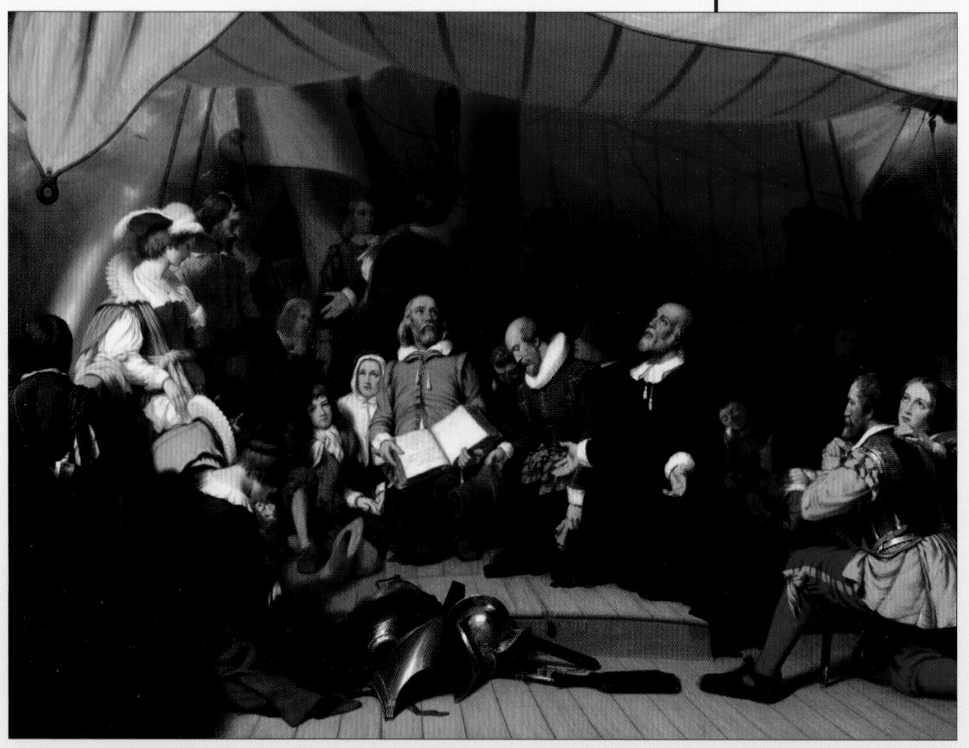

This painting, Embarkation of the Pilgrims, *depicts Governor John Carver (holding his hat) and, kneeling behind him in the background, William Bradford, who would later succeed him. (Robert Walter Weir)*

Landing

The Pilgrims didn't land on "Plymouth Rock." They didn't land on any rock at all. They didn't even land at Plymouth. Their original destination was "Northern Virginia"—but not the same region that currently resides next to Washington, D.C. In the 1600s, many maps referred to the entire eastern seaboard as Virginia, because the Virginia Company laid claim to it. The Pilgrims' actual

The *Palustris hefner* species of rabbit is named for *Playboy* mogul Hugh Hefner.

destination was the Hudson River area in what is now New York, where they had been granted a land claim from the Virginia Company. But they didn't land there, either.

As the *Mayflower* headed for the Hudson, yet another squall tossed and turned the ship, forcing it off course. When one of Master Jones's men sighted a peninsula that they could safely reach, their leader, William Bradford, begged Jones to land there. Jones agreed, so the battered ship immediately turned its rudders and headed for safety. On November 11, 1620, after more than two months at sea, the *Mayflower* dropped anchor off the sandy tip of Cape Cod, near what is now Provincetown, Massachusetts. Bradford described the landing in his journal:

> Being thus arrived in a good harbor and brought safe to land, they fell upon their knees and blessed the God of heaven, who had brought them over the vast and furious ocean, and delivered them from all the perils and miseries thereof, again to set their feet on the firm and stable earth, their proper element.

Tuba Lips and Other Weird Ailments

Fiddler's Neck

The name might sound silly, but according to a study of regular violin and viola players by Dr. Thilo Gambichler of Oldchurch Hospital in London, the friction of the instrument's base against the left side of the neck (for right-handed players) can cause lesions, severe inflammation, and cysts. What's worse, said the study, published in the British medical journal *BMC Dermatology*, it causes *lichenification*—the development of a patch of thick, leathery skin on the neck, giving it a "bark-like" appearance.

Guitar Nipple

A similar report issued in the United States cited three female classical guitarists who suffered from *traumatic mastitis*—swelling of the breast and nipple area—due to prolonged friction from the instrument's body. The condition can strike male players, too.

Bagpiper's Fungus

Recent medical reports have detailed the dangers of playing Scotland's national instrument. Bagpipes are traditionally made of sheepskin coated with a molasses-like substance called treacle. That, the report said, is a perfect breeding ground for various fungi, such as *aspergillus* and *cryptococcus*. Bagpipers can inadvertently inhale fungal spores, which, according to Dr. Robert Sataloff of Thomas Jefferson University Hospital in Philadelphia, can lead to deadly lung—and even brain—diseases.

Tuba Lips

Many long-term tuba players develop an allergic reaction to nickel, an ingredient in brass. The allergy can result in dermatitis of the lips and can sometimes develop into chronic eczema. Strictly speaking, the condition can also affect the chin and hands, and can be contracted from any number of brass instruments (but "tuba lips" is more fun to say).

Ask the Experts

Everyone's got a question or two they'd like answered—basic stuff, like "Why is the sky blue?" Here are a few of those questions, with answers from some of the world's top trivia experts.

Eat Me...Not!

Q: *What would happen if you ate one of those "Do not eat!" silica gel packets found in the packaging of dry goods such as clothing and medicine?*

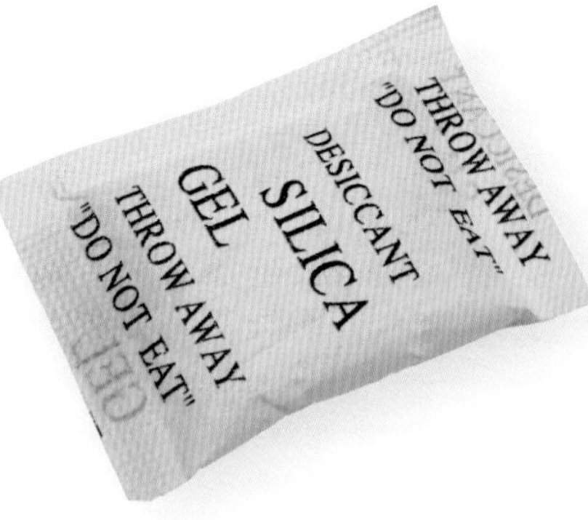

A: "Silica gel absorbs and holds water vapor. While the contents of a silica gel packet are basically harmless, consuming them would be an unpleasant experience. The moisture would be whisked away from the sides and roof of your mouth, your gums, and tongue, giving an all-too-accurate meaning of the phrase 'dry mouth.' If it did happen to get past your mouth—unlikely because you'd probably be making every effort to spit it out—you might suffer a few irritating side effects such as dry eyes, an irritated, dry feeling in your throat, aggravated, dry mucous membranes and nasal cavity, and an upset stomach." (From *Discovery Health*, by Katherine Neer)

Big bowl of silica

Fluid Entertainment

Q: *Do liquid crystal displays (LCDs) actually contain liquid?*

A: "In this case, the term 'liquid' refers to a peculiar quality of a certain type of crystal, not its physical appearance. The twisted nematic liquid crystal is the most common type used in LCD televisions and monitors today. It has a naturally twisted crystalline structure. A particular feature of this crystal is that it reacts to electric currents in predictable ways—that is, by untwisting to varying degrees depending on the current to which it is exposed. Hence the 'liquid' part of the crystal's moniker: Rather than being an oxymoron (How can a solid also be a liquid?), the term refers to the relative pliability of the crystals themselves, which is to say, their twistability." (From *LCD TV Buying Guide*, by Jack Burden)

I just want to be loved...

Cheer Up, Officer!

Q: *Why do police officers wear blue uniforms?*

A: "In 1829 the London Metropolitan Police, the first modern police force, developed standard police apparel. These first police officers, the famous Bobbies" of London, wore a dark blue, paramilitary-style uniform. The color helped

Q: How many days are there in a fortnight? A: 14.

to distinguish them from the British military, who wore red and white uniforms. Based on the London police, the New York City Police Department adopted the dark blue uniform in 1853. Today, most U.S. law enforcement agencies continue to use dark uniforms for their ability to help conceal the wearer in tactical situations and for their ease in cleaning. Dark colors also help hide stains." (From *The FBI Law Enforcement Bulletin*, by Richard R. Johnson)

Prepare for Takeoff

Q: *On commercial airlines, why do you have to put your seat in the upright position before takeoff and landing?*

A: "Should an emergency occur during either of these times, passengers have a better chance of survival if they evacuate the plane immediately. Milliseconds count in these situations, so everyone would be in a mad rush to find an emergency exit. Coach passengers know how difficult squeezing out of a seat mid-flight just to get to the lavatory can be; now imagine that the cabin is filled with smoke and visibility is near zero. Reclined seats, extended table trays, and briefcases in the aisle would cause already panicked folks to stumble and fall, and hamper the evacuation process." (From *Mental Floss magazine's* "7 Burning Questions About Air Travel," *by Kara Kovalchik*)

Don't Get Testy!

Q: *Why do patients have to cough during a hernia exam?*

A: "A hernia occurs when soft tissue, usually part of the intestine, protrudes through a weak point or tear in your abdominal wall. This bulging is most likely to occur when there's increased pressure on your abdomen, such as when lifting, straining, sneezing, or coughing. Forcing a cough during a hernia exam causes your abdominal muscles to contract and increase pressure within your abdomen. This may force a hernia to bulge out, making it easier to detect during examination." *(From the Mayo Clinic's website, by Michael Picco, M.D.)*

I Can't NYC You

Some statistics about the infamous blackout that shut down New York City in 1977.

- Actual fires during the blackout: 1,037
- False alarms: 1,700
- Firefighters injured: between 45 and 55
- Cops on night duty on July 13: 2,500
- Cops on night duty on July 14: 12,000
- Sanitation Department staff mobilized on July 14: 3,800
- Number of 911 calls: 3,000 per hour (70,680 total)
- Amount given to NYC by the federal government to pay for damages: $11 million

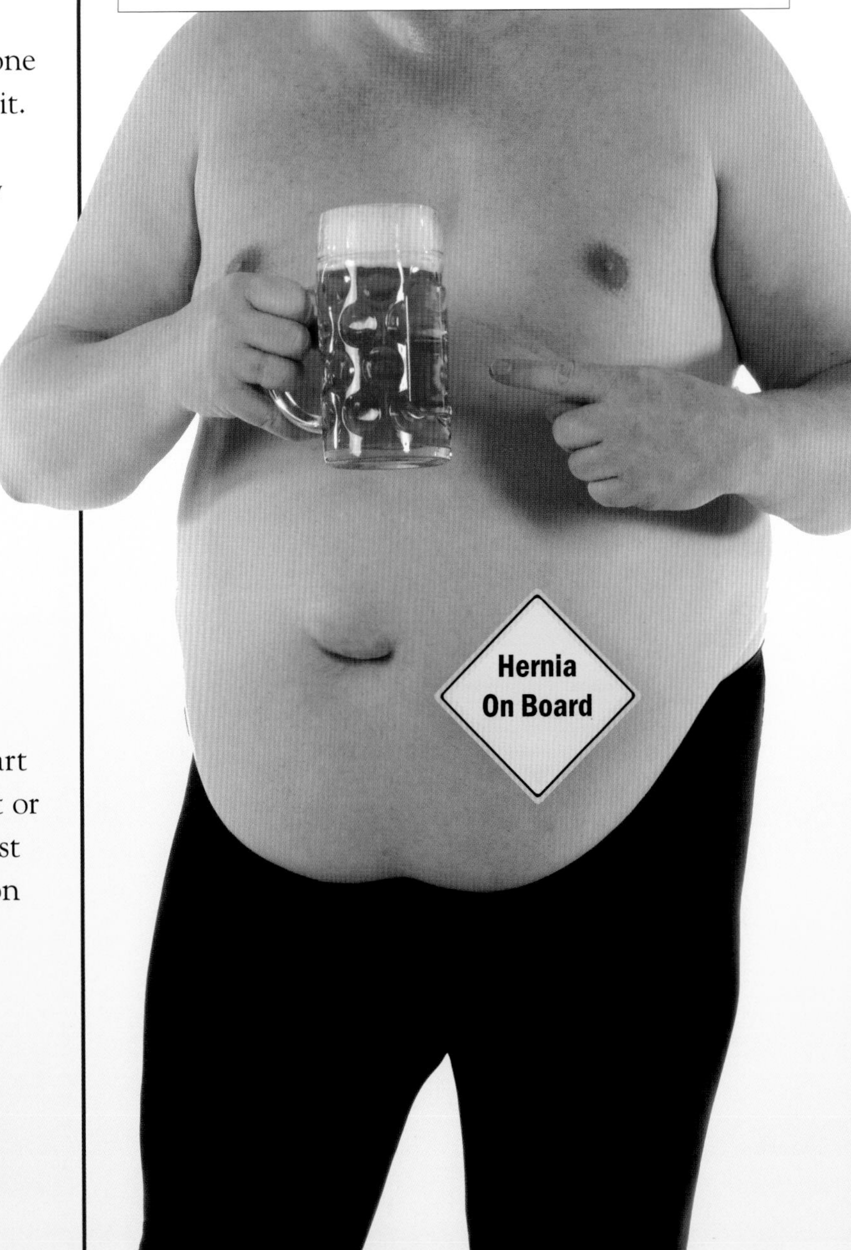

TV Myths and Legends

Our friend's brother's nephew's cousin's friend's brother saw Charles Manson at the Monkees audition, so it must be true, right? Just like these other TV-related urban legends.

Myth: Bill Cosby hated *Amos 'n' Andy*'s stereotypical depiction of African Americans as lazy buffoons so much that he bought the rights to the show…so he could pull it from circulation.

Truth: When the hit radio show *Amos 'n' Andy* moved to TV in 1951, it was heavily criticized by the NAACP for its demeaning portrayal of blacks. The organization urged CBS to cancel the show, but it ran until 1953, at which point reruns were syndicated well into the 1960s. The NAACP and many prominent figures, including Bill Cosby, continued to speak out. While Cosby didn't buy the show to make it disappear, his clout, popularity, and public opposition led CBS to permanently pull *Amos 'n' Andy* from syndication in 1966.

Freeman Gosden and Charles Correll in Amos 'n' Andy

Myth: The kid who played the nerdy Paul Pfeiffer on *The Wonder Years* (1988–93) became shock rocker Marilyn Manson.

Truth: Josh Saviano portrayed Paul on the ABC dramedy *The Wonder Years.* After the show ended, he retired from acting, went to Yale, and became a lawyer. "Marilyn Manson," meanwhile, is the stage name of Florida rock musician Brian Warner. While the two men bear a resemblance, Warner is seven years older than Saviano and was already performing as Marilyn Manson while *The Wonder Years* was on the air. The rumor probably spread because Marilyn Manson found mainstream

Saviano in The Wonder Years *and Manson (not in* The Wonder Years*)*

Hot stuff! The inside of a compost pile can reach temperatures of 150°F.

popularity just as Saviano disappeared from the public eye.

A *new face in* The Monkees?

Myth: Charles Manson auditioned for *The Monkees*.

Truth: Before he became a murderer, Manson was an unsuccessful rock musician. (Music producer Terry Melcher declined to sign him, and Manson may have had Sharon Tate killed because he was looking for Melcher—Tate was renting a house once lived in by Melcher.) Public knowledge about Manson's rock connections (he was also acquainted with Beach Boy Dennis Wilson) led to the urban legend that he'd auditioned for *The Monkees*, the show and the band, in 1965. But he couldn't have—in 1965 he was serving a jail sentence for forgery. (Other future famous musicians who tried out for *The Monkees* include Stephen Stills, Harry Nilsson, and Paul Williams.)

Myth: *Joanie Loves Chachi* was a massive hit in South Korea. The reason: *chachi* is the Korean word for "penis."

Truth: It's been widely reported that the 1982 *Happy Days* spinoff *Joanie Loves Chachi* was the most popular American TV show ever broadcast in South Korea, and scores of curious viewers tuned in because the title translated as *Joanie Loves Penis*. None of it's true. *Chachi* has no meaning in Korean, and *Joanie Loves Chachi* never even aired on South Korean broadcast television. The whole thing started as a joke that creator Garry Marshall told in interviews while promoting the show.

Sandy Duncan's "funny face"

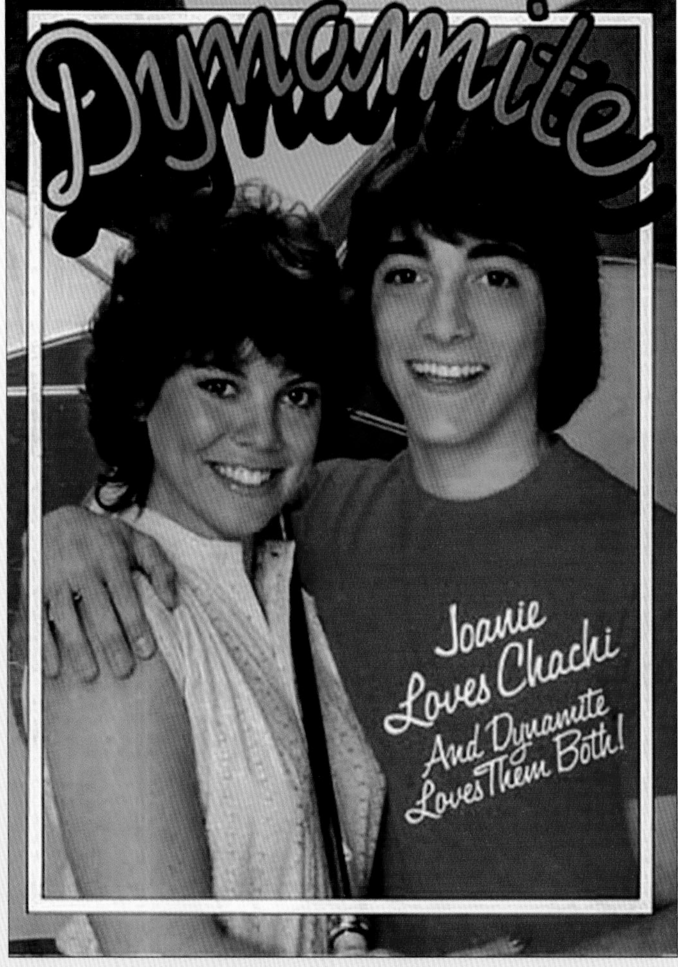

Joanie loving Chachi

Myth: Longtime TV star Sandy Duncan (*Funny Face, The Sandy Duncan Show, The Hogan Family*) has a glass eye.

Truth: Shortly after *Funny Face* debuted in 1971, Duncan's doctor discovered a noncancerous tumor behind her left eye. An operation removed the lump, but it left Duncan blind in that eye. So while it appears "glassy," the eye is real.

Made in China

Have you ever noticed that it seems like everything is made in China? Well, almost everything is made in China. Here's why.

In the Red

Mao Tse-Tung

Prior to World War II, China was a major economic force, exporting huge amounts of raw goods (such as tea and rice) all over the world. When Mao Tse-Tung's Communist government assumed control of China in 1949, it took over all of the country's businesses. Not content with only exporting agricultural goods, Chairman Mao wanted China to become a major industrial power. So he implemented China's first "Five Year Plan" for economic development. Money, resources, and labor were all allocated by the government, which also set wages and prices. Even consumption of food and goods would be controlled through strict rationing. Result: Industry grew rapidly, but agricultural production suffered.

The next Five Year Plan (1958) aimed to revive the agricultural sector to such heights that China could be completely self-sufficient. Farming output increased as planned, but food-storage and transportation technology couldn't keep up with agricultural growth, and much of the nation's huge grain crop went to waste.

An abandoned steel factory in China. (Don't worry—there are plenty more.)

According to folklore, an axe or knife placed under a woman's bed will "cut the pain" of childbirth.

After China publicly criticized the USSR for bowing to American pressure and removing missiles from Cuba during the Cuban Missile Crisis, the Soviet Union withdrew economic assistance in 1962. In the wake of expanding military operations in Southeast Asia and increased Cold War posturing, the West turned its back on China. By 1970, the country was almost completely alone. Self-sufficiency was the goal—but isolation was the result.

Nixon Goes to China

Conditions would begin to improve after President Richard Nixon's 1971 visit to Beijing. China agreed to re-establish ties with the United States on the condition that American troops would leave the region. (They had been stationed in the Chinese province of Taiwan since the Communist takeover.) Nixon agreed; tensions eased between China and the United States.

Out with the Old

Chairman Mao died in 1976 and was replaced by the moderate Deng Xiaoping. Rejecting Mao's failed plans for self-sufficiency, Deng opened China to the world in 1980. To hasten modernization, the government encouraged foreign investment and invited western companies to bring their technology to China in the form of entire state-of-the-art Western factories. State-owned businesses remained the standard, but private ownership of companies became legal. Most revolutionary of all, the government took a capitalist approach to taxing businesses: It took a cut of the business' profits and allowed the remainder to be reinvested into the companies. The result of Deng's policies: China's industry grew at an annual rate of 11 percent in the 1980s and 17 percent in the 1990s, the fastest rate in the world at the time.

But here's what motivated American companies to open factories in China: cheap labor and lots of it. (As of 2011, the Chinese workforce was roughly 785 million people.) China's large population creates huge demand (and competition) for jobs. This drives down wages, and they're made even lower by the government, which keeps pay rates low to control business costs. A worker in China earns less than 10 percent of what a worker doing the same job in the United States would earn. Plus in China, few workers receive benefits, sick leave, or worker's compensation. China's labor laws are very relaxed: Shifts can be 12 hours a day. One of the highest costs of doing business is labor, so low wages means products manufactured in China are unbeatably inexpensive, both to make and to buy.

World Domination

Today Western companies in almost every industry have factories in China. Even with the expense of moving overseas and constantly having to ship materials and goods to Chinese factories, the low wage rates (and lower taxes) still make it highly profitable. Economists

The Pacific Ocean holds about 6,000,000,000,000,000,000,000 gallons of water.

estimate that as much as 90 percent of retail goods available in the United States were made in China.

- Some of the products: Apple computers, Avon cosmetics, Boeing airplanes, Clorox bleach, John Deere tractors, Dow chemicals, General Motors car parts, Hewlett-Packard printers, Johnson & Johnson first aid products, Mattel toys, Motorola cell phones, Toshiba televisions, Black & Decker drills, Intel microprocessors, Maytag appliances, Dell computers, Outboard Marine boats, Head & Shoulders shampoo, Rand McNally maps, Sony PlayStations, Serta mattresses, Sherwin-Williams paint, and Xerox copiers.
- Other companies use Chinese facilities to manufacture satellites, ships, trains, mining machinery, oil drilling equipment, power generators, plastics, pharmaceuticals, bicycles, sewing machines, metal knick-knacks, cement, coffee makers, shoes, and dishes.
- China produces more clothes than any other country. Its industry includes cotton, wool, linen, silk, and chemical fibers, as well as printing, dyeing, knitting, and automatic manufacture.
- China is the largest producer of steel in the world. From stainless steel to sheet metal to pipes, China passed Britain as the world's largest steel producer in the 1960s. The Chinese government increased industrial production so quickly by reassigning millions of farmers to crude backyard furnaces where they made steel from low-grade ore, scrap metal, and even household items.
- The world's six largest producers of American flags are all based in China. Most religious merchandise (like Virgin Mary statues, rosaries, and Buddha figurines) sold in the United States are made in China…a country that is officially atheist.

Where your favorite blue shirt was born

A soap bubble is 10,000 times thinner than a human hair.

Odds & Ends

Some random oddities from our archives.

The Great Bathroom Barbie Mystery

In late 2005, seemingly out of nowhere and without explanation, Barbie dolls suddenly began appearing in the ladies' bathrooms of coffee shops in the Lincoln, Nebraska, area. The first sighting occurred at The Mill, when a barista walked into the ladies' room one morning and found a Malibu Barbie standing on the paper towel holder. A few days later, another was found perched on top of a stall wall. Then more Barbies began showing up at other coffee shops… and it creeped out the staff. "You go to clean and there's a Barbie doll staring up at you. It's scary. I won't go in there anymore," said barista Jamie Yost. All of the Barbies were in pristine condition and came on stands (which pointed toward a collector as the culprit). Shop owners tried everything short of installing video cameras in the bathrooms to catch the woman responsible. But then, a few months after they first appeared, the Barbie visits abruptly stopped (most likely because whoever was putting them there ran out of the dolls).

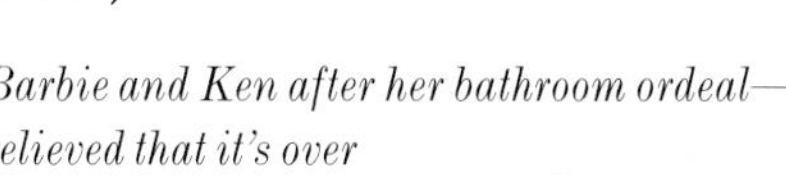

Barbie and Ken after her bathroom ordeal—relieved that it's over

No Laughing Matter

Veteran stand-up comic Buddy Hackett once told film critic Roger Ebert one of the secrets of show business. "Buddy was a student of the science of comedy," recalled Ebert. "His favorite Las Vegas stage was at the Sahara. 'I was offered twice the dough to move to a certain hotel,' he told me, 'but nothing doing. Comics who work that room always flop. There's a physical reason for that. The stage is above the eye lines of too much of the audience. At the Sahara, the seats are banked and most of the audience is looking down at the stage. Everybody in the business knows: Up for singers, down for comics. The people want to idealize a singer. They want to feel superior to a comic. You're trying to make them laugh. They can't laugh at someone they're looking up to.'"

Buddy Hackett

Paper Smash Rock

Did you know there's an international governing body for Rock Paper Scissors? The World Rock Paper Scissors Society sets rules, holds an annual worldwide tournament, and since the 1920s has published *Think Three*, an RPS strategy and lifestyle magazine. Obviously, a rock crushes scissors and scissors cut paper. But why exactly does paper defeat rock? It's the question the World Rock Paper Scissors Society is most often asked. According to them, the answer lays in ancient China. Petitions were given to the emperor for approval. If he accepted it, the document was placed under a rock. If denied, it was draped over the rock. Paper covering rock came to be associated with defeat.

Google's original name was BackRub.

Too Risky for Guinness

If you make it into Guinness World Records *and somebody breaks your record, your name gets taken out. Turns out there's another way to get booted from the book.*

By the Book

If you published a book of world records, what kinds of records would you allow into your book? What kinds would you keep out? The people at the *Guinness Book of World Records* have been asking themselves those questions for more than 50 years. Founding editors Ross and Norris McWhirter took a conservative approach from the start: Anything having to do with hard liquor or sex was out. "Ours is the kind of book maiden aunts give to their nieces," the brothers once explained. Crime was out, too—the brothers didn't want readers breaking laws just to get in the book.

As the years passed and the *Guinness Book* grew into an international phenomenon, a new problem arose: Some categories that were pretty dangerous to begin with—sword-swallowing, fire-eating, etc.—became more so as the winning records climbed ever higher. Do you remember the "Iron Maiden" category? That's where a person lies down on a bed of nails, has another bed of nails placed down on top of him, then has hundreds of pounds of heavy weights piled on top of that. There's a physical limit to how many weights you can pile on a guy sandwiched between two beds of nails before he dies a horrible, crushing death. Sooner or later, somebody trying to get into the book in the Iron Maiden category was going to be killed in the attempt. "We feel that's something we shouldn't encourage," Norris McWhirter said in 1981.

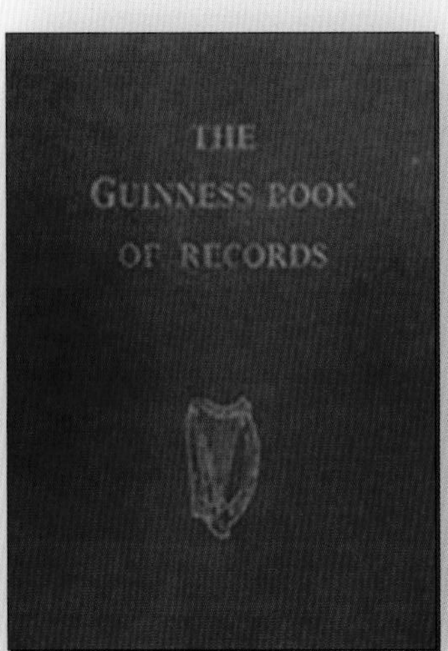

Original 1955 edition

Written Out

So in the late 1970s, the *Guinness Book of World Records* began to close the book on some records that had been around for years. "This category has now been retired," the editors stated after some entries, "and no further claims will be entertained." A few years later, many such categories disappeared from the book altogether.

That might have been it if not for the fact that the *Guinness Book of World Records* had changed hands a few times since then, and each new owner has had their own ideas about what should be included in the book. Some categories that were once deemed too dangerous were brought back… though in a few cases the old world records were forgotten or ignored and replaced with new "world records" that didn't even beat the ones they replaced. So who's back in? Who's still out? What else is new? Here's a look at how some of the more unusual categories have fared.

Iron Maiden

Record Holder: Vernon Craig of Wooster, Ohio, who performed under the stage name "Komar"

Details: Craig set his world record on March

Vernon prepares to nap.

Human urine produced worldwide in one day would take 20 minutes to flow over Niagara Falls.

6, 1977, in Chicago, when 1,642½ pounds of weights were piled on top of him while he was sandwiched between two beds of nails.

What Happened: In the 1979 edition, Craig's record appeared with the following note: "Now that weights in Bed-of-Nails contests have attained ¾ of a ton it is felt that this category should be retired. No further claims for publication will henceforth be examined."

Update: By 2000 the record was reopened for competition; today it's held by Lee Graber of Tallmadge, Ohio, who beat Komar's record by 16½ pounds, for a total of 1,659 pounds on June 24, 2000. According to *Guinness*, the hardest part of Graber's attempt was controlling his breathing, "as he had a lot of weight on his chest and needed to relax to avoid bursting a blood vessel in his head." (Komar retired his Iron Maiden act in 2000 at the age of 68.)

The Long Shower

Record Holder: Arron Marshall of Rockingham Park, Australia

Details: On July 29, 1978, Marshall stepped into his shower, turned on the water, and did not leave again until August 12, setting a world showering record of 336 hours.

What Happened: In the 1982 edition, his world record appeared with the following disclaimer: "Desquamination [skin peeling off in scales] can be a positive danger."

Update: The category was closed and unlike the Iron Maiden, as of 2005 it has not been reopened. (Apparently long showers are more dangerous than the Iron Maiden.)

Car Jumping off a Ramp

Record Holder: Dusty Russell of Athens, Georgia

Details: In April 1973, Russell climbed into his 1963 Ford Falcon, sped up a ramp, and jumped more than 176 feet.

What Happened: The record was still there in the 1981 edition, but in 1982 it was gone.

Update: By 1998 the category was back, but with a slight modification: now a car has to "land on its wheels and drive on afterwards." On August 23, 1998, an Australian named Ray Baumann set a new record, jumping his car 237 feet.

Fire-Eating

Record Holder: Jean Chapman of Buckinghamshire, England

Details: On August 25, 1979, Chapman extinguished 4,583 flaming torches using only her mouth. It took her two hours.

What Happened: For the 1982 edition Chapman's entry was followed with the disclaimer: "Fire-eating is potentially a highly dangerous activity." The category was later dropped.

Update: By 2004 Guinness was accepting entries in a modified (and presumably safer) fire-eating category: most flaming torches extinguished in one minute.

Current record holder: Hubertus Wawra, a comedian/fire-eater from Germany. On February 21, 2011, he extinguished 39 torches in only 30 seconds. Don't try this at home...unless, of course, you know what you're doing.

Hubertus Wawra warms up for the camera.

Amazing Rescue

They risked life and limb to save a trapped whale and were rewarded with the gift of a lifetime.

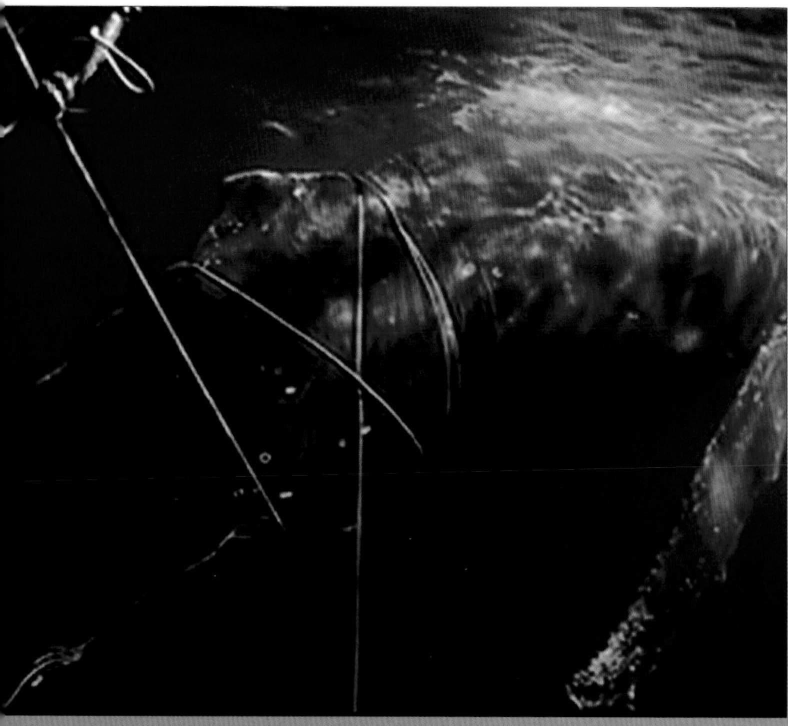

The heartbreaking scene that confronted the divers

Tangled Web

On the brisk Sunday morning of December 11, 2005, a crab fisherman spotted a heartbreaking sight off the coast of San Francisco: a 50-foot humpback whale trapped in a tangle of crab-pot lines. He immediately called for help, and within three hours the Marine Mammal Center had chartered a boat—normally used for whale watching tours—and assembled a rescue team. As soon as they arrived on the scene, they assessed the situation. It didn't look good.

The female humpback was completely entangled in hundreds of yards of ropes that collectively weighed more than 1,000 pounds. To make matters worse, she'd already been struggling for hours to keep her blowhole above water, and they didn't know how much strength she had left. No whale that had been trapped like this off the west coast had ever survived. With time running out, the rescuers knew there was only one way to save her: dive in and start cutting the ropes one at a time.

Into the Water

Four divers went in: James Moskito, Jason Russey, Ted Vivian, and Tim Young. Moskito was the first to reach the whale, and the first to understand the severity of the situation. More than 20 thick lines were wrapped tightly around her tail, flippers, torso, and mouth, all digging deep into her flesh. So, on top of everything else, the whale was losing blood. "I really didn't think we were going to be able to save her," Moskito told the *San Francisco Chronicle*.

Easy Does It

The whale wasn't the only one at risk; her rescuers were in danger as well. They knew that even a small flip of the 50-ton animal's tail could kill any one of them. But once they got to work carefully cutting the ropes with large, curved knives, their fear quickly subsided. The men later said that they could somehow sense the whale knew they were there to help her. While they worked, she barely moved at all, just enough to stay afloat. At one point, Moskito found himself face to face with the animal as he cut the ropes from her mouth. "Her eye was there winking at me, watching me work. It was an epic moment of my life."

Finally, after more than an hour of nonstop cutting, the heavy ropes fell away and the humpback whale was able to move again. She immediately wriggled free of the few remaining lines and started out to sea.

Thank You

But then the whale did something unexpected. She swam in circles near the men, completing a few rotations. And then she swam right up to each of them and, one by one, gently nuzzled against them for a moment.

"It felt to me like she was thanking us, knowing that she was free and that we'd helped her," Moskito recalled. "She stopped about a foot away from me, pushed me around a little bit and had some fun. It was amazing, unbelievable."

The Eruption of Mount Pelée

Here's the tragic tale of a volcano, a town, and some crooked politicians. Or were they crooked? The history books have always painted them that way, but recent findings suggest that the real villain of this story is a lack of basic scientific knowledge.

Rumble Rumble

In late April 1902, Mount Pelée, on the island of Martinique in the Caribbean Sea, began smoking and shaking. Only four miles away lay the town of St. Pierre, the cultural and commercial capital of the French West Indies. More than 30,000 people lived there. They were wary of the rumbling volcano, but it wasn't the first time it had acted up. Since the French had settled the island in the 17th century, Pelée had burped a few times, but always calmed right back down. No one had any reason to believe it would be any different this time, so they stayed put.

But in early May, scalding mudflows began pouring down the slopes and ash fell in the town faster than it could be swept away. Many people changed their minds about leaving and urged the town leaders to start evacuation measures. They didn't. Why? No one knows for sure, because a few days later, nearly everyone in St. Pierre was dead.

Absolute Power

Over the past century, historians and geologists alike have tried to piece together the events that led up to the eruption of May 8, 1902. The most common version: The death toll was so high because of politics. The island's elections were only a few days away. St. Pierre mayor Roger Fouché and Martinique governor Louis Mouttet were more concerned with keeping power than with keeping their constituents safe. Their biggest concern: the growing popularity of a radical political party—led by a black candidate—that stood for equal rights and threatened the white supremacy of the island. With their support starting to slip, Mayor Fouché and Governor Mouttet refused to allow anything to delay the election even a single day. To reassure the people that the mountain would calm down, they planted a story in the local newspaper that a team of "volcano experts" had studied the mountain and deemed there was no danger to the town.

The re-built town of Saint Pierre, Martinique, with Mount Pelée in the background. The beach is volcanic ash.

But Pelée didn't calm down. On May 4, a giant mudslide obliterated the sugar mill on the edge of town, taking 23 workers with it. It caused a tsunami that drowned the seafront district, killing dozens more. As the frightened citizens began packing to leave, they were ordered to stay home. The mayor even told his men to spread rumors that the outskirts of town had been taken over by swarms of poisonous centipedes. Those citizens who did try to leave St. Pierre were met at the borders by armed militia men who turned them back. Only a few people made it out.

Leveled

At dawn on election day, a colossal cloud of superheated gasses, ash, and rock erupted from Mount Pelée...and headed straight for St. Pierre at more than 100 mph. Within three minutes, the entire city was gone. Even ships anchored offshore were set ablaze, killing all those aboard.

Only two people in St. Pierre were left alive. One was a prisoner who was being held in an underground cell with one small window facing away from the volcano. He was horribly burned, but survived and later toured with the Barnum and Bailey Circus as a sideshow attraction. The other survivor was the town cobbler, a religious fanatic who had been hiding in his cellar. He went insane after venturing outside to discover the charred remains of everyone he knew.

The Tower of Pelée. This magnificent spire of felsic lava was generated in the waning stages of the 1902 eruption.

The Truth

Dozens of books published since the catastrophe tell this same basic story, but recently historians have been able to piece together a more accurate version of events: It seems that the governor wasn't quite as concerned about the election as previously thought, and there's no evidence that he and the mayor spread false rumors and forced people from leaving. Even the volcano experts knew Pelée would erupt, but they figured that when it did, townsfolk would have plenty of time to escape the river of lava flowing down the mountain. It was four miles away, after all.

But no one at the time had ever witnessed what is now known as a pyroclastic flow: a wall of gas, ash, and rocks that can travel long distances and instantly consumes everything in its path. So while St. Pierre's leaders were perhaps corrupt, their biggest fault was actually ignorance. They simply didn't see the danger.

If any good has come out of Mount Pelée's eruption, it's that political leaders now take the threat posed by volcanoes much more seriously.

In the Trenches

The use of trenches to conceal military forces predates 1914 by a long time, and in fact, they were called "trenches" from about 1500 on. But their use in World War I, where they far exceeded any prior deployment, gave our language a number of lasting terms.

In the Trenches

During the war being *in the trenches* meant being in action. The same thing today is meant by the term, that is, actively working at something. Thus, "He spent years in the trenches before they made him president of the company."

Digging In

After the trenches were dug, soldiers on both sides lived in them for months on end, with neither side advancing or retreating measurably. From this, *digging in* acquired the meaning of standing firm in one's position or views.

Foxhole

In addition to very long trenches, soldiers occasionally used a small slit trench that housed one or a few men. Although it was used much more rarely, the name given it, *foxhole*, survived. It was to play a much larger role in subsequent wars.

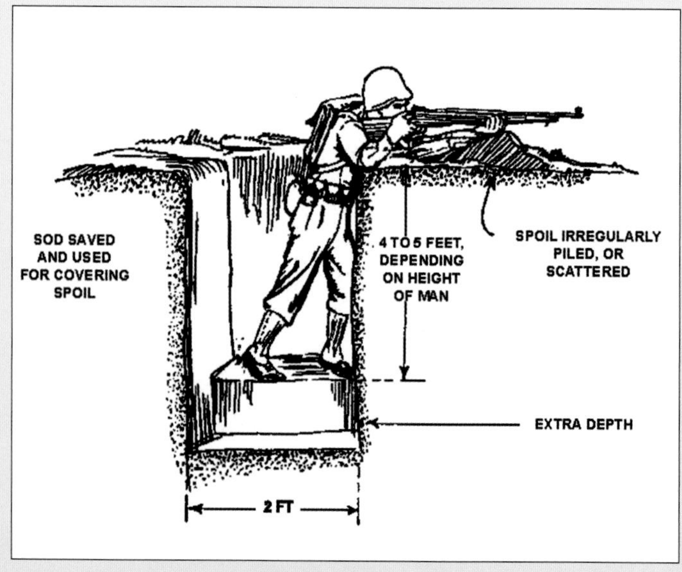

Inside a foxhole

Shell Shock

In addition to physical ailments, soldiers frequently suffered from nervous conditions. One was an acute stress syndrome resulting from exposure to constant shelling by the enemy and therefore called *shell shock*. It was thought to be caused by both the noise of the artillery and the constant fear it engendered. Today this term is still loosely used to describe the after effects of any traumatic experience, as in, "That series of lousy boyfriends gave her a bad case of shell shock."

Screaming Meemies

A similar expression is *screaming meemies*, a term that was coined for German artillery shells that emitted an exceptionally high-pitched whine before exploding. The term was later used to describe a state of extreme nervousness, bordering on hysteria.

Over the Top

When ordered to advance, the soldiers climbed over the parapet of front-line trenches to attack the enemy's front line. The "top" referred both to the trench's top and to the open no-man's-land between them and the enemy. After the war, the term survived, assisted by Arthur Guy Empey's use of the term as the title for his popular World War I account. In civilian use it was extended to mean taking the final plunge and doing something dangerous or notable.

Trench Mouth

The long months in the trenches took a terrible toll on a soldier's health. One condition that afflicted many of them was trench mouth (formerly called

First female national news anchor: Barbara Walters (1976).

Vincent's disease), characterized by painful, bleeding gums and bad breath. It was caused by poor oral hygiene and nutrition, heavy smoking, and stress—all conditions endemic in the trenches. Today trench mouth is readily treated with dental care and antibiotics.

Trench Coat

The trenches were frequently, if not always, wet. Consequently, the officers wore long waterproof coats, or trench coats, a noun later applied to and still used for similar civilian raincoats.

No-Man's-Land

Although *no-man's-land* dates from the 1300s, when it meant the waste ground between two kingdoms, it didn't take on its military meaning until World War I, when it was applied to the territory between the thousands of miles of Allied and German trenches. This area, a virtually stationary battle line for three years, was covered with barbed wire and pitted with shell holes made by the artillery of both sides. Since then, this term also has been used loosely to describe an indefinite situation where one is neither here nor there.

left: Directing the Way to the Front, *Bruce Bairnsfather's World War I illustration of soldiers in trench coats; below: World War I trenches, Flanders Fields, Belgium*

As if enemy fire wasn't scary enough, this poor platoon was "entertained" in the trenches by a grenade-juggling private.

A Cheesy Origin

During the Great Depression, the Kraft Company tried to market a low-priced cheddar cheese powder—but the public wouldn't buy it. One St. Louis sales rep, looking for a way to unload his allotment of the stuff, tied individual packages of the cheese to macaroni boxes and talked grocers on his route into selling them as one item, which he called "Kraft Macaroni and Cheese." When the company found out how well they were selling, it made Kraft Macaroni and Cheese an official part of its product line.

Tripwire

Troops who advanced close to the German line often had to cut through a wire that had been strung to set off a trap or an alarm. The soldiers called it a *tripwire*, because it was meant literally to trip them up. Later the term was used to signify anything that might trip someone up, as in a *New York Times* headline on October 7, 1997, "Looking for Tripwires, Ickes Heads to the Witness Stand." (The term today is also employed for a small military force used as a first line of defense.)

How Insulting!

This page is dedicated to Alice Roosevelt Longworth, who famously said, "If you haven't got anything nice to say about anybody, come sit next to me."

"Someone tried the monkeys-on-typewriters bit trying for the plays of Shakespeare, but all they got was the collected works of Francis Bacon."

—Bill Hirst

"She was good at being inarticulately abstracted for the same reason that midgets are good at being short."

—Clive James, on Marilyn Monroe

"Groucho Marx? He's a male chauvinistic piglet."

—Betty Friedan

"I've been working so hard, I'm about to have a Mariah Carey."

—Usher, referring to Carey's rumored breakdown

"Is he just doing a bad Elvis pout, or was he born that way?"

—Freddie Mercury, on Billy Idol

Billy Idol

"The stupid person's idea of a clever person."

—Elizabeth Bowen, on author Aldous Huxley

"Her voice sounds like an eagle being goosed."

—Ralph Novak, on Yoko Ono

"He's nothing more than a well-meaning baboon."

—General George McClellan, on Abraham Lincoln

"He's like a monkey with arthritis, trying to go on stage and look young. I have great respect for the Stones but they would have been better if they had thrown Keith out 15 years ago."

—Elton John, on Keith Richards

"His writing is limited to songs for dead blondes."

—Keith Richards, on Elton John

"Dan Quayle is more stupid than Ronald Reagan put together."

—Matt Groening

"She's about as modest as Mussolini."

—David Crosby, on Joni Mitchell

"I've got three words for him: Am. A. Teur."

—Charlie Sheen, on Colin Farrell

"He was dull in company, dull in his closet, dull everywhere. He was dull in a new way and that made people think him great."

—Samuel Johnson, on fellow poet Thomas Gray

"Erick Dampier is soft. Quote it, underline it, tape it, send it to him. Don't ask me about that guy ever again."

—Shaquille O'Neal

"He has the vocal modulation of a railway-station announcer, the expressive power of a fencepost, and the charisma of a week-old head of lettuce."

—critic Fintan O'Toole, on Quentin Tarantino

"Shannon [Sharpe] looks like a horse. I'll tell you, that's an ugly dude. You can't tell me he doesn't look like Mr. Ed."

—Ray Buchanan, Atlanta Falcons, three days before Super Bowl XXXIII

"Ray said that? Well, I think he's ugly, but did I ever call him that? No. Tell Ray to put the eyeliner, the lipstick, and the high heels away. I'm not saying he's a cross-dresser; that's just what I heard."

—Shannon Sharpe, Denver Broncos, 20 minutes later

Roman emperor Nero played the bagpipes.

Please Touch the Exhibits

In 2001 Uncle John's older brother started a hands-on science museum called Science Works, right here in our little town of Ashland, Oregon. His inspiration: San Francisco's Exploratorium.

J. Robert Oppenheimer

Brothers in Arms

If you've ever been to a hands-on science museum and enjoyed the experience, you owe a debt of gratitude to famed nuclear physicist J. Robert Oppenheimer and his younger brother, Frank.

Both Oppenheimers had been brilliant nuclear scientists, and both had worked on developing the atomic bomb during World War II. After the war ended, though, and Russia quickly turned from an ally into an enemy, the FBI began focusing on the brothers for their leftist politics. They discovered that in the 1930s, Frank Oppenheimer and his wife Jackie had briefly joined the Communist Party, which was neither illegal nor particularly unusual, at a time when the Communist Party USA had 75,000 members. In the 1932 presidential election, the Communist Party candidate received more than 100,000 votes.

The Oppenheimers had joined the Communist Party because it was the only large organization working to racially-integrate public facilities in their hometown, Pasadena, California, a policy they strongly supported. But after World War II, as Russia took the place of Germany as America's number-one enemy, anybody who had belonged to the party, even in the distant past, was considered a potential spy, saboteur, or traitor. In fact, you didn't even have to be a member, as Robert Oppenheimer soon found out.

Guilt by Association

During his postwar work on the atomic bomb, Robert's strong personality, sophisticated manner, and knack at getting media attention generated some jealousy and enmity among some of his coworkers. The FBI was on the lookout for "disloyalty" in America's defense establishment and leaked information about the Oppenheimers to their enemies, who returned the favor by spreading accusations and rumors. In 1953 Frank lost his security clearance for having been a communist two decades earlier. Shortly after, Robert was informed that he had also lost his security clearance, in large

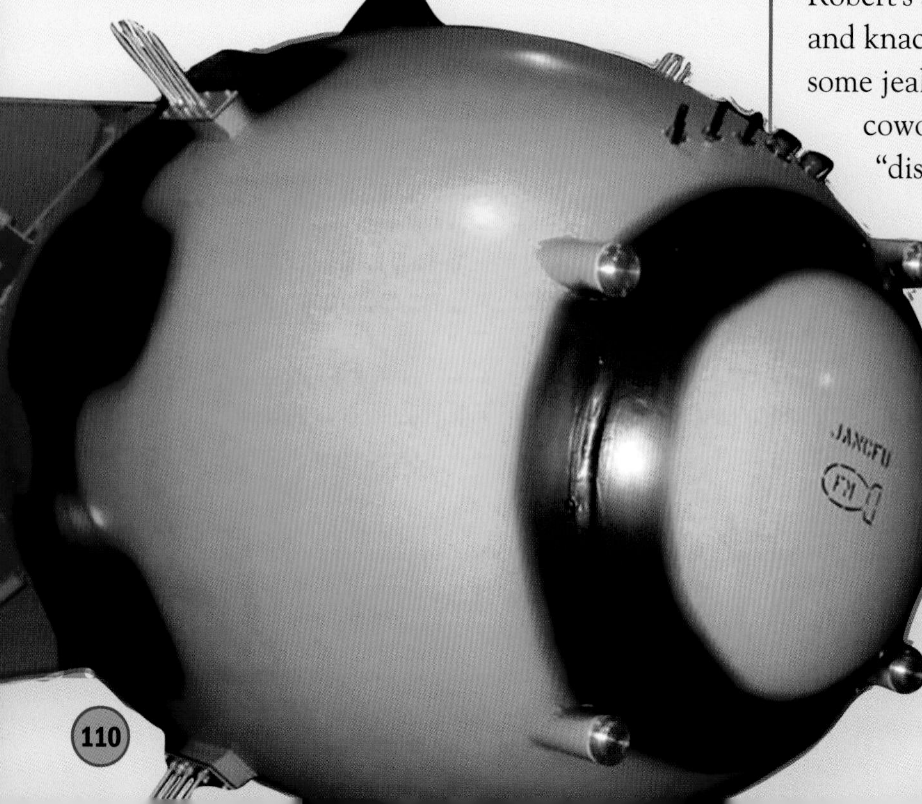

Replica of the "Fat Boy" atomic bomb

Hedgehogs are lactose-intolerant.

part because he associated with his brother and sister-in-law.

Robert Oppenheimer did all right in exile from his career, spending the following years writing and lecturing around the world. (In 1963 he would receive the Enrico Fermi Award from President Lyndon Johnson, partly as an apology for the way he had been treated two decades earlier.) His brother, however, did not do as well.

Out, Standing in His Field

Frank Oppenheimer didn't have as many options as his better-known older brother. He was fired from the faculty of the University of Minnesota and figured he'd probably never work in his field again. So he decided it was time to make a dramatic career change, preferably in a place where his notoriety wouldn't block him. He had inherited a painting by Van Gogh titled *First Steps (after Millet)*, showing a baby being coaxed to walk in a garden bed by proud parents. Perhaps inspired by its rural charm and implicit message of starting anew, he sold it and bought land in Pagosa Springs, Colorado, determined to become a cattle rancher.

Only problem: He knew nothing about cattle ranching. He did, however, have confidence in his ability to learn. He began by reading journals and books and conferring with his new neighbors. He joined the local cattle association and quickly rose to president. By 1957, as his local reputation grew and the Red Scare lost some of its steam, he began teaching a science class at a nearby high school. Two years later, through the urging of some heavy hitters in the field, he was hired by the University of Colorado to teach physics.

Hands On

From working with his hands, Frank Oppenheimer had discovered the importance of direct experience to illustrate what would otherwise just be words on a page. He assembled a series of hands-on, out-of-the-classroom experiments for his students to perform in their free time. Many of the experimental devices and activities were not just informative, but playful and fun. Dr. Oppenheimer began discovering that more than just his students were dropping by to use the equipment: Art

The Exploratorium

students, kids, even other faculty members came by to bounce, spin, compress, race, and otherwise play with the learning tools.

This got Oppenheimer thinking. He became intrigued with the idea of making science education more interesting to younger kids. Thanks to a grant from the National Science Foundation, he developed 100 experiments that elementary-school teachers could use in teaching elementary physics. From the positive reaction to this "Library of Experiments,"

Oppenheimer, now in his 50s, moved to Sausalito, just across the Golden Gate from San Francisco, and began thinking about creating a new kind of science museum.

Having fun with the anti-gravity mirror

Now Museum, Now You Don't

The problem with most science museums, Oppenheimer decided, is that they glorified the accomplishments of a few instead of inspiring people to follow their curiosity and become scientists themselves. He already had a lot of toys, and he began hand-building new ones—interactive experiments that would be big, sturdy enough for many hands, attractive to the eyes and mind, and educational in the process. "Please touch" would be the watchword, a dramatic change from most museums' rules.

Then Oppenheimer got a lucky break. The city of San Francisco had a huge empty space it didn't know what to do with. It was the Palace of Fine Arts, a "temporary" building from the 1915 World's Fair that was intentionally left standing when the Fair's other buildings were destroyed because it was too beautiful to tear down.

Unfortunately, it was also a white elephant: Now sitting in the middle of a residential neighborhood, it was far from the city's other attractions and had inadequate parking. Oppenheimer suggested turning it into a kids' science museum. City officials shrugged, said "Why not?" and leased the space to him for $1.00 per year.

Come See, Came Saw

Dubbed the "Exploratorium," Oppenheimer's museum opened quietly in the summer of 1969. With little budget for publicity, it started slowly. Eventually, a few curious people dribbled in. The exhibits—including a crawl-through sensory adventure for adults only—were unlike anything they'd seen before and word of mouth took over. "The Exploratorium was not designed to glorify anything," explained Oppenheimer in 1972 as his new museum started making waves. "We have not built exhibits whose primary message is 'Wasn't somebody else clever?' or 'Hadn't someone done a great service to mankind and the American way of life?' Nor do we tell people what they are supposed to get out of a particular exhibit or make them feel silly or stupid because they enjoyed it in a way that was perhaps not intended."

In recent years, more than half a million visitors a year have visited the relatively remote location. In 2013 the museum moved to a huge new facility, three times bigger than its old location and on the tourist-friendly Embarcadero downtown. The move seemed overdue to some but a loss to others who loved the old facilities.

Ouch! Hawaiians once used coconut husks for toilet paper.

The Magic of Which Craft?

So, you may say, big deal: A lot of cities have kid-friendly, hands-on science museums. Precisely. The Exploratorium was the first, the prototype of the new museum format. It was a revolution, designed to affect and inspire other museums. Its founder freely gave information and advice to anyone who wanted to start a similar science museum; the Exploratorium workshop even built exhibits for them. Oppenheimer died in 1985, but his spirit lives on.

A tornado you can walk through

Our Favorite Exploratorium Exhibits

- **Anti-gravity mirror:** It's a simple illusion but great for photo ops. A mirror next to a doorway, reflecting your right side as if it's also your left, making it possible to pose with both feet off the ground.
- **Refrigerator pump:** Hand-pump air under pressure into a copper coil that gets warm as you pump. Allow it to cool for a few seconds, and then release it into another coil that suddenly turns very cold. You've just learned how a refrigerator works.
- **Frozen droplets:** Set the timer on a high-speed camera and catch the different stages of a water droplet's splash.
- **Whisper projector:** Sit in a chair in a crowded room; have your friend sit in a chair on the other side of it. Talk softly into the parabolic dish behind each of you—your friend can hear every word.
- **Tornado:** Try standing in or next to an air-and-steam "tornado." Curious folks like trying out what happens when you blow bubbles, release balloons, or spin in the opposite direction.

From the Exploratorium's "After Dark: Resolution" exhibit

Government waste: There are 284 bathrooms in the Pentagon.

Think the Republicans and Democrats are weird? They got nothing on these real (and really odd) political parties.

Party: The Polish Beer Lovers' Party
Country: Poland
Platform: In 1989 Poland's government abruptly switched from communism to democracy. More than 100 political parties hastily formed, including the Polish Beer Lovers' Party (Polska Partia Przyjaciół Piwa, or PPPP). Led by satirist Janusz Rewinski, the PPPP's slogan was "It won't be better but for sure it will be funnier." Their main objective: to encourage the country's vodka drinkers to switch to beer (to combat alcoholism). Partly because of the strange platform, and partly because the Polish people were so thrilled to finally be allowed to discuss politics at the pub, the PPPP received 3 percent of the vote in the 1991 elections and was awarded 16 seats in Parliament. But when party members realized that they'd have to actually govern—and not just talk about how great beer is—they split off into two factions—"Large Beer" and "Small Beer"—and then dissolved as a party. But some of the PPPP's members remained in Parliament as serious politicians...who happen to enjoy beer.

Janusz Rewinski

Polish beer

Party: Party! Party! Party!
Country: Australia
Platform: Who says a party has to win an election to change things? This party's platform was the same as its name: "Party! Party! Party!" Formed in 1989, the PPP received a mere 0.69 percent of the vote in the Australian Capital Territory Legislative Assembly election. To keep similar partying parties away, the legislature passed a new law: For a party to run a candidate, it must have at least 100 members and a constitution.

Party: The Miss Great Britain Party
Country: England
Platform: Formed in 2008 by Robert de Keyser, chairman of the annual Miss Great Britain beauty contest, his goal was "to appeal to the millions of voters who have been reduced to cynical apathy by the dreary and sometimes rather murky world of

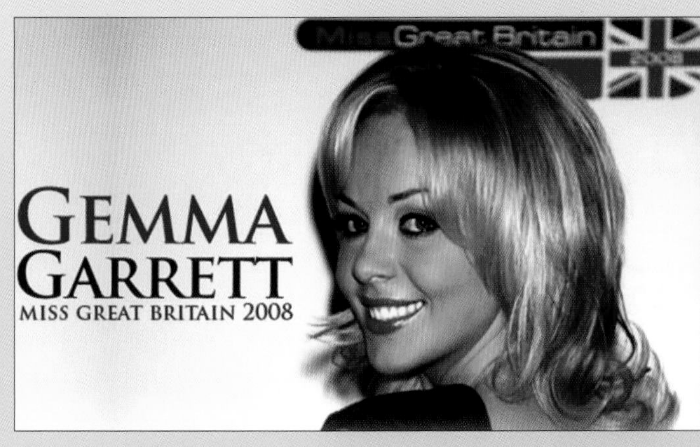

Miss Great Britain, Gemma Garrett, who represented the Great Britain Party...beautifully

Monaco's orchestra has more members than its army.

Westminster and Brussels. We want to bring some fun, glamour, and transparency to the political process but at the same time send the serious message that beauty does have a real power of its own to harness and create positive change." The Miss Great Britain Party ran several candidates—present and former pageant contestants—in local and regional elections. They campaigned on trivial issues, such as a "British Bank Holiday which encourages people to look fabulous for the day," along with more serious ones, such as equal pay for women. However, none of the beauties received enough votes to get elected in any of their races, and the party dissolved a year later.

Party: The Surprise Party
Country: United States
Platform: Gracie Allen (wife of George Burns, and one of Uncle John's favorite comedians) ran for president in 1940. The Surprise Party's slogan: "Down With Common Sense!" Allen took that satirical message on a 34-city whistle-stop train tour along with her mascot—a kangaroo named Laura. Ever the innovative one, Allen claimed to have invented the sew-on campaign pin "so the voter can't change his mind." Like any good politician, she kissed babies, but refused to kiss male babies unless they were "over 21." Among her more memorable campaign promises was to make Congress work on commission. "When the country prospers," she speechified to the delighted crowds, "Congress would get 10 percent of the additional take." Of course, Allen didn't become president, but she was—surprise!—elected mayor of Monominee, Michigan (even though she wasn't on the ballot). Allen politely turned down the opportunity to serve as the town's mayor because she didn't live there.

Gracie Allen

Party: The Donald Duck Party
Country: Sweden
Platform: The Donald Duck Party is a party of one: Bosse Persson. But what he's lacked in members (and votes), he's made up for in longevity: Persson registered the party in the 1980s, and was still running for various offices as recently as 2006. Although Persson has never received more than a handful of write-in votes, he's held strong to his two core values: free liquor for all, and higher curbs so sports car drivers can't park on the sidewalks. So if you travel to Sweden and the liquor is free and the sidewalks are high, you'll know there's a Persson responsible for that.

In Italy, the number 17 is considered unlucky.

The Many Faces of Santa Claus

Time for my next costume change!

You probably think of Santa as a jolly guy in a red suit who hangs out with elves and reindeer. But that's only the American view. Saint Nick, it turns out, is a man of the world, and other countries have their own wildly varying versions.

Kyrgyzstan

In this former Soviet republic, Santa is known as Ayaz Ata ("Snow Father") and he delivers presents on New Year's Eve, not Christmas Eve. Schools host "Christmas Tree Parties" in the week leading up to December 31 to help prepare for Ayaz's arrival. The celebration is part Christmas and part Halloween, as children dress in costumes. Ayaz doesn't have reindeer and elves—he walks with a staff and is assisted by his adopted daughter, Aksha Kar. According to legend, Aksha was once made out of snow, but she began to melt in the spring after Ayaz and his wife adopted her. Then she underwent a magical Pinocchio-like transformation and now serves as his helper.

Italy

In Italy, Santa goes by Babbo Natale ("Father Christmas"), but he typically leaves the gift giving to a witch named La Befana. Italian children place their shoes by the front door of their homes in the hope that she'll stop by and place gifts in them on the night before Epiphany, a holiday that celebrates the 12th day of Christmas (January 5), the day the Three Wise Men arrived in Bethlehem. The legend says that as the Three Wise Men made their way to Bethlehem to greet the baby Jesus, they asked La Befana for directions and invited her to come along…but she declined because she was preoccupied with household chores. Later that night, she spotted a "great, white light" on the horizon, immediately regretted her decision to stay home, and flew off on her broomstick to join them. (She is a witch, after all.) But she got lost, so now she spends every Epiphany Eve searching for Baby Jesus, scattering gifts for kids along the way.

Japan

Fewer than 1 percent of Japan's residents are Christian, so Christmas isn't considered a major holiday there, but many people enjoy it as a secular annual tradition. Children receive presents under their pillows from a Santa dubbed Santakukoru, who has taken on the characteristics of Hotei-osho, a mythological Buddhist monk who, according to legend, was once known for carrying gifts around in a large red bag. And it's become commonplace for couples (and families) to dine at Kentucky Fried Chicken on Christmas Day. The tradition started in the 1980s when Americans living in Japan couldn't find restaurants that served turkey dinners, so they got the next best thing: KFC. Result: Tables for Christmas meals at Japanese KFCs have to be booked months in advance.

La Befana, the Italian gift-giving witch

Read 'em and weep: More than 100 romance novels are published every month.

Statue of Saint Nicolas in Demre, Turkey

Turkey

Santa goes by Noel Baba ("Father Christmas") in Turkey, and his story is similar to the Turkish tales about St. Nicholas, who was born in the town of Patara around A.D. 270. The story goes that Nicholas inherited a large fortune from his father and decided to give it away to the poor, especially needy children. One night, Nicholas encountered a nobleman and three daughters, who had all fallen on hard times. Because their father couldn't provide dowries, the girls had no shot at marriage. One night Nicholas intervened and tossed a sack of gold coins through their window for the first daughter. He returned the following night and tossed in another sack for the second daughter. On the third night, the window was closed. Undaunted, Nicholas climbed onto the roof and dropped more gold down the chimney. The next morning, the daughters found the coins in the stockings they had hung to dry over the fireplace. (Sound familiar?) Now, every Christmas Eve, Noel Baba flies around Turkey delivering more presents via chimneys.

Vintage image of Krampus

Austria

St. Nicholas is the Christmas icon here, and he isn't nearly as forgiving or jolly as the American Santa. Instead of Rudolph, he travels with Krampus, a hairy, demon-like monster with horns and sharp teeth. During the holiday season, children are encouraged to behave themselves: If they do, they get presents. If they don't, Krampus will beat them with his rusty chains. And what happens if the creature finds children still awake on Christmas Eve when Nicholas shows up to deliver gifts? He will toss them into a sack and cart them away. Every December 5, the Austrian town of Schladming hosts an annual "Krampus Karnaval," which features volunteers who dress up as Krampus and march through the streets in a parade, threatening children along the route with tree branches and plastic chains.

The Netherlands

The tales surrounding the Dutch version of Santa may be the strangest of all. Here he goes by Sinterklaas, and he's taller, thinner, and more regal than the American version. He delivers presents on December 5 as part of a holiday called *Sinterklaasavond* ("Santa Claus Evening") or *Pakjesavond* ("Presents Evening"). But before that, on a Saturday in November,

There are 2.2 pounds of salt in every cubic foot of ocean water.

Sinkterklaas's "arrival pageant" is staged and televised across the country. Mounted atop a white horse, an actor dressed as Sinterklaas rides through a randomly selected Dutch city before he makes his deliveries. (Sinterklaas lives not at the North Pole, but in the distant, exotic land of…Madrid.) Accompanying him on his journey (via steamboat, not sleigh) is a group of African servants called the *Zwarte Pieten*, or "Black Peters."

During the televised event, white Dutch actors wear black makeup and bright red lipstick to portray the Black Peters. They march alongside Sinterklaas, performing pratfalls while handing out candy to good children. Bad children are threatened with brooms, and according to Dutch legend, *really* bad kids are carted in sacks back to Spain to make the toys that Sinterklaas delivers to the good children.

To keep up with the "politically correct" times, many Dutch parents now tell their children that the Pieten aren't really black—they're just covered in soot from sliding up and down so many chimneys. In 2006 the Dutch Program Foundation went even further and attempted to replace Sinterklaas's helpers with rainbow-colored Pieten. It proved so unpopular that they reverted back to the traditional, all-black Pieten for the 2007 celebration.

Sinter-dog

What Does It Take?

Well, if you must know, it takes…

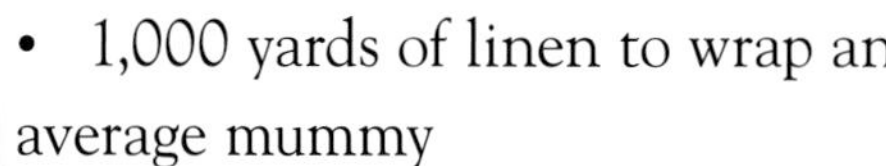

- 1,000 yards of linen to wrap an average mummy
- 50,000 words to use up the lead in one pencil
- 600 grapes to make one bottle of wine
- 30 to 40 gallons of maple tree sap to make one gallon of maple syrup
- 24 to 26 hours for a hen to produce an egg
- 72 muscles to speak one word
- eight weeks for the average man to grow a one-inch-long beard
- one acre of soybeans to produce 82,368 crayons
- one bushel of corn to sweeten 400 cans of soda pop
- 25 tomatoes to make one bottle of ketchup
- one acre of trees one year to remove 13 tons of dust and noxious gases from the air
- seven years for a lobster to grow to one pound
- 345 squirts of milk from a cow's udder to make one gallon of milk
- 18 hummingbirds to weigh an ounce
- 42,000 tennis balls for a Wimbledon tournament
- one cherry tree to produce enough cherries for 70 pies
- about 100 cherries to make a cherry pie
- 2 million visits to 2 million flowers for a honeybee to make one pound of honey.

Which sport has first slips, silly points, and fine legs? Cricket—they're all fielding positions.

Rituals of Death

The treatment and disposal of a dead body is a sacred ritual in every culture, but each one does it a little bit differently.

A Hindu funeral on the Ganges in northern India

- In **India**, custom calls for a body to be burned on a funeral pyre near a riverbank and a temple; the ashes are thrown into the river. Some adherents to Zoroastrianism place bodies atop towers; after the flesh is eaten by vultures, the bones are thrown into a pit at the center of the tower.
- In the **Solomon Islands** of the South Pacific, a body was traditionally placed on a reef where it would be eaten by sharks.
- **Inuit people** constructed small igloos around a corpse (like an "ice tomb"). The cold protected and preserved the body (unless a polar bear found its way in).
- The **Navajo** feared being haunted by the dead, so the body was burned and the deceased's house was destroyed. On the way back from the funeral, relatives took a long, circuitous route to confuse the spirit into not following them.
- At a **Viking** funeral, the dead man was placed on a small boat at sunset. As it drifted out to sea, it was lit on fire. If the color of the sunset was the same as that of the fire, it meant the deceased was bound for Valhalla (Viking heaven).

The American way, known as "bagging and tagging"

- **Muslims** do not use caskets (unless required by law). The body is washed three times, wrapped in a white shroud, and placed directly in the ground with the head pointed toward Mecca.
- The **Iroquois** buried corpses in shallow graves, but exhumed them after a few months. Relatives then placed the bones in a community burial plot.
- In **modern Japan**, bodies are washed in a Buddhist temple, dressed (men in suits, women in kimonos), and put in a casket with a white kimono, sandals, and six coins, all for the spirit's crossing into the afterlife. After a funeral, the body is cremated. Relatives pick bones out of the ash, put them in an urn, and bury it.
- In **ancient Egypt**, it took 70 days to make a mummy. Priests removed all the internal organs except the heart, which the Egyptians thought housed a person's intelligence and personality. Then they covered the body with salt and let it sit until all the moisture was removed. They added false eyes, puffed out any sunken-in parts with linen, covered the body with resin, and then wrapped it in a shroud. (And they didn't just mummify people—cat, ram, and even alligator mummies have been found in various tombs.)

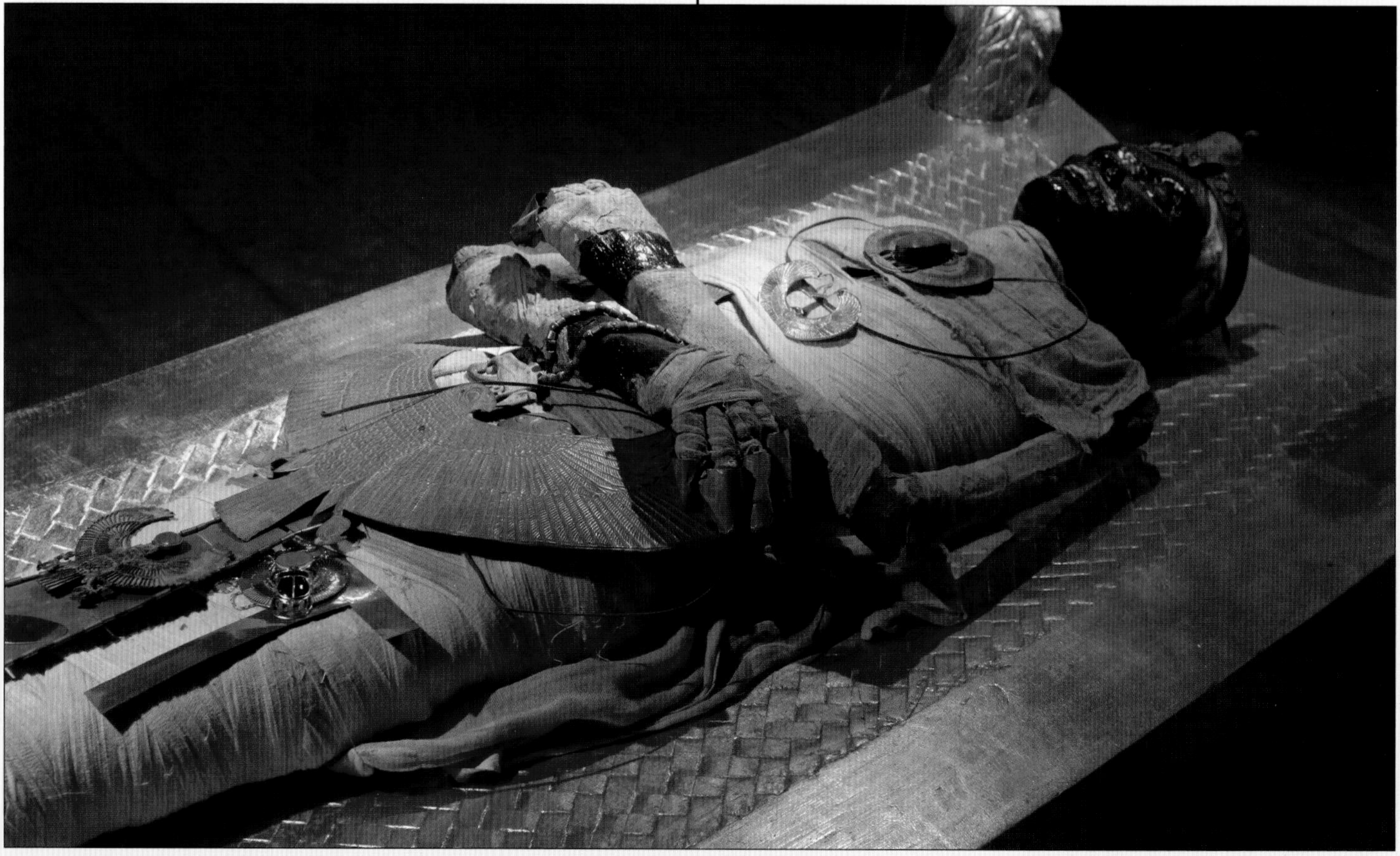

Funeral, Japanese style

An Egyptian Mummy–all dressed up and no place to go

Every second, 100,000 chemical reactions occur in your brain.

Musical eBay

Want to own a piece of your favorite musician? Check the online auction sites for stuff that used to belong to them. Just don't be too picky.

- Wanna rock? Somebody sold a stone with an image they claimed looked like Jerry Garcia of the Grateful Dead on it. Price: $450,000 (The rock came with a free yacht.)
- A chair owned by Nirvana bassist Krist Novoselic, with a sweat stain attributed to bandmate Kurt Cobain, sold for $15,000.
- A plastic Christmas tree with ornaments, garland, and lights once owned by Syd Barrett of Pink Floyd. Someone paid $1,600 for it.
- A clock made of ivory elephant tusks purchased in the 1950s by country music star Jim Reeves ("He'll Have to Go") sold for $1,500.
- Remember the one-hit wonder Rednex, who had a hit with the country/disco song "Cotton Eye Joe" in 1995? In 2007 the band and everything that came with it—trademark, record deals, back catalogue—went on sale on eBay for $1.5 million. (No takers.)
- Baseball isn't popular in England, which makes a baseball autographed by Paul McCartney rare (and strange). It sold in 2005 for $2,500.
- Somebody asked $5,000 for a wooden sake drinking box used by Bon Jovi guitarist Richie Sambora. (It didn't sell.)

Oi! Who's got my bat?

Paul McCartney

- A coat hanger used to hang the suit that Elvis Presley was buried in fetched $15,000. (Suit not included, obviously.)
- A microphone autographed by Britney Spears's ex-husband and failed rapper Kevin Federline, along with the words "America's most hated." Asking price: $100.
- A program from Prince's 1996 wedding to Mayte Garcia called "Coincidence or Fate?" outlining the many spooky reasons why the two should marry. (Example: Her middle name is Jannell, his father's first name and initial is John L.) Asking price: $600.

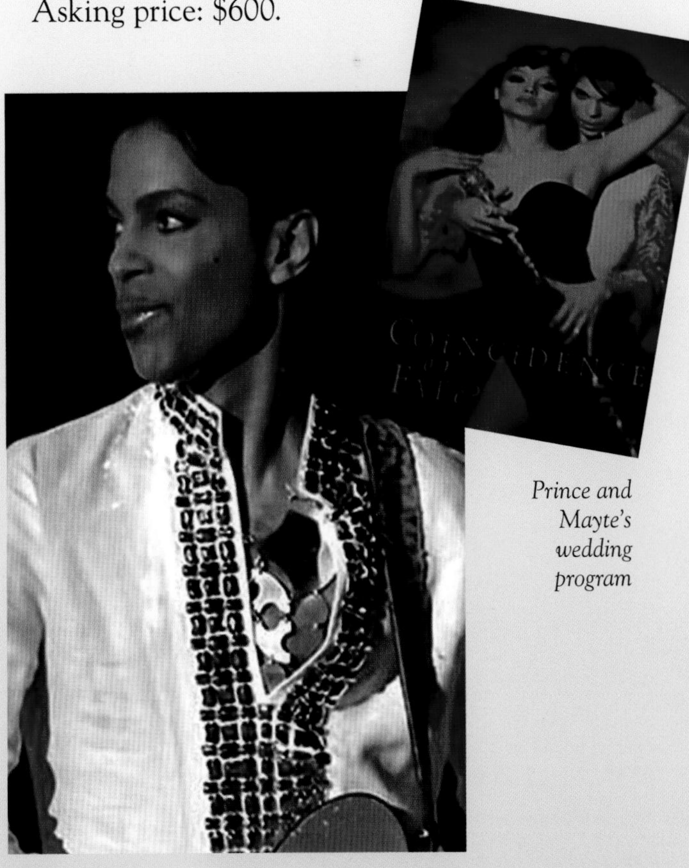

Prince and Mayte's wedding program

Prince

The English horn was invented in France.

Mohawk Skywalkers

Meet the unsung heroes who built New York City's skyscrapers.

Fearless Wonders

In 1886 the Dominion Bridge Company (DBC) of Canada was hired to build a cantilever railroad bridge across the St. Lawrence River near Montreal. The north end of the bridge lay in the village of Lachine; the south end fell on the preserve of a Mohawk band called the Kahnawake. In order to get permission to build the bridge on Indian land, DBC agreed to employ as many Mohawks as possible as laborers. As work progressed, the bridge builders noticed something unusual about the Mohawks: They were fascinated by the bridge. In fact, the company couldn't keep them off it. They walked all over it, scrambling along the narrow spans hundreds of feet above the river with a grace and agility that wowed DBC's seasoned riveters, most of whom were former sailors, used to working high above the ground on flimsy ropes. Word quickly spread that the Mohawks had something special—no fear.

Do the "Shuffle Up"

As an experiment, one of the foremen decided to train some of the local boys as riveters. Riveting was the most dangerous job in high steel construction, and good riveters were hard to find. He hired 12 Mohawks, all teenagers, and began teaching them the job. As the foreman recounted later, "Putting riveting tools in their hands was like putting ham with eggs." The Mohawk teens were naturals—so good, in fact, that they became known as "The Fearless Wonders." When the bridge was completed, the Fearless Wonders were split into three teams, or "gangs," and hired to work on another bridge, the Soo, spanning Lake Superior between Ontario and Michigan. Each Mohawk gang arrived with a young apprentice. As soon as the gang trained the new recruit, another new one would be summoned from the reservation. When there were enough men to create a new gang, the Mohawks had what they called a "shuffle-up": Old hands were pulled from the existing gangs to buddy up with the new guy, creating a new gang. The demand for Mohawk gangs grew, and by 1907 there were more than 70 skilled Mohawk bridgemen working all across Canada, or, as they called it, "booming out."

Alex Mayo (Mohawk, Kahnawake) on a column at Second Avenue between 47th and 48th streets, New York, 1971

Mark Twain called the accordion the "stomach Steinway."

Disaster Strikes

On August 29, 1907, while building the Quebec Bridge across the St. Lawrence River near Quebec City, 84 bridgemen died when a span collapsed. Thirty-five of the dead were Kahnawake. It was a horrifying blow to the band, and builders feared that the Mohawks would abandon steelwork forever. Instead, young Mohawk men wanted to boom out with the gangs working the high steel. Why?

It was the appeal of danger itself. A Mohawk man's place in his community was determined by the respect he earned for acts of bravery. Traditionally those moments had occurred during hunting or in battle. With those avenues largely taken away from them, young men had no way to prove their manhood. But now Mohawk men were wanted by the world for precisely the thing they valued most: their courage. That's what really attracted the Mohawks to "skywalking." The idea that they had no fear of heights was a myth; they were as frightened as anyone else. But by mastering their fear, the Mohawks earned the respect of their community and the entire world. Best of all, they were paid handsomely for their skills. As a white bridgeman observed, "Men who want to do it are rare, and men who *can* do it are even rarer."

However, there were changes after the disaster. The Kahnewake women insisted that the gangs no longer work together on one single project. From then on they had to split up to spread the risk of widowhood. The men agreed and went back to work. And the work kept coming, fast and furious. The skywalkers decided to boom out across the border, where the skyscraping phase of American architecture was just getting under way in New York City.

Falling Down

The first attempt by Mohawk bridgemen to work in Manhattan ended in tragedy. John Diabo, known as "Indian Joe" to his Irish coworkers, worked on the Hell Gate Bridge in 1915. He soon formed his own gang with three fellow tribe members. They'd been on a job for only a few weeks when Diabo fell off a scaffold and plummeted hundreds of feet to his death in the East River below. When asked what happened, one of the other Mohawks said tersely, "He got in the way of himself." The Mohawks quit and went back to the reservation in Canada, and that was it for almost a decade.

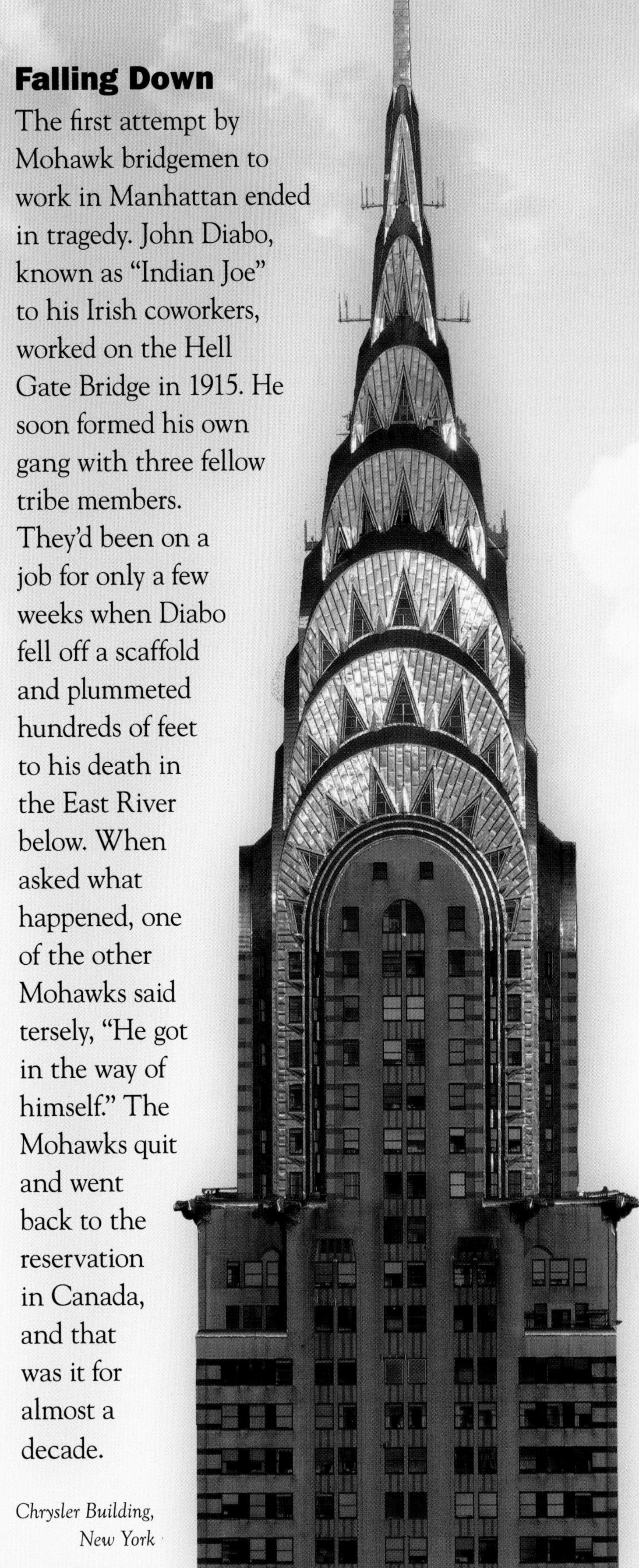

Chrysler Building, New York

below: Construction workers shaping the New York skyline, c. 1931

Climbing Back Up

By 1926 New York was experiencing a frenzy of steel construction, and high-flying riveters were in hot demand. That's when a few Kahnewake gangs came down from Canada to work on the George Washington Bridge, followed by more teams to build Rockefeller Center, the Chrysler and Empire State buildings, and every other significant high-rise and bridge. The Mohawk gangs joined the Brooklyn branch of the International Association of Bridge, Structural and Ornamental Steel Workers, and settled their families in the North Gowanus neighborhood. Other Mohawk bands joined the original Kahnawake, and together they created the legend of the fearless Mohawk skywalkers, one that has endured for more than 80 years.

A Riveting Job

Skywalkers building a bridge or skyscraper during the heyday of high steel construction (1920–1950) fell into three groups:

- **Raising Gangs:** Buildings were (and still are) put together like gigantic Erector sets—girders, beams, and columns arrived at the construction site with pre-bored holes labeled with chalk marks indicating where each piece went. The raising gang hoisted the steel piece up to the right spot with a crane, and then attached it to the framework with temporary bolts.

- **Fitting-up Gangs:** This unit was split into plumbers and bolters. The plumbers worked with guy wires and turnbuckles to align the girders and beams into perfect position. The bolters added extra bolts to secure the piece more firmly.
- **Riveting Gangs:** These gangs had four workers: a heater, a sticker-in, a bucker-up, and a riveter.
- **Setting up:** The heater was responsible for the small coal-fired stove that heated the rivets. He'd lay a few boards across some beams near the piece to be riveted, set the stove on it, and put the rivets in the stove. While the rivets heated, the other three team members hung a plank scaffold—ropes looped over the beam that was to be worked on, with wooden planks for the men to stand on either side. Then they'd grab their tools and climb onto the scaffold, an unnerving prospect at any height but especially several hundred feet above the ground. There was very little room to move: Any misstep meant almost certain death.
- **Preparing for the rivet:** The sticker-in and bucker-up would get on one side of the beam, the riveter on the other. Once the rivets were red-hot, the heater grabbed one with a pair of metal tongs and tossed it to the sticker-in, who'd catch it in a metal bucket. The bucker-up had already unscrewed one of the temporary bolts, which was about to be replaced with the rivet.
- **Putting the rivet in place:** The sticker-in took the hot rivet out of his bucket with his own set of tongs and slid it into the empty hole (at this point the rivet looked like a mushroom, with a round "buttonhead" and a stem). The sticker-in then stepped out of the way (carefully), and the bucker-up slipped a backing brace called a hold-on over the buttonhead.
- **Riveting:** The stem of the red-hot rivet protruded through the hold-on and out the other side, where the riveter placed the cupped head of a pneumatic hammer against the stem and smashed the almost-molten metal into a matching buttonhead. The team then walked down the scaffold, repeating the process until they ran out of beams. Then they moved the scaffold and repeated the process until every hole was riveted. Every man on the team knew how to do each other's jobs, and they switched often because the pneumatic hammer was a bone-jarring tool to use. As for the heater, he stayed put, tossing hot rivets with (hopefully) unerring accuracy anywhere in a 30-foot radius from his platform.

Riveting is no longer the preferred method of assembling pieces of structural steel—advances in welding and bolting made those techniques safer and equally effective—so the Mohawk skywalkers simply learned the new skills and stayed at work high over the city. More than 100 Mohawks were aloft at construction sites across lower Manhattan when the World Trade Center came down in 2001. They were among the first rescuers at the scene and worked for months to help clear away the rubble of the great towers they had helped erect.

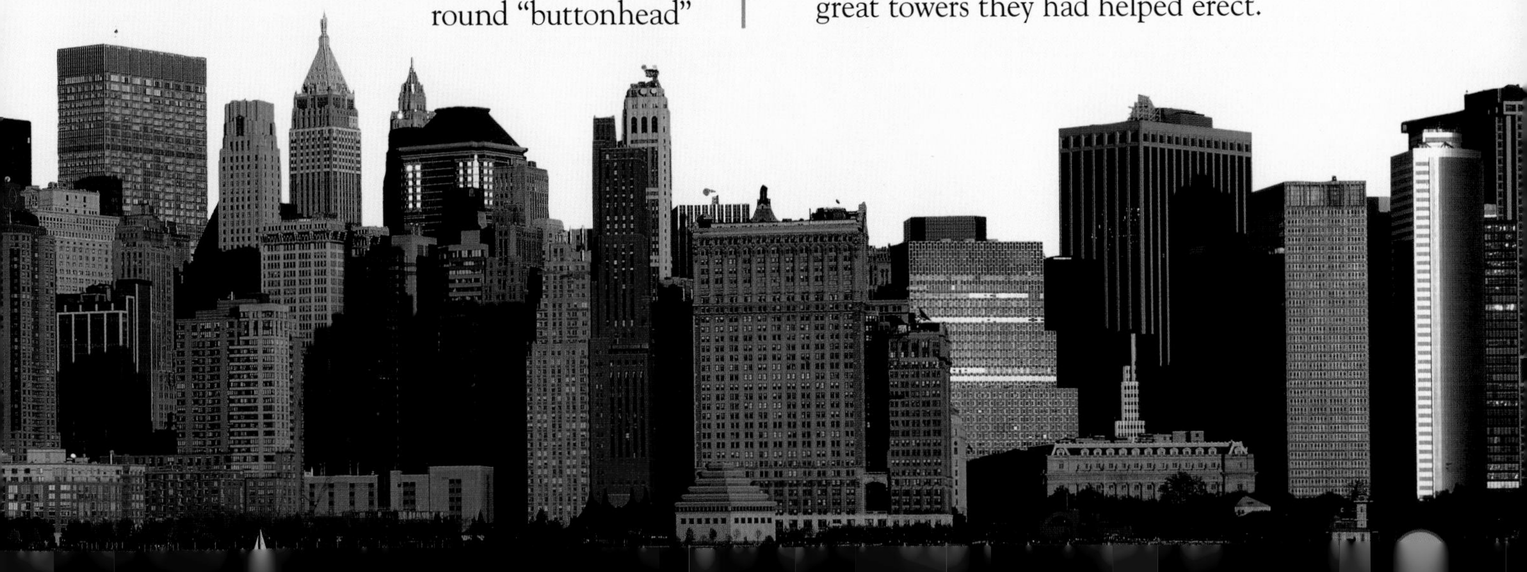

Govern-mental

Five-time presidential candidate Eugene McCarthy said, "The only thing that saves us from bureaucracy is inefficiency. An efficient bureaucracy is the greatest threat to liberty." (Looks like our liberty is safe.)

Secret Treasure

Did you receive a piece of junk mail in the spring of 2008, addressed to "Resident" and labeled "National Household Travel Survey"? Don't remember? Then you probably threw it away, as did thousands of others who received the mailer from the Department of Transportation requesting that you take part in a survey about your travel habits. If you'd opened the mailer, you would've found a crisp $5 bill inside (a "token of appreciation"). Had the DOT sent out checks for $5, they could have tracked how many people cashed them and canceled all the checks that weren't cashed. But because they sent out cash, there was no way to trace how many people got the money…or how many $5 bills ended up in the trash.

Gator Aid

According to the book *Great Government Goofs*, compiled by Leland Gregory, "Members of the Georgia State Game Commission were fiercely debating the pros and cons of regulating 'alligator rides' when one alert member noticed a typographical error on the agenda—the commission was actually supposed to be discussing whether or not they should regulate 'alligator hides.'"

Kicked the Bucket

From 1999 to 2005, the USDA awarded more than $1 billion to farmers who were no longer living. Farm families are eligible to receive money for two years after the head of the household dies in an effort to help them get back on their feet. After an investigation, however, the Government Accountability Office discovered that the USDA has no steps in place to stop the payments—families continue receiving payments until an heir of the deceased farmer informs the USDA to stop. According to the GAO's findings, few of the dead farmers' families have contacted the USDA…so most continue receiving checks to this day.

Going Postal

As part of the 2008 economic stimulus package, the IRS decided to inform citizens that their checks were coming, so they sent out letters to 130 million taxpayers. Cost of sending the letters: $42 million. A few weeks later the IRS spent that amount again to send the real checks.

Princess Diana's favorite band was Duran Duran.

Me Me Me!

In 2007 Rep. Charlie Rangel (D-NY) requested funds for three construction projects at City College of New York. They include the "Charles B. Rangel Center for Public Service," the "Rangel Conference Center," and the "Charles Rangel Library." Cost to taxpayers: $2 million. When freshman congressman John Campbell (R-CA) railed against the politician for naming buildings after himself while still in office, Rangel, who's been in Congress since 1971, responded, "I would have a problem if you did it, because I don't think that you've been around long enough to inspire a building." The library, incidentally, will only display memorabilia that pertains to Rangel. According to a CBS News report, "It's kind of like a presidential library, but without a president."

Naming Wrongs

As president, Ronald Reagan preached smaller government and less spending. So why not name one of the biggest and most expensive projects in government history after him? The Ronald Reagan Building and International Trade Center opened in Washington, D.C., in 1998, and it's the largest federal building in D.C. (The only larger federal building is the Pentagon, located in Virginia.) And at the time, the Ronald Reagan Building boasted the heftiest price tag for a single structure in U.S. government history: $768 million. (Another ironic naming fact: In 1981 the nation's air-traffic controllers went on strike—and President Reagan fired them all. In 1998 National Airport in Washington was renamed…Ronald Reagan National Airport.)

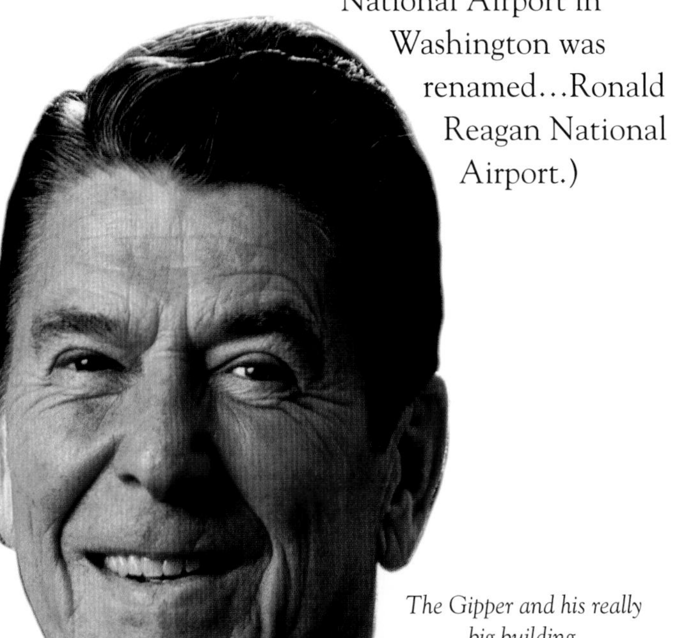

The Gipper and his really big building

Long-Distance Taxi Service

In 2008 an accused thief named Mark Bailey was being arraigned in Northampton, England. After a brief hearing, the judge ordered that Bailey be sent to the magistrate's courtroom—located in a building across the street—to plead his case. One problem: The prisoner transport van wasn't available (it had "gone on to do other things"). So police officers offered to escort Bailey to the courthouse, about 200 yards away, on foot. Court officials said that the public walk would "violate Bailey's human rights," so they were forced to call for another van… the closest one being in Cambridge, nearly 60 miles away. Two and a half hours later, the van showed up, and Bailey took the 30-second trip to the courthouse. The van then drove the 60 miles back to Cambridge. "I've never heard such nonsense," said Conservative MP Brian Binley. "Why we should have to suffer such ludicrous incompetence, and pay for it, is beyond me."

The Tip of the Ice Cube

In the aftermath of Hurricane Katrina in 2005, the Federal Emergency Management Agency (FEMA) purchased 112,000 tons of ice for $24 million. Unfortunately, they were unable to distribute all of it to those in need, so they stored the unused ice in cold warehouses. Two years later, it was still in storage—and the cost to keep it cold all that time totaled more than $11 million, nearly half of what it cost to purchase. Even more embarrassing, it was announced that because FEMA didn't know the "shelf life" for ice, the stockpile couldn't be reused and had to be melted. The cost of the melting operation: another $3.4 million. (FEMA subsequently announced that they are no longer in the business of buying and storing ice for disasters.)

No More Mr. Nicely

In 2012 Tennessee state congressman Frank Niceley became upset when one of his constituents—a 39-year-old nurse named Meredith Graves—was arrested while visiting the Ground Zero Memorial in New York City. Why? Because she brought a loaded pistol. Although Graves had a permit to carry in Tennessee, it's illegal to bring a gun to Ground Zero. Nicely drafted an official motion in the Tennessee Legislature admonishing New York City officials for their lack of "common sense." But what put the motion in the news was the final sentence: "Be it further resolved that we remind the citizens of New York City to drive carefully through the great State of Tennessee, paying extra attention to our speed limits." New York mayor Michael Bloomberg viewed it as a not-so-veiled threat that traveling New Yorkers would be singled out and pulled over. Bloomberg retorted: "Common sense also includes checking gun laws before traveling." Nicely said he was just kidding about the speeding-ticket threat: "You've got to inject a little humor to get attention." Mission accomplished.

Bloomberg talks about gun safety.

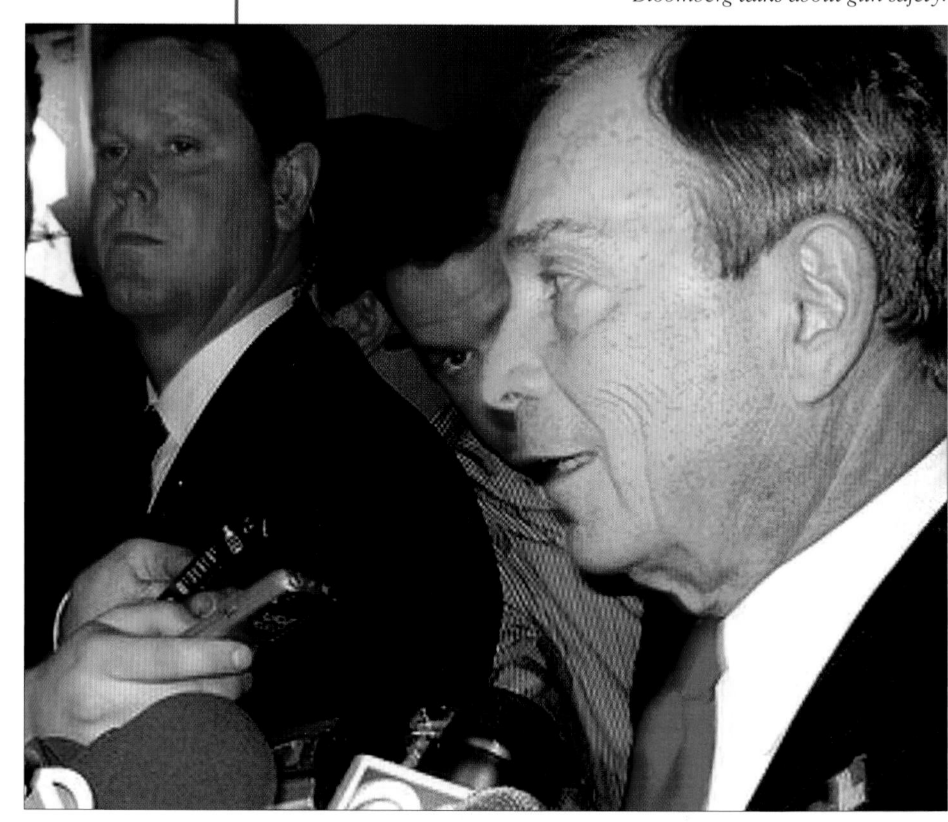

According to a 2005 Bristol University survey, birds prefer to poop on white cars.

Weird Bar Sports

Here's a look at some of the more unusual ways that bar owners have tried to keep customers busy and entertained while they drink.

Dwarf Tossing

How It's Played: A dwarf dresses up in body padding, a crash helmet, and a harness. Then contestants hurl him across the room into a pile of mattresses. The "winner" is the person who throws the dwarf the farthest. In some contests, dwarfs have been thrown as much as 30 feet. Why do the dwarfs do it? They can make as much as $2,000 a night.

History: Invented at a Queensland, Australia, bar in 1985. It later produced an offshoot—dwarf bowling: "A helmeted dwarf is strapped to a skateboard or mechanic's creeper and rolled headfirst into bowling pins, which are made of plastic." In 1987 a few American bars tried out this "sport," and it was a commercial success. But the bad publicity—combined with lobbying by groups like Little People of America—killed it.

The Human (Bar) Fly

How It's Played: Wearing a velcro suit, bar patrons sprint down a runway, leap on a small trampoline, and hurl themselves onto a wall covered with velcro hooks. First prize goes to the person whose feet stick highest on the wall. Getting off the wall can be fun, too. "One of our rules is that the men peel off the women, and the women peel off the men," says a bar owner. "Sometimes it takes three women to peel off one guy."

History: Inspired by David Letterman, who performed the stunt on his show in 1984. The Cri Bar and Grill in New Zealand began holding "human fly" contests in 1991, and other New Zealand bars followed suit. *Sports Illustrated* covered it in 1991; it quickly spread to the United States, where it flourished for a few years.

Sumo Suit Wrestling

How It's Played: Participants don 43-pound rubberized vinyl and nylon suits that make them look like 400-pound sumo wrestlers—complete with the traditional Japanese sumo "diaper" and a crash helmet with a sumo wig glued on the outside. Then they slam into each other on a big padded mat. (Not to be confused with human cockfighting, in which—no kidding—people dress up in padded chicken costumes and peck, bump, and scratch each other.)

History: Englishman Peter Herzig invented the suits after seeing sumo wrestlers in a Miller Beer commercial. Miller then bought hundreds of the suits and began promoting the "sport" in nightclubs in the early 1990s.

Human Bowling

How It's Played: Like real bowling, you have to knock down as many pins as you can…but in this sport, the pins are five feet tall and made of canvas and styrofoam; the bowler is strapped inside a huge metal-frame bowling ball. A partner rolls him or her down the 30-foot lane toward the pins. "Just because you're in the ball doesn't mean you have no obligations to the team," says Lori Fosdick, a regular bowler. "I've seen some pretty maneuvers—but I've also seen people who seemed to be going straight and rolled right around the pin."

History: Creator Thomas Bell got the idea in the early 1990s after watching some gerbils running on an exercise wheel. He figured humans might enjoy doing the same thing. "Bowling has always been a competitive sport," he says straight-faced. "We're just taking it to a more competitive level."

Gerbil Racing

How It's Played: Eight gerbils race in a portable racetrack that's set up on the wall behind the bar. Betting is not allowed, but customers who pick the winning gerbil win free drinks.

History: Invented in 1992 at a bar in Alberta, Canada, with the blessings of the Canadian SPCA. "My gerbils live to the age of two, unlike wild gerbils, which have a lifespan of only eight months," says Morley Amon, owner of the Alberta track. "They aren't running against their will. They run just to see what's on the other side."

Chances That…

- You'll survive for another year: 99.8 percent
- You'll get married: 64 percent
- Your car will be recalled for something: 60 percent
- You'll have to wear glasses: 52 percent
- Your drinking water is contaminated: 20 percent
- A recovering alcoholic staying sober for good: 9 percent
- A bill introduced into U.S. Congress will pass: 8 percent
- You'll have a supernatural encounter: 5.9 percent
- Your kid's a genius: 4 percent
- You'll marry someone of another race: 2 percent
- A pregnancy will result in twins: 2 percent
- You'll be injured in a car accident: 1.33 percent
- An asteroid will crash into the Earth and destroy all life sometime in the next 100 years: 0.02 percent
- You'll win an Academy Award: 0.0083 percent
- Your kid will earn a doctorate: 0.008 percent
- You'll be killed by terrorists in a foreign country: 0.000015 percent
- You'll win the big lottery: 0.000019 percent
- You'll die from your pajamas catching on fire: 0.000003 percent.

I've got the NEED for SPEED!

There are 200,000 more people on Earth today than there were yesterday.

Funny Money

Years ago, Uncle John owned a toy store. One day a customer tried to pay him with a photocopy of a $20 bill. Did Uncle John fall for it? Well, let's just say he doesn't think these stories are funny.

A Million to One

In 2004, 35-year-old Alice Pike tried to pay for $1,671.55 worth of merchandise at a Covington, Georgia, Wal-Mart with a $1 million bill. The clerk sensibly refused it ($1 million bills don't exist). Unfazed, Pike offered to pay with a Wal-Mart gift card worth $2.32...plus the $1 million bill. The clerk then pretended to take it, and while Pike was waiting for her $998,331.17 change, Wal-Mart called the cops. When they arrested her on forgery charges, they found two more $1 million bills on her.

A Fistful of Yen

Police in Saitama, Japan, discovered more than 400 phony 1,000-yen bills in vending machines, but they don't know who made them—or why. Real 1,000-yen bills have three colored strips. On the fake bills, one strip is a photocopy, but the other two are real, lifted from real currency. In other words, the counterfeiter cut up real 1,000-yen bills to make fake ones. Police can't figure out why someone would make counterfeit money that cost more to produce than it was worth.

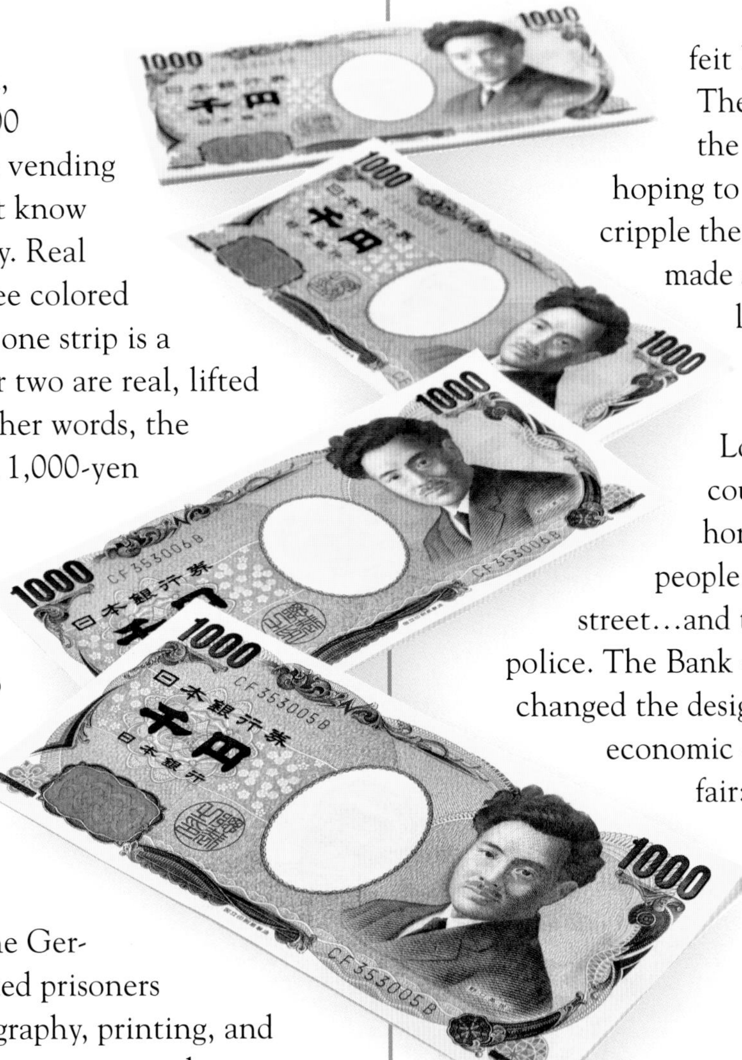

We Did Nazi that Coming

During World War II, the German government recruited prisoners with experience in typography, printing, and forgery for a special assignment: to make counterfeit British money.

The Nazis planned to flood the world market with it, hoping to devalue the pound and cripple the British economy. They made £134 million ($377 million) in phony £5, £10, £20, and £50 notes and then dropped them over London. But they didn't count on one thing: the honesty of the Brits. Most people picked the cash up off the street...and turned it over to the police. The Bank of England quickly changed the design of its bills, and an economic crisis was averted. (All's fair: At the same time, the United States and England were counterfeiting German currency.)

Japanese yen

Doooooom!

The phrase "You're destroying the planet!" is all too common (especially when a plastic bottle gets thrown in the trash). In reality, destroying the planet is very difficult. But not impossible. You could...

Blow It Up with Hydrogen Bombs

In order to split apart a planet, you have to apply enough force to overcome its gravitational binding energy. To overcome the Earth's GBE, you'd need a force of 224,000,000,000,000,000,000, 000,000,000,000 Joules (units of energy). A hydrogen bomb generates a tiny fraction of that, so you'd need to simultaneously set off about 107 trillion of them in order to obliterate Earth.

Build a Black Hole

Black holes are super-dense vacuums that suck in and absorb whatever happens to be near them. You could make your own black hole by cramming together a bunch of neutronium atoms (although you'd need far more than exist on Earth). Your black hole would then systematically devour the planet, and anything else in the vicinity, until nothing was left.

Use an Antimatter Collision

Star Trek was right: Antimatter is the most explosive substance in the universe. It's the opposite of matter (i.e., everything), so when the two collide, they explode, vaporizing both. You can create a small amount of antimatter in a particle accelerator, but to make enough to destroy Earth (using current technology), it would take you roughly 500 years.

Dig and Shoot

This involves breaking off chunks of the planet and shooting them into space with enough force to break the planet's escape velocity, to ensure the chunks don't start orbiting the planet. Even so, and at a rate of only a billion tons of materials shot into space per second, it would take about 100 million years to dispose of Earth.

Boil It

First, intercept thousands of asteroids. Then turn the raw materials—aluminum, nickel, and iron—into gigantic reflective surfaces. About two million square miles' worth should do it. Train them on the sun and redirect enough heat toward Earth to boil it into a cloud of gases. Bwaha-ha-ha!

Oh, Baby!

Birds do it. Bees do it. Here's how the rest of the animal world does it. (And what happens after that.)

- Female mayflies of the *Dolania americana* species have five minutes after their final molting stage to zoom out of the water, find a mate, do the mating, and then fall back into the water to lay their eggs. After that, they die.
- The longest gestation period for any animal is the alpine black salamander, which can be pregnant for more than three years.
- A newborn blue whale calf is about 23 feet long, weighs up to four tons (slightly less than an adult elephant), and can swim within 10 seconds of being born.
- Elephant calves are the largest infants on land, weighing as much as 300 pounds.
- The gestation period for the American opossum is just 13 days.
- Kangaroos are born extremely premature and hairless, and are only about an inch long. Immediately after birth, they crawl up their mother's fur (she licks a path) and into her pouch where they attach to a teat and stay for several weeks. Mother kangaroos come back in heat almost immediately after giving birth, so any new embryos go temporarily dormant until the first baby can live on its own and there's room for a new one in the pouch.
- Rabbits can have a litter of babies every 30 days or so.
- Female alligators lay their eggs in a compost pile to keep them warm. If the temperature in the compost stays at or below 86°F, the eggs will hatch female gator babies. If it gets to 93°F or hotter, the embryos will turn out to be boys.

- Hibernating female bears often sleep through their babies' births.

Ol' Jay's Brainteasers

Uh-oh. Looks like Jay has written the BRI team into a another batch of puzzles. Let's see how we do. Answers are on page 287.

1. Hungry Bookworm

Kim found this conundrum in an old *Bathroom Reader For Kids Only!* and tried to stump us: "Three *Bathroom Readers* are stacked vertically next to each other on a bookshelf, with their spines facing out. The covers of the books each measure 1/8". The pages of each book measure 2". If the bookworm starts eating at page one of the book on the left, then eats through the books in a straight line until he gets to the last page of the book on the right, how many inches of book will he have eaten?"

2. The 5th Condition

Uncle John strolled into the office and announced, "Civics quiz, everybody!" After we whined a bit, he asked a question that sounded tough, but he assured us it was not. "According to the U.S. Constitution," he said, "five conditions must be met in order for a candidate to become president. He or she must:

1. be born in the United States,
2. be 35 years old or more,
3. be an American citizen, and
4. have resided in the U.S. for the last 14 years.

What's the fifth condition? You may think you don't know it, but you do."

3. Surrounded

Trina is riding a horse. Directly to her left is a hippo going the same speed. In front of her is an elephant, also traveling at the same speed. Behind her at the same speed is a lion. And to her right is a ledge. How will Trina make it to safety?

4. Builder Blunder

JoAnn, Melinda, and Monica each purchased a new home in Porcelain Estates, an exclusive community consisting of nine shiny houses. But the builders forgot to add an important part to the houses, forcing the three new homeowners to buy the part at the hardware store. One thousand would have cost $4. Fifty would have cost $2. But JoAnn, Melinda, and Monica needed only one each and paid a combined total of $3. What did the builders forget to add?

Dumb Crooks

Here's proof that crime doesn't pay.

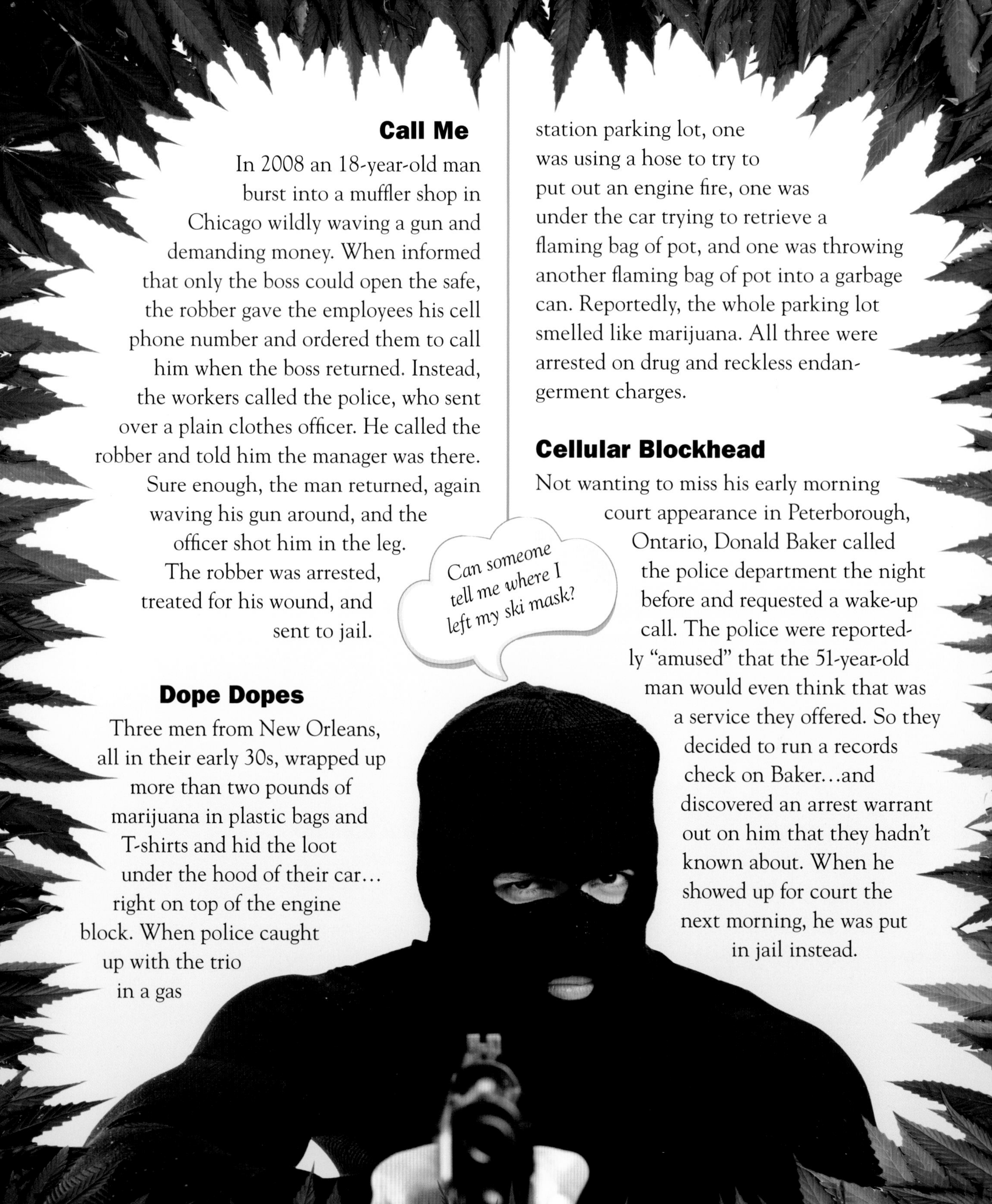

Call Me

In 2008 an 18-year-old man burst into a muffler shop in Chicago wildly waving a gun and demanding money. When informed that only the boss could open the safe, the robber gave the employees his cell phone number and ordered them to call him when the boss returned. Instead, the workers called the police, who sent over a plain clothes officer. He called the robber and told him the manager was there. Sure enough, the man returned, again waving his gun around, and the officer shot him in the leg. The robber was arrested, treated for his wound, and sent to jail.

Dope Dopes

Three men from New Orleans, all in their early 30s, wrapped up more than two pounds of marijuana in plastic bags and T-shirts and hid the loot under the hood of their car… right on top of the engine block. When police caught up with the trio in a gas station parking lot, one was using a hose to try to put out an engine fire, one was under the car trying to retrieve a flaming bag of pot, and one was throwing another flaming bag of pot into a garbage can. Reportedly, the whole parking lot smelled like marijuana. All three were arrested on drug and reckless endangerment charges.

Cellular Blockhead

Not wanting to miss his early morning court appearance in Peterborough, Ontario, Donald Baker called the police department the night before and requested a wake-up call. The police were reportedly "amused" that the 51-year-old man would even think that was a service they offered. So they decided to run a records check on Baker…and discovered an arrest warrant out on him that they hadn't known about. When he showed up for court the next morning, he was put in jail instead.

Hanging Out

In Aachen, Germany, a sales clerk at a clothing store noticed a man with a pronounced triangle-shaped bulge protruding from underneath the back of his coat. "Do you need any help, sir?" she asked. "No," he told her. "I won't be buying anything today." The clerk quickly alerted security, who caught the man with a stolen suit...still on its clothes hanger. "Only a sign saying 'Stop me, I'm a thief!' would have made him look more unprofessional," said the arresting officer.

Here I Am

A 40-year-old man from Janesville, Wisconsin, named Lem Lom was walking down a neighborhood street one day in September 2003 when he saw a fancy electronic device about the size of a brick on a front doorstep. Unaware that it was a $2,500 GPS transmitter that served as a "base" to an ankle monitor (worn by a woman under house arrest), Lom snuck up, stole the box, and then took it to his apartment. A short time later, the police were knocking on his door. "Apparently he didn't know what he had because he'd have to be awfully stupid to steal a tracking device," said correctional officer Thomas Roth.

Gone in 60 Seconds

On a Saturday morning at around 11:40 a.m. in March 2008, Christopher Koch parked his car in a bank parking lot in Liberty, Pennsylvania. It took him 20 minutes to get up the nerve to rob it—at 12:01 p.m. he burst out of his car wielding a shotgun and wearing an orange ski mask and gloves. Unfortunately for Koch, the bank closed at noon. He banged on the door, got frustrated, and left, never having seen the employees inside. But they saw him and wrote down the license number of his car. Police quickly caught up with Koch and arrested him.

All the Latest from the News Stream

Facts for the Road

- The United States has almost 4 million miles of roads and streets.
- Each mile of a four-lane freeway takes up more than 17 acres of land.
- Fifteen percent of drivers get 76 percent of all traffic tickets.
- The worst day for automobile accidents is Saturday.
- Longest Main Street in the United States: the one in Island Park, Idaho. It's more than 33 miles long.
- Forty percent of car-theft victims left their keys in the ignition.
- According to statistics, yellow cars and bright blue cars are the safest to drive.
- If you're an average American, you'll spend about six months of your life waiting at red lights and five years stuck in traffic.
- Odds of winning if you challenge a traffic ticket in court: about one in three.
- Accident rates rise 10 percent in the first week of daylight saving time.

New York's Broadway—once known as Bloomingdale Road.

Average top speed of a racehorse: 30 mph. Average top speed of a greyhound: 43 mph.

Hi-Tech Underwear

Who says underwear should only be clean and comfortable? Here's a look at some skivvies with extra built-in features.

Indomitable Underwear

Special Feature: They're (pre)scented underwear for men.

Details: Manufactured by the French firm Le Slip Français, the Indomitable line of boxers and briefs is made of cotton fabric that has been impregnated with microcapsules containing musk and pear-scented perfume. The capsules, which last for up to 30 washes, release their scent when the wearer walks or moves around. But that pleasant smell doesn't come cheap! The briefs sell for $46 apiece; the boxers sell for $52.

A smoking Fembot displays the ultimate in self-defense lingerie (New Line Cinema)

Self-Defense Lingerie

Special Feature: Protects the wearer from an assailant, then automatically reports the incident to the police

Details: Designed by a team of Indian engineering students in 2013, the ladies' undergarment contains built-in pressure sensors around the bust area. When these detect "unwanted force," the garment delivers a 3,800-kilovolt shock to the assailant (the wearer is protected by a layer of insulating material), then uses its built-in text messaging and GPS capabilities to report the incident and location to police and to the wearer's relatives. The garment can deliver up to 82 electric shocks before it needs to be recharged.

Scannable Underwear

Special Feature: Contains "radio frequency identification" tags that allow the underwear to be sorted by machines

Details: On Russian military bases, underwear from different soldiers is typically co-mingled and washed in giant industrial laundries, making it unlikely that the wearers will get back the same skivvies they turned in for washing. Introduced on an experimental basis in May 2013, the new undergarments will contain personalized RFID tags and bar codes that allow machines to identify the owner of each piece of underwear and sort them accordingly. "Each serviceman will know for sure that he has been given his own underwear," making military service "more hygienic," says a spokesperson for Voentorg, the Russian company that is introducing the technology. If the program is successful, the Ministry of Defense hopes to one day make it possible for everyone in the Russian military to wear his or her own underwear.

Smart-E-Pants

Special Feature: They prevent bed sores.

Details: When a person is bedridden or in a wheelchair and remains in one position for too long, skin tissue can become compressed in places where the bone is close to the skin, such as in the hips, shoulders, and portions of the back. The tissue compression can restrict blood flow to these areas or cut it off entirely, causing injuries known as "pressure ulcers," or bedsores. Smart-e-Pants, developed by researchers at the University of Calgary and the University of Alberta, deliver a mild electric shock to the wearer's buttocks for ten seconds every ten minutes. The jolt is just

Snowmelt from Montana's Triple Divide Peak can end up in 3 oceans: Pacific, Atlantic, and Arctic.

enough to stimulate the muscles to move slightly, simulating fidgeting and thereby allowing blood and oxygen to flow to the areas that would other-wise become compressed. During a two-month study of 33 patients, none developed bed sores while wearing the underwear. The next step is a larger clinical trial; if that's successful, Smart-e-Pants could hit the market as early as 2015.

Moisture-Sensing 'Smart' Underwear

Special Feature: It vibrates and sends a text message to the wearer if it detects any unwanted moisture.

Details: The underwear is intended for incontinence sufferers. One big fear they have is that their protective undergarments may be leaking without their knowing it. Senior citizens, whose sense of smell may be poor, often have the accompanying fear that they are beginning to smell bad, but that they themselves cannot detect it. This experimental underwear, developed by scientists in the UK, has moisture-sensing conductive threads embedded in the fabric surrounding the absorbent incontinence pads. If the moisture leaks from the pads onto the threads, a buzzer is activated, alerting the wearer. Other models being tested use Bluetooth to send a text message to the user's cell phone, or in the case of patients in a nursing home, to a central station to alert staff that the patient may need fresh underwear.

Chastity Pants

Special Feature: They're designed to prevent extramarital affairs.

Details: Invented by one Mr. Jeong in Gwangju, South Korea, in 2012, the men's briefs are treated with temperature-sensitive paint that is invisible at normal body temperature. But if the temperature of the underwear drops below 88° F., such as when they are removed during the consummation of an extramarital affair, the briefs turn irreversibly darker, providing evidence of the affair. Only problem: The underpants can't be removed for any reason, such as to work out or to go swimming, because these activities would also cause the underwear to test positive for adultery. (And there's nothing to stop a philanderer from keeping his underwear on during trysts or from storing it in a warm place, such as a preheated oven.) Even peeing outdoors in cold weather could cause potential marital problems for the wearer. At last report Mr. Jeong was still waiting for his patent to be approved; no word on whether he plans to bring his underpants into production.

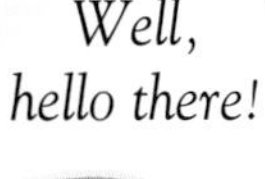

An armadillo flirts with an armored cup.

The Nutshellz Armored Cup

Special Feature: It's bulletproof.

Details: The U.S. military estimates that as many as 1,000 soldiers serving in harm's way suffer injuries to the groin area each year. This product, which was being tested for use in combat in 2013, is strong enough to protect the wearer from bullets fired from 9 mm and 357 magnum handguns. "The cup is designed to 'swallow' the round, not deflect it," says inventor Jeremiah Raber. "This is very important, because if a bullet slid off the cup, it would likely go into the thigh and hit the femoral artery, causing a bleed-out." Stronger cups, designed to protect against even more powerful rounds, are in the works.

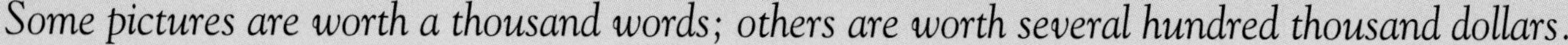

Some pictures are worth a thousand words; others are worth several hundred thousand dollars.

Out of Film

Polaroid was founded in 1937 by Edwin H. Land. The company fell victim to the digital revolution and tried to regroup in 2001, but finally went bankrupt in 2008. To pay off creditors, it was ordered to sell a portion of its collection of 400 photographs. These photos were part of the Artist Support Program started by Land. He provided some of the world's best photographers with equipment and film in return for some of their work. In June 2010, Sotheby's conducted a sale that netted more than $7 million and brought a record price for an Ansel Adams picture. According to Sotheby's auction website, the top money-getters were as follows:

1. Ansel Adams, "Clearing Winter Storm" (flash-only), Yosemite, $722,500
2. Ansel Adams, "Moonrise," Hernandez, New Mexico, $518,500
3. Ansel Adams, "Aspens," New Mexico, $494,500
4. Ansel Adams, "Winter Sunrise," Sierra Nevada, $482,500
5. Ansel Adams, "The Tetons and Snake River," Grand Teton National Park, Wyoming, $350,500
6. Ansel Adams, similar/same as above, $326,500
7. Chuck Close, "9-part Self Portrait," $290,500
8. Andy Warhol, "Self Portrait" (eyes closed), $254,500
9. Harry Callahan, "Trees and Mist," Chicago, $254,500
10. Robert Rauschenberg, "Japanese Sky" (The Bleacher Series), $242,500

Edwin H. Land demonstrates Polaroid photography.

Ansel Adams

The bones of a pigeon weigh less than its feathers.

Second-Rate Sequels

All sequels are not created equal. Some are great, like The Godfather, Part II; The Empire Strikes Back; *and* Superman II. *Some, like the ones reviewed here, are unworthy. But don't take our word for it.*

***The Bad News Bears Go to Japan* (1978)**

"And they can stay there."

—Ken Hanke, *Mountain Xpress*

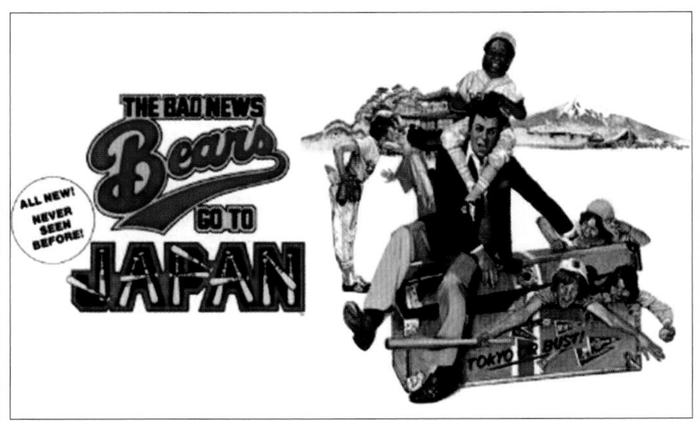

***Grease 2* (1982)**

"The story can't even masquerade as an excuse for stringing the songs together, which are…so hopelessly insubstantial that the cast is forced to burst into melody about pastimes like bowling."

—Janet Maslin, *The New York Times*

***Arthur 2: On the Rocks* (1988)**

"This film never happened. Don't ask me about it again."

—Widgett Walls, *Needcoffee.com*

***Staying Alive* (1983)**

"So horrific are the musical sequences in this movie that you'll swear you were having nightmares directed by Satan himself."

—Scott Weinberg, *Apollo Guide.com*

***Return to the Blue Lagoon* (1991)**

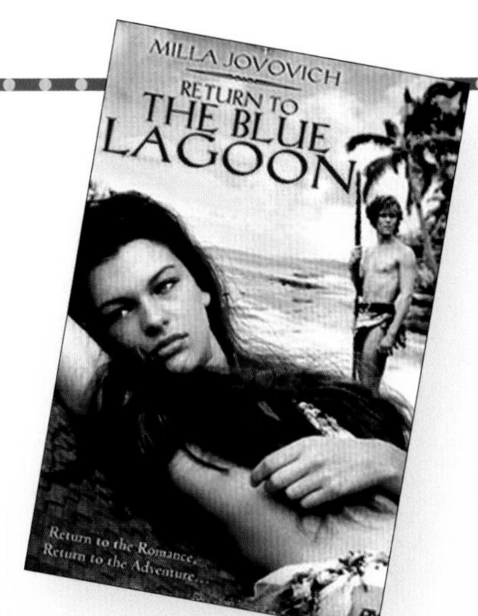

"*Return to the Blue Lagoon* aspires to the soft-core porn achievements of the earlier film, but succeeds instead in creating a new genre, 'no-core porn.'"

—Roger Ebert, *Chicago Sun-Times*

***Superman IV: The Quest for Peace* (1987)**

"More sluggish than a funeral barge, cheaper than a sale at Kmart, it's a nerd, it's a shame, it's *Superman IV*."

—Desson Thomson, *The Washington Post*

***Batman and Robin* (1997)**

"Holy creative breakdown, Batman!"

—Robin Dougherty, *Salon.com*

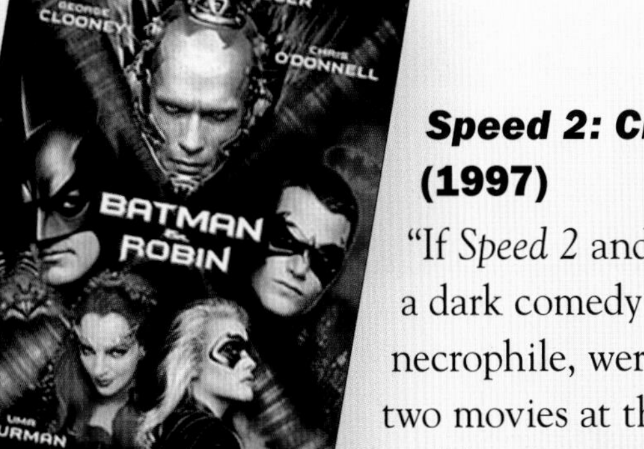

***Speed 2: Cruise Control* (1997)**

"If *Speed 2* and let's say, *Kissed*, a dark comedy about a woman necrophile, were the very last two movies at the video store, I would pick *Kissed*."

—Judith Egerton, *Louisville Courier-Journal*

***Child's Play 3* (1991)**

"Slow, stupid and cheap, the ending effectively kills off any reason for *Child's Play 4*. We hope."

—Richard Harrington, *The Washington Post*

Kenny G.'s real last name is Gorelick.

When the Big One Hit

The Great San Francisco Earthquake was one of the costliest—in both lives and money—natural disasters to hit the United States in the 20th century. Here's the story.

A Tuesday Like No Other

Most of San Francisco's 450,000 people were asleep at 5:13 a.m. on Tuesday, April 18, 1906. Firefighters lay exhausted in their beds after fighting a fire at the California Cannery Company the night before. The *Daily News* was about to go to press with an article noting that San Franciscans had collected $10,000 for the victims of the recent earthquake in Formosa. It mentioned that committees had been meeting in town to discuss how to handle such a disaster should it ever happen in San Francisco.

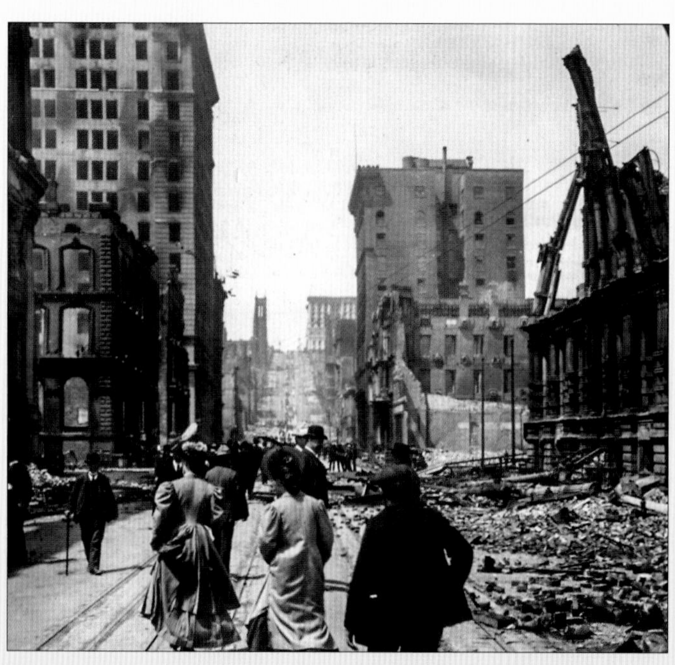

After the earthquake in San Fanrisco: California St.

Then it happened. The jolt from the earthquake was felt from Los Angeles to Coos Bay, Oregon, a distance of 730 miles. San Francisco stood at the epicenter. It's not known how high on the Richter scale the quake was—some estimates say more than 8.5—but when the earth shook, electric lines came down, trolley tracks twisted, water pipes shattered, bridges collapsed, and buildings crumpled. In some areas, the ground moved 20 feet. It was over in 48 seconds. All services—including communication, transportation, and medical—were either completely gone or heavily damaged. The city lay in ruins, and the casualties mounted. The situation was bad...and it was about to get worse.

Ignition

Smaller earthquakes had hit the town in 1857, 1865, 1868, and 1890. As the city was reconstructed over the years, people built their homes out of wood, knowing it withstood shaking better than brick. But there was a problem with wood: it burned. So anywhere a gas line was ruptured, a stove was upset, or a lantern was overturned, there was enough ready fuel to start a serious fire...and that's exactly what happened.

People reported more than 50 fires within the first half hour following the quake, but because

Ruins of San Francisco after earthquake and fire, 1906

Will Ferrell's father was a longtime keyboard player for the Righteous Brothers.

the city's alarm system was out, San Francisco's 585 firefighters had no way of pinpointing the locations. And even if they could, there was little they could do because most of the water mains were broken. Worse yet, Fire Chief Dennis Sullivan lay dying of injuries suffered in the quake. The fires quickly began to consume San Francisco.

San Francisco mayor Eugene E. Schmitz

Here Comes Funston

Brigadier General Frederick Funston, stationed at the Presidio, an army outpost on the northern edge of San Francisco, was flung from his bed by the quake. He immediately sprang into action. Funston knew that army troops were needed to help with the disaster, but he also knew that federal law prevented soldiers from entering the city without first being invited by local authorities. So he headed to City Hall to find Mayor Eugene Schmitz. What he found instead was the building in ruins, fires in the distance, and no sign of the mayor. He decided that troops were needed—whether or not the proper channels were followed. He sent messengers to the Presidio and to Fort Mason, which was also at the north end of the city, and less than two hours after the quake the first of 500 soldiers were on their way into the stricken city. Later they would be joined by sailors, marines, and the National Guard.

Funston organized survivors, ordering some people to gather and distribute all the food that they could find. Others were sent to find wagons and go to neighboring towns for food and supplies. More were sent in search of any bakeries still standing with orders to help get them back in business. And still others were ordered to begin collecting and burying the dead. At 10:15 a.m., Funston sent a telegram to Washington, D.C., asking Secretary of War William Howard Taft for emergency assistance and tents for 20,000 people. It wasn't long before he revised the request to 100,000. Even that wouldn't be enough.

Displaced survivors had to cook their meals in the street.

The Old United States Mint, one of the few buildings that survived the earthquake.

PROCLAMATION

BY THE MAYOR

The Federal Troops, the members of the Regular Police Force and all Special Police Officers have been authorized by me to KILL any and all persons found engaged in Looting or in the Commission of Any Other Crime.

I have directed all the Gas and Electric Lighting Co.'s not to turn on Gas or Electricity until I order them to do so. You may therefore expect the city to remain in darkness for an indefinite time.

I request all citizens to remain at home from darkness until daylight every night until order is restored.

I WARN all Citizens of the danger of fire from Damaged or Destroyed Chimneys, Broken or Leaking Gas Pipes or Fixtures, or any like cause.

E. E. SCHMITZ, Mayor

Dated, April 18, 1906.

Mayor's Orders

Mayor Schmitz finally arrived at City Hall at 7 a.m., as bodies were being pulled from the rubble. He immediately moved into the Hall of Justice and later moved his headquarters four more times as the fires grew and spread. His first order of business was to send out messengers—one to find a telegraph office that was still operating, one to Oakland to ask for fire engines, hoses, and dynamite, and one to the governor requesting that food and water be sent with all possible haste. He also ordered troops to shoot looters on sight, a rule that was so strictly enforced, it was claimed people were shot while searching through the rubble of their own homes. Others claimed the troops did most of the looting.

Nowhere to Run

Fires continued to pop up, grow, and join with other blazes to become huge walls of flame. By 9:00 a.m., a fire was moving across the city, devouring entire blocks at a time. In some areas, the flames advanced as fast as a human can run. By noon, 11 blocks had burned and Market Street had turned into a flaming tunnel. Meanwhile, the streets became clogged with refugees, soldiers, firefighters, and police. Sightseers coming from outlaying areas to view the damage soon found themselves trapped by the crowds and confusion. And before long they were all trapped by the flames. The entire city of San Francisco and many of its citizens were in danger of being reduced to ashes.

Turn to page 220 to find out how the city was saved.

People have been playing board games for more than 4,000 years.

Rejected...Almost

Thinking about giving up on your big dream? Think again.

These went down the toilet... almost!

- Korean War veteran H. Richard Hornberger spent 12 years writing a novel about his war experiences.

  Seventeen publishers turned it down before it was finally published in 1968. Written under the pseudonym Richard Hooker, the novel—*MASH*—became a bestseller.

H. Richard Hornberger

- Barnstorming pilot Richard Bach received 26 rejection slips for his book about an enlightenment-seeking bird before it was published in 1970. *Jonathan Livingston Seagull* went on to sell more than 30 million copies worldwide.

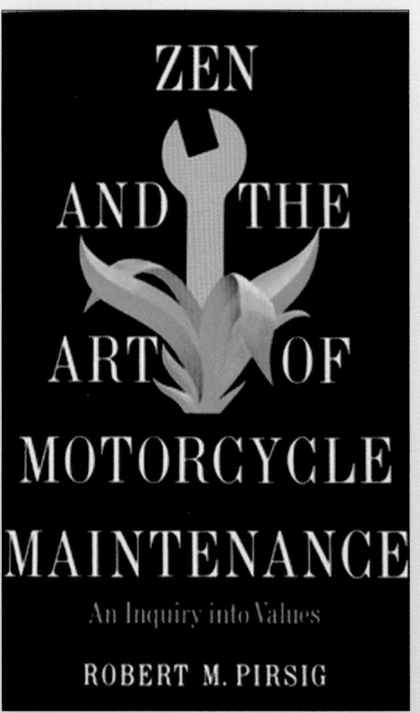

A first edition of Zen and the Art of Motorcycle Maintenance

- Robert M. Pirsig wrote a book about a cross-country motorcycle trip—and the meaning of life. 121 publishers rejected it, but the 122nd didn't. Now there are more than four million copies of *Zen and the Art of Motorcycle Maintenance* in print.

- Jerry Boyd was a boxing "cornerman," one of the people who tend to boxers. He wrote short stories all his life, and for 40 years tried unsuccessfully to get them published. Finally, in 1999 one appeared in a small magazine. A literary agent happened to read it, tracked Boyd down, and got *Rope Burns* published. Hollywood later bought the rights. Several of Boyd's stories were combined into the 2004 film *Million Dollar Baby*, which won four Oscars, including Best Picture.

- When poet e. e. cummings couldn't get a collection of poems published in 1935, he published it himself. He titled the book *No Thanks*, and the dedication page read "WITH NO THANKS TO," followed by the names of the 14 publishers who had rejected the work. Cummings became one of the most popular American poets of all time.

- After Uncle John created the first *Bathroom Reader* in the late 1980s, he received rejection after rejection from publishers who were all so sure that "a book with a toilet on the cover won't sell." Twenty-five years later, nearly 20 million *Uncle John's Bathroom Readers* have sold. So nyah-nyah-nyah!

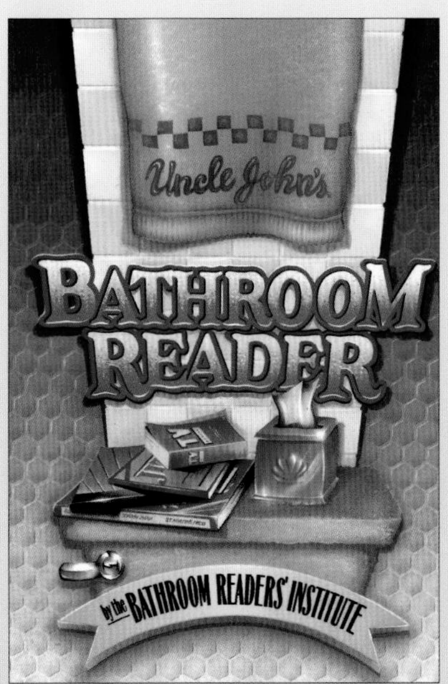

The book that launched it all—Uncle John's Bathroom Reader, *1988*

The Jeep vehicle was named for an animal in O. C. Segar's "Popeye" comic strip.

$neaky Corporations

Powerful corporations often set up fake "institutes" and programs that sound like independent foundations promoting the public good... when in fact they're just the opposite. Here are four examples.

Very Inconvenient

The documentary film *An Inconvenient Truth* received a lot of attention and attracted huge audiences when it was released in May 2006. The film argues that global warming caused by industrial pollution is slowly altering the Earth's climate and melting the polar ice caps, and will eventually flood major cities and leave the planet uninhabitable. But shortly after the movie came out, "public service" commercials began appearing on TV, calling global warming a myth and claiming that carbon dioxide—a byproduct of industrial pollution and automobile emissions (and the "villain" of the movie)—is actually not a pollutant at all, because "plants breathe it." They went on to say that industrial waste is not only harmless, it's essential to life.

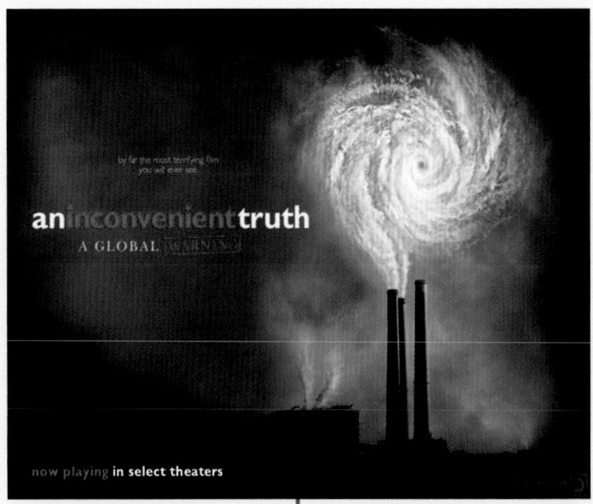

So who made the "public service" ads? A think tank called the Competitive Enterprise Institute, whose members are almost exclusively oil and automobile companies, including Exxon, Arco, Ford, Texaco, and General Motors.

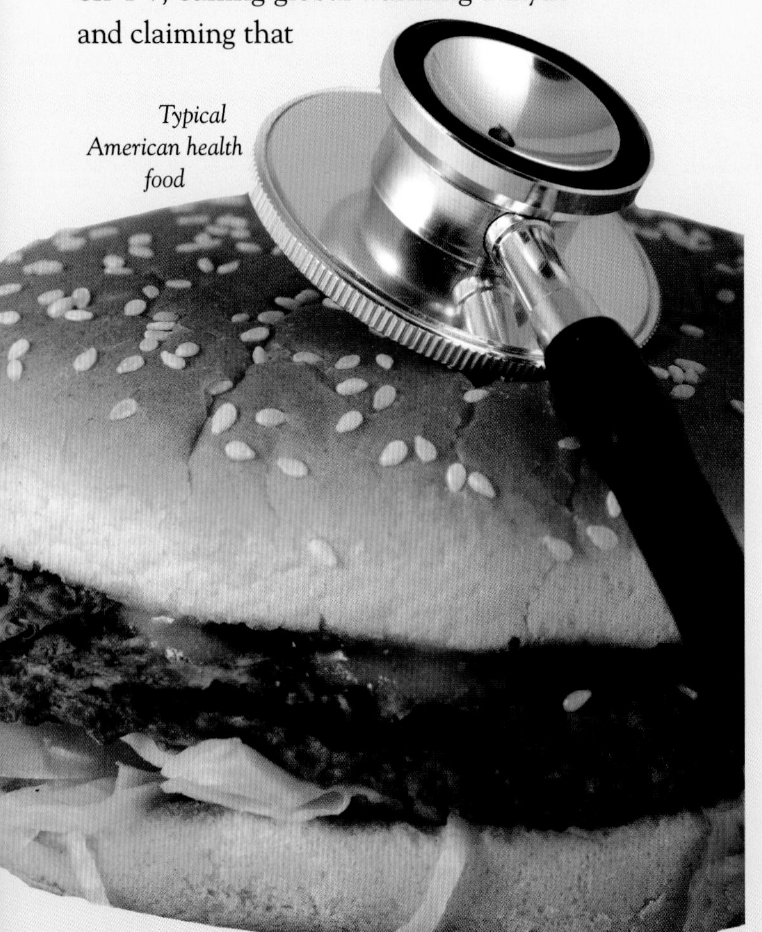

Typical American health food

Junk Food = Fitness

The American Council for Fitness and Nutrition was formed in 2003 to combat the United States' growing obesity problem. At least that's what they said. Shortly after its formation, the Council held a press conference to announce its latest findings: Contrary to numerous government and medical studies, they reported, too much fast food and vending machines filled with junk food did not make children fat.

Turns out the ACFN's interest in childhood obesity is purely business related. The ACFN is actually a lobbying group...for snack-food makers and fast-food restaurants. Its members include Pizza Hut, Taco Bell, Sara Lee, Pepsi, Nestle, McDonald's, Hershey, Coca-Cola, and the Sugar Association.

Chemicals are Cool!

In 1997 students in hundreds of high schools across America got a few hours off from class to attend

Uranus has 27 moons.

"Chem TV." Supposedly designed to get kids excited about chemistry and science, it was a traveling multimedia extravaganza featuring loud music, videos, lasers, games, skits, dancers, free T-shirts, a huge set with giant TV screens, and a cast of enthusiastic performers. Educational? Sort of. Chem TV (meant to sound like "MTV") said it was about chemistry, but it was really about the chemical industry. It was part of a million-dollar public relations campaign by Dow Chemical—one of the world's biggest polluters—to help change their image. Dow had a controversial history: It supplied napalm and Agent Orange to the U.S. government during the Vietnam War, and lawsuits over faulty breast implants nearly bankrupted the company in 1995.

The horrible effects of Agent Orange

Critics charged that the Chem TV presentations were misleading (in one example, an actor took off his clothes to demonstrate that "your entire body is made of chemicals"). Chem TV didn't differentiate between a chemical (a man-made, often toxic combination of ingredients) and an organic compound (molecules that fuse together naturally—like water). Despite the criticism, the program toured schools for three years and won numerous awards. (And it was tax exempt because it was "educational.")

Independent Thought

In May 1998, the federal government filed a lawsuit against Microsoft, accusing the software giant of monopolistic behavior. In June 1999, the Independent Institute, a California-based legal think tank, ran full-page ads in the *New York Times* and *Washington Post* that staunchly defended Microsoft. In the form of an open letter (signed by 240 "economists"), it stated that prosecuting Microsoft would hurt consumers and weaken the economy. What exactly is the "Independent Institute"? It's not independent at all. Though its mission statement says it is "dedicated to the highest standards of independent scholarly inquiry," in 1998 it had exactly one source of funding: Microsoft.

Uncle John's Stall of Fame

We're always amazed by the creative ways people get involved with bathrooms, toilets, toilet paper, etc. That's why we've created Uncle John's "Stall of Fame."

Honoree: Henry Pifer, a truck driver from Arkansas

Notable Achievement: Standing up for the rights of workers who are sitting down…you know where

True Story: In June 1999, Pifer was hit by a coworker's truck while he was at work. His injuries were serious enough that he had to take time off from his job, so he applied to the state Workers' Compensation Commission for benefits…and was turned down. The reason? At the time of the accident, Pifer was returning from a bathroom break. "Doing your business" at your place of business doesn't count as work, the commission concluded, because it is not an "employment service." Your boss isn't paying you to poop.

Rather than take the decision sitting down, Pifer fought it all the way to the Arkansas Supreme Court…and won. In March 2002, the court ruled that Pifer's bathroom break "was a necessary function and directly or indirectly advanced the interests of his employer." Little Rock attorney Philip Wilson called the ruling "a landmark decision, because it's the first time the Supreme Court has defined employment services with respect to going to the bathroom."

Composer Max Reger got a little behind in his work.

Honoree: Max Reger, a German composer (1873–1916)

Notable Achievement: Being best remembered for something he composed…in the bathroom

No one ever asks for my opinion.

Top 6 Pet Peeves of Sharing a Bathroom

Rank	Peeve
1	Not replacing the toilet paper when it runs out
2	Leaving the seat up (according to women)
3	Too many cosmetics on the counter (according to men)
4	Leaving toothpaste globs in the sink
5	Leaving spots on the mirror
6	Leaving dirty clothes on the floor

The frequency of twin births has almost doubled since 1980.

True Story: Have you ever heard of Max Reger? Probably not; his name isn't even that familiar to music buffs. In fact, Reger is remembered less for his music than for his response to a scathing review of his work written by a critic named Rudolph Louis in 1906. "Dear sir," Reger wrote in reply, "I am sitting in the smallest room of my house. I have your review before me. In a moment it will be behind me."

Honoree: The Toto Company of Japan, the world's largest manufacturer of toilets and plumbing fixtures

Notable Achievement: Creating the "Miracle Magic Pavilion"

True Story: In 2002 Toto wanted to make a big impression at Japan's Kitakyusyu Expo trade show, so they spent a lot of money making a promotional movie touting the company's plumbing fixtures. Rather than just project it onto an ordinary boring movie screen, the company commissioned the "Miracle Magic Pavilion," also known as the "Toilet Theater." It's just what it sounds like it is: a toilet so big that it can be used as a movie theater. Viewers enter through a door built into the side of the huge toilet bowl, then sit on genuine life-sized toilets to watch the film. Have you ever been at a movie and had to use the bathroom really bad, but you didn't want to leave your seat for fear of missing an important scene? Even in the Toilet Theater, you'd still be out of luck—none of the toilet-seat theater seats are actually hooked up to plumbing. More bad news: Toto has no plans to screen feature films in its enormous toilet, either. You get to watch Toto infomercials. That's it.

Random Bathroom Stats

You'd be surprised how many corporations and other organizations finance surveys of bathroom-related opinions and behaviors...just to see what you're doing in there. Some recent findings:

At Home

- 30% of people suffer from *nocturia*—they have to get up at least once a night to pee.
- 74% of people read in the bathroom (Go team!); 47% talk on the phone; 11% eat in there.
- When watching the Super Bowl, 38% of viewers go to the bathroom during the commercials, so they won't miss the game; 23% go during the game, so they won't miss the commercials.

Away from Home

- 74% perform some type of "maintenance" task—wiping the seat, flushing, putting down a seat cover—before using a public toilet. Nearly a third say they bring their own materials—Kleenex, sanitizing wipes, etc.—to perform the task.
- 7% suffer from paruresis—shy bladder syndrome.
- 40% flush restroom toilets with their feet instead of their hands.
- 38% of people say they've peeked into someone else's medicine cabinet. (4% of these snoops say they were caught in the act.)

Paper Trail

- Most valued quality in toilet paper: softness (absorbency is #2).
- Survey respondents are almost equally divided on how they use toilet paper: 51% "crumple or wad" it; 49% "fold" it.
- 60% are annoyed by scratchy toilet paper in public restrooms.
- A poll conducted by the Bathroom Readers' Institute found that 70% of our fans prefer to hang their TP over the top.

A Barrel of Laughs

What goes up must come down...and up...and down...

This letter is a classic piece of American humor and has been around in various forms for nearly a century, appearing in dozens of books and movies, and even in a *Saturday Night Live* sketch in 2004. This version is a memo to an insurance company, but there are many others. The tale has now been passed around so often that it's achieved urban legend status—in other words, some people believe it's true. It's not. In fact, it was written in 1902 by Will Rogers. (Not really, we just thought we'd add to the legend.)

Dear Sir:

I am writing in response to your request for additional information in Block 3 of the accident report form. I put "poor planning" as the cause of my accident. You asked for a fuller explanation, and I trust the following details will be sufficient.

I was alone on the roof of a new six-story building. When I completed my work, I found that I had some bricks left over which, when weighed later, were found to be slightly more than 500 pounds.

Earliest use of the flashback in Western literature: Homer's *Odyssey*.

Rather than carry the bricks down by hand, I decided to lower them in a barrel by using a pulley that was attached to the side of the building on the sixth floor.

I secured the rope at ground level, climbed to the roof, swung the barrel out, and loaded the bricks into it. Then I climbed back down and untied the rope, holding tightly to ensure a slow descent of the bricks.

You will notice in Block 11 of the accident report form that I weigh 135 pounds. Due to my surprise at being jerked off the ground so suddenly, I lost my presence of mind and forgot to let go of the rope. Needless to say, I proceeded at a rapid rate up the side of the building.

Somewhere in the vicinity of the third floor, I met the barrel, which was now proceeding downward at an equally impressive speed. This explains the fractured skull and the broken collar bone, as listed in section 3 of the accident form. Slowed down slightly, I continued my rapid ascent, not stopping until the fingers on my right hand were two knuckles deep into the pulley. Fortunately, by this time I had regained my presence of mind and was able to hold tightly to the rope—in spite of beginning to experience a great deal of pain. At approximately the same time, however, the barrel of bricks hit the ground and the bottom fell out of the barrel. Now devoid of the weight of the bricks, the barrel weighed approximately 50 pounds. (I refer you again to my weight.)

As you can imagine, I began a rapid descent down the side of the building. Somewhere in the vicinity of the third floor, I met the barrel coming up. This accounts for the two fractured ankles, the broken tooth, and the lacerations of my legs and lower body. Here my luck began to change slightly. The encounter with the barrel seemed to slow me enough to lessen my injuries when I fell on the pile of bricks; fortunately, only three vertebrae were cracked.

I am sorry to report, however, that as I lay there on the pile of bricks—in pain and unable to move—I again lost my composure and presence of mind and let go of the rope; I could only lay there watching as the empty barrel begin its journey back down towards me. This explains the two broken legs. I hope this answers your questions. Sincerely, Gordon J.

Two Eccentric Artists

- American painter **James Whistler** believed that art should concentrate on the proper arrangement of colors, not on realism. Putting that theory to work, he once dyed a dish of rice pudding green so it would better match the green walls of his dining room.
- Nineteenth-century French poet **Gerard de Nerval** kept a pet lobster. He liked to take it on walks around Paris on a leash made out of ribbon. Nerval defended his choice of pet, saying, "He was quiet and serious, knew the secrets of the sea, and did not bark."

The Year of Living Festively

Want to have the most fun year of your life? If you've got the time, the money, and a spirit of adventure, we've found 12 of the world's most bizarre festivals, gatherings, and sporting events for you to attend.

January

Festival: Camel Wrestling Championship, Turkey

Description: You're standing among a crowd of thousands of cheering fans. The main event begins when two elaborately saddled bull camels are walked to the center of a dirt field. Then, to get them in the mood, a lavishly decorated female is paraded in front of them. The animals' nostrils flare, their saliva froths, and the little bells on their humps jingle as they trip, push, and sit on each other in a battle for dominance. A winner is declared when one of the animals falls down or runs away. But more often than not, the camels just stand there. Or they both run away. Or their handlers become so worried that their prized animal will get injured that they pull it from the competition.

Camels pretending to wrestle in Turkey

History: This pastime has been a tradition throughout Turkey for centuries, but is now limited mostly to the region bordering the Aegean Sea. The annual championship takes place in Selçuk every winter during camel mating season.

Don't miss: The owners trash-talking each other during the prefight camel parades through the city. But watch out for saliva and urine—anyone within 10 feet of a camel is at risk of getting hit with one of these projectiles.

February

Festival: Ivrea Carnevale, Italy

Description: Your next stop is the largest food fight in Italy, held annually in the town of Ivrea a few days before Lent. You and about 10,000 other "rebels" are divided into nine "combat teams." Then you run through the streets throwing oranges at each other and at hundreds of "aristocrats," who defend themselves from chariots and balconies. By the end of the battle, the peels and pulp blanket the town's streets in a foot-deep layer of orange goop.

History: According to legend, a 12th-century maiden named Violetta fought back against the tyrannical ruler Count Ranieri when he tried to claim the "right" of the local duke to sleep with every new bride on her wedding night. In the struggle, Violetta

In 1966 singer Joan Baez sued cartoonist Al Capp for parodying her in one of his comic strips. She lost.

Tomatoes on the fly in Italy

decapitated him. Upon hearing the news that the hated tyrant was dead, the townspeople stormed the castle and threw rocks at the guards.

Afterward, an event was held annually to reenact the rebellion—some participants played the castle guards, others played the rebels, and they all ran around and threw beans at each other. In the 19th century, imported oranges became the preferred weapons.

Don't miss: Not only is participation free, so is the food. Locals serve regional specialties such as fagioli grassi (beans boiled with sausages and pork rinds), cod with polenta, pastries, and Italian wines.

March

Festival: Hokitika Wildfoods Festival, New Zealand

Description: Ever eaten fried lamb testicles? You and about 15,000 other tourists can sample that and other "gourmet" foods at this feast provided by Hokitika's "Coasters" (people who live on the thinly populated west coast of New Zealand's South Island).

The menu is different every year; past feasts have featured grasshopper bruschetta, smoked eel, "huhu grubs" served on toothpicks, and, for dessert, wasp larvae ice cream followed by mealworm Jell-O shots. What will they serve next year? It could be just about anything.

History: During New Zealand's 1860s gold rush, the Coasters learned to make do with whatever protein-rich foods they could find. In 1990, to celebrate the 125th birthday of the town of Hokitika, a winemaker named Claire Bryant came up with the idea of a festival that honors the diverse local fare.

Don't miss: The gorgeous sunsets, live music… and mimes.

Bugs on bread in New Zealand

April

Festival: Beltane Fire Festival, Scotland

Description: Every April 30, also known as the Eve of May, thousands of people gather near Calton Hill above Edinburgh and wait for the sun to go down. As it does, a fire is lit that will provide the spark for the dozens of ritualistic fires to follow. Then there's a procession—an actor dressed as the "May Queen" emerges from the ground, and hundreds of performers march together as thousands of drums beat in unison. The May Queen is brought to her King, the "Green Man." As darkness falls, more players perform dramatic reenactments of the lives of ancient gods and goddesses. It all culminates with a giant bonfire, and everyone dances the night away.

History: Although this particular festival—the largest of its kind in the world—is only about 30 years old, the Gaelic festival of "Beltane" dates back thousands of years, as farmers celebrated the end of winter by lighting bonfires to honor the fertility of the land.

In the late 1980s, a group of musicians formed the Beltane Fire Society, a nonprofit organization that puts the festival on every year.

Don't miss: A chance to participate as one of the performers. (Contact the Society a few months ahead of time to join in.)

Heading out in Colorado

May

Festival: Mike the Headless Chicken Days, Colorado

Description: The town of Fruita celebrates its most famous historical figure, Mike the Headless Chicken, with an annual weekend of fun and chicken. First there's a lawnmower race, followed by fried chicken. Then a classic car show, followed by chicken tenders. There's also a chicken dance, followed by more chicken.

History: As longtime *Bathroom Reader* fans may know, Mike the Chicken's neck

Heating up the night in Scotland

Family affair: Worldwide, about 20% of all married couples are first cousins.

went under farmer Lloyd Olsen's axe in 1945. Miraculously, the rooster lived for 18 months after his head was chopped off (he still had a brain stem, and his keepers fed him by dropping liquefied food down his neck). Mike became famous and toured the U.S. and abroad as a star attraction. "Mike's will to live remains an inspiration," it says on his official Web site. "It's a great comfort to know you can live a normal life, even after you've lost your mind." Mike died in 1947.

Don't miss: The "Run Like a Headless Chicken 5K Race."

June

Festival: Toe Wrestling Championships, England

Description: Each June, competitors assemble in Staffordshire to lock big toes and try to force their opponent's foot off of a custommade podium known as a "toesrack." If you think you can go toe-to-toe with one of the sport's superstars, such as Alan "Nasty" Nash or Paul "Tominator" Beech, it's free to join the competition. All you need are clean feet and strong ankles.

History: Toe wrestling was invented in the 1970s by a group of bored pubbers at Ye Olde Royal Oak Inn in Wetton, Derbyshire. Today it's an internationally recognized sport, attracting big-name sponsors such as Ben & Jerry's Ice Cream.

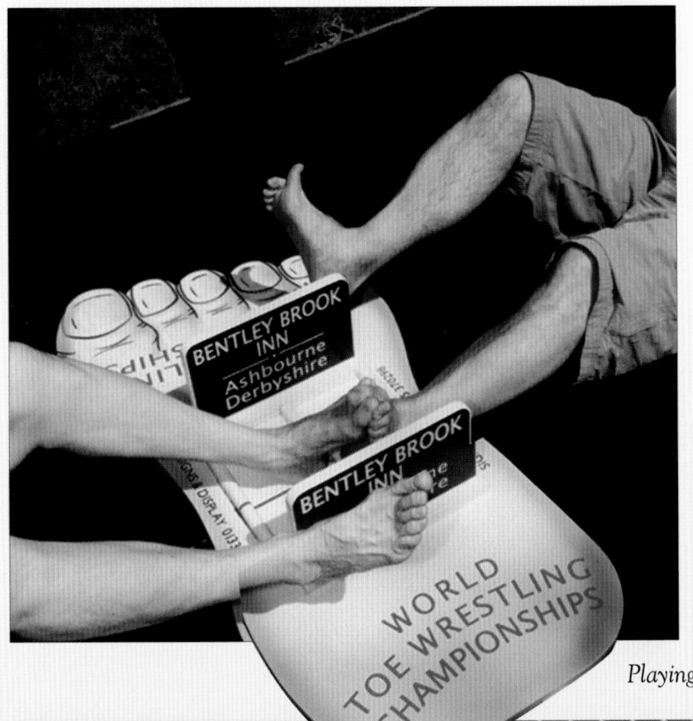

Playing footsies in the U.K.

Don't miss: Also in June and just a few hours' drive away is the annual Summer Solstice Festival at Stonehenge, a celebration that's much larger and, in many ways, weirder—but features little, if any, toe wrestling.

Flinging mud in South Korea

July

Festival: Boryeong Mud Festival, South Korea

Description: At this festival, you can frolic in the mud with more than 1.5 million revelers in the coastal city of Boryeong. The sixday celebration attracts as many foreigners as locals, making it not only the largest festival in Korea, but also one of the biggest in the world. Enter the Mud King contest, enjoy a mud massage, ride on a mud slide into a giant tub of mud, and when you're done, take a mud shower.

History: This festival was founded in 1998 to take advantage of the town's unusually silty soil. Because it isn't suitable for agriculture, marketing-savvy civic leaders concocted a plan to push the mud's beauty benefits. With high concentrations of germanium and other minerals, Boryeong mud is said to be great for the skin and hair.

Don't miss: The opportunity to take some of Boryeong home with you in the form of mud soap, mudpacks, and mud cosmetics for sale at the festival.

For the rest of the year, go to page 242.

He Slud into Third

Sometimes the most entertaining things you'll find on sports broadcasts don't come from the field of play, but from the mouths of the broadcasters.

"That's Hendrick's 19th home run. One more and he reaches double figures."

—Jerry Coleman

"The racecourse is as level as a billiard ball."

—John Francome

"He fakes a bluff."

—Ron Fairly

"Stern John had the easy task of rolling it into the net from six yards. He made it look easy, although it wasn't!"

—Chris Kamara

"Hawaii doesn't win many games in the United States."

—Lee Corso, football analyst

"It's a partial sellout."

—Skip Caray

"Aw, how could Jorge Orta lose the ball in the sun? He's from Mexico."

—Harry Caray

"That is the most unheard-of thing I've ever heard of!"

—Harry Neale, after the Washington Capitals lost two consecutive hockey games in the final three seconds

In a sense, it's a one-man show—except there are two men involved, Hartson and Berkovic, and a third man, the goalkeeper."

—John Motson, BBC

"Bruce Sutter has been around for a while, and he's pretty old. He's 35 years old. That will give you some idea of how old he is."

—Ron Fairly

"Next up is the Central African Republic...located in...central Africa.

—Bob Costas, during the 2000 Summer Olympics

"He was a dead man walking—he didn't have a leg to stand on."

—Malcolm Boyden, after a soccer player was ejected

"Fans, don't fail to miss tomorrow's game."

—Dizzy Dean

Will the real Harry Caray please stand up?

Sounds fishy: In the U.S., anchovies always rank last on the list of favorite pizza toppings.

Political Squirming

Few people have mastered the fine art of the excuse/apology as well as seasoned politicians have. Let's all watch as they try to squirm their way out of some embarrassing political predicaments.

Politician: Rep. Frank Chopp (D-WA)
Offense: In 2007, during debates over whether a taxpayer-funded NASCAR raceway should be built near Seattle, a reporter asked Chopp, who opposed the raceway, if he was aware that racing legend Richard Petty was currently in town to promote it. Chopp's response: "You mean that guy who got a DUI?" Realizing his mistake, Chopp quickly started backtracking.
Squirm: "By the way, on that last point, I was told that—so I'm not sure. You better check to make sure it's accurate."
Aftermath: Not only was it inaccurate, but Petty has long advocated against drunk driving—he even refuses sponsorship from any company that sells alcohol. The next day, Chopp invited Petty to his office to apologize personally. Petty hadn't heard what Chopp had said; he figured the congressman was simply apologizing for his opposition. But when Petty found out later, he said, "I'm glad you didn't tell me that before because I might have went off on him. I don't drink, okay?" He then joked, "I'm not saying I don't run over people when I'm sober, though."

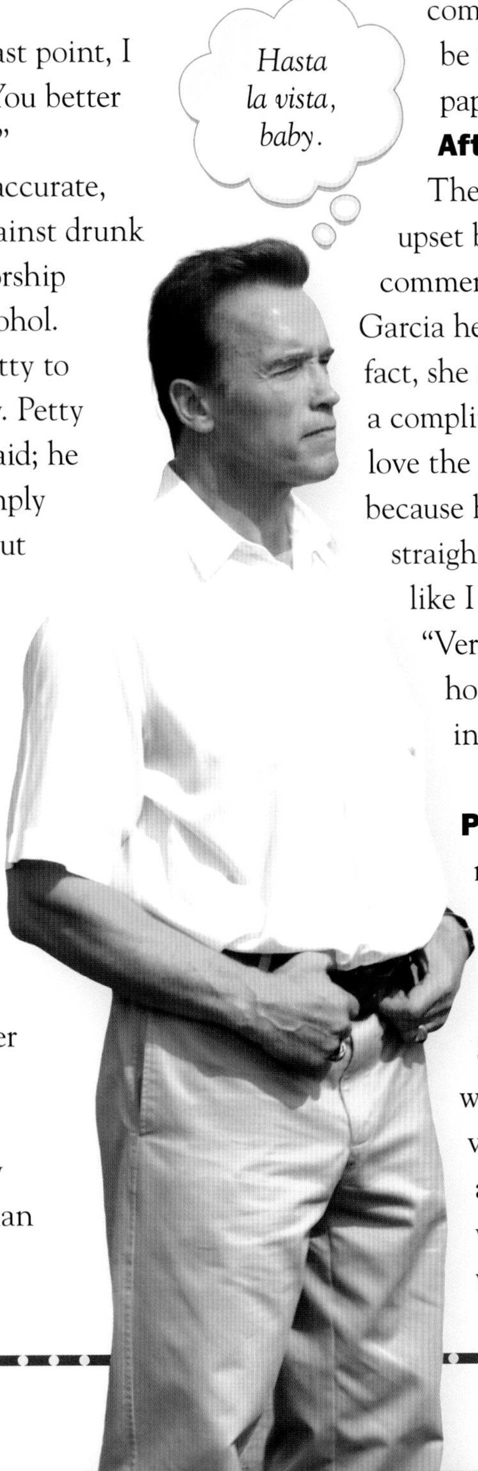

Hasta la vista, baby.

Politician: California governor Arnold Schwarzenegger
Offense: During a closed-door policy meeting in 2006, the Governator made a few racy statements about Assemblywoman Bonnie Garcia. He joked that Garcia's "black blood" and "Latino blood" made her "very hot." The tape was leaked to the press, and Schwarzenegger's comments were printed in newspapers all over the United States, prompting this apology.
Squirm: "Anyone out there that feels offended by these comments, I just want to say I'm sorry. The fact is that if I would hear these kinds of comments in my house, by my kids, I would be upset, and today, when I read it in the papers, it made me cringe."
Aftermath: The person least upset by the comments was Garcia herself. In fact, she saw it as a compliment. "I love the governor because he is a straight talker, just like I am," she said. "Very often I tell him, 'Look, I am a hot-blooded Latina,' and this is kind of an inside joke that I have with him."

Bonnie Garcia

Politician: Tom DeLay (R-TX), House majority leader
Offense: In 2005 DeLay commented on the controversial rulings of the federal judges in the case of Terri Schiavo, a brain-damaged Florida woman who spent 15 years in a persistent vegetative state and was at the center of a battle between family members over whether to maintain her life support. "We will look at an arrogant, out-of-control,

unaccountable judiciary that thumbed their nose at the Congress and the president," said DeLay, who then added, "The time will come for the men responsible to answer for their behavior." Critics on both sides accused DeLay of advocating violence against the judges, prompting him to elaborate…more on the wording itself than the implications it suggested.

Squirm: "I said something in an inartful way. I shouldn't have said it that way, and I apologize for saying it that way. It was taken wrong. I didn't explain it or clarify my remarks, as I'm clarifying them here. I am sorry that I said it that way, and I shouldn't have."

Aftermath: DeLay weathered that storm, but soon found himself at the heart of another scandal—receiving gifts from a lobbyist in exchange for favorable legislation. In January 2006, he resigned from his post as House Majority Leader, and in April resigned from his seat in congress.

Ray Nagin

Politician: Ray Nagin, mayor of New Orleans

Offense: During the aftermath of Hurricane Katrina, the African American mayor spoke of his plans for rebuilding his hometown. "This city will be chocolate at the end of the day," he proudly announced. "You can't have New Orleans no other way—it wouldn't be New Orleans." The remark "chocolate city" outraged not only his fellow politicians, but also many New Orleans citizens who felt it was a limited and racist portrayal. Nagin needed to save face, and quick, as he was up for reelection.

Squirm: "How do you make chocolate? You take dark chocolate, you mix it with white milk, and it becomes a delicious drink. That is the chocolate I am talking about. New Orleans was a chocolate city before Katrina. It is going to be a chocolate city after. How is that divisive? It is white and black working together and making something special."

Aftermath: Nagin won reelection.

Politician: Cynthia Hedge-Morrell (D), New Orleans city councilwoman

Offense: Late for a meeting with FEMA officials in February 2007, Hedge-Morrell checked out a government-issued SUV and sped down the highway at nearly 100 mph with the vehicle's blue lights flashing, weaving in and out of cars and driving on the shoulder. When a state trooper pulled her over, Hedge-Morrell refused to exit the vehicle, yelling, "Do you know who I am? What the hell are you stopping me for?" After waiting a few minutes for a police supervisor to show up, Hedge-Morrell was released without a speeding ticket. New Orleans citizens, still weary of their elected officials' bungled response to Hurricane Katrina, demanded that Hedge-Morrell not be given special treatment just because she's on the city council. Said Gary Russo, the driver who called 911 on the former elementary school principal, "We all have to deal with traffic, simple as that. She ain't the president."

Squirm: "I deeply regret the incident, and I will be a more careful driver in the future. I take responsibility for my actions, because when I taught children, I always told them to step up and take responsibility when you make a mistake. Admit what you did, and use the word 'I.'"

Aftermath: Hedge-Morrell was never issued a ticket, remained on the city council, and kept using the taxpayer-funded SUV (with a driver).

A parody coloring book inspired by Nagin's colorful remarks

In the United States, Frisbees outsell baseballs, basketballs, and footballs combined.

Politician: Former U.S. Rep. Rick Santorum (R-PA)

Offense: While running for president in January 2012, Santorum was speaking at a fund-raiser in Iowa. According to the video of the event, Santorum appears to have said, "I don't want to make black people's lives better by giving them somebody else's money." His critics, including the NAACP, charged that the comment was racist because it singled out African Americans as the only ones living off the welfare state.

Rick Santorum

Squirm: "I looked at the video. I'm pretty confident I didn't say 'black.' What I think—I started to say a word and then sort of changed and it sort of said—'blah'—mumbled it and sort of changed my thought."

Aftermath: Despite a drubbing in the press—*"SANTORUM HATES BLAH PEOPLE!"*—he went on to win the Iowa caucus.

MMM...Words

The Simpsons has been on the air for more than 25 years, and in that time the show's writers have invented dozens of words (some of which have actually made it into common usage). Here's a sampling.

File photo of Homer Simpson

Meh: An expression of indifference, first uttered by Lisa when Homer wanted to take the family to a Legoland-like theme park.

Yoink: In a 1993 episode, Homer yanks a wad of money right out of Marge's hand and says "yoink" as he does so. It's since been said by other characters when they're stealing something, and has become part of the vernacular—half slang for "stealing," half sound effect.

Glaven: An interjection used by the wacky scientist Professor Frink to express any grand emotion, from joy to wonder to terror. The character is based on Jerry Lewis's Nutty Professor, and Simpsons writers thought the sing-songy "GLAY-ven" sounded like something Lewis would've said.

Kwijibo: To wrap up a game of Scrabble, Bart puts all his letters on the game board to form the imaginary word *kwijibo*, which he defines as "a big, dumb, balding North American ape with no chin and a short temper" (i.e., Homer).

Senseless Dunderpant: Montgomery Burns's old-timey term for a "stupid person."

Smarch: In a 1995 episode, Springfield Elementary receives misprinted calendars that include an extra month called Smarch. (Smarch is almost always included in Simpsons calendars.)

Embiggens: Springfield town founder Jebediah Springfield coined the town's motto, "A noble spirit embiggens the smallest man."

Cromulent: Lisa questions whether the founder of Springfield ever really said the town motto, especially the made-up sounding *embiggens*, but is reassured by her teacher that *embiggens* is a "perfectly cromulent word."

The Death Ray

We see a lot of crazy contraptions in science fiction movies. But real scientists—some crazier than others—have actually tried to build them.

Machine: Death Ray

What It Does: Vaporize enemy planes

Scientist: Nikola Tesla (1856–1943)

Story: Tesla was one of the greatest inventors of all time. His genius is the reason we use alternating current (AC) to power electric appliances. He invented the first radio, radar, radio-controlled ships, and the speedometer. He also invented the "Tesla Coil," familiar from Frankenstein movies for its arcing bolts of electricity, but still used today for sending radio and TV signals over long distances.

Nikola Tesla

In 1943 the 87-year-old Tesla contacted the U.S. War Department and offered to sell them his secret "teleforce" weapon, a cosmic ray gun that would shoot a narrow stream of accelerated atoms at enemy airplanes up to 250 miles away…and melt them. The War Department thought Tesla was crazy and declined the offer.

Tesla then offered the weapon to several European nations, but before any could take him up on it, he passed away. Tesla was said to have stored a compact prototype of the "death ray" in a trunk in the basement of his hotel. After his death a Russian spy purportedly raided his room and stole a safe containing the plans for the device, along with the prototype. In 1943 Tesla was thought to be a lunatic, but 40 years later, President Ronald Reagan successfully pitched the same basic idea to Congress and called it "Star Wars."

Machine: Orgone Energy Accumulator

What It Does: Collects energy to use as a power source

Scientist: Wilhelm Reich (1897–1957)

Story: Reich was famous for his pioneering studies in sex and psychology. In 1939 he became convinced that an endless supply of invisible "life force" energy, which he called orgone, surrounded the Earth in vast moving currents. He invented a special box, or "accumulator," to trap the orgone. Reich's orgone accumulator was a six-sided box built of alternating layers of organic and metallic materials. The organic layers attracted the Earth's orgone and the metallic layers radiated the energy toward the center of the box. Patients would sit inside the box and absorb the orgone into their skin and lungs, which was supposed to improve the flow of life energy and release any energy blocks that might be making the patient ill.

Reich used the orgone accumulator as part of a controversial cancer therapy and opened several clinics to deliver it. But the FDA charged him with violating the Food, Drug, and Cosmetic Act by making false and misleading claims to the public.

Have a seat in the Orgone Energy Accumulator.

Bare fact: ***Gymnastics*** **is from a Greek word meaning "to exercise naked."**

A judge ordered that every orgone accumulator be destroyed and Reich thrown in jail, where he died of heart failure in 1957. Since his death, Reich's followers have looked for a way to turn orgone into usable power, but without success. The problem, they say, is that Reich ordered his research papers to be sealed for 50 years, because he felt the world wasn't ready for his advanced ideas. His papers were unveiled in 2008, but the age of orgone energy has yet to arrive.

Machine: Anti-Gravity Flying Saucer
What It Does: Flies by repelling gravity
Scientist: Thomas Townsend Brown (1905–85)
Story: Brown was an American physicist best known for his attempts to use gravitational fields as a means of propulsion. In the 1920s, he found that when he charged a capacitor to a high voltage, it moved toward its positive pole, creating an "ion wind." He claimed that this effect proved a link between electrical charge and gravitational mass, and could be harnessed to create flight. In 1953 Brown demonstrated his "electrogravitic" propulsion for the U.S. Army at Pearl Harbor by flying a pair of metal disks around a 50-foot course. Energized by 150,000 volts, the disks, which were three feet in diameter, purportedly reached speeds of several hundred miles per hour.

According to Brown, the military immediately classified the project and no more was heard about it. But throughout the 1950s, Brown's work was cited as a possible explanation for how UFOs might be able to fly.

Machine: Project Habbakuk
What It Does: Unsinkable aircraft carrier made of ice
Scientist: Geoffrey Pyke (1894–1948)

Artist's rendition of Project Habakkuk

Story: In 1943 Pyke, a science advisor to the British military, made a radical proposal: build unsinkable aircraft carriers out of ice to protect Atlantic convoys against attacks from German U-boats. The scale of these floating landing strips would be immense: 2,000 feet long with a 50-foot-thick hull and a displacement of 2 million tons. And since they were to be made out of ice, the vessels would have been virtually unsinkable, but easy to repair if damaged by torpedoes. A 1,000-ton prototype was being built on Patricia Lake in Alberta, but the project was abandoned when the British were informed that it would cost $70 million and take 8,000 people working for eight months to build it. The refrigeration units were turned off and the hull sank to the bottom of the lake, where it melted.

Machine: Newman Motor/Generator
What It Does: Produces an almost endless supply of energy
Scientist: Joseph Newman (1936–)
Story: Accepted laws of physics say that you can't get more energy out of a generator than you put

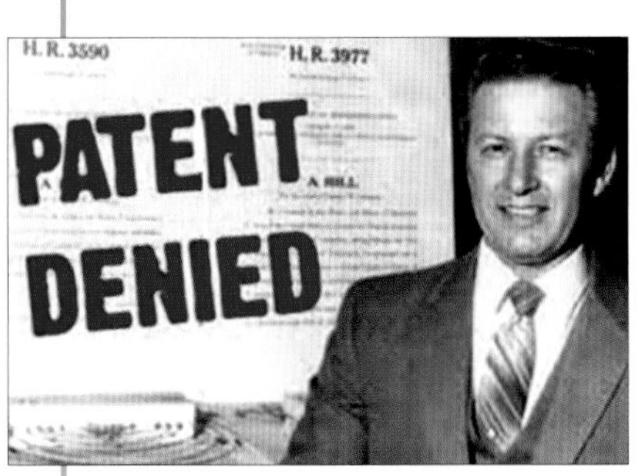

Joseph Newman

into it. Newman, a self-taught scientist from Louisiana, thinks otherwise. He's patented a generator that he claims operates at over 100 percent efficiency, effectively generating more energy than it uses. If his machine works as he describes it, that would mean all powered machines—cars, boats, home appliances, airplanes—could run forever on a single fuel charge. Unfortunately, Newman has been unable to convince the scientific community that his generator works. The National Bureau of Standards tested his machine and found that his generator only delivered 33 percent to 67 percent of the energy put into it. Another test by engineers from Mississippi State University had the generator working at 70 percent efficiency. Have these reversals sent Newman back to the drawing board? Not at all. He continues to tinker with his generator, raising money for future work by auctioning off scale models of it.

Running on Newman power

What two cities combined to form Budapest, the capital of Hungary? Buda and Pest.

Bar Codes

Here are a few spirited facts—shaken, not stirred.

Whiskey. The word comes from the Gaelic *uisce beatha*, meaning "water of life." It's alcohol distilled from fermented grains such as barley, rye, corn, wheat, or a combination. In Ireland and the United States, whiskey is spelled with an "e." In Scotland, Canada, and Japan, it's spelled *whisky*.

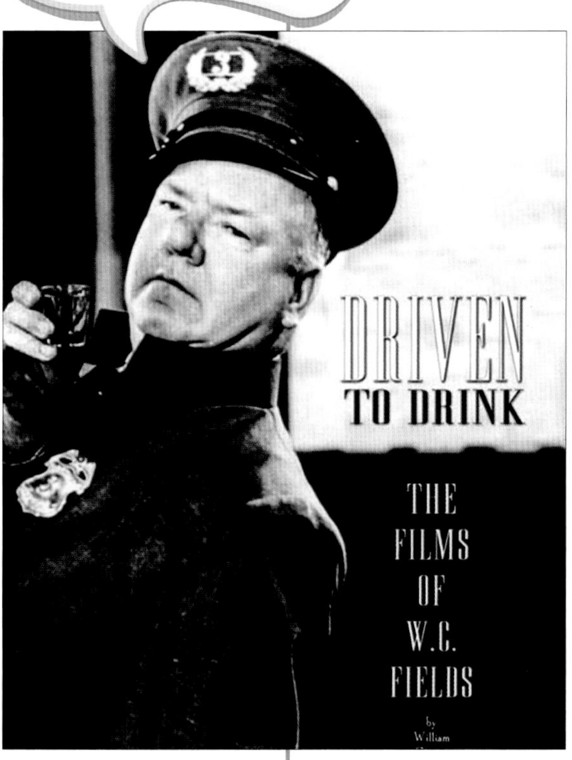

Scotch. Whiskey made in Scotland. According to international law, only whiskey made in Scotland may be called Scotch.

Bourbon. American whiskey of the type originally made in Bourbon County, Kentucky, typically made from 70 percent corn and 30 percent wheat, rye, or other grains. Tennessee whiskey is similar to bourbon, except that it's produced in—you guessed it—Tennessee. It is filtered through a ten-foot layer of maple charcoal, which gives it a milder, distinctive flavor.

Brandy. Alcohol distilled from fermented fruit juices. Brandy is short for brandywine, which comes from the Dutch *brandewijn*, which means "burnt wine." It can be made from grapes, blackberries, apples, plums, or other fruits. Cognac is a type of brandy produced in the Cognac region of France.

Gin. Distilled grain alcohol flavored with juniper berries. Sloe gin is gin flavored with sloe berries from the blackthorn bush instead of juniper berries.

Rum. Alcohol distilled from molasses and sugarcane juice, both of which are by-products of the process used to turn sugarcane into refined sugar.

Vodka. Distilled alcohol originally made from potatoes, but today mostly made from grain. "Vodka" is the diminutive form of *voda*, the Russian word for water, and means "little water." All vodka produced in the United States is required by law to be colorless, odorless, and nearly tasteless, which accounts for its popularity in mixed drinks.

Sherry. White wine that has been fortified by the addition of distilled spirits. It gets its name from *Shareesh*, the Arabic name for the town of Jerez in southwestern Spain, where it originated.

Port. Fortified red or white wine. It gets its name from the city of Porto in northern Portugal, where it originated.

Vermouth. Fortified white wine flavored with aromatic herbs and spices. It's no longer true, but the flavorings were originally used to mask the flavor of inferior wines. Vermouth gets its name from *wermut*, German for "wormwood," one of the traditional flavors.

Cordials. Distilled spirits combined with sweetened fruit pulp or fruit juices. Liqueurs are similar to cordials, except that the flavoring is provided by flowers, herbs, seeds, roots, or the bark of plants. Many traditional cordial and liqueur recipes are centuries old and started out as medicinal products.

Lions sleep 17 hours a day.

The Toxic Travel Guide

Bored with Disneyland? Had enough of the Bahamas? Have a real *vacation at one of these exotic—and toxic—locales.*

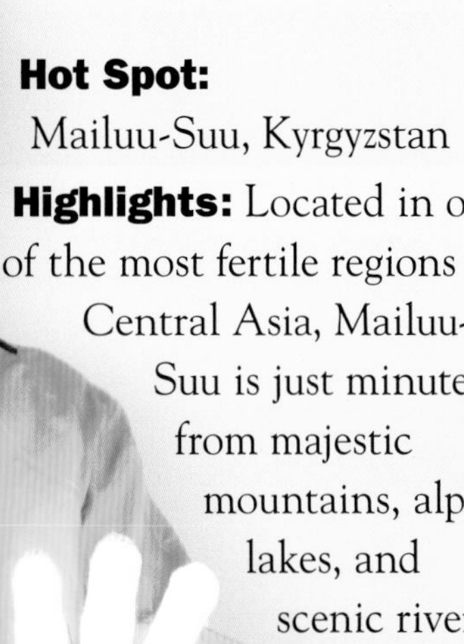

Hot Spot: Mailuu-Suu, Kyrgyzstan

Highlights: Located in one of the most fertile regions of Central Asia, Mailuu-Suu is just minutes from majestic mountains, alpine lakes, and scenic rivers.

Travel Tips: Bring a Geiger counter. Once part of the Soviet Union, from 1946 to '67 Mailuu-Suu processed uranium for the U.S.S.R.'s nuclear power and weapons programs. Today, nuclear waste—millions of pounds of it—is buried in pits in the hills surrounding the town.

Bonus: It's an earthquake and floodprone region. Since many of the storage containers are already damaged, the area is overdue for a disaster of unprecedented proportions.

Lodging: There's little employment in the town of 24,000, so many people have just up and left. You can probably rent an empty (radioactive) house for next to nothing.

Hot Spot: Linfen, China

Highlights: This out-of-the-way city of four million is located in Shanxi Province. Widely considered the ancient birthplace of Chinese culture, Linfen is home to the Yao Miao temple, the Yao Tomb, and the Iron Buddha Monastery.

Travel Tips: If you're not fond of inhaling coal dust, wear a mask. Linfen lies in the heart of China's coal country, and everything there is covered in black soot. How bad is it? In 2008 *Time* magazine named Linfen the "Most Polluted City in the World." Tourism officials will even give you a mask emblazoned with the words "I Can Breathe!"

Lodging: Consider the four-star Tang Yao Hotel, which features a "pavilion in the yard which makes you linger on with no thought of leaving when you enter just as in fairyland!"

Hot Spot: La Oroya, Peru

Highlights: This mountain paradise offers stunning views of the Andes from its perch at 12,000 feet above sea level.

Travel Tips: Bring all the water, food—and air—that you'll need. La Oroya processes copper, zinc, and lead—and the massive smokestack in the

An airbag deploys at about 250 mph.

center of town has been spewing out black smoke and dust for 80 years. The once-lush hills have gone gray from decades of acid rain, which has contaminated the area with toxic levels of lead, arsenic, and sulfur dioxide.

Lodging: Rent an airtight Winnebago… and a haz-mat suit, should you want to take a walk.

Chemical structure for chromic acid, which contains hexavalent chromium

Hot Spot: Ranipet, India

Highlights: Nestled in the southeastern state of Tamil Nadu, Ranipet sits on the banks of the majestic Palar River, and the city teems with Indian history and folklore.

Travel Tips: It also teems with *hexavalent chromium*—a carcinogen (made famous by the movie *Erin Brockovich*) that's a waste product of the leather tanning business, which the town is famous for. More than half the leather in all of Asia moves through Ranipet's factories—and it pollutes the groundwater at the highest levels on Earth. Local farmers say the water they use for irrigation actually "stings like insect bites" if it gets on their skin.

Lodging: There are many fine hotels in Ranipet; just think twice before drinking the water.

Hot Spot: The Irish Sea, located between England and Ireland

Highlights: Boating, scuba diving, whale watching—the foggy Irish Sea has it all for the coldwater-loving adventurer!

Travel Tips: Don't go in the water. Since the 1950s, the Sellafield nuclear power plant on the coast of Cumbria, England, has discharged untold amounts of radioactive waste into the Irish Sea. It's still at it, too—dumping an estimated two million gallons per day, giving the Irish Sea a dubious honor: "the most radioactive sea in the world." So don't go fishing, either, as the fish contain dangerously high levels of plutonium-239 and cesium-137.

Lodging: Since you're going to be exposed to radiation anyway, why not go all the way and book a nuclear submarine?

Sellafield Nuclear Reprocessing Plant: artist's impression of the possible effects of unchecked industrial pollution

What It Cost in 1980

Remember when you could take the whole family to the movies for $20?

- A Commodore VIC-20 computer cost $299.95. It boasted a maximum of 5 KB of memory and didn't include a monitor.
- Ticket for a Los Angeles Dodgers game featuring Mexican rookie pitching sensation (and future MVP) Fernando Valenzuela: $4.50
- Cost of one of the year's most popular novels, Stephen King's *Firestarter:* $13.95
- The price of a pack of cigarettes (people still smoked in 1980): about $1.00
- A ticket to see *The Empire Strikes Back* cost $2.75
- A gallon of leaded gasoline, which is now banned but was still available then, cost about $1.20
- In 1980 a new house cost, on average, just under $69,000. Barbie's Dream House cost around $100
- This year, McDonald's expanded its menu with the first fast food chicken sandwich, the McChicken (deep fried boneless patty on a bun). Price: 80 cents
- A 1980 Chrysler Cordoba, memorably advertised by Ricardo Montalban as being upholstered in "rich Corinthian leather," cost $6,745.

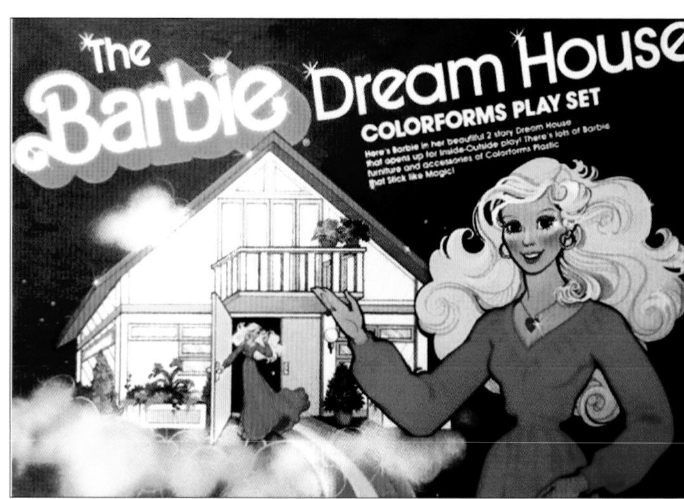

- The Sears Catalog offered a UHF- and VHF-enabled 19-inch "big-screen" color TV with a hot feature—a wood-paneled remote control with four buttons—for just $485.
- Irene Cara's title song from the movie *Fame* won an Oscar for Best Original Song. The soundtrack LP cost about $6.
- New in the candy aisle: Big League Chew, shredded bubble gum invented by a former minor league pitcher as a chewing-tobacco substitute. A package cost 25 cents.
- A state-of-the-art VHS machine—on which you could watch pre-recorded movies at home!—cost $699. Renting one of the few dozen titles Hollywood had released cost about $8 at one of the many new "video stores" around the country, some of which required membership fees or deposits of up to $50.

Ricardo Montalban and the Chrysler Cordoba (above), and another model (without Montalban)

 The Love Boat **was based on a novel.**

Delusions of Grandeur

This is by far the finest, most fascinating, most incredible page of quotations in any book in the history of publishing, period!

"I can't think of a comparable level of cultural excitement about something since Neil Armstrong landed on the Moon in the 1960s."

—Gil Schwartz, CBS publicist, on the *Survivor* finale

"It's probably the most famous phrase said by a human being in history."

—Michael Buffer, on why he trademarked his catchphrase, "Let's get ready to rumble!"

"The Bible had 20, 30, 40, 50 characters in it. You don't think that I would be one of the characters of today's modern Bible?"

—Kanye West

"I don't know what my calling is, but I want to be here for a bigger reason. I strive to be like the greatest people who have ever lived. Like Jesus."

—Will Smith

"Gingrich—primary mission: Advocate of civilization, Teacher of the rules of civilization, Arouser of those who form civilization, Leader of the civilizing forces."

—Newt Gingrich

Kanye being Kanye

"Iconic"? Really?

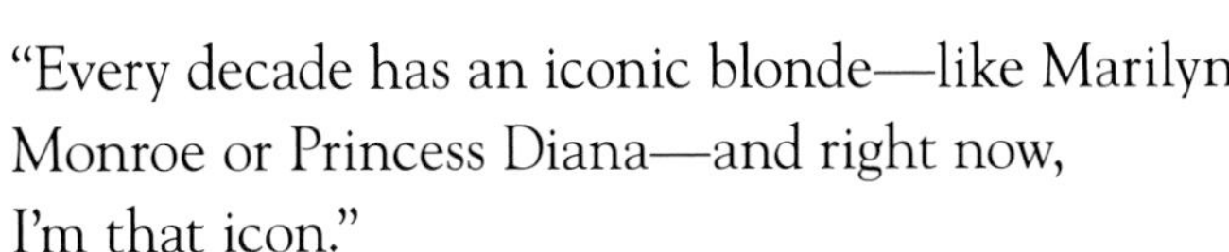

"Every decade has an iconic blonde—like Marilyn Monroe or Princess Diana—and right now, I'm that icon."

—Paris Hilton

"My greatest competition is, well, me. I'm the Ali of today. I'm the Marvin Gaye of today. I'm the Bob Marley of today. I'm the Martin Luther King. And a lot of people are starting to realize that now."

—R. Kelly

"The only difference between me and the other presidential candidates is that I'm more honest and my women are more beautiful."

—Donald Trump

"I have 100 billion dollars...You realize I could spend 3 million dollars a day, every day, for the next 100 years? And that's if I don't make another dime. Tell you what—I'll buy your right arm for a million dollars. I give you a million bucks, and I get to sever your arm right here."

—Bill Gates

Sweet Special Effects

Ever see an old movie where someone crashes through a glass window? There's shattered glass everywhere, but the actors don't have a scratch on them. How do the Hollywood magicians do it? Uncle John's got the answer.

Glass Act

Jagged glass is dangerous—especially glass from a broken window. In reality, anyone flying through a glass window risks severe injury, including severing a limb. So how do actors and stunt people avoid getting mangled or even scratched up? The answer lies in the nature of the "glass" itself. The windows the actors fall through, and even the prop bottles and glasses that are broken over people's heads, aren't made of glass at all. Today, innovations in the development of plastics and polymers have put new, safe glasslike materials at filmmakers' disposal. But until very recently, stunt coordinators used a much more homey substance for their glassy feats.

A stuntman safely jumping through safety glass

Clear and Pleasant Danger

In older movies, those windows and bottles are made of candy—hard, glossy, shiny sugar candy that shatters like glass...just without all those sharp, dangerous edges and shards. The similar molecular structures of candy and glass allow them to look alike and break alike. But glass is harder than candy because it's mostly made of silica (that's ordinary sand), soda ash, and lime, and has a very high melting point (1,292 degrees), which makes it sharper and more dangerous when it breaks. Since candy is softer because it's made of sugar and water, and has a much lower melting point (367 degrees), its edges aren't as dangerous. And this difference not only makes the candy safer but also much easier to produce. To make the candy look like real glass, it is formed exactly the way the glass would be. It is melted, blown, and then shaped into objects or panes by a "glass" blower.

Have Your "Glass" and Eat It, Too

Interested in making your own stunt glass? Then just follow this recipe for candy glass:

- 7 cups sugar
- 3 cups corn syrup
- 2 cups water

Smallest motorized car ever made: Denso Micro-Car. It's the size of a grain of rice.

Mix all ingredients together in a clean, metal pot. Gently bring the mixture to a boil (don't stir it) and let it reach 300 degrees on a candy thermometer. While you're waiting for the mixture to heat up (it should take about 40 minutes), line a cookie sheet (or jellyroll pan) with wax paper. Once the solution has reached 300 degrees, immediately pour it carefully onto the cookie sheet. Let the "glass" cool completely before peeling off the wax paper. And voilà, sugar glass.

Note: Always take proper caution when following this recipe. Be very careful while pouring your "glass" onto the cookie sheet.

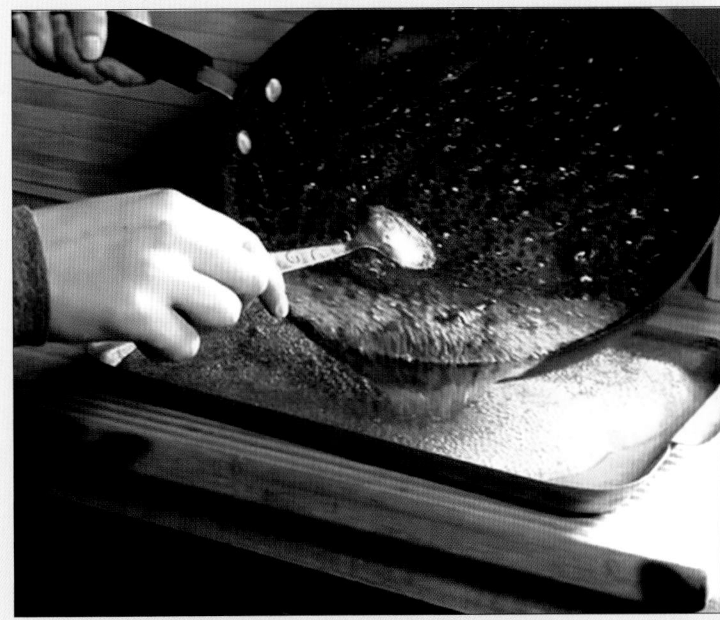

Pouring the "glass" into a jellyroll pan

Facts to Make You Spew

- A tapeworm in your intestines can reach 50 feet in length and live for 25 years.
- The average city water treatment plant processes enough human waste every day to fill 72 Olympic-sized swimming pools.
- According to a survey, more than 10% of Americans have picked someone else's nose.
- Tears are made up of almost the same ingredients as urine.
- Your mouth slows production of bacteria-fighting saliva when you sleep, which allows the 10 billion bacteria in your mouth to reproduce all night; "morning breath" is actually bacterial B.O.
- Astronauts have to exercise daily to keep their muscles in shape. So where does the sweat go? It doesn't drip off their faces or run down their armpits—it collects in a puddle about the size of a dinner plate on their backs. The astronaut has to wipe it off quickly or the sweaty puddle will float away.
- Your eyes will change color after you die, most likely to a greenish-brown.

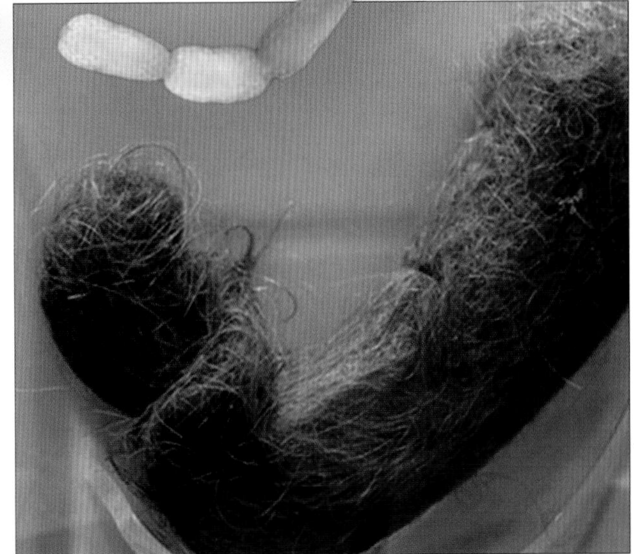

This stomach-shaped bezoar was removed from the stomach of a 12-year-old girl who ate her hair for six years.

- Bezoars look like dark stones, but they're actually compacted balls of hair, saliva, and other stuff that collects inside your stomach. They take years to form, can grow as big as baseballs, and can require surgery to remove. The best way not to get a bezoar: Don't eat your hair!
- If you're average, you'll fart out enough gas today to fill a small balloon. Try not to pop it.

Waaaaah! The average newborn baby spends 113 minutes a day crying.

Throne of Games

The bathroom is more than a great reading room—it can also be a great game room!

Toilet Ten Pin

What You Need:

- ten golf tees, or other objects that can serve as bowling pins
- a few rubber bands to serve as bowling balls.

What You Do:

- Set the golf tees up in a triangle like bowling pins as far from the toilet as you can while still having them within reach—that way you can set them up over and over again and bowl as long as you want.

How to Play:

Have you ever shot a rubber band like a gun? Make your hand into a pistol—curl your pinkie around the rubber band, then stretch the rubber band around the back of your thumb and over the tip of your index finger. Hold the pistol square in the center of your chest, lean back as far as you can, and when you're ready to shoot, release your pinkie. Aim for the pins—try to knock them all down.

Trash Can Frisbee

What You Need:

- a wastepaper basket (if the wastepaper basket isn't big enough to hold the paper plates, use a cardboard box or a paper shopping bag)
- some paper plates

What You Do:

Place the basket on the bathroom floor as far from the toilet as you can.

How to Play:

Fling the paper plates like Frisbees—see if you can throw them into the wastepaper basket. For a bigger challenge, try to ricochet them off a wall into the basket.

Bathroom Darts

What You Need:

- a pie tin
- a saucer
- a small glass
- small objects you can throw (coins and caps from discarded toothpaste tubes work well)

What You Do:

Put the glass in the center of the saucer, and put the saucer in the center of the pie tin. Set them all down on the bathroom floor a few feet from the toilet. That's your "dartboard."

How to Play:

Toss the coins ("darts") at your target—if they land in the glass, you get 10 points; if they land in the saucer, you get 5; if they land in the pie tin, you get 1. If you score too well, move the target farther away to make it more challenging.

Bathroom Blow Gun

What You Need:

- a soda straw
- some wooden matches
- a hat

What You Do:

Turn the hat upside down and place it on the bathroom floor a good distance away from the toilet.

How to Play:

Turn the hat upside down and place it on the bath-room floor a good distance away from the toilet. Put a match in the straw, hold the straw up to your mouth, and blow. Try to shoot all the matches into the hat.

Fun with a Funnel

What You Need:

- a rubber ball
- a funnel

What You Do:

Hold the pointy end of the funnel.

How to Play:

Bounce the ball off the wall opposite the toilet and try to catch it in the funnel on the rebound.

Bathroom Bouncy Ball

What You Need:

- an egg carton
- some Ping-Pong balls

What You Do:

Write different point values in each of the 12 cups of the egg carton, then place it on the bathroom floor a few feet from the toilet.

How to Play:

Try to bounce the Ping-Pong balls into the egg carton. Start with one bounce, then, as your skills improve, move the carton farther away and bounce the balls twice before they go into the cups. Add up the values for your scores.

Bathroom Broken Neck Preventer

What You Need:

All the stuff you just spread out all over the bathroom floor to play all these games we just taught you.

What You Do:

Leave it all over the floor.

How to Play:

Now pick it up all up—before somebody gets killed!

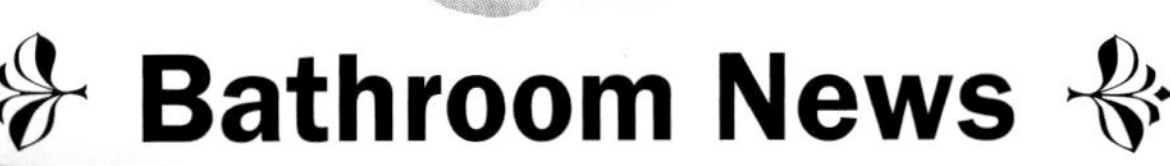

Bathroom News

Iron Chef

In March 2009, a housing unit of Washington State's Clallam Bay Corrections Center was evacuated when a guard noticed smoke pouring out of a sewer vent pipe. One hundred and thirty inmates had to evacuate their cells and wait in the dining hall until guards finally tracked down the source of the smoke: a fire in a stainless-steel toilet, set by an inmate who was trying to heat up a snack sausage he bought in the commissary.

Face Time

In 2010 a Florida man named Pat McCourt ran for election to the Bonita Springs Fire Rescue District board. Shortly after he proposed cutting the fire department's budget, his campaign started getting some undesirable publicity: Urinal cakes bearing his photograph appeared in the men's room urinals of several local bars and restaurants. The proprietors of the establishments hadn't given permission for their urinals to be used in that way, and when customers complained ("Whose face am I peeing on?" was a common query), the offending cakes were removed. But it didn't matter. "As soon as we take them out they're being replaced," Gary Maurer, manager of the Landsdowne Street Pub, told reporters. Local firefighters denied any involvement: "Nope. It's not the firefighters, the union, or the fire department," said a spokesperson for Firefighters Union Local 3444. (McCourt lost the race.)

Pat's piece of cake

The Golden Age of Quackery

Go ahead and scoff at the cure-alls and tonics concocted in the 1800s, but know this: Taken in large enough quantities, they'd make people forget what ailed them.

The Way We Were

You'd think our ancestors had cornered the market on gullibility. They'd take kickapoo juice, swamp root, ocean weed, or just about anything else to cure their ills. They must have been crazy! Or were they?

In the 19th century, doctors were few and far between—which may have been a good thing, since medical practices weren't anywhere near an exact science. Patients took their chances: Bloodletting, purging, sweating, and freezing were standard operating procedures. Blistering was also in vogue, based on the notion that a body could harbor only one ailment at a time. The theory was that the pain of raw blisters would drive out the pain of just about anything else. Many doctors carried a supply of acid and other skin scorchers. If they ran short, a hot poker from the hearth worked just as well.

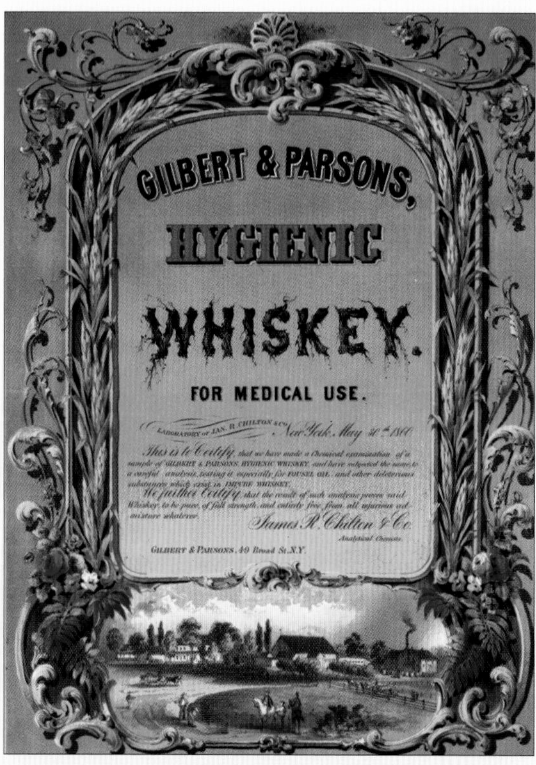

No doubt Gilbert & Parsons Hygienic Whiskey was a popular and trusted cure-all.

On the Cutting Edge

Amputations were also popular; hence the nickname "sawbones" for doctors. There also was something called "trepanning" that involved drilling holes in the patient's skull to relieve pressure on the brain. When electricity came into everyday use in the late 1800s, doctors quickly discovered the healthy jolt it could provide to their incomes. One doctor advertised a range of electric brushes, corsets, hats, and belts to cure everything from constipation to malaria.

Is There a Doctor in the House?

Calling the doctor was a last resort. In some communities, the doctor moonlighted as the local undertaker. Mothers, who made their own home remedies, did most of the doctoring. Sometimes an apothecary, who could grind together a more exotic medication, was consulted. But in the 19th-century spirit of unbridled and unregulated American capitalism, it wasn't long before Mom got a little mass-produced help from the medicine men.

Doctor Chilton offered a guaranteed "Fever and Ague Cure"; Doctor Rowell sold an "Invigorating Tonic...unrivaled as a cathartic"—a fancy name for a bowel loosener. One of the most successful medicine men was Doctor Ayer, who used saturation newspaper ads to create product demand, and mail order to meet it. No prescriptions were needed to buy Ayer's Cherry

English astronomer Fred Hoyle coined the term "Big Bang" in 1949.

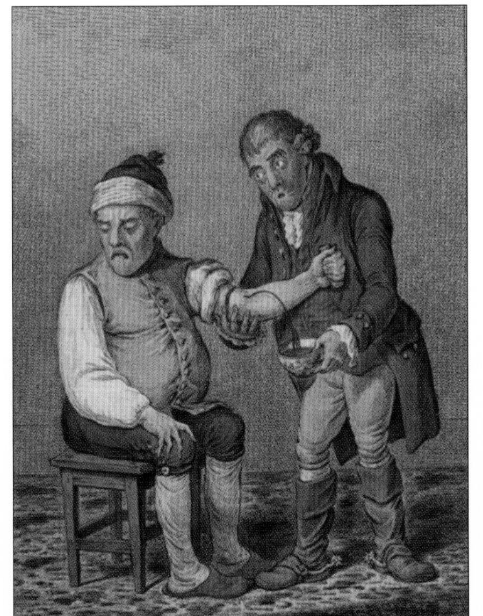

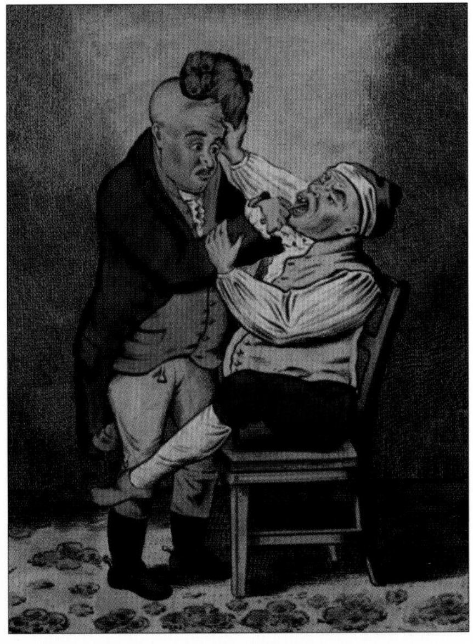

Left: "Breathing a vein," also known as "blood-letting," was used in the early 19th century to release disease and ease the suffering of ill patients. Right: The cure for a toothache may well have been worse than the toothache itself.

Pectoral for coughs, colds, asthma, consumption; Ayer's Cathartic Pills for constipation, dyspepsia, biliousness; Ayer's Sarsaparilla, a surefire blood purifier; or Ayer's Hair Vigor to put an end to gray hair.

Opiate of the People

Ayer and company had plenty of competition: Parker's Tonic was among the toughest, a cure for just about any internal ailment. The tonic definitely provided a quick fix—it contained 40 percent alcohol. For children's coughs, colds, and runny noses, Allen's Lung Balsam was a staple; for adult ailments there was Perry Davis's All-Purpose Pain-Killer. Doctor Thomas' Eclectic Oil was guaranteed to cure everything from a toothache (five minutes) to a backache (two hours) to lameness (two days) and deafness (two days). All of these tonics shared one characteristic: they contained opium. The Eclectic Oil was also laced with alcohol and chloroform.

Grove's Tasteless Chill Tonic suggests obesity was not quite the growing problem back then that it is today.

Slime Fever Syndrome

This army of humanitarians busily relieving the suffering of the masses contained a few charlatans and swindlers. Take the Killmer brothers, Andral and Joseph, for example. Doctor Killmer's U & O Meadow Plant Anointment allegedly eased suffering from more than 45 ailments—some of which he invented himself. Doctor Killmer's Swamp Root Kidney, Liver, and Bladder Cure worked its magic on pimples, diabetes, syphilis, and something called "internal slime fever." But best of all was Doctor Killmer's Ocean-Weed Heart Remedy, which was advertised to cure "sudden death." Maybe it worked. There's no record of anyone demanding a refund on the money-back guarantee.

Marketing Magic

The Killmer brothers became millionaires, as did several other patent-medicine moguls. These "wholesale druggists" refined print media advertising, product packaging, and direct mail sales—all hallmarks of American mass-market retailing. Their free samples and revolutionary one-time only introductory offers were very popular. They also

Only nation with a plain, solid-colored flag: Libya. (It's green.)

Doctor Ayer's tonics treated a wide range of ills.

came up with the discreet "plain brown wrapper" for milady's feminine products, many of which contained alcohol, opium, morphine, cocaine, and even arsenic (in some beauty aids). But the newly minted millionaires couldn't have had as much fun as the hucksters who operated the traveling medicine shows that went from town to town like a small carnival, complete with bands, dancers, jugglers, magicians, and skit actors. The entertainment was free, but the inevitable hard sell of exclusive elixirs—a specially blended sarsaparilla, a balsam brew, or a genuine kickapoo cure-all—paid the bills.

Snake Oil in Your Face

Snake oil cures were very popular on the medicine show circuit until exposés by muckraking reporters decreed them to be not only useless but also lacking in authentic snake oil—about the same time that the term *snake oil salesman* took on its shifty connotation. But that did nothing to stop the self-styled Rattlesnake King, Clark Stanley, from selling his snake oil at the 1893 World Columbian Exposition in Chicago. His routine was to kill and process the rattlesnakes right in front of potential customers.

The Government Gets in on the Act

By the turn of the century, the great cure-all period was drawing to a close. Germs and bacteria had been discovered; bona fide medical doctoring was on the rise. There were pill-making machines that could turn out millions of pills daily, and some large wholesale drug companies were evolving into pharmaceutical giants and retail chains. In 1906 the federal Pure Food and Drug Act was passed; advertising codes of ethics and ingredient labeling weren't far behind. Now the ailing public had to go to a drugstore to get their cure. The soda fountain—a fixture in most drugstores—served mineral water (which was thought to be curative) from carbonation machines. Though the medicinal connection withered away, when Prohibition was enacted, the soda fountain's success was assured—at least for a little while. Root beer and ice cream sodas were the order of the day. Unfortunately, in the long run, soda fountains couldn't compete with the money brought in by shelves and shelves of mass-produced cold, headache, and heartburn relievers—to say nothing of the beauty aids, school supplies, canned goods, and batteries. Welcome to the drugstore of today.

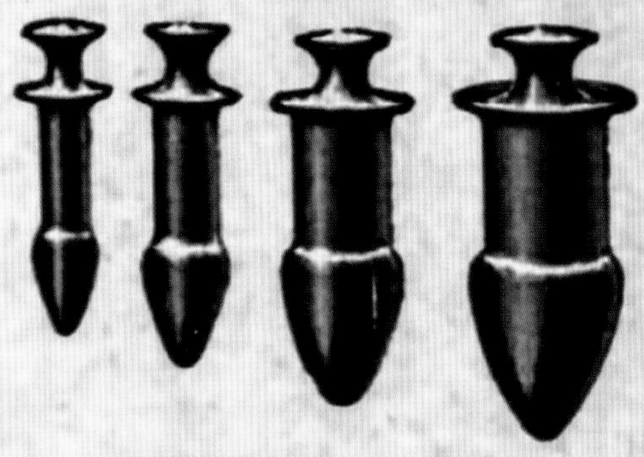

A curious cure for chronic constipation

Antarctica is the only continent that does not have land areas below sea level.

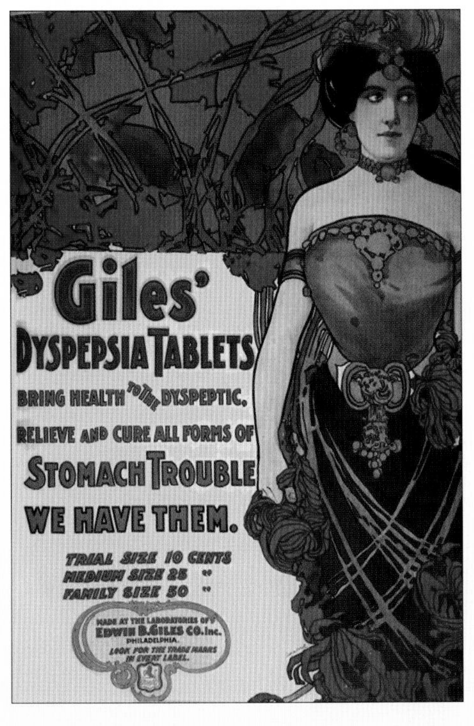

"Don't get mad. Don't get even. Just get elected…then get even."
—**James Carville**

"Don't take life too seriously. You'll never get out alive."
—**Tex Avery**

"Don't marry a man to reform him—that's what reform schools are for."
—**Mae West**

"Don't just do something, stand there."
—**Dean Acheson**

"Don't worry if you're a kleptomaniac, you can always take something for it."
—**Robert Benchley**

"Don't blame God. He's only human."
—**Leo Rosten**

"Don't worry about people stealing an idea. If it's original, you'll have to ram it down their throats."
—**Howard Aiken**

"Don't meet trouble halfway. It's quite capable of making the entire journey."
—**Stanislaw Jerzy Lec**

"Don't carry a grudge. While you're carrying the grudge, the other guy's out dancing."
—**Buddy Hackett**

"Don't steal. The government hates competition."
—**Anonymous**

"Don't dig for water under the outhouse."
—**Cowboy proverb**

"Don't judge each day by the harvest you reap but by the seeds that you plant."
—**Robert Louis Stevenson**

"Don't ever send a man window shopping. He'll come back carrying a window."
—***A Wife's Little Instruction Book***

Some 6,000 battles, skirmishes, and engagements were fought during the U.S. Civil War.

It's a Weird, Weird World

Here's proof that truth is stranger than fiction.

A Cryin' Shame

The 2011 Bar-B-Que cookoff in Houston came to an abrupt halt after one of the grillers, 51-year-old Mike Hamby, threw a canister of tear gas into a rival team's tent. The noxious fumes quickly spread to other tents. Dozens of people were sickened, and the contest was postponed. It's unclear why Hamby threw the canister, but apparently there was a "disagreement." After the smoke cleared, he was taken into custody...and later fired from his job as an officer with the Houston Police Department.

Scene of the canister incident

Checking You Out

For one day in November 2010, the Toronto Public Library allowed patrons to check out an actual human being. Officials explained that the project was a way for people to spend half an hour of one-on-one time with someone they'd never normally get to interact with—including a stand-up comedian, a homeless person, a Buddhist monk, and a former prostitute.

Hang on, Yan!

Extreme Napping

In 2012 Yan Yan Ch'eng, a 28-year-old Chinese student, was sunbathing when she fell asleep on a narrow concrete ledge five stories above the ground. Then she rolled over. Luckily, she woke and was able to grab hold of the ledge and hang on. Too scared to climb back up, she screamed for help as a crowd of people watched from below. Firefighters eventually pulled her to safety.

Witch Way Did She Go?

Eilish De'Avalon, a 40-year-old Australian woman, was pulled over in 2010 for talking on her cell phone while driving. When officer Andrew Logan gave her a citation, De'Avalon told him that she was exempt from traffic rules because she's a witch. "Your laws and penalties do not apply to me. I'm sorry, I must go. Thank you." As she started to drive away, Logan tried to take her keys, but his arm got caught in the window, and he was dragged 300 feet before he could pull the keys out of the ignition. De'Avalon was sentenced to two months in jail for severely injuring Logan's shoulder. She

Magic carpet: A high-quality Persian rug can last for 500 years.

apologized and offered him "spiritual healing and a massage." He declined.

Dying to Be on TV

Law Lok-lam died five times in one day in April 2011. The popular Chinese actor appeared on five different shows as five different characters—each of whom met his end. Two of the deaths occurred off-screen. One—a Ming emperor—died of an illness. The other two characters met their ends in martial arts dramas with Law coughing and spitting up blood as he perished. According to his fans, five TV deaths in a single day is a world record.

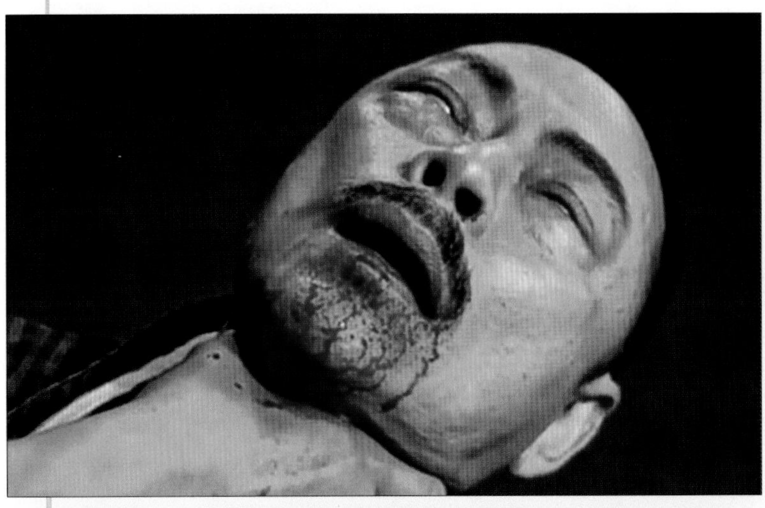

Don't worry—Law Lok-lam is only pretending.

Gender Bender

Jenny Johnsson, a preschool teacher in Stockholm, Sweden, has banned the use of the words "him" and "her" in her classroom. Instead, the children must refer to each other as "friend." "That way," said Johnsson, "they can be whoever they want to be!" Some of the parents have criticized the taxpayer-funded school for "brainwashing" their boys and girls, but Johnsson claims she is simply following the state-approved national curriculum in Sweden, which aims to eliminate "oppressive" gender stereotypes.

Is this meteorite a "message" from aliens?

Chicken Little Was Right

Radivoje Lajic's house in Bosnia has been struck by six meteorites: the first in 2007, another a few months later, and four more over the next three years. Scientists from Belgrade University confirmed that the six objects are indeed space rocks. What makes the strikes more curious? They only occur when it's raining heavily. "I don't know what I have done to annoy the aliens, but there is no other explanation that makes sense," said Lajic, 50. "The odds of being hit by a meteorite are so small that getting hit six times has to be deliberate. They are playing games with me." Lajic sold one of the meteorites to a school in the Netherlands and used the money to install steel reinforcements in his roof for protection.

Random Origin: The Kazoo

Similar instruments, called mirlitons, had been used in Africa for hundreds of years, either for hunting (to imitate animal sounds) or in religious rituals. The famous kazoo sound comes from the user humming (not blowing air) across a membrane, which causes it to vibrate. In the 1840s, an African American man named Alabama Vest form Macon, Georgia, based the modern kazoo on these instruments. They were mass-produced to Vest's specifications by German clockmaker Thaddeus von Clegg and were first demonstrated at the 1852 Georgia State Fair.

Try it yourself: When an ice cube melts, it doesn't raise the water level in the glass.

Bizarre Crooks

Over the years, we've written about all kinds of criminals—dumb ones, nice ones, even clever ones. But these peculiar law breakers defy classification.

When Art Really Bombs

In 2002 Luke Helder, a University of Wisconsin art student, was arrested for planting 18 pipe bombs in mailboxes in half a dozen states. It was all part of a bizarre "art" project: When plotted on a map, the bomb sites formed a "smiley face," with the "eyes" in Nebraska and Iowa and the left side of the "mouth" in Colorado and Texas. The right side remained unfinished because police caught Helder after his father turned him in. (Nobody died.)

The happy face bomb locations; the red line shows the incomplete part of the smile.

Sleepy Crime

Two women approached a man in a park in Sibu, Romania, and struck up a friendly conversation with him, during the course of which they asked him to let them hypnotize him. He agreed, thinking it might be fun. A half hour later the man woke up from his trance. The women were gone, and so was his wallet.

Stressling

Simon Andrews of Osbaldwick, England, was sentenced to six months house arrest in 2003. The crime: Andrews had attacked four random men on the street, wrestling them to the ground and taking off—but not stealing—their shoes and socks. Why'd he do it? Andrews, an accountant, says he was "stressed out."

Crime Plague

A biological terror alert went out in January 2003 when Dr. Thomas Butler, an infectious disease researcher at Texas Tech University, informed police that 30 vials of bubonic plague were missing from his lab. Police feared the vials were stolen by terrorists who could convert the samples into a chemical weapon. Even President George W. Bush was briefed about the incident. A day later, Dr. Butler was arrested when it was discovered he'd accidentally destroyed the plague vials himself, and had lied to cover up the error.

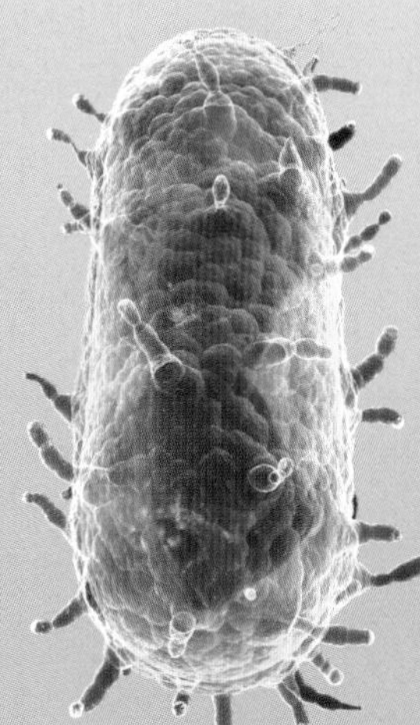

Bubonic plague

Life on Mars

Dusco Stuppar, 32, of France was able to con an old childhood friend, known only as "Christophe H." into giving him 650,000 francs (about $62,000) to help fund the construction of a city to be built under a secret river on the planet Mars. Stuppar informed Christophe that he was part of a secret society of ultra-intelligent people who had the technology required to make

Yeehaw Junction, Florida, used to be called Jackass Junction.

the underwater space city possible. Even more bizarre: Stuppar claimed his evil clone (also part of the Mars project) had injected him with explosives. If Christophe didn't hand over the money, he said, the clone would blow up Stuppar. Christophe told the story to a psychiatrist, leading to Stuppar's arrest and an 18-month jail term.

Breaking and Delivering

A couple living in Dorset, England, called the police in 2001 when they realized their home had been broken into while they were out. An investigation revealed that the thief hadn't actually stolen anything, but had left behind a new television and an unopened bottle of Zima.

It's Electric

In fall 2005, a strange crime wave hit Baltimore, Maryland: Over a period of six weeks, 130 light poles were stolen. Each pole measured 30 feet tall, weighed 250 pounds, and cost $1,200. There were no witnesses and police were baffled. More baffling is why the thieves were so neat—when they stole the poles, they left all the high voltage wiring cleanly wrapped in black electric tape.

Oh, That's Where I Left Them

In 2003 a 23-year-old woman from Tyrol, Austria, went to a police station to report that her expensive pair of ski pants had been stolen. Officers quickly solved the case—they pointed out to the woman that she was wearing the pants. "I was so nervous that I forgot to take them off," she said.

The Last Laugh: Epitaphs

Some grave humor collected by our wandering tombstone-oligists.

- **In Massachusetts:**
  Here lies as silent as clay
  Miss Arabella Young
  Who on the 21st of May 1771
  Began to hold her tongue.
- **In Ohio:**
  I thought it was a mushroom when
  I found it in the woods forsaken
  But since I sleep beneath this mound,
  I must have been mistaken.
- **In England:**
  Here lies Will Smith
  And, something rarish,
  He was born, bred, and hanged,
  All in the same parish.
- **In New Jersey:**
  She drank good ale, good punch and wine
  And lived to the age of 99.
- **In England:**
  Here lies the father of 29.
  There would have been more
  But he didn't have the time.
- **In Arizona:**
  Here lies Lester
  Moore,
  Four slugs from a .44,
  No Les
  No More.
- **In Colorado:**
  Bill Blake
  Was hanged
  by mistake.
- **In Texas:**
  I told you
  I was sick.

HERE LAYS BUTCH.
WE PLANTED HIM RAW.
HE WAS QUICK
ON THE TRIGGER,
BUT SLOW
ON THE DRAW.

Invented Words

Most English words took decades, even centuries, to achieve their modern form. But not these—they were invented overnight.

Factoid

Coined by: Norman Mailer

Story: In 1973, while writing his biography of Marilyn Monroe, Mailer was trying to describe made-up facts that are believed because they're printed in a magazine or newspaper. He combined the word "fact" with the suffix -oid, which means "like." The term held this "invented fact" meaning until the 1990s, when CNN Headline News began displaying trivia and statistics on the screen beneath the title "Factoid." Result: Now it also means "little fact."

Marilyn Monroe factoid: She was buried in a green Pucci dress.

Agnostic

Thomas H. Huxley

Coined by: Thomas H. Huxley, 19th-century biologist

Story: Huxley's belief that people can only truly understand what they can see with their own eyes earned him the "atheist" label, and no matter how hard he tried, he couldn't distance himself from it. So one night at a party in 1860, "I invented the word 'agnostic' to denote people who, like myself, confess themselves to be hopelessly ignorant concerning a variety of matters." Huxley combined the prefix a-, meaning "without," and gnostic, a word derived from the Greek *gnostos*, meaning "knowable," and used by early Christian writers to mean a "higher knowledge of spiritual things." The definition has since changed subtly from "admitted ignorance of spiritual things" to the "questioning of spiritual things."

Yes-Man

Coined by: Tad Dorgan, American cartoonist

Story: In 1913 Dorgan drew a cartoon called "Giving the First Edition the Once-Over," which featured a newspaper editor and his assistants. Attempting to show how weak-kneed the assistants were, above each of them was the word "yes-man." The term quickly expanded to include any subordinate—in business, sports, or politics—who always agrees with the boss, regardless of whether it's justified. (Also credited to Dorgan: "23-skidoo," "cat's meow," "dumbbell," "for crying out loud," "hard-boiled," and "Yes, we have no bananas.")

Realtor

Coined by: Charles N. Chadbourn, president of the Minneapolis Real Estate Board

Story: What do you call a person who sells homes? A realtor? Wrong—a real estate agent. Not all real

In golf, a score of 8 on a single hole is called "making a snowman."

estate agents are REALTORS®. The term is what's called a collective membership trademark, so only members of the National Association of Realtors (NAR) can legally use it. Chadbourn invented the word in 1916 after reading the headline: "Real Estate Man Swindles a Poor Widow." "The advantage of a distinguishing mark," he said, "is so that the public may know the responsible, expert real estate man from the curbstoner who possesses no such qualifications." He sold the rights of the word to NAR for $1.

Grok

Coined by: Robert A. Heinlein, science-fiction writer

Story: It appears in Heinlein's 1961 novel, *Stranger in a Strange Land*, as a Martian word that means "to understand so thoroughly that the observer becomes a part of the observed—to merge, blend, intermarry, lose identity in group experience. It means almost everything that we mean by religion, philosophy, and science—and it means as little to us (because of our Earthly assumptions) as color means to a blind man."

Although the humans in the novel never really grokked the meaning of the word, it has since been adopted by popular culture "to understand a concept, opinion, or philosophy on a deep, profound level."

Gobbledygook

Coined by: Maury Maverick, U.S. Congressman

Story: To Maverick, a straight-talking Texas politician (and grandson of Samuel Maverick, from whom we get the word "maverick"), most other politicians were like turkeys: "always gobbledy gobbling and strutting around with ludicrous pomposity." While chairman of Smaller War Plants Corporation in 1944, Maverick sent out a memo: "No more gobbledygook language! Anyone using the words 'activation' or 'implementation' will be shot."

Cheesy Does It

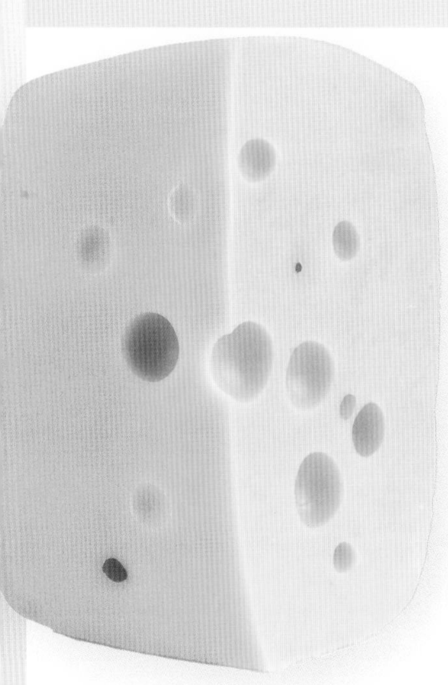

"The early bird gets the worm, but the second mouse gets the cheese."

—**Jon Hammond**

"A corpse is meat gone bad. Well, and what's cheese? Corpse of milk."

—**James Joyce**

"McDonald's double cheeseburgers are a weapon of mass destruction."

—**Ralph Nader**

"Swiss cheese is a rip-off. It's the only cheese I can bite into and miss."

—**Mitch Hedberg**

"Right now, I'm as single as a slice of American cheese."

—**Nick Cannon**

"When cheese gets its picture taken, what does it say?"

—**George Carlin**

Robigus is the Roman god of mildew and grain rust.

Edifice Complex

Think the old woman who lived in a shoe had weird taste in housing? It turns out she was just ahead of her time. Buildings can look like all sorts of things. Even...

An Igloo

Crouched on the Parks Highway about 180 miles outside of Anchorage, Alaska, is a hulking four-story igloo. Its dome can be spotted from an airplane flying at 30,000 feet. Built in the 1970s, the igloo was meant to give tourists a chance to visit a "real" Alaskan igloo. Igloo City, as it's known, has been a convenience store, a gas station, a makeshift triage clinic for a man attacked by a grizzly bear, and an emergency airplane refueling stop (a small plane once landed on the highway and taxied in for gas). But other than part of the ground floor, the igloo itself has never been used. It was supposed to be a motel, but the couple who built it forgot something important: building codes. The structure never passed inspection, and its owners went broke.

A Chicken

A 56-foot-tall chicken head juts from the roof of the Kentucky Fried Chicken at the corner of Roswell Street and Cobb Parkway in Marietta, Georgia. Locals use it as a landmark when giving directions: "Turn right, after you pass the Big Chicken." The architectural whimsy, built in 1963, was a Johnny Reb's Chick, Chuck and Shakes fried-chicken restaurant until 1966, when the owner, Tubby Davis, sold it to his brother, who turned it into a KFC. In 1993 the chicken suffered wind damage and might have been demolished were it not considered too important to be axed. Reason: Pilots use the building as a reference point when approaching Atlanta and nearby Dobbins Air Reserve Base.

An Egg

The owner of a European ad agency wanted to add an office next to her lakeside house in Belgium, and hired the design firm dmvA to come up with something organic-looking that could be built without cutting down a single tree. Local authorities refused to issue a building permit because city council members thought the design was too weird: The building—nicknamed "the blob"—looked like a giant white egg. To get around the council, the designer turned the egg into a mobile unit so it would qualify as a work of art, not a

The "blob" house—and open and shut case

Hi, neighbor: TV's Mr. Rogers and golfer Arnold Palmer were high school pals.

building. The structure consists of a wooden frame with a polyester skin and an ultra-modern grid of niches molded into the interior for storage. The interior features lighting, a sleeping shelf, a kitchen, and a bathroom. The pointy end of the egg (the egg is on its side) opens up to create a porch. After the project, known as the Blob VB3, was completed, the unique structure appeared in a Belgian newspaper under the heading "Art skirts building regulations." The next day, someone at the building council showed up to warn the owner that if the egg was placed near the house, there would be consequences. Dubbed the "rovin' ovum" by its fans, the Blob VB3 went on the auction block in 2010. (No word as to whether anyone had the huevos to buy it.)

A Peach

The 150-foot-tall water tower outside Gaffney, South Carolina, was built to catch the eye of motorists speeding along I-85. It looks like a gigantic peach. In 1981, when the tower went up, the local economy depended on peach orchards. Townspeople wanted it known that Cherokee County, where Gaffney is located, grew more peaches per year than the whole state of Georgia (the "Peach State"). Macro-artist Peter Freudenberg studied local peaches for many hours and used 50 gallons of paint

That's no moon—it's a peach!

in 20 different colors to make the peach hyper-realistic. Features include a 7-ton, 60-foot-long leaf and an enormous vertical cleft in its backside, leading to the nickname "Moon Over Gaffney."

A Nautilus Shell

In 2006 a young family in Mexico City decided to ditch their conventional home and build one more in harmony with nature. From above, their new house looks like the perfect spiral of a nautilus shell. From the front lawn, it looks like a soft-serve ice cream sundae. The frame for the building consists of steel-reinforced chicken wire that's covered in a two-inch layer of stucco, inside and out. Stained-glass bubbles in the walls sparkle like sunlight on water. A stone walkway spirals from room to room on a bed of live plants, creating the sensation of floating above the ocean floor. The bathroom's sandy walls and blue tiles offer users the illusion of being underwater. Family members say the Nautilus House makes them feel "like a mollusk in its shell, moving from one chamber to another."

Mr. Roboto

In 1986 Thai architect Sumet Jumsai designed the new Bank of Asia in Bangkok to reflect the computerization of banking going on at the time. Result: The $10 million, 20-story building looks like a giant LEGO robot. The "robot" has two antennae that serve as lightning rods, and glass eyes with louvered metallic lids that serve as windows. Jumsai wanted the building to "free the spirit from the present architectural intellectual impasse and propel it forward into the next century." So what was the inspiration for what's been called a "post-high-tech marvel?" His son's toy robot.

A House on Stilts

Architect Terunobu Fujimori has a weird way of getting approval for his unique designs. He invites clients to join him in his tiny *Takasugi-an*—his "Too-High Teahouse." Perched 20 feet in the air, the 30-square-foot private teahouse in Chino, Japan, balances on two forked tree trunks that resemble spindly chicken legs. Once clients have climbed the ladders to the house, he shows them his hand-drawn plans. "If they don't like my design, I shake the building!" he says with a laugh.

The World's Largest Chest

In the 1920s, the High Point, North Carolina, Chamber of Commerce built its first building-sized chest of drawers. Twenty feet tall, the giant chest served as the chamber's Bureau of Information and helped to promote the city's image as the "Furniture Capital of the World." In 1996 the chest was augmented, making it 38 feet tall. In 2010, upset with the city's refusal to help with the upkeep of the landmark, Pam Stern, the building's owner, had the chest measured for a giant bra: 20 feet of silk, spandex, and underwiring. (Get it? A chest of drawers.) HanesBrands Inc., maker of Playtex bras, sent engineers over to take the chest's measurements. Whether the city will permit the chest to wear the bra remains unknown at this time.

Paul Bunyan's missing sock?

In 17th-century America, the average married woman gave birth to 13 children.

Executive Decisions

They may be in positions of responsibility...they may be captains of industry...they may be among the world's most successful business people. But that doesn't mean they can't make really dumb decisions, just like the rest of us. Here are some classics.

Should We Buy This Invention?

Executive: William Orton, president of the Western Union Telegraph Company

William Orton

Background: In 1876 Western Union had a monopoly on the telegraph, the world's most advanced communications technology. This made it one of America's richest and most powerful companies, "with $41 million in capital and the pocketbooks of the financial world behind it." So when Gardiner Greene Hubbard, a wealthy Bostonian, approached Orton with an offer to sell the patent for a new invention Hubbard had helped to fund, Orton treated it as a joke. Hubbard was asking for $100,000!

Decision: Orton bypassed Hubbard and drafted a response directly to the inventor. "Mr. Bell," he wrote, "after careful consideration of your invention, while it is a very interesting novelty, we have come to the conclusion that it has no commercial possibilities...What use could this company make of an electrical toy?"

An "electrical toy": replica of an 1876 Bell "Centennial" Telephone

Impact: The invention, the telephone, would have been perfect for Western Union. The company had a nationwide network of telegraph wires in place, and the inventor, 29-year-old Alexander Graham Bell, had shown that his telephones worked quite well on telegraph lines. All the company had to do was hook telephones up to its existing lines and it would have had the world's first nationwide telephone network in a matter of months.

Alexander Graham Bell

Instead, Bell kept the patent and in a few decades his telephone company, "renamed American Telephone and Telegraph (AT&T), had become the largest corporation in America....The Bell patent—offered to Orton for a measly $100,000—became the single most valuable patent in history."

Ironically, less than two years after turning Bell down, Orton realized the magnitude of his mistake and spent millions of dollars challenging Bell's patents while attempting to build his own telephone network (which he was ultimately forced to hand over to Bell). Instead of going down in history as one of the architects of the telephone age, he is instead remembered for having made one of the worst decisions in American business history.

How Do We Compete with Budweiser?

Executive: Robert Uihlein Jr., head of the Schlitz Brewing Company in Milwaukee, Wisconsin

Background: In the 1970s, Schlitz was America's #2 beer, behind Budweiser. It had been #1 until 1957 and has pursued Bud ever since. In the 1970s, Uihlein came up with a strategy to compete against Anheuser-Busch. He figured that if he could cut the cost of ingredients used in his beer and speed up the brewing process at the same time, he could brew more beer in the same amount of time for less money...and earn higher profits.

Decision: Uihlein cut the amount of time it took to brew Schlitz from 40 days to 15, and replaced much of the barley malt in the beer with corn syrup—which was cheaper. He also switched from one type of foam stabilizer to another to get around new labeling laws that would have required the original stabilizer to be disclosed on the label.

Impact: Uihlein got what he wanted: a cheaper, more profitable beer that made a lot of money...at first. But it tasted terrible, and tended to break down quickly as the cheap ingredients bonded together and sank to the bottom of the can—forming a substance that "looked disconcertingly like mucus," Philip Van Munching writes in *Beer Blast*.

Suddenly Schlitz found itself shipping out a great deal of apparently snot-ridden beer. The brewery knew about it pretty quickly and made a command decision—to do nothing. Uihlein declined a costly recall for months, wagering that not much of the beer would be subjected to the kinds of temperatures at which most haze forms. He lost the bet, sales plummeted, and Schlitz began a long steady slide from the top three.

This stuff gave me the Schlitz.

Schlitz finally caved in and recalled 10 million cans of the "snot beer." But their reputation was ruined and sales never recovered. In 1981 they shut down their Milwaukee brewing plant; the following year the company was purchased by rival Stroh's. One former mayor of Milwaukee compared the brewery's fortunes to the sinking of the *Titanic*, asking, "How could that big of a business go under so fast?"

If They Married...

This may be the stupidest wordplay game ever invented.

- If America Ferrera married Billy Idol, she'd be **America Idol**.
- If Paula Abdul married Kareem Abdul-Jabbar, she'd be **Paula Abdul-Abdul-Jabbar**.
- If Portia de Rossi married Bob Costas, then divorced him and married Giorgio Armani, then divorced him and married Adrian Legg, she'd be **Portia Costas-Armani-Legg**.
- If Naomi Watts married Sir Thomas Moore, then divorced him and married Eddie Money, she'd be **Naomi Moore-Money**.
- If Philip Seymour Hoffman married Ebeneezer Scrooge, then divorced him and married Minnie Driver, he'd be **Philip Scrooge-Driver**.
- If Scarlett Johansson married Dr. Johnny Fever (character on WKRP in Cincinnati), she'd be **Scarlett Fever**.
- If Amanda Seyfried married Bob Huggins (basketball coach), then divorced him and married Zoltán Kiss (Hungarian athlete), she'd be **Amanda Huggins-Kiss**.

Queen Victoria was one of the first women to use chloroform as anesthesia during childbirth.

There's nothing like a good dose of irony to put the problems of day-to-day life in proper perspective.

Beastly Irony

- The crow population of Woodstock, Ontario, grew so large that residents started complaining to the city council about the noise. The council's solution: frequent bursts of noisy fireworks to scare the crows away.
- Tired of the other hunters who crowded into his favorite squirrel hunting grounds, in 1963 Pete Pickett strapped on some fake gorilla feet and tramped all over the place, hoping the prints would scare everyone else away. Instead, the footprints drew mobs of Bigfoot hunters.

Ironic Deaths

- English novelist Arnold Bennett died in Paris in 1931. Cause of death: He drank a glass of typhoid-infected water to demonstrate that Parisian water was perfectly safe to drink.
- In 1955 James Dean made an ad warning teens about driving too fast. "The life you save may be mine," he said. Shortly after, he died when his Porsche Spyder, going 86 mph, hit another car.
- In 1871 attorney Clement Vallandigham was demonstrating to a jury that the man his client was accused of shooting could have accidentally done it himself. Vallandigham took out a gun, held it as it was held at the scene of the crime, and pulled the trigger. The gun was loaded; he proved his point.
- Elizabeth Taylor outlived Mel Gussow by six years. Mel who? He was the *New York Times* writer who penned Taylor's obituary.
- Michael Anderson Godwin was sentenced to death in the early 1980s for murder. After six years and numerous appeals, the South Carolina death-row inmate got his sentence reduced to life in prison. Not long after, Godwin was sitting on the metal toilet in his cell, watching TV. He was wearing nothing except a pair of headphones, which started to crackle. Trying to fix them, Godwin bit into the wire. He was electrocuted and died.

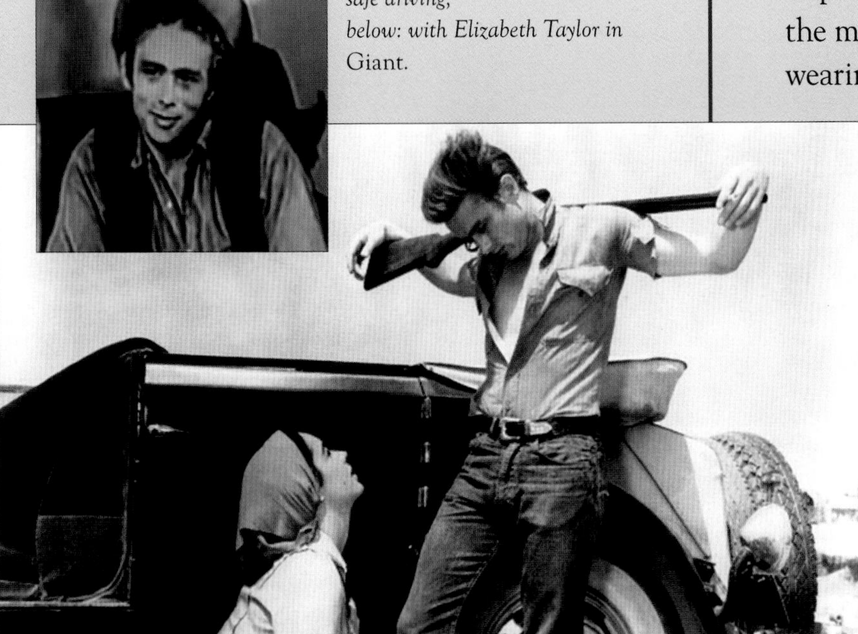

left: James Dean promoting safe driving;
below: with Elizabeth Taylor in Giant.

Irony and Public Safety

- In 1974 the Consumer Product Safety Commission ordered 80,000 buttons promoting toy safety. They said: "For Kids' Sake, Think Toy Safety." The buttons were recalled when the agency found out they had "sharp edges, parts a child could swallow, and were coated with toxic lead paint."

Tom Cruise writes with his right hand, but does almost everything else left-handed.

Creepy Cryptids

We asked our friend Andy the Talking Humpback Whale to settle this once and for all: Do these creatures exist or not? We'd tell you what Andy's answer was… but then we'd have to krill you.

Background

Cryptozoology is the study of animals that some people think exist, but whose existence has yet to be proven. Of course, the field includes a lot of wackadoodle creatures (uh-oh—here comes the angry letters from Bigfoot and Chupacabra!), but there's some serious science involved, too. That includes the study of animals that are believed to be extinct…but not by everybody. Meanwhile, take these possibly imaginary creatures...please.

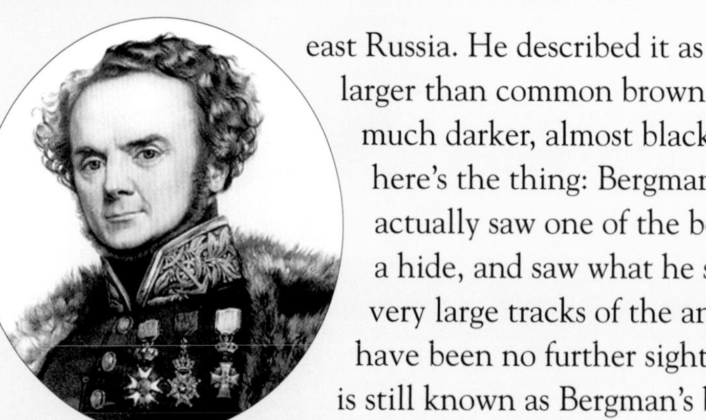

Joseph Paul Gaimard

Bergman's Bear

In the 1920s, Swedish zoologist Sten Bergman identified what he claimed was a subspecies of the brown bear on the Kamchatka Peninsula in northeast Russia. He described it as significantly larger than common brown bears, and much darker, almost black in color. But here's the thing: Bergman never actually saw one of the bears. He saw a hide, and saw what he said were very large tracks of the animals. There have been no further sightings of what is still known as Bergman's bear.

Rhinoceros Dolphin

This odd cetacean (a marine mammal such as a porpoise, dolphin, or whale) was first sighted in the Mediterranean Sea in the 1800s. The reports, which claimed the animal was a dolphin with two dorsal fins—hence the name "rhinoceros dolphin"—were not taken seriously, because no

Cryptologists believe Bergman's Bear may reside in Russia's Kamchatka Peninsula.

A newborn baby's brain weighs only 3 ounces; the average adult's weighs 3 pounds.

This old photograph may prove the existence of Bergman's Bear (or of a tiny race of people).

other known cetacean has two dorsal fins. (They all have either none or one.) That would have been that, but in 1819 two respected French naturalists, Joseph Paul Gaimard and Jean René Constant Quoy, backed up the story when they reported seeing very similar creatures while sailing the South Pacific: "Every one on board was surprised to perceive that they had a fin on their head bent backwards, the same as that on their backs," they wrote. The naturalist duo even gave the creature the scientific name *Delphinus rhinoceros*. Sightings of similar two-finned dolphins have been recorded over the years since, but none have been confirmed. (If you see one—take a picture and send it to us!)

Giglioli's Whale

On September 4, 1867, Italian zoologist Enrico Hillyer Giglioli was on the Italian warship *Magenta* in the Pacific Ocean, about 1,200 miles off the coast of Chile, when a whale surfaced very close to the ship and stayed alongside for several minutes. Giglioli wrote that it looked like a member of the baleen whale family, which includes blue whales and humpbacks, was about 60 feet long—and had two dorsal fins. Again: No known cetaceans have two dorsal fins, and no such creature has ever been captured. But (also again) there have been other sightings since, one of the most recent in 1983, when sailors on a boat between Corsica and France reported that a large whale with two dorsal fins followed their ship for several hours. Whale experts still think it very unlikely such creatures exist, mostly because large whales were so heavily hunted during the whaling era that surely at least one whale with two dorsal fins would have been seen.

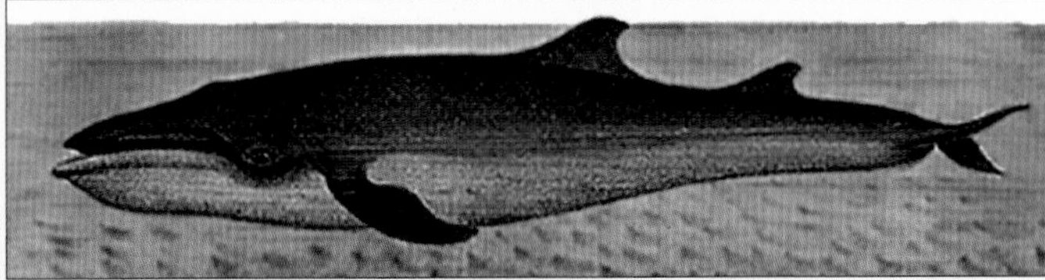

Giglioli's Whale

Irkuiem

The story of Bergman's bear was understandably mostly forgotten—until the 1980s, when Russian biologist N. K. Vereshchagin heard that native peoples in Kamchatka were talking about having seen a strange bear there. They called it *irkuiem*, meaning "trousers pulled down" because it had bunches of fat that hung down between its rear legs, which made it look like it was wearing falling-down trousers. The reports revived the stories of Bergman's bear, but Vereshchagin suggested the animal might be something much more remarkable: a surviving strain of *Arctodus simus*, one of the largest

Arctodus simus, *reconstruction*

Artist's impression of the Dingonek

bears that ever lived. Before it went extinct, the bear inhabited North America for millions of years, from Mississippi to Alaska—right across the land bridge from Russia, where the locals were telling their irkuiem stories.

Dingonek

This fanciful creature is supposed to resemble an anteater, except that it lives in rivers and lakes, can grow to 18 feet in length, has a horn on its head, a poison-secreting tail like a scorpion, and tusks like a walrus (hence its other name: the "jungle walrus"). According to legend, dingoneks inhabit the jungles of western Africa, where they prey on crocodiles, hippos, and people.

They're best known from a description by British explorer John Alfred Jordan, who claimed to have seen and shot at one in the River Maggori in Kenya in 1907. Alas, it got away. (The origin of the name "dingonek" is unknown.)

Illustration of the Agogwe

Nandi Bear

The forested mountains of eastern Africa are the supposed home of this supposed creature, whose name is taken from the Nandi people of Kenya. It's been described as about four feet tall at the shoulders, with reddish-brown fur, and much longer forelegs than hind legs, which makes it look more like a hyena than an actual bear. According to legend, it's a ferocious carnivore that eats only the brains of its victims, which include humans (a "zombie bear"?). Sightings have been reported for centuries, but no Nandi bear has ever been captured or photographed. Some cryptozoologists say it may be a surviving *Pachycrocuta brevirostris*, or "giant hyena," which most paleontologists say went extinct 500,000 years ago. Others say it could be a relative of the Atlas bear, Africa's only known native bear, which roamed the Atlas Mountains of northwest Africa before being driven to extinction by overhunting in the late 1800s. Even famed paleoanthropologist Louis Leakey added his two cents to the debate, wondering if the Nandi bear could be related to the *Chalicotherium*, which according to fossil evidence has been extinct for more than 7 million years, and rather than being a brain-eating carnivore (zombie bear!) was an herbivore.

Agogwe

The earliest credible sighting of this small, humanlike biped was reported by British explorer Captain William Hichens. Writing in the British magazine *Discovery*, Hichens claimed he saw two of the creatures in what is now Tanzania in the 1920s. He described them as standing about four feet tall, covered in russet-colored hair, and walking upright

Walruses get bald as they age.

like humans. His local guide called them *agogwe*, explaining they were legendary creatures that would, for example, work in people's gardens in exchange for food and beer. Similar creatures with a variety of names are said to exist all across the region. There have been many reported sightings of small, bipedal "humans" over the years, but no solid confirmation. Some say agogwes could be ancient hominids long thought to be extinct, many of which were small in stature, like the agogwe. If they exist, that is.

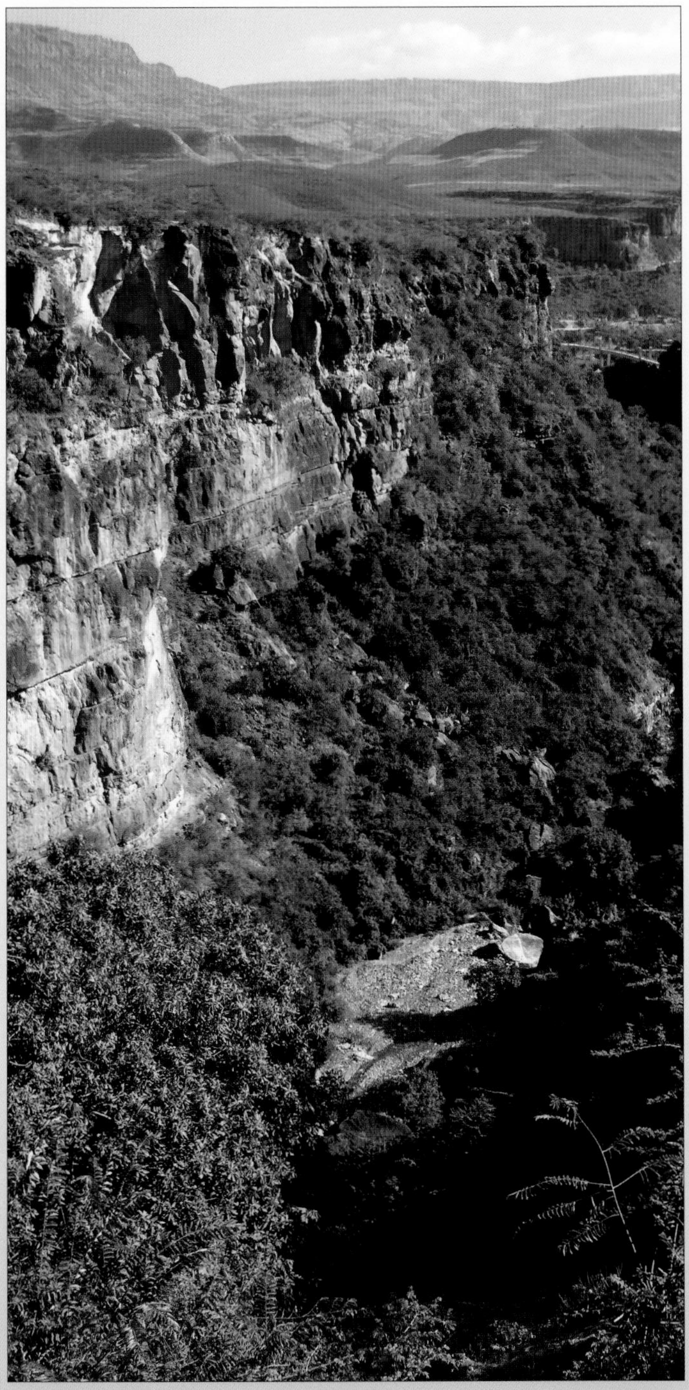

Could these remote forests in eastern Africa be home to the Nandi bear?

All the Latest from the News Stream

 **Bathroom News** 

It's in the Bag

According to complaints made to their union, 25 male field technicians for Qwest, a telecommunications company in the western United States, were told by a supervisor in Montrose, Colorado, to bring "urine bags" out to the job to cut down on "lengthy bathroom breaks" (the workers generally go all the way back to the garage to do their business). The union claims the workers were ordered to use the bags; the company counters that there's no set policy—the bags are simply provided for the workers' convenience, should they need them.

Down the Drain

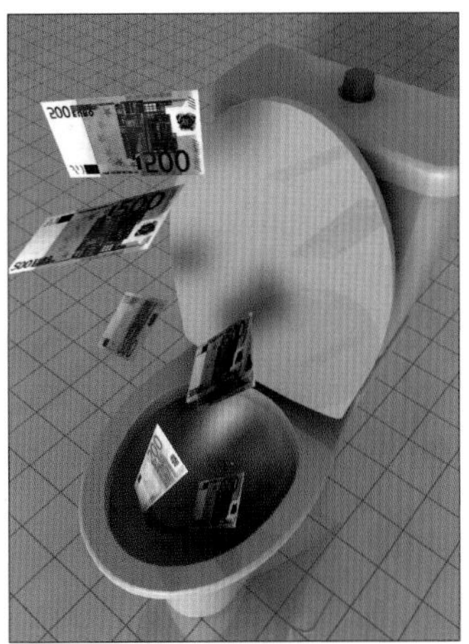

When the euro took over as Europe's official currency in 2002, many people believed—incorrectly—that their old money would be worthless. A man in Berlin, Germany, believed it...and flushed 60,000 Deutsche marks down his toilet. When informed that he could have exchanged the cash for about 30,000 euros ($37,000 U.S.), the man (his name was withheld—wouldn't you want yours withheld if you were him?) called the city public works department and begged them to retrieve his money for him. The workers had to go out to the man's street anyway...because the sewer line was clogged with his money. After working for hours, they were able to pull some of the man's cash from the sewage, which he then painstakingly dried and cleaned before exchanging it.

Bad Trip

For decades, rumors have swirled around the CIA's testing of lysergic acid diethylamide (LSD) in the 1960s. In seeking a knockout drug weapon, did the CIA slip substances to unsuspecting patsies? The answer is yes. And Frank Olson was the man who paid the heaviest price. Here's the story of the CIA's Electric Kool-Aid Acid Test and how it went horribly wrong.

Behind Closed Doors

The Olson family—Alice, Frank, and their three young children—lived an all-American, idyllic life in Frederick, Maryland. B unbeknownst to everyone, Frank had a secret li developing ways of efficiently distributing deadl strains of diseases during bacteriological warfar for the Special Operations Division (SOD) of tl army's Chemical Corps.

Lab Rats

While Frank Olson was busy creating ways to hide delivery systems in shaving cream and bug spray cans, a CIA researcher and official, Dr. Sidney Gottlieb, was developing very different weapons with his team, called MK-ULTRA. For years Gottlieb had been studying the use of narcotics such as cocaine and mescaline, hoping that he could come up with a pharmacopoeia of substances that could be used as tactical weapons. In the early 1950s, he believed he had found something that might work—lysergic acid, aka LSD. LSD seemed perfect for Gottlieb's purposes. It was colorless, odorless, and capable of reducing sane people to babbling, disoriented idiots.

Everybody Must Get Stoned

Besides conducting experiments at universities and prisons, the MK-ULTRA team tested LSD on themselves, slipping it into each other's food and drinks without warning. But Gottlieb wasn't interested in LSD's effects on willing subjects; he needed to know how average folks would react when fed the drug without their knowledge. Gottlieb's bosses had put the kibosh on furtive civilian experiments, but Gottlieb had a better idea. Every year the MK-ULTRA team met up with the SOD (Frank's group) for a brainstorming weekend. These were men who worked around hazardous chemicals all the time. Surely it would be okay to doctor their cocktails.

Experiment in Error

Two days into the meeting, November 19, 1953, Gottlieb struck. He gathered a group together—eight colleagues including himself and Olson—and made everyone a cocktail. Twenty minutes later he let them in on his little secret: Their drinks were spiked. Within an hour, Olson began acting strangely. He was paranoid, convinced there was a CIA plot to discredit him. He wept, laughed, ranted, and howled. Gottlieb was nonplussed. None of his test subjects had acted this way before. And it went on and on. The next morning, all the other unwitting trippers had come down, but Frank was still disturbed and fearful. Not knowing what else to do, Gottlieb allowed him to return home.

Tuned-in, Turned-on, Dropped-out

A new Frank Olson came back to his family. Instead of the loving and cheerful husband and father, Frank was suspicious and depressed. Gottlieb took responsibility. He sent Olson to a Manhattan psychotherapist who for years had administered LSD to his patients in order to study its effects on sex and addiction.

Dr. Harold Abramson tried to talk Olson down—the patient was holding forth on the CIA's plans to get him, humiliate him, and slip him drugs to keep him awake. He was afraid he'd be made to disappear; he heard voices and believed that agents were waiting everywhere to arrest him. Stymied, Abramson and Gottlieb agreed that Olson should be put in a psychiatric hospital. Just before he was to be admitted, Olson was sharing a hotel room with a CIA scientist who'd brought him to New York. In the middle of the night, just nine days after Frank ingested the LSD, the agent awoke in time to see Frank Olson dashing across the room and crashing through the window. By the time the agent was able to reach the window and look a long 10 stories down, Frank Olson was dead.

Cover-up Exposed

CIA officials soon found out what had happened. In the interest of national security, they elected to cover it up. Alice Olson was told that her husband had died of a "classified illness," and she received two-thirds of his salary as a pension. The CIA admonished Sid Gottlieb but didn't halt his experiments—instead they ordered that LSD be tested instead on street prostitutes and other people who they figured wouldn't much be missed if they went astray. The LSD experiments continued for 10 more years. But Frank Olson's unusual death didn't remain a secret. In December 1974, the *New York Times* broke the story of the CIA's mind-control experiments, and eventually it was revealed that at least one subject had died after being fed LSD. The Olson family realized that subject was Frank. They told his story to the national media, winning a $750,000 settlement in 1976—and a personal apology from President Gerald Ford.

Hogwarts motto: *Draco dormiens nunquam titillandus* ("Never tickle a sleeping dragon").

Sequoia and the Cherokee Alphabet

The story of the man who single-handedly brought the written word to his entire culture.

The Height of Human Achievements

Most people accept written language as a given, but archaeologists believe writing was invented independently by only a few ancient cultures, and that almost every subsequent writing system was derived from these originals. That writing developed at all is a testament to human ingenuity. So the fact that one man invented a completely original writing system in the early 19th century is pretty remarkable.

What makes it even more remarkable is that he did it without ever having read or written a single word in any preexisting alphabet. The only language he had ever spoken was Cherokee. His name was Sequoia.

Taking up the Pen

Few details of his life are known, but Sequoia is believed to have been born sometime between 1750 and 1775, a time when settlers from the growing region around Georgia, South Carolina, and Tennessee were beginning to threaten Cherokee independence. He was a part of the last generation of Cherokees to live freely in their ancestral homeland, the same generation that was eventually forced west over the infamous Trail of Tears. Recognizing that the European culture had an advantage in being able to communicate through writing, Sequoia became determined to level the playing field by devising a similar system for his own language.

Sequoia with a tablet depicting his writing system for the Cherokee language (Henry Inman)

Beginning in 1809, he created an 85-character system of syllables, which differed from the English alphabet in that the characters depicted full syllables instead of individual sounds. It took him 12 years. When he was finished, he had created a writing system still marveled at today for the ease with which it can be learned. Previously illiterate speakers of Cherokee were able to master it within a matter of weeks. And they could teach it to others just as quickly.

Power of the Press

Sequoia introduced his syllabary in 1821. Within just five years, the Cherokees were operating what the Boston *Missionary Herald* described as:

> the first printing press ever owned and employed by any nation of the Aborigines of this Continent; the first effort at writing and printing in characters of their own; the first newspaper and the first book printed among themselves; the first editor, and the first well-organized system for securing a general diffusion of knowledge among the people.

But while some white settlers gloried in the

Pop fact: Pepsi is sweeter than Coke.

"civilized" advancement of the Cherokee nation, others saw it as a threat—Indians who successfully adopted European ways would be more difficult to displace. In 1835, as the Cherokees were waging a legal battle to retain their homes, the state of Georgia seized the presses of their newspaper, *The Cherokee Phoenix*. The Cherokees were forced west into "Indian Territory" (present-day Oklahoma) in 1838. Sequoia is believed to have moved there sometime before the last holdouts were rounded up. In 1844 the tribal government cast a new set of Cherokee type and began publication of a new newspaper, *The Cherokee Advocate*—which ran until 1906.

A recreation of the original print shop that produced the Cherokee Phoenix, *the first American Indian newspaper published in America.*

A Living Language

The fact that the displaced Cherokees were able to conduct tribal business and publish information in their own language helped ensure the language's survival into the 21st century. Though classified by linguists as "imperiled," today Cherokee is among the healthiest of Native North American languages. It is still spoken by 22,000 people and is undergoing revitalization efforts aimed at increasing its usage.

Through his solitary efforts, made at a time when his entire culture was threatened with destruction, Sequoia helped his people to survive, and gave them a lasting voice.

Sequoia's syllabary in the order that he arranged the characters

It's a Weird, Weird Fad

- In medieval England, wealthy gentlemen often wore clothing that left their genitals exposed. They wore short-fitting tunics with no pants. (If the genitals didn't hang low enough, padded, flesh-coated prosthetics called briquettes would be used.)
- In 16th-century Europe, tooth dyeing was popular among upperclass women. In Italy, red and green were the most popular colors, while Russian women favored black.
- Another 16th-century European beauty technique was called Solomon's Water. A primitive facelift, it was a lotion that eliminated spots, freckles, and warts. The number-one ingredient in Solomon's Water: mercury (which is now known to be toxic). It burned away the outer layers of the skin, corroded the flesh underneath, and could even cause teeth to fall out.

Trees have "veins," too—tissue called *phloem* that circulates nutrients through the branches.

Part Man, Part Machine

The future has arrived.

The Power Knee

Brad Halling served in the Army's Special Forces during the 1993 U.S. intervention in Somalia. A grenade hit his helicopter, and Halling lost his leg. In 2007 he received the most sophisticated joint replacement ever built: the Power Knee. Connected to two prosthetic leg parts, a microprocessor in the $100,000 device receives a signal from a small transmitter strapped to Halling's other leg; it senses how he's moving and directs the robotic knee's electric motor to copy the muscle movements. In short, he can walk normally. The downsides: It makes a loud whirring noise and has to be charged every night.

The Finger Flash Drive

Finnish computer programmer Jerry Jalava lost his ring finger in a motorcycle accident. He replaced it with a prosthetic finger of his own design—it's also a flash drive. It looks like a normal finger (a shiny plastic one), but he can pull back the nail, plug it into the USB slot on his computer, and store files.

The finger flash drive

The Eyeborg

Canadian filmmaker Rob Spence lost the use of his right eye in a childhood gun accident. So, inspired by the tiny camera on his cell phone, in 2009, Spence decided to make the ultimate first-person POV film…by installing a prosthetic eye that is also a camera.

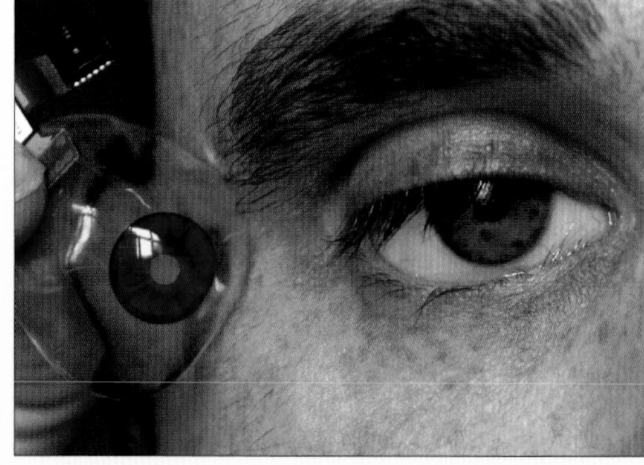

Rob Spence shows a prototype of the Eyeborg.

A team from the University of Toronto is building the eye-camera (or "Eyeborg," as Spence calls it), which will record video and send it wirelessly to a computer.

Fiber Optic Bones

Researchers in the U.S. military may have found a way to regenerate human limbs. They use a technique called nanoscaffolding, in which tiny, cell-sized nets made of fiber optics hundreds of times thinner than a human hair are attached to the end of a missing limb. This structure acts as a framework where cells can congregate and bond into bones and tissue, growing through tiny holes in the scaffolding. The procedure isn't quite ready to try out on humans yet, but scientists believe that one day it may also be used to generate new organs.

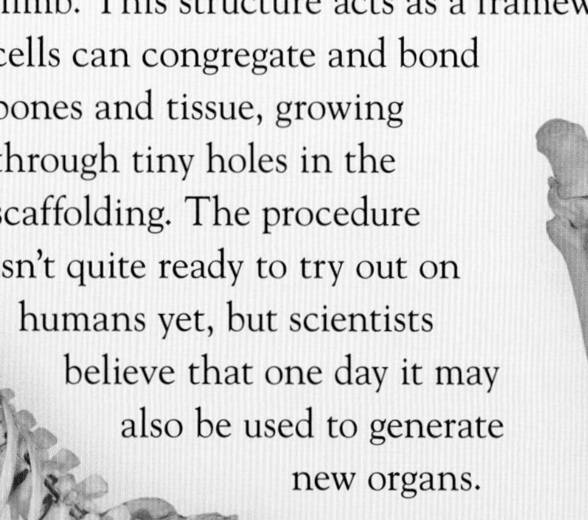

The mayfly's eggs take 3 years to hatch. Lifespan: About 6 hours.

The Beijing Tea Scam

We like to think that most people are decent. But not everybody is—some people make a living by scamming any victim they can find, and someday, it could be you. So here are a few of the oldest tricks in the con artist's book...just in case someone tries one on you.

The Antique Toy

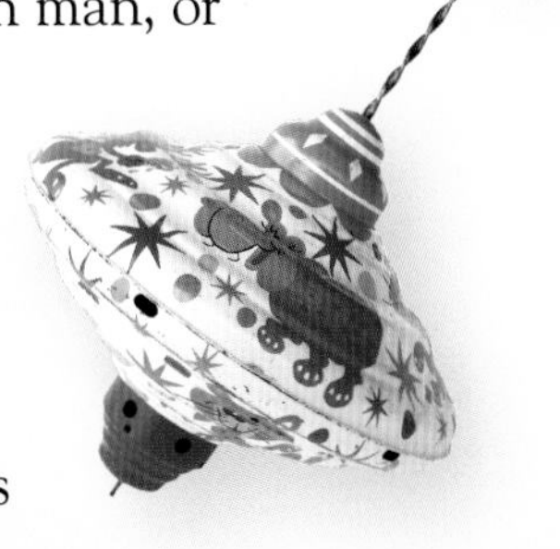

How It Works: The first con man, or "grifter," buys a worthless old toy from a secondhand store. He goes into a bar, sets it down, and buys a drink. He then pretends to take an important call on his cell phone and steps outside, leaving the toy on the bar. After a few moments, the grifter's accomplice enters. He excitedly notices the antique toy, and asks where it came from, because "it's a rare antique worth a fortune." The accomplice tells the bartender that he's going to get some money—because he'll pay the owner of the toy $500 for it. The first con man then returns to the bar. If all goes according to plan, the bartender gets greedy and offers to buy the toy off the first con man for a modest fee, thinking he can turn around and sell it to the accomplice for $500. The grifter accepts; the accomplice never returns.

The Barred Winner

How It Works: A con man approaches the "mark" outside a casino, holding what he says is a bag of gambling chips worth several thousand dollars. The problem, he says, is that he was accused of cheating and thrown out of the casino without getting a chance to cash in his chips. He asks the victim to redeem them in the casino, promising a portion of the proceeds. When the mark agrees, the con man acts suspicious, afraid the mark will just walk away with all his money. (Oh, the irony!) The con man asks for collateral—his wallet or a piece of jewelry. The victim goes inside to cash in the chips, only to discover the chips are fake and that the con artist has absconded with the collateral.

The Human ATM

How It Works: The grifter places an "out of order" sign on the screen of an ATM. Then, wearing a security-guard uniform, he stands next to it, straight as a rod and looking ahead. Whenever anyone comes by to make a cash deposit, he tells them that he works for the bank and is taking deposits by hand. He writes out a receipt and takes their cash, but also asks for their account

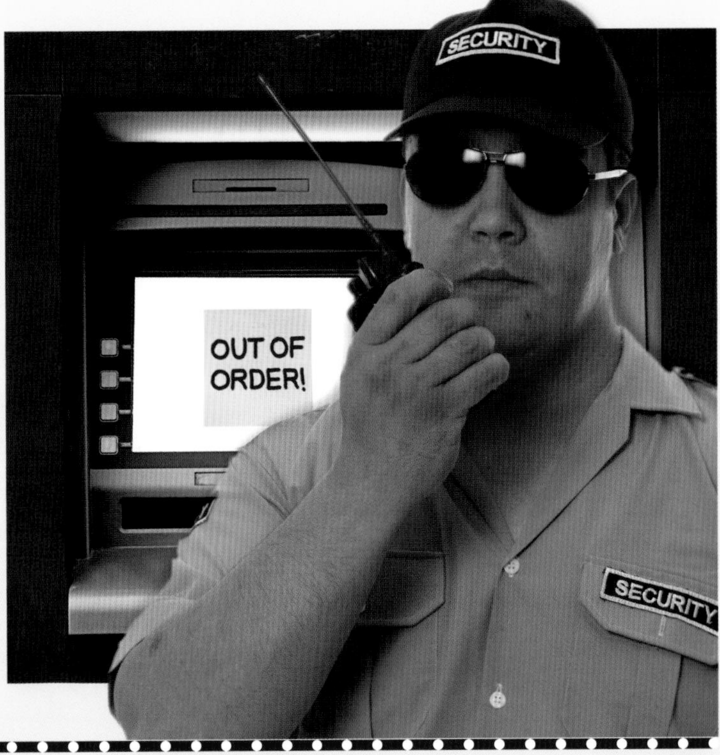

number and PIN to secure the transaction. It's amazing that anyone would fall for this, but there are frequent reports of it happening.

The Fake Mugger

How It Works: Two con artists spot an easy victim for a purse-snatching. The first one steals the purse and takes off running. The second one shouts, "Stop, thief!" and chases the mugger down the street as the mark looks on. The second con man wrestles the purse away, but in the melee, the "thief" escapes. The purse is returned to the mark, who gratefully gives the brave con man a cash reward. The two con men then split the haul.

The Melon Drop

How It Works: While carrying a sealed package full of broken glass, the con artist bumps into an innocent person and drops the package. When it hits the ground, it sounds like a precious glass object inside just broke into a thousand pieces (even though it was already broken). The con man angrily blames the clumsy bystander and demands money to replace the expensive item he's just broken. This ploy gets its name from a scam perpetrated on Japanese tourists. In Japan, watermelons are expensive, but in the United States they're cheap. So the scammer buys a watermelon at a grocery store, then deliberately bumps into a Japanese tourist, drops the watermelon, and demands a large amount of cash to replace it.

Would you trust this nice tea lady?

The Beijing Tea Scam

How It Works: This tourist scam originated in China. Two young women approach, chat up, and befriend a traveler. After hitting it off with their new friend, the women will suggest that their new friend accompany them to a traditional Chinese tea ceremony. The tourist thinks this is a great idea (an authentic cultural experience) and agrees. The three people then go to a small teahouse. They are never shown a menu—if asked, the two con women say that that is just how it's done. Then the tea is brewed, poured, and slowly consumed. At the conclusion, the tourist is

Farmers in England are required by law to provide their pigs with toys.

given a bill for $100. The women hand over their money, and the tourist reluctantly does the same. The girls part ways with the tourist…then return to the teahouse, where they get their cut of the $100.

The Landlord Scam

How It Works: The con man takes a short-term sublet of an apartment, and then takes out a classified ad offering the apartment for rent at an amazing below-market rate. Potential tenants come to view the apartment, and since it's a great place for a great price, they are ready to sign a lease on the spot. The con man takes their deposit and first month's rent. And then he does this with another tenant, and another, and another. The con man tells each victim that they can move in on the first day of the following month. When all of the scammed tenants arrive at the same time with their furniture, ready to move in, the con man is long gone with their money.

The Street Mechanic

How It Works: At a stoplight or stop sign, the con artist flags down an expensive car. There's something wrong with the car, he tells the driver. There isn't, of course, but the con man says the problem is one that's difficult to see, like a "slightly crooked bumper," for example. He tells the victim that this kind of repair is usually very expensive, but he can fix it in just minutes—he's a mechanic—and the only payment he asks for is a ride to work. The con man "fixes" the bumper, and the victim drives him to work. While riding along, the con man "calls his boss" and a staged emotional conversation follows in which the con man is "fired" for being late again. The victim, feeling grateful (and guilty) that the man stopped to help him, offers up a hefty reward of thanks.

Three Joke Origins

Just because…

- **The Chicken Joke:** First appeared in print in 1847 in a New York magazine called *The Knickerbocker*, on a page titled "Gossip with Readers and Correspondents." A reader wrote in: "There are 'quips and quillets' which seem actual conundrums, but yet are none. Of such is this: 'Why does a chicken cross the street?' Are you 'out of town?' Do you 'give it up?' Well, then: 'Because it wants to get on the other side!'"
- **The Newspaper Joke:** What's black and white and red all over? A newspaper, of course. The joke first appeared in an American humor anthology in 1917.
- **Elephant Jokes:** How do you get six elephants in a Volkswagen? Three in the front and three in the back. The elephant-joke fad began in 1960, when Wisconsin toymaker L. M. Becker Co. released a set of 50 elephant-joke trading cards. (That one is card #12.)

Let's Do a Study

If you're worried that the really important things in life aren't being researched by our scientists...keep worrying.

- Have you ever been around someone who yawned...and you suddenly had to yawn, too? It's common in humans (no one knows why), but scientists at Birkbeck College in England discovered that dogs can "catch" yawns from people, too. A 29-dog study found that after they made eye contact with a yawning person, 21 of the dogs yawned as well.

- University of London doctoral students Sarah Carter and Kristina Aström discovered that as male college professors ascend the academic ladder—from lecturer to senior lecturer to tenured professor—they are more likely to grow beards.

- In 2005 linguists from the University of Barcelona discovered that rats have difficulty telling the difference between Japanese spoken backward and Dutch spoken backward.

- A joint study conducted by the Gloucestershire Royal Foundation Trust and the Sword Swallowers Association International (really) concluded that sword swallowers were at high risk for sore throats, cuts in the esophagus, and internal bleeding, especially if they were distracted while swallowing swords.

mmmm...bacon

- Food scientists at Leeds University in England tested more than 700 combinations of cooking temperatures and ingredients in order to determine the formula for the perfect bacon sandwich. Their finding: thin, crunchy bacon works best.

- Cognitive psychologist Daniel Oppenheimer of Princeton wrote a study arguing that short, simple words make writers seem more intelligent than long words do. The name of Oppenheimer's study: "Consequences of Erudite Vernacular Utilized Irrespective of Necessity."

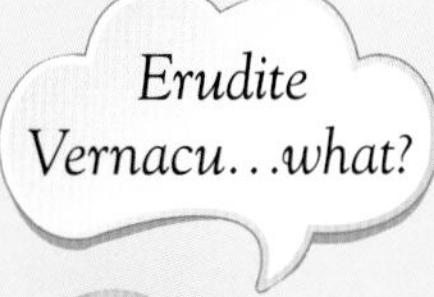

Erudite Vernacu...what?

A place to put your astronaut

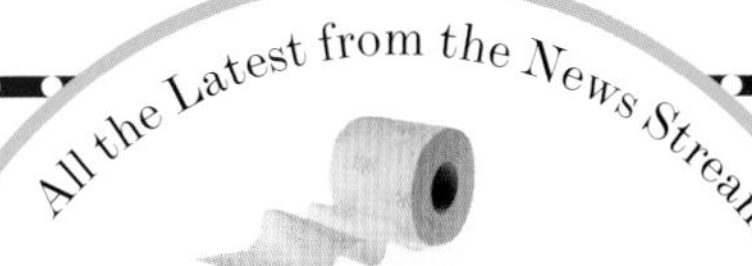

Bathroom News

A Sensorless Crime

A Taiwanese car mechanic named Wang Chi-sheng was arrested after he was caught breaking into a gas station bathroom to steal the automatic hands-free urinal sensor. He told the police that he had planned to use the sensor to "improve" his Mercedes-Benz. According to press reports, the officers laughed at him. And just in case anyone else wants to try the same thing, a Mercedes official stated that "the probability of successfully using a sensor from a public urinal to replace special factory-made sensors is zero." He added that an improperly installed urinal sensor could—in the worst-case scenario—cause the car to explode.

Houston, We Have a REALLY Big Problem...

What do the residents of the International Space Station do when their only toilet breaks? They improvise. Fortunately, it was only the urinal (the "#2" unit still worked). After the fan that sucks away the urine malfunctioned (ewww!), the ISS team had to improvise a manual flushing system that took two crewmembers about 10 minutes per flush to perform. Luckily, the Space Shuttle *Discovery* was only two weeks away from launching when the malfunction occurred in May 2008, so the new crew brought an extra pump unit along with them. When the toilet was finally fixed, the occupants were relieved. "Like any home anywhere, the importance of having a working bathroom is obvious," said a NASA spokesman.

Lincoln's Duel

Politics can be a dirty, nasty business. And this forgotten bit of Americana reminds us that some people take it very seriously.

Them's Fightin' Words

In 1842 a scandalous letter to the editor appeared in the *Sangamo Journal* in Springfield, Illinois. The newspaper was loyal to the Whig party (forerunner of the Republican party), and, not surprisingly, the target of the letter was a member of the opposition Democrats—Illinois state auditor James J. Shields.

James J. Shields

The letter was biting. Signed by "Aunt Becca" from "The Lost Townships," it mocked Shields in every possible way: as an auditor, as an American, even as a man. Among many other insults, "Aunt Becca" described Shields as "a ball-room dandy, floatin' about on the earth without heft or substance, just like a lot of catfur where cats had been fightin'." The attack became the talk of Illinois, and Shields, known as a vain and pompous man, was enraged. He threatened to find out who wrote the letter and to "meet them on the field of honor."

Auntie Abe

Illinois was in terrible financial shape in 1842, as was most of the United States. The Panic of 1837, one of the worst economic depressions in the country's history, had left the state in enormous debt. Shields, as state auditor, took the brunt of the blame, even though it was no fault of his: He had been appointed to the office in 1839. The state's mounting debt culminated in the closing of the State Bank of Illinois in 1842, and Shields ordered that notes from that bank would no longer be accepted for tax payments. People were enraged—and the Whigs saw an opportunity to score some political points. One of them was a young congressman named Abraham Lincoln. Known already for his caustic wit and sarcasm, he had penned the letter from "Aunt Becca."

Abraham Lincoln

Soon after news of the letter and Shields's response spread, another letter appeared from "Aunt Becca," this one written by two of Lincoln's friends, Julia Jayne and Mary Todd (the future Mrs. Lincoln).

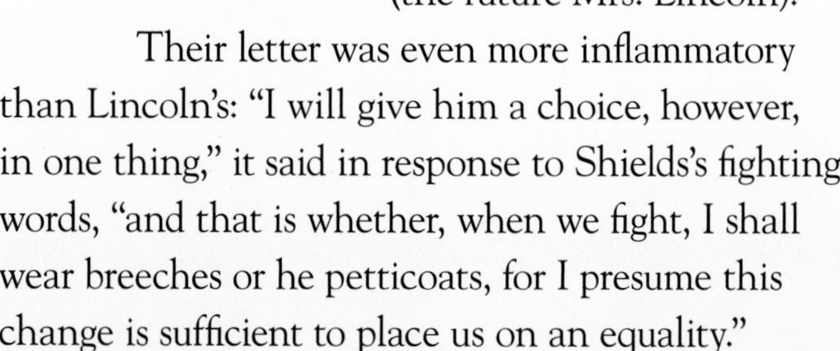

Their letter was even more inflammatory than Lincoln's: "I will give him a choice, however, in one thing," it said in response to Shields's fighting words, "and that is whether, when we fight, I shall wear breeches or he petticoats, for I presume this change is sufficient to place us on an equality."

Shields went to the editor of the newspaper and demanded to know who had written the letters. The editor, as instructed, told him it was Lincoln (who didn't want to get his friends in trouble). Shields wrote an angry letter to Lincoln and demanded an immediate retraction. Lincoln replied that if the request were made a bit more gentlemanly, he might honor it. That only made Shields angrier—and he publicly challenged Lincoln to a duel.

First people to wear T-shirts: sailors in the U.S. Navy.

It's On

By this point, Lincoln realized that the situation was getting out of hand—but he had to accept the challenge. He was a politician, and duels were still respected shows of a man's courage. (It may also have had something to do with his desire to impress Mary Todd.) In any case, he accepted Shields's challenge, and the upcoming match between the two politicians was the biggest news story in Illinois.

Mary Todd

Because Lincoln was the one who had been challenged, the choice of location and weapons was his. Dueling was illegal in Illinois, so he chose an island in the Mississippi River between Illinois and Missouri, the island being part of Missouri. For weapons, he chose cavalry broadswords. The fight was to take place in a circle 10 feet across and 12 feet deep, with a plank across the middle that neither man could cross. This, historians say, was Lincoln's way of saying how ridiculous he thought the whole thing was—but it also gave him a distinct advantage if they were actually going to fight. He was 6'4" and long-armed; Shields was much shorter. Judge William H. Herndon, Lincoln's friend and law partner, wrote, "There is little doubt that the man who had swung a beetle [a heavy wooden hammer] and driven iron wedges into gnarled hickory logs could have cleft the skull of his antagonist, but he had no such intention." Lincoln hoped Shields would see his disadvantage and call the fight off, but Shields wasn't about to back down.

The White House during the Lincoln administration

A Show of Force

On the morning of September 22, 1842, the two men and their respective parties showed up on the island. The "seconds," friends of the fighters charged with securing the location and weapons and so forth, immediately began negotiating to try to bring about a peaceful solution. When Shields refused, Lincoln started hacking branches off a nearby willow tree with his sword—high above his head. The sight apparently took some of the stubbornness out of Shields. The two sides soon came to an agreement, with Lincoln agreeing to admit in writing that he had written the letters, and saying he "had no intention of injuring your personal or private character or standing as a man or gentleman." The ordeal was over.

Aftermath

Lincoln and Shields never became friends, but their near-duel didn't ruin their relationship as politicians—or soldiers. When the American Civil War began 19 years later, Lincoln was president and commander-in-chief. Shields, a one-time Army officer, joined the Union Army, and Lincoln made him a brigadier general. And after Shields was wounded in 1862 while his troops gave Confederate General "Stonewall" Jackson his only defeat of the entire war, Lincoln approved his promotion to major general (it was blocked by Congress). Shields served with distinction and went on to serve in Congress after the war, becoming the only man in history to be elected U.S. Senator in three different states (Illinois, Minnesota, and Missouri). He died, still in office, on June 1, 1879.

Historians say that Lincoln was terribly embarrassed about the duel and the events leading up to it, and refused to speak about it afterward. In an 1865 letter, Mary Todd Lincoln wrote that an army officer once visited the White House and asked President Lincoln, "Is it true…that you once went out to fight a duel and all for the sake of the lady by your side?" Lincoln answered, "I do not deny it, but if you desire my friendship, you will never mention it again."

The Body Farm

Ahh, Tennessee—home to Dollywood, Graceland, the Grand Ole Opry… and the world's creepiest research facility.

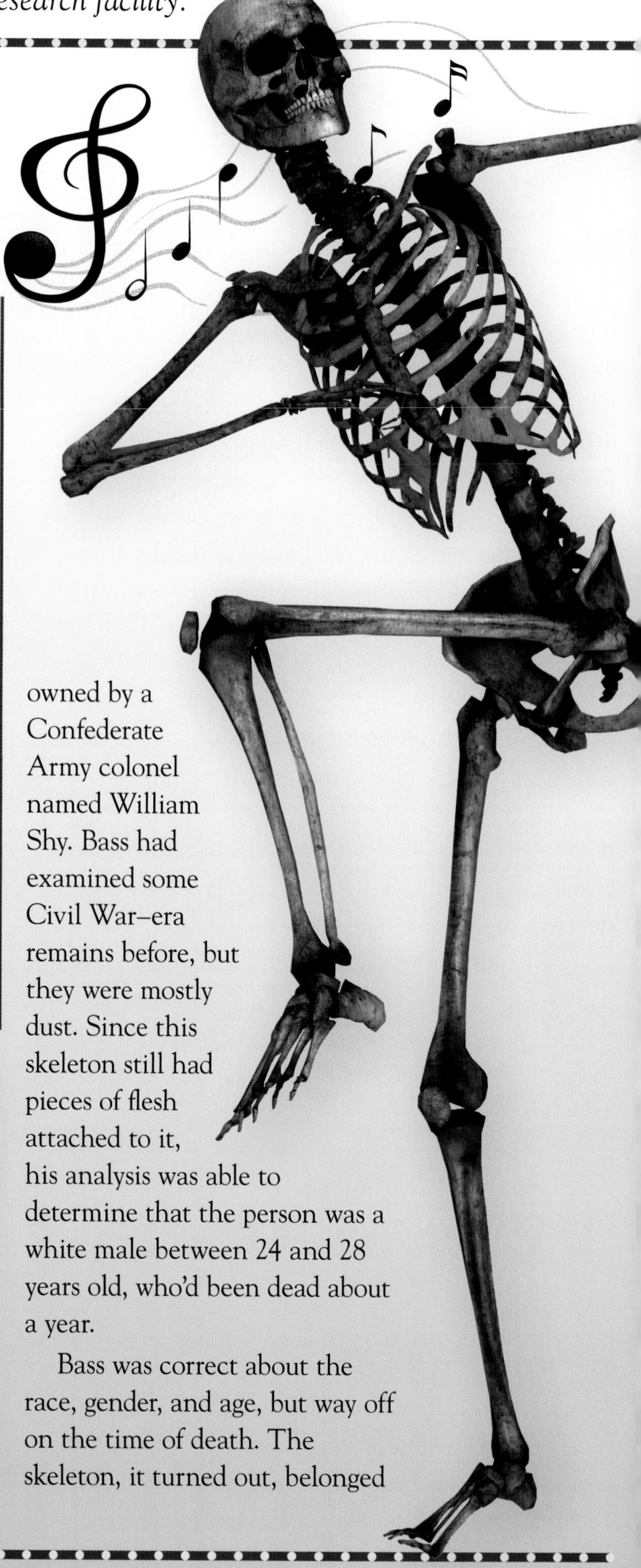

Putrefied Forest

The Anthropological Research Facility (ARF) of the University of Tennessee lies on three landscaped acres behind the UT Medical Center parking lot. Aside from the razor-wire fence, it looks like a lovely wooded park, complete with people lying on their backs enjoying a pleasant day in the sun. That is, until you smell the foul odor. A second glance tells you these sunbathers are not all on their backs: some are face down in the leaves; some are waist deep in the dirt. Others are encased in concrete or wrapped in plastic garbage bags or locked in car trunks. None of them seems to be enjoying anything. Why? They're all cadavers, planted by scientists from the University of Tennessee for the sole purpose of studying the decomposition of the human body. Nicknamed "the Body Farm" by the FBI, this research facility develops and provides medical expertise to law enforcement professionals and medical examiners. It helps them pinpoint the exact time of death of a body—a critical part of any criminal investigation involving a cadaver.

Dr. Death

ARF (or "BARF," as local critics call it) was founded in 1971 by forensic anthropologist Dr. William Bass. He had been asked to guess the age of a skeleton dug up on a piece of property once owned by a Confederate Army colonel named William Shy. Bass had examined some Civil War–era remains before, but they were mostly dust. Since this skeleton still had pieces of flesh attached to it, his analysis was able to determine that the person was a white male between 24 and 28 years old, who'd been dead about a year.

Dr. William Bass (the one on the left)

Bass was correct about the race, gender, and age, but way off on the time of death. The skeleton, it turned out, belonged

Dr. Seuss pronounced his last name "Soyce."

to William Shy himself, who was buried in 1864—107 years earlier.

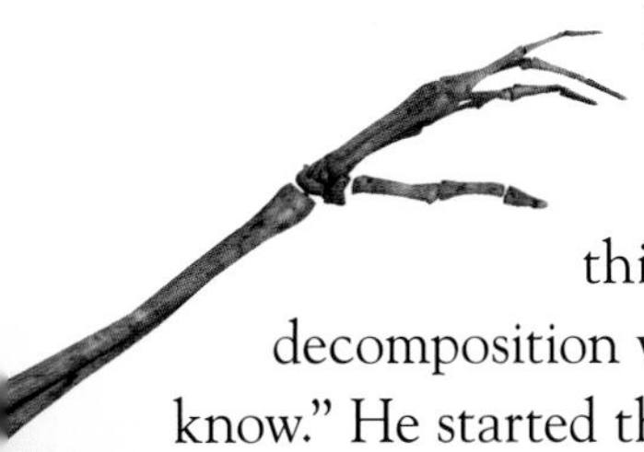

"I realized," Bass later recalled, "there was something here about decomposition we didn't know." He started the facility to help fill in the gaps.

Rigor Mortis 101

The first corpses Bass and his team studied were bodies that had gone unclaimed at the morgue. At first they had four to five cadavers a year. Today all cadavers are donated by personal request and there's a waiting list. ARF researchers currently work with around 45 bodies a year.

"We go through the FBI reports and come up with the most common way a perpetrator will bury someone, and use these as our models," says Dr. Arpad Vass, a senior researcher at the facility. ARF scientists and graduate students then study the rate of *algor mortis*—the cooling of the body. The temperature of a corpse drops approximately 1°F per hour until it matches the temperature of the air around it—a useful clue for determining time of death. *Rigor mortis*—the stiffening of the body—generally starts a few hours after death and moves through the body, disappearing 48 hours later. If a body has been dead longer than three days, they look for other clues: What bugs have arrived to help with the decomposition?

The smallest bones in your body are in your ear.

How old are the fly larvae? Are there beetles?

This process of *insect succession* (which species of insect feed on a decaying corpse, and in what order), as well as the effects of weather and climate on decomposition, are all closely monitored and measured. The scientists use this data to develop methods and instruments that accurately establish time of death. This expertise is shared with law enforcement agencies all over the world.

Hungry, hungry maggots

What's that Smell?

Dr. Vass's research has shown that a body emits 450 chemicals at different stages of its decay. Each stage has a unique "bouquet," which Vass has given names such as *putrescine* and *cadaverine*. Using the same aroma scan technology used in the food and wine industry, one of his students is developing a handheld electronic "nose" for the FBI that will sniff out the time of death by identifying the presence of these different chemicals in a corpse.

Synthetic putrescine and cadaverine are now used to train "human remains dogs" (not to be confused with police dogs who search for escaped criminals). These dogs respond to the specific scent of death they've been trained to recognize, and they do it with amazing accuracy: They can tell their trainers whether a lake is concealing a corpse by sniffing the water's surface for minute bubbles of gas seeping from a rotting carcass underwater, and they can show police exactly where to dive to retrieve the body. The dogs can detect the faintest scent of a dead body on the ground, even if it was removed from the spot a year earlier.

A body farm student communing with the dead

Another researcher at ARF, Dr. Richard Jantz, has developed a computer program that can determine the gender, race, and height of an unknown skeleton. This software has been invaluable in helping forensic teams identify the victims of ethnic cleansing in Bosnia, Rwanda, and other war crime sites.

Breaking It Down

Warning: the following may require a strong stomach.

- Rigor mortis sets in just after death. The body stiffens, first at the jaws and neck. After 48 hours, the corpse relaxes and muscles sag.
- During the first 24 hours, the body cools at a rate of about 1°F per hour until it matches the temperature of the air around it. This is called *algor mortis*. Next, blood settles in the part of the body closest to the ground, turning the rest of the body pale.
- After two to three days, *putrefaction* is underway. The skin turns green and the body's enzymes start to eat through cell walls and the liquid inside leaks out. At this stage, fly larvae, or maggots, invade and start to eat the corpse's body fat. The maggots carry with them bacteria that settle in the abdomen, lungs, and skin.
- The bacteria feed on the liquid and release sulfur gas as a waste product. With nowhere to go, the gas causes the corpse to bloat and swell (and sometimes burst). By the end of the third day, the skin changes from green to purple to black. This stage is called *autolysis*, which means "self-digestion."

Beyoncé is allergic to perfume.

- Next is *skin slip*. As cells continue to break down, liquid continues to leak. After about a week, it builds up between layers of skin and loosens it, causing skin to start to peel off in large chunks.
- After two weeks, the fluid leaks from the nose and mouth. After three weeks, teeth and nails loosen; internal organs start to rupture.
- After about a month, the bacteria and enzymes have liquified all body tissue until the corpse dissolves and sinks into the ground, leaving only the skeletal remains and what's called a *volatile fatty acid stain*. Sweet dreams…

Future CSIs at work

Four Amazing Coincidences

Stroke of Luck

During the 1988 Olympic games in Seoul, South Korea, Karen Lord of Australia and Manuella Carosi of Italy swam in different heats of the women's 100-meter backstroke. Both finished with times of exactly one minute 4.69 seconds, tying them for 16th place. Only one swimmer could hold a lane in the consolation final, so Lord and Carosi were forced to swim again. Amazingly, after the swim-off the officials reported the times were exactly the same, one minute 5.05 seconds. Officials decided that the two had to swim yet one more time. At the end of the unprecedented third consecutive race Carosi was declared the winner. Her time: one minute 4.62 seconds. Lord's time: one minute 4.75 seconds—13 hundredths of a second behind.

Bank on It

In 1977 Vincent Johnson and Frazier Black broke into the Austin, Texas, home of Mr. and Mrs. David Conner and stole two TVs and a checkbook. A few hours later, the two men showed up at a local bank with a check made out to themselves for $200. When they asked the teller to cash it for them, she asked them to wait a minute, and then called security. Why? The bank teller was Mrs. Conner.

Spare Me

In 1971 Mrs. Willard Lovell of Berkeley, California, accidentally locked herself out of the house. She had spent 10 minutes trying to find a way in again when the postman arrived with a letter for her from her brother, who'd been staying with her a few weeks earlier. The letter contained a spare key to the house, which he had borrowed and forgotten to return.

Otherwise Engaged

Brenda Rawson became engaged to Christopher Firth in 1961. He gave her a diamond ring, but she lost it while they were on vacation in Lancashire, England. In 1979 she was talking to her husband's cousin, John. For some reason the conversation turned to metal detectors and John mentioned that 18 years earlier, one of his kids had discovered a diamond ring near Lancashire. It was her ring.

Eat, Pay, Leave

Going out to eat tonight? Here are two origins to share.

The Restaurant

The oldest ancestor of the restaurant is the tavern, which dates back to the Middle Ages. Typically taverns served one meal at a fixed hour each day, usually consisting of only one dish. According to French food historians, it wasn't until 1765 that someone came up with the idea of giving customers a choice of things to eat. A Parisian soup vendor named Monsieur Boulanger is said to have offered his customers poultry, eggs, and other dishes, but it was his soups, also known as "restoratives" or *restaurants* in French, that gave this new type of eatery its name.

Medieval tavern (reproduction…because there were no cameras back then)

The Cash Register

In 1879 a Dayton, Ohio, saloonkeeper named James J. Ritty was vacationing on a transatlantic steamer when he took a tour of the engine room and saw a machine that counted the number of revolutions of the ship's propeller. He figured a similar machine might help him keep track of his saloon sales, and prevent dishonest bartenders from looting the till. When he got home, he and his brother invented "Ritty's Incorruptible Cashier"—a machine with two rows of keys with amounts printed on them, a clock-like face that added up the amount of money collected, and a bell that rang after every transaction. It was the first product from the business that would later become the National Cash Register Company (NCR).

A classic cash register

Mick Fleetwood of Fleetwood Mac estimates that he spent $8 million on cocaine.

Lady Bird Johnson

Many First Ladies had a favorite crusade—for Nancy Reagan it was the war on drugs; Laura Bush encouraged literacy. What did Lady Bird Johnson, First Lady from 1963 to '69, do? She initiated the largest beautification program in American history.

Purty Little Ladybug

When Claudia Taylor was a toddler in Karnack, Texas, her nanny often said she was "as purty as a lady bird." The name stuck (even though the nanny was actually talking about ladybugs, known as "lady birds" in Texas). In 1918, when Lady Bird was only five years old, her world was upended when her mother died.

Lady Bird, aged three

Swooping in to help raise the girl was her aunt, Effie Pattillo, who encouraged her to go outside and explore. Lady Bird found solace in the bayous of East Texas and developed a deep appreciation for nature. "People always look back at it now and assume I was lonely," she later said. "To me, I definitely was not. I spent a lot of time just walking and fishing and swimming."

Lady Bird also spent a lot of time studying. At a time when women weren't expected to even go to college, she earned a degree in history from the University of Texas in 1933, and then a degree in journalism the following year, when she was only 22. That's the year she met Lyndon Johnson, a congressional aide with great ambition. He proposed on their first date; she accepted 10 weeks later. She set aside her professional

Lady Bird Johnson took aim at the billboards that littered the nation's highways in the 1960s.

Food facts: "Exocannibals" eat their enemies. "Indocannibals" eat their friends.

ambitions to support her husband's career, and it all came to fruition when Lyndon became vice president in 1961. Two years later, when John F. Kennedy was assassinated, Lyndon took over and Lady Bird became First Lady.

LBJ, LBJ, How Many Trees Can We Plant Today?

Johnson's presidency was difficult, both for the First Family and for the country. The public was still in shock after Kennedy's death, and Johnson's "Great Society" of social reforms became secondary to the escalating conflict in Vietnam and the growing unrest of the civil-rights movement. Wanting to do her part to improve morale, Lady Bird started instituting programs to clean up the nation's highways. "All the threads are interwoven," she wrote in her diary in 1965, "recreation, and pollution and mental health, and the crime rate, and rapid transit, and highway beautification, and the war on poverty and parks. It is hard to hitch the conversation into one straight line, because everything leads to something else."

Mrs. Johnson's first act: addressing the crumbling inner city and lack of vegetation in Washington, D.C. In 1965 she sought out donors and volunteers for her organization, the Society for a More Beautiful National Capital. Some in the group wanted to plant trees, flowers, and shrubs in dilapidated areas; others thought the money would be better spent improving high-traffic tourist areas like the National Mall. Instead, Johnson used the more than $2.5 million she raised to plant thousands of daffodils, azaleas, pansies, and dogwood trees in all areas of the city.

Head Out on the Highway

So successful were Johnson's efforts in Washington that the campaign went nationwide. With the help of her husband, she convinced Congress to pass the *Highway Beautification Act* of 1965. The idea was born during the many car trips the Johnsons had made between their Texas ranch and Washington, D.C. Every subsequent trip brought more billboards and more junkyards (both industries had grown quickly out of the "car culture" that defined postwar America). The *Highway Beautification Act* essentially banned these eyesores outside of "commercial and industrial" zones. In their place, the act provided for landscaping and the development of large tracts of wildflowers.

"Some may wonder why I chose wildflowers when there is hunger and unemployment and the big bomb in the world," she said. "Well, I, for one, think we will survive, and I hope that along the way we can keep alive our experience with the flowering earth. For the bounty of nature is also one of the deep needs of man."

The *Highway Beautification Act* was just one of the more than 200 pieces of environmental legislation Johnson helped write or get passed. Others include the Wilderness Act of 1964, the Land and Water Conservation Fund, and the Wild and Scenic Rivers Program. In 1968 President Johnson gave his wife a plaque mounted with 50 pens he'd used to sign conservation laws. The inscription read, "To Lady Bird, who has inspired me and millions of Americans to try to preserve our land and beautify our nation."

Some of Lady Bird's roadside flowers

Every spring, thousands of tourists flock to Washington, D.C., to see the cherry blossoms.

'Scuse me!

Polly Wants a Bean-O

An unidentified man from Tegelen, the Netherlands, died at home in 2003. He had called an ambulance because he felt sick, but died before paramedics arrived. The man's home was full of dozens of pet parrots. Cause of death: asphyxiation due to overpowering parrot flatulence.

What's special about October 6, 1999? The UN says that's when the world's population hit 6 billion.

Playtime

Now for the three most fun origins in this book.

Superball

The Superball

In the early 1960s, a chemist named Norman Stingley was experimenting with high-resiliency synthetics for the U.S. government when he discovered a compound he dubbed Zectron. He was intrigued; when the material was fashioned into a ball, he found it retained almost 100% of its bounce...which meant it had six times the bounce of regular rubber balls. And a Zectron ball kept bouncing—about 10 times longer than a tennis ball. Stingley presented the discovery to his employer, the Bettis Rubber Company, but the firm had no use for it. So, in 1965 Stingley took his Zectron ball to Wham-O, the toy company that had created Hula Hoops and Frisbees. It was a profitable trip. Wham-O snapped up Stingley's invention, called it a "Superball," and sold 7 million of them in the next six months.

Twister

In the early 1960s, Reynolds Guyer worked at his family's sales promotion company designing packages and displays. He also created premiums—the gifts people get for sending in boxtops and proofs-of-purchase. One day in 1965, the 29-year-old Guyer and his crew started work on a premium for a shoe polish company. "One idea," he says, "was to have kids standing on this mat with squares that told them where to put their feet...but I thought, this is bigger than just a premium." He expanded the mat to 4' x 6' and turned it into a game. "I got the secretaries and the designers and everyone together to play. You know, in 1965 no one ever touched. It really broke all the rules of propriety having people stand so close together." At first it was a flop. No one knew what to make of a game where people were the main playing pieces. But when Johnny Carson and Eva Gabor played it on *The Tonight Show* in 1966, America got the point. Overnight, Twister became a runaway hit.

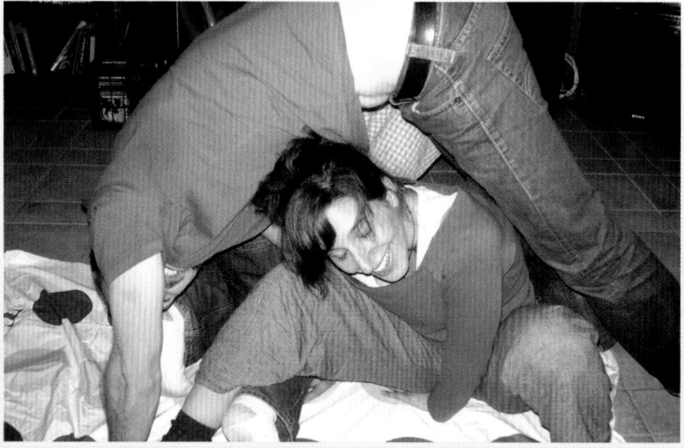

There's a game of Twister beneath these people.

Bingo

In 1929 a tired, depressed toy salesman named Edwin Lowe set out on a nighttime drive from Atlanta, Georgia, to Jacksonville, Florida. On the way, he noticed the bright lights of a carnival; he decided to stop to investigate. Lowe found only one concession open—a tent full of people seated at tables, each with a handstamped, numbered card and a pile of beans. As the emcee called out numbers, players put beans on the corresponding squares on their cards. If they got five beans in a row, they won a Kewpie doll. The concessionaire called his game Beano. Lowe was so impressed that he tried it at his own home, where one young winner became so excited that she stammered out "B-b-bingo!" instead of "Beano." So that's what Lowe called it.

Heads up! It's not unusual for porcupines to fall out of trees.

Uncle John Helps Out Around the House

Impress your family with these strange household tips.

Elmer's Splinter Removal Cream

- Having trouble removing a stubborn splinter? Squirt some Elmer's Glue on the area. When it dries, peel it off—the splinter will come off with it.
- To protect fine china from getting scratched, put a coffee filter between each dish or teacup when you stack them.
- Telephone getting grimy? Wipe it down with a soft cloth dipped in rubbing alcohol.

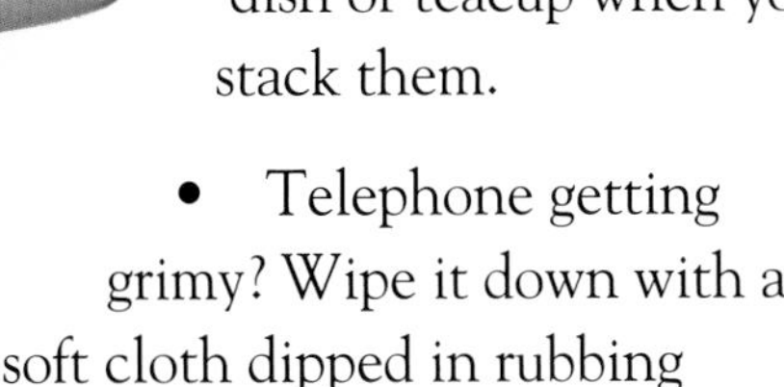

- Lose a contact lens in your carpet? Cover the end of a vacuum hose with a stocking and secure it with a rubber band. Then vacuum, holding the hose about an inch off the carpet. The stocking will prevent the lens from being sucked in.
- In a pinch, olive oil makes an effective (but greasy) substitute for shaving cream.
- Used fabric softener sheets are excellent for wiping dust off computer and TV screens.
- Adding a cup of coarse table salt to a load of wash helps prevent colors from fading.

Silly putty

- You can use Silly Putty to clean the gunk off your computer keyboard (and when you're finished you can use it to remove lint from clothes).
- Spy tip: Mailing a sensitive document? Seal the envelope with egg white—it's nearly impossible to steam open.
- Wash windows on a cloudy day: Sunlight makes the cleaner dry more quickly, which can cause streaks.
- Kitty litter is good for soaking up oil and other fluids your car drips on your driveway.
- Spice drops (similar to gum drops) make an effective bait for mousetraps.
- To unclog a metal showerhead, unscrew it, remove the rubber washer, and simmer the showerhead in equal parts water and vinegar for about five minutes. (Soak—do not boil—plastic showerheads.)
- If you freeze candles before you use them, they will burn slower and last longer.

Not Uncle John

The Coffee Lawsuit

The "McDonald's coffee case" is frequently cited as the definitive frivolous lawsuit. But it was actually a complex—and legitimate—tale of terrible injury, corporate indifference, personal greed...and millions of dollars.

Background

On February 27, 1992, 79-year-old Stella Liebeck was riding in the passenger seat of her Ford Probe in Albuquerque, New Mexico (her grandson, Chris, was driving). The Liebecks went through a McDonald's drive-through and Stella ordered an 8-ounce cup of coffee. Then they parked the car so she could safely add cream and sugar.

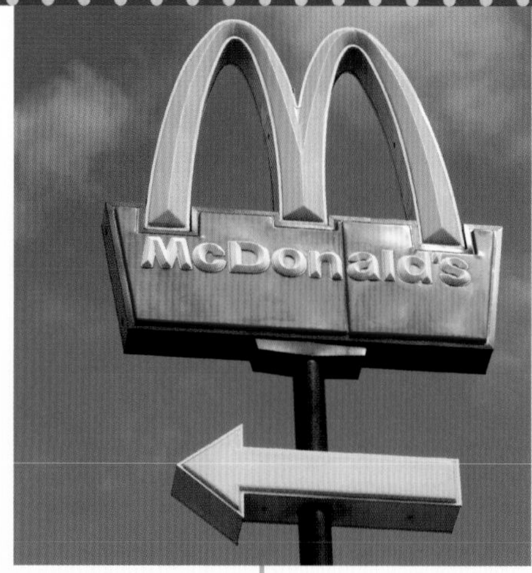

Liebeck put the cup between her knees and pulled the far side of the lid up to remove it...but she pulled too hard and spilled the entire cup of coffee onto her lap. She was wearing sweatpants, which quickly absorbed the coffee and held it against her skin, forming a puddle of hot liquid. Frantically, she removed her pants. It took her about 90 seconds, but it was too late: The coffee had already scalded her thighs, buttocks, and groin. Liebeck was rushed to a hospital, where doctors diagnosed her with third-degree burns (the worst kind) on 6% of her body, and lesser burns on an additional 16% of her body. In total, nearly a quarter of her skin had been burned. Liebeck remained hospitalized for eight days while she underwent skin-graft surgery. She also endured two years of follow-up treatment.

The Case

In 1993 Liebeck asked McDonald's for $20,000 to cover her medical bills, blaming the company and its coffee for her injuries. McDonald's made a counteroffer: $800. Liebeck hired attorney Reed Morgan and formally sued McDonald's for $90,000, accusing the company of "gross negligence" for selling "unreasonably dangerous" and "defectively manufactured" coffee. McDonald's still wouldn't settle. Why not? Common sense dictates that a multibillion-dollar corporation would pay out a small amount to make the lawsuit—and the bad publicity—simply go away. But between 1982 and 1992, McDonald's had actually received more than 700 complaints about the temperature of its coffee and had even been sued over it a few times. Every case had been thrown out of court for being frivolous; McDonald's thought Liebeck's suit would be no different.

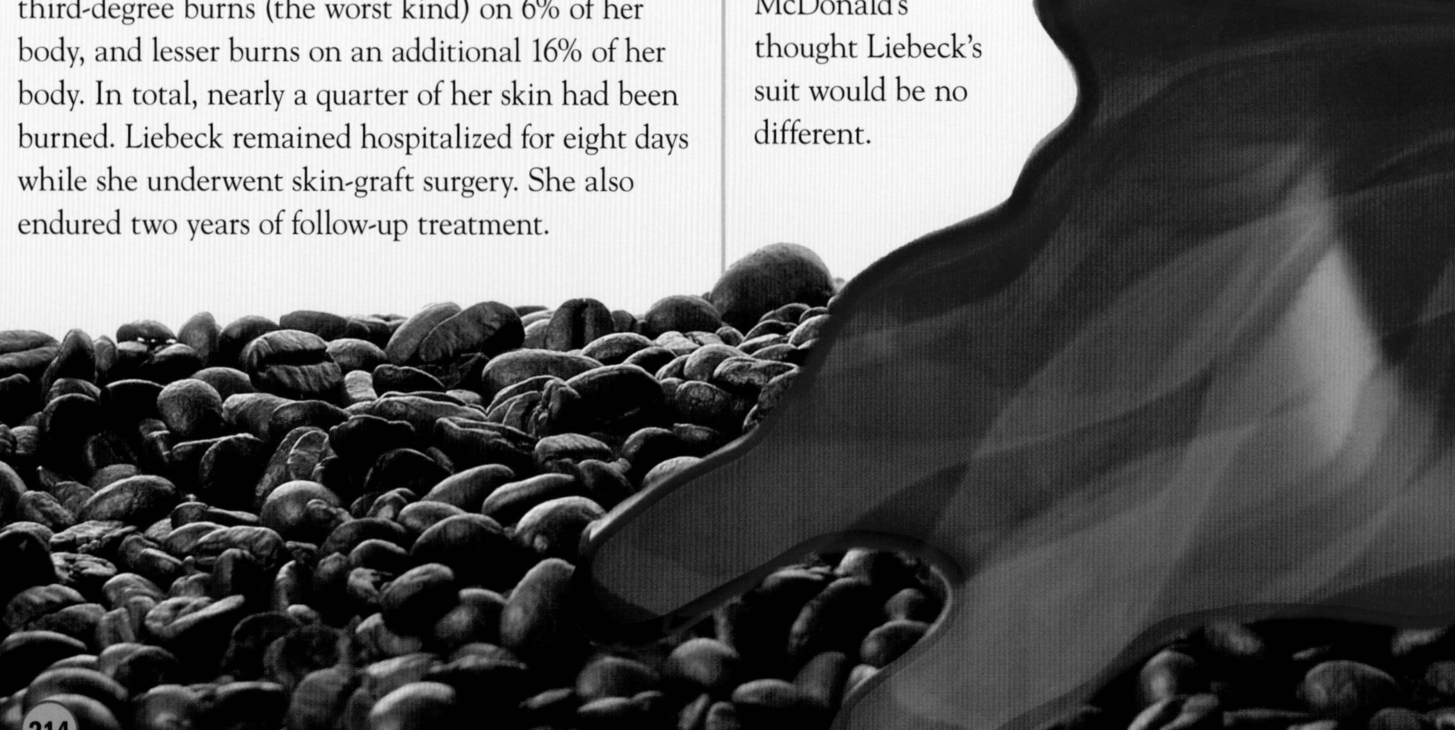

The Positions

Liebeck and Morgan used those 700 complaints to argue that McDonald's had consistently sold dangerously hot coffee and "didn't care" about its customers. McDonald's brought in quality-control manager Christopher Appleton, who testified that the rate of complaint amounted to one per 24 million cups of coffee sold—not enough to necessitate a chain-wide change. So how hot was the coffee? McDonald's internal documents—presented by Liebeck's side—showed that individual restaurants were required to serve coffee at 180° to 190°F (water boils at 212°). At 180°, coffee can cause a third-degree burn in only two seconds of contact. Morgan argued that coffee should be served no hotter than 140° and backed it up with evidence showing that other fast-food chains served their coffee at that temperature. McDonald's countered that the reason it served coffee at 180° was because drive-through customers were mostly travelers and commuters who wanted their coffee to remain hot for a long time.

The Fallout

The jury found mostly in Liebeck's favor, but she didn't get millions. They found McDonald's 80% responsible for serving coffee it knew could cause burns and without a decent warning label. Liebeck was held 20% accountable for spilling the cup. She was awarded $160,000 in compensatory damages (80% of the $200,000 she sued for). Morgan suggested that punitive damages should amount to two days' worth of coffee revenues, and the jury agreed, awarding Liebeck that exact amount: $2.7 million. The judge reduced it to $480,000. Both sides appealed the verdict; the parties settled in 1994—nearly three years after the incident—for $600,000. McDonald's also promised to reduce the temperature of its coffee to about 160°, which it did. But since 1994, McDonald's admits that it has slowly raised it back up to 180°, the same temperature that gave a 79-year-old woman burns on a quarter of her body. So sip carefully.

Despite the fact that it wasn't Stella's fault, her name will forever be associated with frivolous lawsuits.

Weird Canada

Canada: land of beautiful mountains, clear lakes, bustling cities...and some really weird news reports. Here are some of the oddest entries from the BRI newsfile.

Snow Day

In January 2002, a 30-year-old Ontario man named Nona Thusky was charged with public drunkenness and violation of probation. He was kept in custody awaiting sentencing on a previous conviction for assaulting a police officer when, two weeks later, he was suddenly released. Why? Because it snowed. Mr. Thusky is a member of the Algonquin tribe from the Barriere Lake reservation, and he's the only community member who knows how to operate the snowplow. After a severe February snowstorm, Judge Jean-Francois Gosselin decreed that "community service"—i.e., clearing snow from the streets—made more sense than jail time.

The Plop Thickens

One of the most popular events at the state provincial fair in Calgary, Alberta, is Cow Patty Bingo. They divided a field up into squares, painted numbers on them, and let people bet on the numbers. Then they let the cows into the field. The person whose square got the first "lucky patty" won a prize. Organizers denied claims that the cows had been given laxatives to speed the game up.

The good old days—when shaking hands with a Hells Angel was the most scandalous thing a Toronto mayor could do.

I Thought They Were a Hockey Team

Toronto Mayor Mel Lastman found himself in a storm of criticism in January 2002. He had staged a photo session shaking hands with and receiving a T-shirt from a member of the Hells Angels. Members of the notorious motorcycle gang had been involved in a vicious six-year drug war with rival gangs in Quebec in which more than 150 people were killed. Police organizations, city officials, and citizens blasted the mayor for the move, calling it grossly insensitive. Mayor Lastman threw the T-shirt away and apologized, saying he didn't

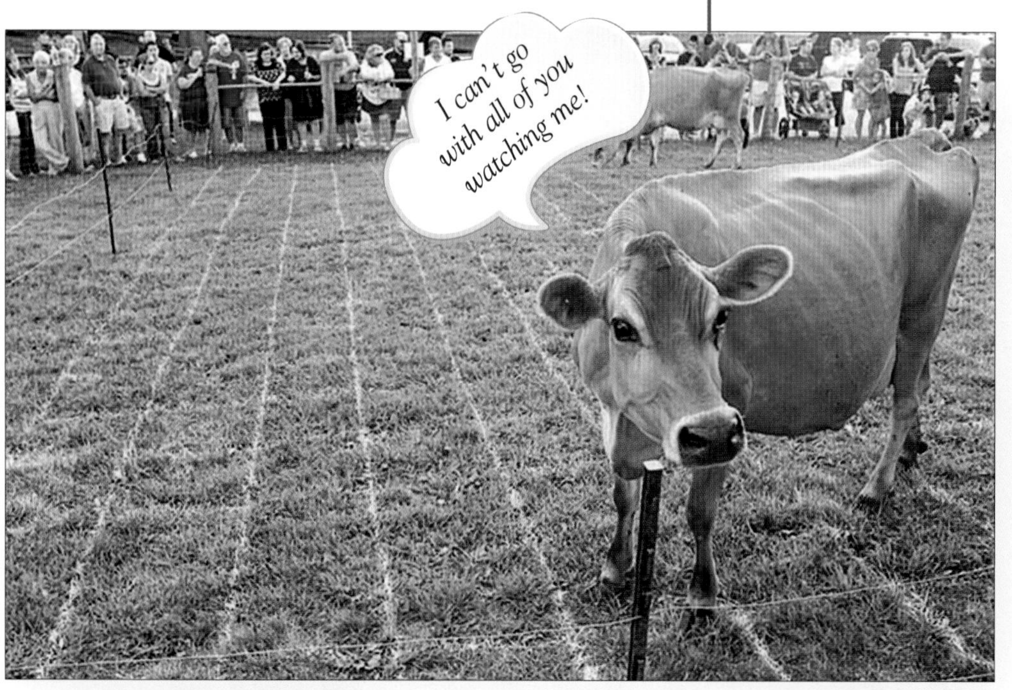

Cows taking part in Cow Patty Bingo

Between 2000 and 2005, more than 1,000 American baby girls were named Unique.

know that the Hells Angels dealt drugs. Afterwards, the gang demanded an apology from the mayor—for throwing away the present they gave him.

Beyond the Call of Dooty

In 1943, 17-year-old Hugh Trainor enlisted in the army and passed a preliminary test in his hometown on Prince Edward Island. He then traveled by ferry to an army barracks in Halifax, Nova Scotia. Once there, he failed his medical test and never officially became a member of the armed forces. But Trainor claimed that his time on the ferry—about a 10-mile ride—qualified as "war service," because German submarines had previously attacked ships in Canadian waters. In 2002 the Federal Court of Canada ruled that 75-year-old Trainor was entitled to veteran's benefits for his service and awarded him $1,000 a month for the rest of his life.

Hoot off the Press

Wanted

"Salespeople needed. If you are now employed but wish to improve your position, or in a dead-end job, call now for opportunity in cemetery sales."

—*Toronto Star*

"Career opportunity for a firefighter position: 'We offer a smoke-free work environment.'"

—*Calgary Herald*

Announcements

"All residents will now be collected on Thursday."

—**Ontario waste-systems company notice**

"At a meeting of the cemetery commission, the burial rates were increased slightly to reflect the higher cost of living."

—**Nova Scotia church bulletin**

Classifieds

"Visitors are needed for a man having trouble with blindness and a German-speaking woman."

—*The Ottawa Citizen*

"Lots of stuff! All ex-hubby's remains."

—*South Delta Today,* **B.C.**

"Wedding gown worn once by mistake. Size 9–10. Asking $20."

—*Oshawa Times*

News Flash

"A third grain-elevator fire in east-central Alberta has investigators wondering if there's a cereal arsonist at work."

—*Calgary Herald*

Two Amazing Coincidences

Needs Work

While eating dinner at Notting Hill Gate restaurant in 1992, a London publisher had her car broken into. One of the things taken from the car was a manuscript she had been reading and found extremely promising. Apparently the thieves weren't interested in literature, though—they threw the manuscript over a fence while driving away. On Monday morning she was desperately trying to come up with a way to explain how she lost the manuscript when the author called. Before she got a chance to apologize, the author asked, "Why did you have my manuscript thrown over my front fence?"

Long Shot

In 1893 Henry Ziegland of Texas jilted his fiancé, and she killed herself over it. Her brother swore revenge. He took his gun and went after Ziegland, shot him in the face and then turned the gun on himself. But the bullet only grazed Ziegland and then got lodged in a tree. Twenty years later, Ziegland was removing the tree that had the bullet buried in it, using dynamite to make the job easier. The explosion blasted the bullet out of the tree… striking Ziegland in the head and killing him.

Fictional Vacation

Check out these real tourist attractions based on fictional places.

- Tourists can take a ***Sopranos*** tour in suburban New Jersey. Stops include Satriale's Pork Store, the place where Livia Soprano is "buried," and the Bada Bing nightclub. The tour includes cannolis and a meeting with actor Joe Gannascoli, who plays Vito on the show.
- ***Gunsmoke*** was filmed in California, but set in Dodge City, Kansas. Since the 1960s, about 100,000 people a year visit the real Dodge City to see replicas of buildings from the show.
- ***The Wizard of Oz*** takes place in Kansas, but neither the book nor the movie say where in Kansas. So the town of Liberal decided that it was there, and in 1981 opened a museum they call Dorothy's House—an old farmhouse that kind of looks like the one in the 1939 movie.
- The 1990s TV series ***Northern Exposure*** took place in the fictional town of Cicely, Alaska, but was filmed in the real town of Roslyn, Washington. The Roslyn Museum houses artifacts and memorabilia from the show.
- People still visit Fort Hays, Kansas, setting of the 1990 movie ***Dances with Wolves***. Only problem: The movie was filmed in South Dakota.
- ***Twin Peaks*** was filmed in Snoqualmie, Washington, and North Bend, Washington. You can visit the show's Mar-T Cafe in North Bend, where they sell cherry pie, "a damn fine cup of coffee," and official Log Lady logs.

Sadly, you won't see Tony Soprano on The Sopranos *tour.*

- What do ***The Breakfast Club***, ***Ferris Bueller's Day Off***, and ***Sixteen Candles*** have in common? All were written by John Hughes and all take place in Shermer, Illinois. It's a fictional place, based on Hughes's hometown of Northbrook, Illinois. Landmarks from the movie, however, are real. Fans can see the "Save Ferris" water tower and the high school used in *The Breakfast Club*.
- Visiting New York? Take the ***Seinfeld*** tour. It's led by Kenny Kramer, who inspired Michael Richards's Kramer character on the show. Stops include the Soup Nazi's restaurant, Monk's Diner (Tom's Restaurant in real life), and the building used to film exterior shots of the office where Elaine worked. It's a great way to spend Festivus.
- Sam Spade, the detective in Dashiell Hammett's ***The Maltese Falcon***, kept his office in the Hunter-Dulin Building at 111 Sutter Street, San Francisco. The building is real; the office is fictional.

The road's still there, but the sign is long gone.

Pumice is the only rock that floats.

The "Soup Nazi" calls his restaurant Soup Man (for obvious reasons).

- Bedrock City in Custer, South Dakota, is a re-creation of the town of Bedrock from ***The Flintstones***. It includes the Flintstone and Rubble homes, the main street (with a bank being held up by a caveman), and Mt. Rockmore, a mini Mt. Rushmore (with Fred, Barney, and Dino instead of presidents).

- ***Little House on the Prairie*** (the books and the TV show) is based on author Laura Ingalls Wilder's life, growing up in the 1860s near Wayside, Kansas. People who visit Wayside can see modern replicas of the show's schoolhouse, post office, and the Ingalls's cabin.
- Fans of ***Gone With the Wind*** can't visit Tara—it's fictional. But they can visit the Road to Tara Museum in Clayton County, Georgia. Highlights include replicas of some costumes used in the 1939 movie, such as Scarlett's drapery dress, two seats from the Atlanta movie theater where stars of the movie saw the film's premiere, and a copy of the novel autographed by the author, Margaret Mitchell.
- Andy Griffith was born in Mt. Airy, North Carolina, which became the model for Mayberry on ***The Andy Griffith Show***. Every September, Mt. Airy holds "Mayberry Days" (cast members attend). There's a statue of Andy and Opie and replicas of Floyd's Barber Shop, the jail, and Andy's house. But don't look for the fishing hole seen in the opening credits—that's in Beverly Hills.

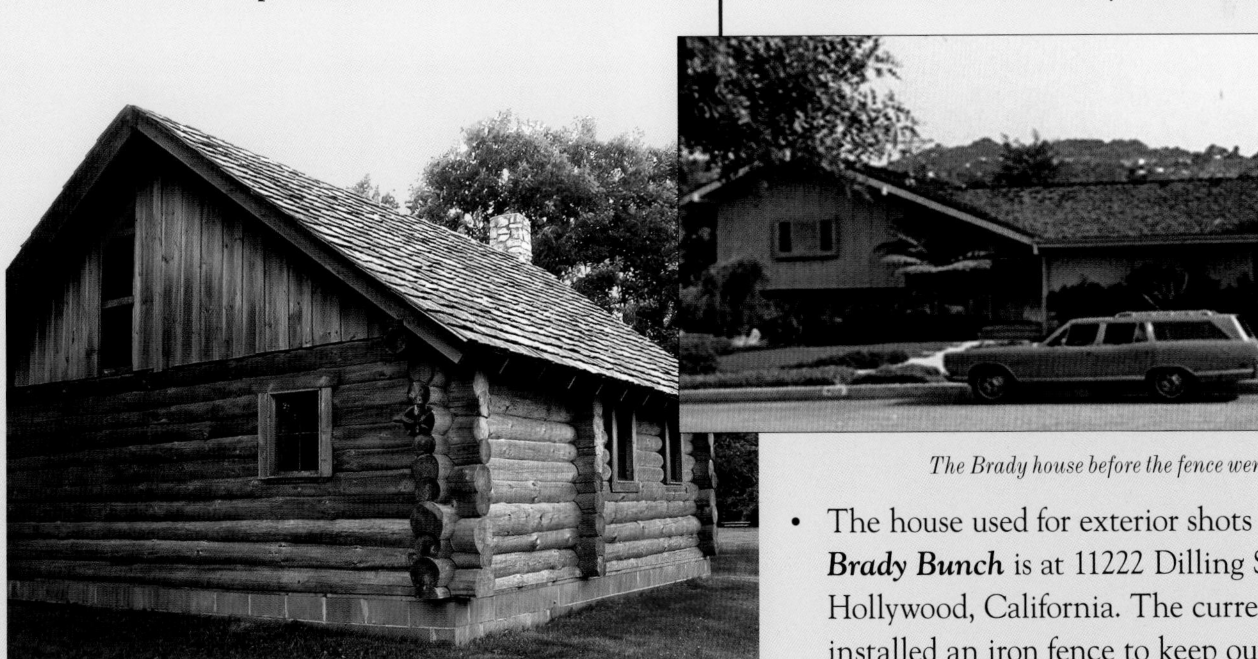

The Brady house before the fence went up

- The house used for exterior shots of ***The Brady Bunch*** is at 11222 Dilling Street, North Hollywood, California. The current residents installed an iron fence to keep out fans hoping to catch a glimpse of the Bradys.

Several towns across the United States boast original "Little Houses"—this one is in Wisconsin.

After the Quake: The Fire War

The Great San Francisco Earthquake of 1906 set off massive fires around the city. Here's how the flames were fought. *(Part I is on page 142.)*

Blasting the Blaze

Within hours after the San Francisco earthquake, fires had broken out all over the city. The fires had many allies: the San Francisco hills, a steady breeze, the slow-burning redwood that composed 75% of the city's structures, numerous aftershocks, and insufficient water to fight them. So as a last resort, Mayor Schmitz came to a decision: Fight fire with fire.

What San Franciscans *did* have a lot of was dynamite—so they used it to build firebreaks, the theory being that disintegrating a building before the flames could reach it would cut off the fire's fuel supply. But this plan only partly worked; new fires sprouted up from the explosions. By noon much of downtown was engulfed in flame. The destruction continued: The Army Medical Supply Depot went up in flames, taking with it material that could have been used in the disaster. One of the city's highest skyscrapers, the Call Building—which had withstood the quake—was reduced to ashes.

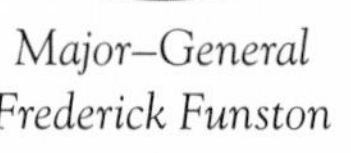

Major–General Frederick Funston

Also leveled were the St. Ignatius Church (which housed a priceless pipe organ), the *Examiner* building, the Emporium department store, the Hall of Justice, Chinatown, the Columbia Theater, the

California Academy of Sciences, and the Opera House, where world-famous Italian tenor Enrico Caruso had sung the previous night. One by one, San Francisco's most beloved buildings, including more than 30 schools, were destroyed. By midnight on Wednesday, most of the downtown district was in ruins, and there was more destruction to come.

One Step Forward...

Wherever firefighters stopped the path of the fires, other avenues of fire opened up. The city streets were so narrow and the buildings so close together that there was more than enough fuel for the flames. One place where firefighters almost got the upper hand was Powell Street. Because it was very wide, the flames couldn't reach both sides and couldn't create the dangerous tunnels of fire that were spreading elsewhere in the city. And the massive St. Francis Hotel formed a huge firebreak. Surrounded by vacant lots, it gave the firefighters room to work and the flames no place to go. It looked like the fire might run out of real estate.

It would have, too, if it hadn't been for a few tired and hungry soldiers on the other side of the firebreak. They went into the empty Delmonico Restaurant to rest and find something to eat. They decided they wanted hot food, so they built a small fire to cook with. Bad idea: The "Ham and Eggs Fire," as it was later called, got out of hand and quickly spread. Soon the entire restaurant was in flames, followed by the Alcazar Theater next door, followed by every building on Geary Avenue. Then it headed toward Powell Street, scattering enraged firefighters and forcing them to regroup elsewhere.

"Thank God for the Soldiers," San Francisco earthquake aftermath, 1906 (H. Charles McBarron)

The city in ruins, April 18, 1906

...Two Steps Back

At this point, Mayor Schmitz decided the next fire line would be drawn at Van Ness Avenue. He ordered troops to start dynamiting homes to form another firebreak—an unpopular decision because many of the town's wealthiest and most influential people lived there. While one Army officer was sent to begin evacuation procedures, another was sent to take the fastest boat to the nearest city to replenish the town's exhausted stock of dynamite.

But somehow the message was misconstrued and the boat never left. With Van Ness Avenue completely evacuated and firefighters forming a line, they waited for the arrival of the dynamite...and waited...and waited. In disgust, Brigadier General Funston finally commandeered another boat and sent it on its way—but by then it was too late. In desperation, some firemen tried to set a backfire, but it failed to stop the advance of the flames, and Van Ness was on fire before the boat returned.

Next, the firefighters fell back to Franklin Street. It was narrow, but it was their only hope. Once again, residents were evacuated and firefighting forces were gathered. Demolition teams detonated home after home. Then the wind changed and it appeared that the fire was stopped. Bystanders rejoiced—until they realized the flames were just being pushed in a new direction. The exhausted firefighters had to drum up the energy to make yet another stand.

On the other side of the city, 20th Street was chosen as a firebreak. It was a fairly wide street with some open ground downhill from a large cistern that still had some water in it. Buildings on the north side of the street were quickly dynamited, and the engines pulled by horses were taken up the hill to the cistern. When the horses gave out, dozens of citizens pushed the engines up the hill themselves to get the water. Their efforts worked. The fire was stopped at 20th street.

After four days of battling the blazes, the firemen slowly began to get the upper hand. By Saturday, only remnants of the great fire were left smoldering in pockets around the city. Late that night a much-needed rain began to fall, and the smoke finally began to clear.

Aftermath

About 700 people died as the result of the quake and the fires, but countless more were saved by General Funston, Mayor Schmitz, and all of the brave men and women who stayed to fight the fires and help others. Property losses topped $500 million. Some 497 city blocks covering 2,831 acres lay in ruins. Twenty-eight thousand buildings were gone. Half of the city's population, amounting to a quarter of a million people, were homeless. But San Franciscans were determined to save their city; rebuilding began almost immediately.

Secretary of War Taft rushed a bill through Congress requesting half a million dollars in relief funds for the city. It was passed the same day. He ordered 200,000 rations sent from the

Damage from the 1989 San Francisco earthquake

Vancouver, Washington, Army Base, and ordered every military post in the nation to send all tents without delay. Then he sent another bill through Congress increasing his request for financial aid to $1 million. It was approved. In addition, $10 million more poured in from 14 nations. Fundraisers for San Francisco were held all over the nation. Songwriter George M. Cohen sold souvenir newspapers for $1,000 per copy, and boxing champion Jim Jeffries sold oranges for $20 each. Relief distribution centers provided aid—the Red Cross served over 313,000 meals on April 30 alone.

Getting Back to Normal

Ten days later, water service was restored. Soon after came the lights along the main streets and the trolley cars. And the rebuilding continued nonstop. Within three years, 20,000 of the 28,000 ruined buildings had been replaced, and this time most of the buildings were made of brick and steel—not wood. In 1915 San Francisco hosted the World's Fair, and by then there was barely any evidence left of the Great San Francisco Earthquake and fires.

A Tragic Legacy

San Franciscans got a rude reminder of the big quake on October 17, 1989. An earthquake hit the area, and although it was much smaller, it was big enough to cause extensive damage. Way back in 1915 when they were still rebuilding, many new structures were built in the Marina District. Engineers used rubble, mud, and sand to fill in the shallow bay. But the new land wasn't properly compacted before the buildings went up. After the Exposition ended, homes and other buildings were constructed on top of this unstable base. Without solid ground to stand on, the Marina District was severely damaged in the 1989 quake.

Lottery Losers

What if you won the lottery and became an instant millionaire? Would you lose your head and burn through the money? Or would you keep your cool and invest? (Tip: Uncle John would invest in toilet futures.)

What Are the Odds?

Your odds of winning the Florida Lotto jackpot are one in 22 million. But don't despair—that's better than your odds of winning the California SuperLotto Plus, which are one in 41 million. According to experts, if one person purchases 50 Lotto tickets each week, he or she will win the jackpot…about once every 5,000 years. Still, many people do beat those odds and win. But here's the big question: Do their lotto winnings make them happy?

Windfall

- When Juan Rodriguez won $149 million in a New York lottery, his wife of 17 years immediately filed for divorce and claimed half of his winnings.
- Michael Klingebiel was sued by his own mother in 1998 because he failed to share his $2 million jackpot.
- Ken Proxmire, a machinist from Michigan, took his $1 million winnings to California to start a car business with his brothers. Five years later he was bankrupt and back working as a machinist.
- Against all odds, Evelyn Adams won the New Jersey lottery not once, but twice—in 1985 and 1986. Her total winnings: $5.4 million. But she gambled those millions away, and today she lives in a trailer. "Everybody wanted my money," said Adams. "Everybody had their hand out. I never learned one simple word in the English language—'No.'"

Living Large

It seems like big money just means big trouble. It certainly did for Jack Whittaker of West Virginia. On Christmas 2002, Whittaker won the largest undivided jackpot in United States history—$314 million. Since then he's had hundreds of thousands of dollars in cash stolen from his cars, home, and office. He was arrested twice for drunken driving and pleaded "no contest" to a misdemeanor

assault charge against a bar manager. Though Whittaker gave $20 million to churches, charities, and schools, it never seemed to be enough. On a daily basis, strangers rang his doorbell, eager to tell their stories and ask for financial help. The sudden wealth took a toll on his wife and family, too. His 16-year-old granddaughter, Brandi Bragg, who stood beaming by his side at the initial press conference, died of a drug overdose almost two years to the day after the big win. Whittaker's wife told the Charleston *Gazette* that she regrets everything. "I wish all of this never would have happened," said Jewel Whittaker. "I wish I would have torn the ticket up."

It looked like their troubles were over, but...

Crash Landings

- Willie Hurt of Belleville, Michigan, won $3.1 million in 1989. He divided his fortune between his ex-wife and cocaine, and by 1991, he was penniless and in jail, charged with murder.
- Victoria Zell, who shared an $11-million Powerball jackpot with her husband in 2001, was broke by 2006 and serving seven years in a Minnesota prison for vehicular manslaughter after killing a friend in a drug-and-alcohol-induced car crash.
- Thomas Strong, winner of $3 million in a Texas lottery in 1993, died in a shootout with police in 2006.
- In 1993 Janite Lee won $18 million in the Missouri Lottery. She spread the wealth around, donating huge sums to schools, political

campaigns, community organizations, and charities. But Lee was too generous: She filed for bankruptcy in 2001 with just $700 left.

If You Think that's Bad...

Jeffrey Dampier won $20 million in the Illinois lottery in 1996. After buying houses and cars for his siblings and parents, and treating 38 of his nearest and dearest friends to a Christmas Caribbean cruise, he was kidnapped and murdered by his own sister-in-law.

What if You Win?

What if you are one of the rare few struck with "sudden-wealth syndrome"? What should you do with all that money? Enough people have faced this dilemma that organizations like the "Sudden Money Institute" and "The Affluenza Project" have formed to help winners through this life-altering event. Here's some advice from the experts:

- Don't do anything rash. Don't make any promises to *anyone*.
- Get out of the house. Better yet, get out of town until the media interest calms down.
- Get an unlisted phone number.
- Talk to a tax expert first to find out how much money you'll really get.
- Talk to two or three financial planners/CPAs before choosing the one that seems like the best fit for you.
- Create a budget and try to stick with it. Think long-term.
- Don't invest in anyone's business unless you know something about business.
- Take a small percentage of the money, say 5%, and do something just for fun.

Bathroom Facts

- The flushing toilet came into being in 1596 in England. It was invented by Sir John Harrington for Queen Elizabeth I.
- Thomas Crapper capitalized on the invention, establishing a plumbing company to manufacture them for the British public. Given a royal warrant, Crapper's name was forever associated with flush toilets.
- British King George II died falling off a toilet in 1760.
- *Psycho* (1960) was the first movie to show a toilet being flushed, a scene that drew indecency complaints.
- Statistics show that more Americans flush their toilets at halftime during the Super Bowl than at any other time of the year.

In the densest jungle, only 1% of sunlight ever reaches the forest floor.

Random Origins

More stories behind the stories.

The Tape Measure

In Sheffield, England, in the late 1820s, James Chesterman manufactured long steel bands that were rolled into continuous loops for use as frames in hoop skirts. But when the hoop skirt fashion fell out of favor, Chesterman was left with a lot of light-weight, bendable steel bands. Solution: He put notches into them at incremental distances and sold them to surveyors as "Steel Band Measuring Chains." He even built a special casing with a spring inside that would roll up the band. In New Haven, Connecticut, in 1868, Alvin Fellows improved on Chesterman's design by adding a clip that locked the tape in any desired position. Tape measures have changed little since then.

The Periodic Table of Elements

In 1868 Russian chemist Dmitri Mendeleev, a professor at the University of St. Petersburg, set out to categorize the 60 known elements. Although scientists didn't know what atoms were made of, they knew that elements were different kinds of atoms, each with its own unique atomic weight. Mendeleev made a little card for each element, complete with all of its physical and chemical properties. Then he laid them all out on a table and tried different ways of arranging them. He noticed that when he started with the lightest weight, a pattern emerged: Basically, certain types of elements would always follow each other based on their reactivity. Although Mendeleev had only 60 of what we now know to be 110 elements—and much of what was assumed about them was wrong—he was able to predict most of the ones that had yet to be discovered, and as such, his periodic table is still in use today.

Hamsters

The natural habitat of Golden or Syrian hamsters, as the pet variety is known, is limited to one area: the desert outside the city of Aleppo, Syria. (Their name in the local Arabic dialect translates to "saddlebags," thanks to the pouches in their mouths that they use to store food.) In 1930 a zoologist named Israel Aharoni found a nest containing a female and a litter of 11 babies in the desert and brought them back to his lab at the Hebrew University of Jerusalem. The mother died on the trip home; so did seven of her babies. Virtually all of the millions of domesticated Golden hamsters in the world are descended from the four that survived.

The Slot Machine

Other types of gambling machines date back as far as the 1890s, but the first one to really catch on was a vending machine for chewing gum introduced by the Mills Novelty Company in 1910. Their machine dispensed three flavors of gum—cherry, orange, and plum—depending on which fruits appeared on three randomly spinning wheels. If three bars reading "1910 Fruit Gum" appeared in a row, the machine gave extra gum; if a lemon appeared, it gave no gum at all (which is why "lemon" came to mean something unsatisfactory or defective). You can't get gum in a slot machine anymore—the 1910 Fruit Gum machine was so popular that the company converted them to cash payouts—but the same fruit symbols are still used in many slot machines today.

The Privy Man

Here is the story of a man who saw millions of people suffering and made it his life's mission to help them. How? By building a better toilet.

Bindeshwar Pathak

Caste-Aways

When Bindeshwar Pathak was a boy growing up in a wealthy Indian family in the 1940s, he was punished for breaking a cultural rule—he touched the arm of a family servant. The punishment: Bindeshwar's grandfather forced him to take a ritual bath in which every inch of his body was painfully scrubbed clean, and then he had to swallow a nugget of cow dung mixed with cow urine to "flush out the filth from within."

The boy didn't understand why the punishment was so severe, so his grandfather explained that the servants were "untouchables"—people so filthy and dirty that they weren't even given a place in one of India's four main castes. It was their lifelong duty to clean up the waste of their masters, to carry it away in buckets and dispose of it in holes. And they had to live in small huts with no running water.

The lesson of that day stayed with Bindeshwar. He knew in his heart that there had to be a better way for these people. So he decided that he would use his stature and schooling to help the untouchables live a better life. But first, he needed a plan.

Building a Better Toilet

After graduating from college with a degree in sociology, Dr. Bindeshwar Pathak traveled throughout India and lived with the poorest families to study them. He found that the worst problem they had to deal with was sanitation. Of the 500 million people living in India at the time, nearly 75 percent either defecated in the open or used bucket latrines. And only a tiny fraction of India's 4,800 towns and cities even had sewers. Bindeshwar saw that two things needed to happen: "First, every single house in India should

Rooms with a view

The Sulabh International Museum of Toilets, dedicated to the history of sanitation and toilets. Sulabh International, founded by Dr. Pathak, houses the museum in Delhi.

have a proper toilet and adequate toilet facilities. Secondly, the untouchables in India should be adopted into mainstream lives."

He researched different plumbing systems and consulted with engineering experts around the world, and in 1970 came up with a simple but ingenious solution: the *sulabh shauchalaya*, a toilet consisting of two pits with a sealed cover.

The Sulabh's Benefits

It is very inexpensive, so every family can afford one. Waste can be cleaned without direct contact. It saves water by requiring only half a gallon for flushing instead of the usual four gallons needed for a bucket. It eliminates ground contamination by recycling human waste into fertilizer right there in the sealed pit.

- Because there are two pits, the toilets will never be out of service—one can be used while the other is being emptied.
- It eliminates the need for costly septic tanks, which use much more water and emit foul odors.

Making a Difference

In the four decades since its introduction, the sulabh has drastically altered India's cultural landscape. Hundreds of thousands of former untouchables no longer have to be exposed to waste.

The second part of Pathak's plan—to rehabilitate former untouchables into society—has been successful as well. In centuries past, no education or job training was available to these people. But now, thanks to the money that comes in from the public sulabhs (as well as some government funding), Pathak has set up vocational schools that train people in fields such as computer technology, typing and shorthand, electrical engineering, and other skilled trades. There is still much work to be done. Although hundreds of thousands of lives have been improved, there are still millions of people in India whose job it is to clean toilets with their bare hands. And although the name "untouchable" has fallen into disuse in recent years, the stigma against them still exists, especially in rural areas.

But thanks to Bindeshwar Pathak, change has begun and continues to spread. "Let us save these people from squalid conditions," he says, "and in doing so we will be saving the national conscience."

These plush toy characters, Pee and Poo, were given to the Sulabh International Museum of Toilets by Benjamin Zilberman, a French documentary filmmaker.

Boneheads

What's the difference between horns and antlers? Which animals have which? And why do they have them? Inquiring minds want to know.

Rack 'em Up

Many different mammals in many parts of the world have what is known as headgear—horns or antlers. All the species that have them have unique varieties which grow in their own special way: Some are straight as an arrow, some spiral like vines, some are only inches long, and some weigh more than 40 pounds each. Nearly all headgear comes in the form of true horns and antlers, but there are some rare exceptions: keratin horns and pronghorns.

- **Horns** are found only on *bovids* such as cattle, sheep, goats, and antelopes. They are made of compressed *keratin*—the same thing that human hair and fingernails are made of. True horns grow in a single tine—they have no branches—and are permanent fixtures that keep growing throughout the animal's life. In most species they appear on both the male and the female.

- **Antlers** are found only on *cervids*, members of the deer family. They are made of solid bone and always branch out to form several tines or "points" (as in a five-point buck). While antlers are still growing they're covered by a layer of soft, very sensitive skin, known as *velvet*. The velvet contains veins and nerves that actually "grow" the antlers. They're the fastest growing bone on any animal—up to an inch a day on some species—and only the males have them (the caribou is the one exception). Antlers are *deciduous*. Just before mating season the velvet dries up and the antlers stop growing. The animal scrapes off the dry velvet on trees or bushes, and the antlers become hard and sharp. After mating season the antlers fall off, and within a few months they start growing again. Each year (on healthy animals) they will grow a little larger.

- **Keratin horns** only appear on some species of

Elk horn pile

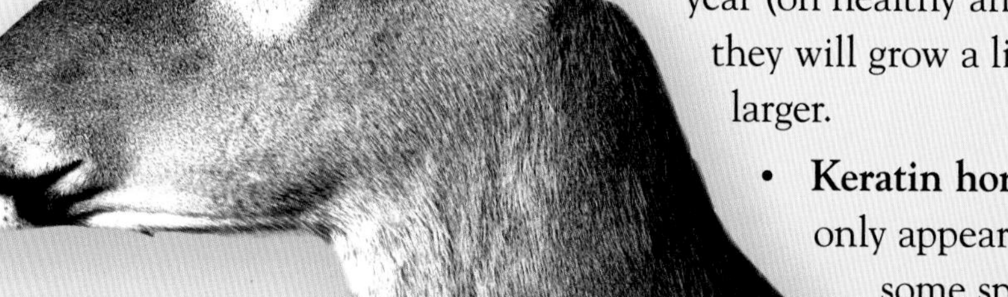

White-tailed deer buck with velvet antlers

Virtual hookers: 40,000 Americans participate in "fantasy fishing" leagues.

Battle of the bull elks

rhinoceros. Just like horns, they are permanent and appear on both sexes. They don't grow in pairs—they jut out from the midline of the snout.

- **Pronghorns** are only found on…the *pronghorn* (often called the *pronghorn antelope*, although it is not a true antelope) found in western North America. Their headgear is a unique mix of both horns and antlers. They have the bone core and the keratin sheath of a horn, but they're not permanent—the keratin falls off each year like antlers do, leaving only the bone core.

No, you're the bonehead.

Bighorn sheep

So That's Why They Call it "Horny"

The most important role of headgear: sex. It's no coincidence that antlers grow to prominence just in time for mating season and then fall off when the work is done. Males of nearly all species with headgear use it to fight off rivals for mates. It's usually done in harmless, ritualistic ways, but can sometimes get brutal and bloody. And sometimes the bull with the mightiest headgear doesn't even have to fight—his display alone can ward off contenders and impress the females.

Bambi Bites Back

All animals with headgear are herbivores, or plant-eaters; they are prey, not predators, which means they lack the sharp claws or teeth of carnivores. Their headgear is their weapon—nature's way of providing them with "teeth." Take the bull elk for example: His first instinct is to flee, but if necessary he will stand down a 150-pound mountain lion, with dagger-sharp antlers up to five feet across. (And not just lions: The elk at Yellowstone National Park have been known to gore careless visitors. A few have even attacked automobiles, poking holes right through car doors with their antlers.) Headgear can also be used for marking trees, digging in the ground for food, or scratching a hard-to-reach itch.

Headgear Standouts

- **Big Horn Sheep** have thick, stout horns that curve back around, beneath their ears, and then forward again. And the horns can weigh more than all the other bones in their bodies put together. Each mating season the males fight for social dominance, running into each other and bashing the thick bases of their horns together—at speeds of over 20 mph with a force of 2,000 pounds per square inch. Their battles can be heard up to a mile away.

- **The Moose** is the largest member of the deer family, often reaching seven feet at the shoulder. Every year the male grows a set of palmate antlers. They spread out like the palm of a hand with large flattened areas and tines sticking out of the flats. His antlers can span more than six feet, have as many as thirty spikes, and can weigh 40 pounds each.
- **Elk** antlers grow to five feet, with six to ten spikes on each side. During mating season their battles get fairly violent: Some stab wounds can kill outright or cause so much damage that the loser cannot escape from danger. Worst-case scenario: Two bulls interlock their antlers and are unable to get them apart. Both animals will eventually die of starvation or be killed by predators.
- The **Indian Water Buffalo** has the longest horns of all. In 1955 a bull's horns were measured from tip to tip around their long, sweeping curve. Length: 13 feet, 11 inches.
- The **Chousinga** is a member of the true-horned bovid family, but instead of two horns, it has four. Also known as the four-horned antelope, this small creature lives in India and Nepal and grows an extra set of horns on its forehead, just above its eyes.
- **Giraffes** are unique: Their horns aren't covered with keratin—they're covered with skin.

Get to the Point

- The **Asian Musk Deer** is one of the few members of the deer family that have no antlers. What do they have instead? Tusks—long, fang-like teeth that grow down over their lower jaw.
- Imagine seeing a tusked animal only 20 inches long that looks like a cross between a deer, antelope, and a pig. That's the **mouse deer** from Malaysia.
- The **Irish Elk** is the name given to an extinct species of deer. Their antlers measured over 13 feet across, and weighed up to 100 pounds—each.
- Not only are all of the animals with headgear herbivores. They also share one other characteristic: They all have hooves.
- Animals with headgear are native to every continent except Antarctica and Australia. No native Australian mammals have antlers, horns, or hooves.

Bull moose

Harvard's library has three books bound in human flesh.

The Swat Team

It's so natural to want to take a whack at the fly buzzing around your head, it's hard to think of fly swatters as something somebody actually invented. But someone did.

Weapon of Meshed Destruction

On January 9, 1900, the U.S. Patent Office granted patent number 640,790 to Robert R. Montgomery of Decatur, Illinois, illustrated with a detailed drawing of a piece of windowscreen, folded precisely at one end and attached to a wooden handle with two rivets. The design turned out to be so perfect that it has remained essentially unchanged for more than a century, even down to the helpful hole (also shown on the patent application) on the end of the handle for hanging on a nail.

Today, the occasional fly that gets into the house is an annoyance, but not much more. It's difficult to imagine how serious a health hazard flies were before modern medicines and pesticides, when horses were used for transportation, outhouses used for bathrooms, fresh manure used as fertilizer, and open windows used as "air conditioning." Animal dung was everywhere—not only on the farm, but also in big cities, where the streets were literally paved with layer upon layer of horse droppings. Populations of houseflies would explode each year. But flies do not live by poop alone, and at a time when open windows and doors were the only way to cope with sweltering summers, flies came from the street (and outhouse) into the home with impunity, landing on food, sleeping babies, pets, and anything else that would stand still. And they weren't just unappetizing houseguests—although they do not bite, houseflies are carriers of dozens of diseases, including typhoid, cholera, dysentery, anthrax, tuberculosis, and salmonella.

Invented on the Fly

People had long been whacking at flies with rolled-up newspapers or whatever else was at hand, but nothing had ever accomplished the task with the elegant efficiency of Robert Montgomery's fly swatter. Besides stealth, speed, and accuracy, Montgomery's meshed screen brought forward enough bulk to kill the fly without damaging what was beneath it. The flexible "whiplike" killing surface worked on irregular and angular surfaces, and the mesh allowed a large enough surface area to thwart last-second fly evasions without creating wind resistance. And best of all, the thin, sharp edges of the swat surface tended to slice into the fly's body instead of smashing it flat, minimizing the mess on walls, furniture, paintings, wallpaper, and unlucky bystanders.

Pest Asides

Montgomery may have been a genius

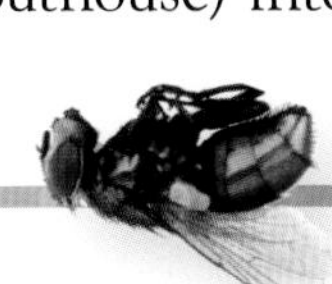

Why is honey so easy to digest? Because it has already been digested by the bee.

Old-style fly spray pump

in fly-killing technology, but he wasn't really that interested in manufacturing the swatter. Three years after his patent was granted, with the public buying up half a million fly swatters a year, Montgomery and his overworked partners (his two sons) decided it was time to turn the invention over to somebody else. That somebody was a local manufacturer named John L. Bennett. Bennett would later take credit for making "dramatic improvements" to the fly swatter, but his contribution was literally "tinkering around the edges." He added stitching around the outside of the netting to keep it from fraying. (He'd later have a more legitimate claim to pop-culture fame as the man who patented the beer can.)

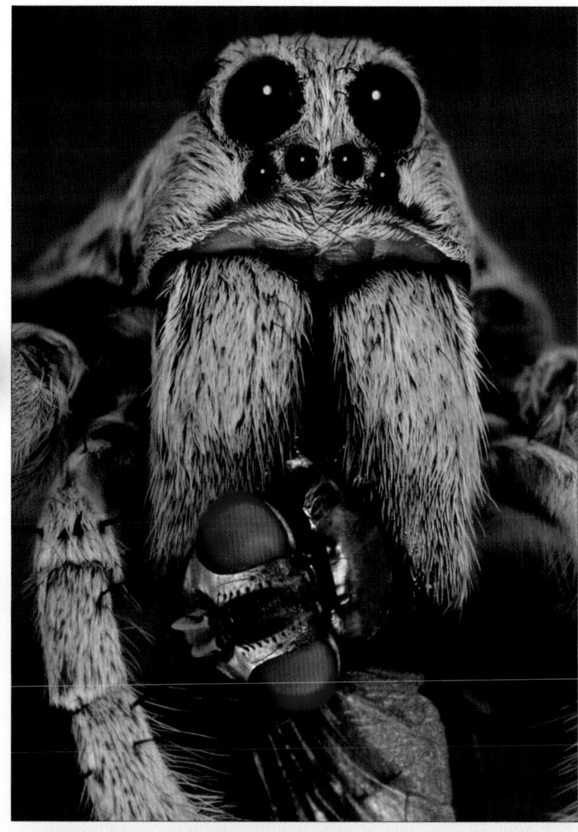

A natural app: a wolf spider holds a fly in its fangs.

Killer App

There have been many attempts to improve on fly-swatting technology, from fly guns that shoot swatting disks to electrified fly zappers, but the most popular anti-fly weapon remains the classic fly swatter, unchanged in basic design (except that they're now made of plastic instead of wood and metal). They're inexpensive, well-suited for the job intended, and still weirdly satisfying when you make solid contact. Who but the flies could ask for anything more?

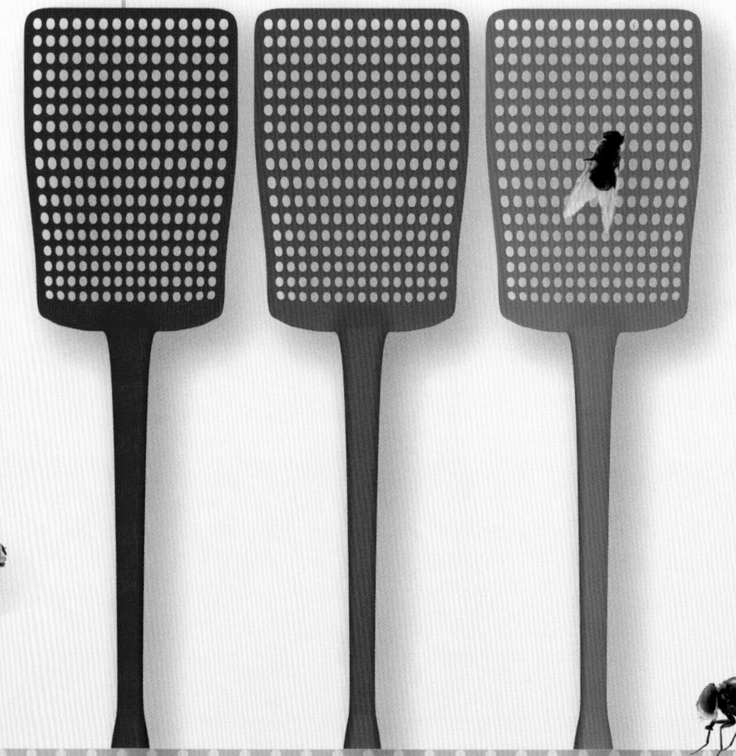

Bad boy! One in four British veterinarians say they've treated a drunk dog.

Food Styling Secrets

Ever drooled over a juicy cheeseburger or a frosty milkshake on a TV commercial? Here's some bad news: You probably wouldn't want to eat them. Why? Because they've been pumped up, glued, and painted to look tasty by a "food stylist."

Fake Soup's On!

Food doesn't look good for long. Right after it hits the plate, it starts to melt, cool, deflate, dry out, wilt, perspire, or brown. And the degeneration begins even faster under hot TV lights. That's why commercial producers and cooking shows hire food stylists, people who know how to work around these challenges and make food appear delicious and perfect. As stylist Lisa Golden Schroeder says, "Taste is of little concern, but looks are everything." Here are some of the tools of the trade:

- **Brown shoe polish** is painted onto steaks and burgers to make them look like they're perfectly cooked, just out of the oven or off the grill.
- **Blowtorches** are used to quickly brown and sear the surfaces and edges of raw meats, to brown chicken skin, and to "fire roast" vegetables.
- **Scissors** are used to cut a triangle out of the unseen back of a burger patty. The meat is then spread apart to give the illusion of a very large patty.
- **White glue** glistens under hot studio lights and produces a glossy, buttery look. It's also used as a substitute for milk in cereal commercials, and for mayonnaise on sandwiches because it stays thick and creamy.
- **Hair spray** prevents lettuce and vegetables from wilting, and can also temporarily revive dry-looking foods—particularly breads and cakes.
- **Spray deodorant** is how stylists get the look of tiny, frosty ice crystals on the outside of an ice cream container. It also makes delicate fruits—particularly grapes—shine.
- **Motor oil** is probably what you're seeing if the commercial features maple syrup. Its color and consistency mimic those of the edible stuff.
- **Spray-on fabric softener** keeps foods from blending together, or from soaking into each other. Cold pancakes are sprayed with this before the stage syrup is applied.
- **Syringes** are used to pump water or air into foods to make them look full and plentiful. Water is used to inflate chicken skins; air is injected into mashed potatoes for fluffiness.
- **Cardboard squares** keep food from sinking or falling. They're placed between a bun, burger patty, and condiments to make the hamburger look taller. They also soak up excess liquid.
- **Glycerin** is painted on "food" to provide the perfect amount of shine and desired wetness. (It works especially well with seafood.)

Sweet, oily pancakes

Fastest tennis serve by a woman ever recorded: 130 mph, by Venus Williams.

I Toast You!

On a recent trip to Ireland, Uncle John spent many an evening going from pub to pub collecting traditional toasts (and many a morning after, begging for aspirin). Here are some favorites.

May you have food and clothing,
A soft pillow for your head;
May you be forty years in
heaven,
Before the devil knows you're
dead.

For every wound, a balm.
For every sorrow, a cheer.
For every storm, a calm.
For every thirst, a beer.

May misfortune follow you
the rest of your life,
But never catch up.

May the roof above us never fall in,
and may we friends gathered below
never fall out.

Here's health and prosperity,
To you and all your posterity,
And them that doesn't drink with
sincerity,
That they may be damned for all
eternity!

May we live to learn well,
And learn to live well.

May your right hand
always be stretched out
in friendship
And never in want.

May the people
who dance on your grave
Get cramps in their legs.

Here's to warm words
on a cold evening,
A full moon on a dark night,
And the road downhill all the way to
your door.

Success to the lover,
Honor to the brave,
Health to the sick,
And freedom to the slave.

May I see you gray,
Combing your grandchildren's hair.

Wood to burn,
Old books to read,
Old wine to drink,
Old friends to trust.

Champagne to our real friends,
And real pain to our sham friends.

May you live as long as you want,
And never want as long as you live.

Health and long life to you,
The woman of your choice to you,
A child every year to you,
Land without rent to you,
And may you die in Ireland.

Gentlemen, start your livers!

Praying mantises eat their victims alive.

I Curse You!

Save these classic curses to use against people who refuse to toast you.

May you be transformed
into a chandelier,
To hang by day and burn by night.

May the seven terriers of hell
Sit on the spool of your breast
and bark in at your soul-case.

May I live just long enough
to bury you.

May you be afflicted
with the itch
And have no nails to scratch with.

May your daughter's beauty be admired
by everyone in the circus.

All your teeth should fall out
except one,
And you should have a toothache
in that one.

Your nose should grow so much hair
it strains your soup.

May fire and brimstone
never fail to fall in showers on you.

May you live in a house of 100 rooms,
And may each room have its own bed,
And may you wander every night from
room to room,
And from bed to bed,
Unable to sleep.

May you have devoted children
to chase the flies off your nose.

May you go stone-blind
so that you can't tell your wife from
a haystack.

May the curse of Mary Maline
and her nine blind children
Chase you so far over the hills of Damnation
that the Lord himself won't find you
with a telescope.

May you win a lottery
and spend it all on doctors.

May the devil swallow you sideways.

May you back into a pitchfork
And grab a hot stove for support.

May those who love us love us.
And those that don't love us,
May God turn their hearts,
And if He cannot turn their hearts,
May He turn their ankles
so we'll know them by
their limping.

Weird Beauty Pageants

If you think the Miss America contest is a little strange, put on your bikini and high heels and read about these ones.

Title: Miss Artificial Beauty

Background: When 18-year-old Yang Yuan was barred from competing in the 2004 Miss Beijing pageant because she was "an artificial beauty" (the Chinese expression for someone who has had plastic surgery), she sued pageant organizers and lost. Consolation prize: they created the 2004 Miss Artificial Beauty pageant.

The Pageant: To qualify, entrants had to provide a doctor's certificate as proof that they had actually undergone plastic surgery. There were 19 finalists, ranging from age 17 to 62, including one transsexual. They competed in several different categories, including "Best Body" and "Biggest Physical Change." (The transsexual, 21-year-old Liu Xiaojing, won in the "Most Newsworthy" category.)

And the Winner Is: Feng Qian, 22, a medical student, underwent four procedures—eyelid surgery to get "Western eyelids," facial sculpting, Botox injections, and liposuction on her cheeks and waist—not only to look beautiful, but also to "understand the psychology of someone who does this." Feng won $6,000 and a trip to Japan to attend a plastic surgery conference.

Miss Artificial Beauty finalists, 2004

Miss Beauty in Epaulettes, 2003

Title: Miss Beauty in Epaulettes

Background: This pageant is for women in the Russian army. (An "epaulette" is a shoulder ornament on military uniforms.)

The Pageant: Sixteen finalists from army posts all across Russia participated in the 2003 pageant. Beauty was only one area of competition—in addition to modeling evening gowns and combat fatigues, the women also competed in cooking, ballroom dancing, and target shooting.

And the Winner Is: Junior Sergeant Tatyana Posyvnina, a radio engineer from the St. Petersburg military district.

Title: Miss Captivity

Background: Probably the world's first beauty pageant held in a women's prison: Lithuania's high-security Panevezys Penal Labor Colony. TV producer Arunas Valinskas, who came up with the

Carpenter's pencils are square so they don't roll off roofs.

idea, says he wanted to prove that "you can find beauty even where you might think there isn't any."

The Pageant: Thirty-eight inmates competed in a wedding dress competition, a formal dress competition, and two bikini swimsuit competitions (one with a black leather theme and a second one featuring exotic furs). Contestants used pseudonyms instead of real names and details of their criminal records were not released to the press.

And the Winner Is: "Samanta," a 24-year-old inmate who hopes to start a modeling career when she gets out of prison. She won a silver crown and about $2,000, which will be held for her until she is released. What are her hopes for the future? "I'd like to get out of prison right now." Stay tuned: A Hollywood movie is in the works and there's even talk of a Miss Captivity Europe pageant.

Title: Miss Besieged Sarajevo

Background: When Bosnia-Herzegovina declared independence from Yugoslavia in 1992, the Serbian separatists placed the Bosnian capital under virtual siege. People trapped in Sarajevo were under constant threat of sniper and artillery attack. Yet for many this only made them more determined to live life as normally as possible. Hence the Miss Besieged Sarajevo beauty pageant, held in May 1993.

Miss Besieged Sarajevo, 1993

The Pageant: Thirteen semifinalists, some with shrapnel scars, competed in two events: evening dress and swimsuit competitions. Reminders of the siege were everywhere: whizzing bullets and exploding artillery shells could be heard in the background. When the contestants came onstage during the swimsuit competition, they unfurled a banner that read, "Don't let them kill us."

And the Winner Is: Seventeen-year-old Imela Nogic, who won a trip to Madrid. (She had to wait until the siege ended in 1995 to redeem it.) When asked by a reporter what her plans were after the pageant, she replied, "Plans? I have no plans. I may not even be alive tomorrow."

Imprisoned beauty queens in Colombia

Mothers of Inventio

There have always been women inventors...even if they've been overlooked by the history books. Here are a few you may not have heard of.

A typical New York winter—made a little easier to endure thanks to Mary Anderson's invention

Mary Anderson

Invention: Windshield wipers

Story: In 1903 Anderson, an Alabaman, took a trip to New York City. One snowy afternoon she decided to tour the city by streetcar, but instead of sightseeing found herself staring at the streetcar conductor, who had to keep stopping to wipe the snow off his windshield. On the spot, Anderson made a drawing in her sketchbook of a device consisting of a lever that "activated a swinging arm that mechanically swept off the ice and snow" from the windshield. She got her patent the following year; ten years later windshield wipers were standard equipment on automobiles.

Sojourner Mars Rover *(above right) and artist's impression of a later Rover,* the Curiosity Rover *(right)*

Donna Shirley

Invention: *Sojourner Mars Rover*

Story: In 1991 Shirley, an aerospace engineer, was appointed manager of NASA's Mars Explorer Program. Her team was charged with developing the rover vehicle that would go to Mars aboard the unmanned *Pathfinder* spacecraft. The rover was to be about the size of a pickup truck, with rockets to blast it off the surface of Mars and back to the *Pathfinder* for its return to Earth. They'd already built a one-eighth-scale prototype; now they were using it to design the full-scale rover. There was just one problem: Sending a truck-sized rover to Mars and then returning it to Earth was too expensive. The craft only had a budget of $25 million. That may seem like a lot but, says Shirley, "for a planetary spacecraft it's incredibly cheap; $25 million would pay for a few commercials for the Super Bowl."

That's when Shirley got the

Popular pizza topping in Brazil: green peas.

idea that saved the mission. "While her male colleagues were ready to scrap the whole project, Shirley suggested that perhaps size was not that important," Ethlie Vare writes in *Patently Female*. "Could not the prototype of the rover become the vehicle itself?" It could and it did: On July 4, 1997, the *Sojourner Rover* landed on Mars and began exploring the surface. It's going to be there a while, too—the rockets that were supposed to send it home got cut from the budget.

Laura Scudder

Invention: Potato chip bag

Story: Before a Southern California businesswoman named Laura Scudder came along in the mid-1920s, potato chips were sold in bulk in large barrels. When you bought chips at the store, the grocer scooped them out of the barrel and into an ordinary paper bag. If you got your chips from the bottom of the barrel, they were usually broken and stale.

It was Scudder who hit on the idea of taking wax paper and ironing it on three sides to make a bag, then filling it with potato chips and ironing the fourth side to make an airtight pouch that would keep the chips fresh until they were eaten. Scudder's self-serve, stay-fresh bags were instrumental in turning potato chips from an occasional treat into a snack food staple.

Martha Coston

Invention: Signal flare

Story: Martha Hunt was only 14 when she eloped with a Philadelphia engineer named Benjamin Coston...and only 21 when he died bankrupt in 1848, leaving her destitute with four small children. Not long after his death she found something interesting among his possessions: a prototype for a signal flare.

She hoped that if it worked, she could patent it and use it to restore her family's fortunes. But it didn't—so Martha started over from scratch, and spent nearly 10 years perfecting a system of red, white, and green "Pyrotechnic Night Signals" that would enable naval ships to communicate by color codes over great distances at night. (Remember, this was before the invention of two-way radio.) The U.S. Navy bought hundreds of sets of flares and used them extensively during the Civil War. They are credited with helping maintain the Union blockade of Confederate ports, and also with saving the lives of countless shipwreck victims after the war.

Rommy Revson

Invention: Scünci

Story: In 1987 Revson was divorced from Revlon cosmetics heir John Revson, and the divorce settlement was so bad that she had to find a job to support herself. Appearances count, so she had her hair bleached before she started applying for jobs. Big mistake—the chemicals damaged her hair to the point that "it was coming off in handfuls," Revson remembers. She decided the only thing to do was pull her hair back into a ponytail, but it was so brittle that she couldn't use rubber bands. She came up with something better: an elastic band covered with soft fabric.

So did Revson ever get around to applying for a job? Who knows—she decided to patent her ponytail holder instead, naming it the Scünci after her Lhasa Apso puppy. Today they're better known as "scrunchies," and at last count Revson has sold more than two billion of them.

The Year of Living Festively

On page 152 we took you to some of the world's weirdest festivals. You're not done yet!

Burning the Man in Nevada

August

Festival: Burning Man, Nevada

Description: Each year during the week before Labor Day, nearly 50,000 people gather in the Black Rock Desert, a flat tract of fine sand 80 miles north of Reno. But don't expect to be able to buy supplies there; the only things for sale at Burning Man are coffee and bags of ice, both available at what's known as "Center Camp." Everything else—food, water, fuel, tents—you have to bring yourself.

You'll also need some very sturdy tent poles to keep your homestead secure during one of the inevitable dust storms and wind gusts that often blow over 50 mph. And during the day, the temperature regularly tops 100°F; at night, it can drop down to the 30s. Why put yourself through all of that? To see mechanical fire-breathing dragons lurch by on hydraulic legs, or take a ride on a life-size clipper ship sailing over the sand, or just get to know the thousands of artists, performers, and ordinary people who make Burning Man an annual pilgrimage. Plus there are 24-hour dance parties, live music from all over the world, a Thunderdome (just like the one from Mad Max), and the ceremonial burning of the 40-foot-tall Man on Saturday night.

History: In 1986 two friends from San Francisco, Larry Harvey and Jerry James, went to a nearby beach and built an 8-foot-tall wooden man—and a wooden dog—and burned them. Inspired by the crowd that had gathered to watch their "spontaneous act of radical self-expression," they did it again the following year. More people came. The next year, even more people came. Finally, it got too big for the beach. After a long search, in 1991 the organizers moved the event to the Black Rock Desert.

Don't miss: The chance to take part in Burning Man's "gifting society." Bring extra trinkets and supplies to give away to other attendees.

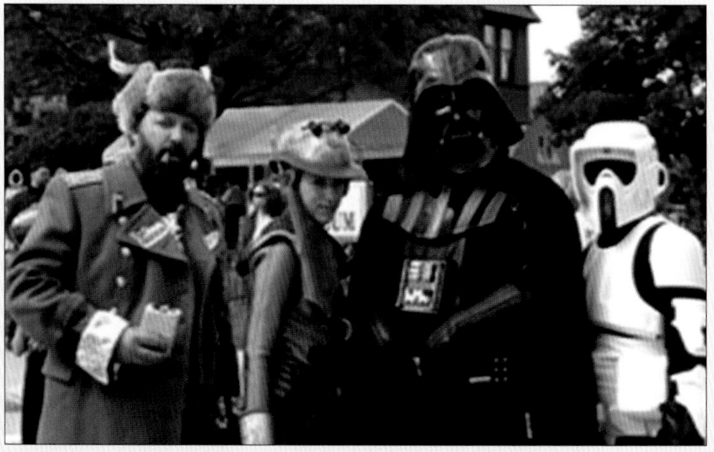

Joining the dark side in Wisconsin

September

Festival: Sputnikfest, Wisconsin

Description: Enjoy the fried cheese, cold beer, and friendly people dressed as big-eyed aliens, and see local celebrities get soaked in the "Splashdown" dunk tank.

The iVoodoo application lets you use your iPhone as a voodoo doll.

History: Around 5:30 in the morning on September 5, 1962, hundreds of early risers in northern Wisconsin reported a spectacular sight: dozens of bright, burning objects streaking through the clear dawn sky. Around the same time, two patrolmen in the town of Manitowoc noticed a strange object in the middle of a street: a 20-pound chunk of metal that had embedded itself in the pavement. They went to remove it—but it was too hot to touch. It turned out to be a piece of *Sputnik IV*, a Russian satellite that had gone off course shortly after it was launched two years earlier, and had finally disintegrated in the skies over Wisconsin. In 2008 the town decided to turn the odd incident into a reason for a celebration—and Sputnikfest was born.

Don't miss: The tinfoil-suit fashion show, the "Miss Space Debris" beauty contest, and for the kids, the Alien Autopsy Room.

October

Festival: Phuket Vegetarian Festival, Thailand

Description: Squeamish? Then stay far, far away from this festival. Every autumn, Chinese and Thai religious devotees called *Mah Song* parade through Phuket's streets in trance-like states, their bodies pierced with, among other things, bicycle wheels, saw blades, and metal skewers of varying sizes—all protruding into and out of their arms, legs, noses, lips, ears, and eyebrows. There's also hot-coal firewalking and a ladder made of sharpened blades. Why? The Mah Song believe that those who are truly devoted feel little, if any, pain, and aren't left with scars. You don't have to participate in the self-mutilation, but like the Mah Song, you're asked to adhere to a vegetarian diet all week. Luckily, that's not hard because the festival's food is excellent.

Getting poked in Phuket

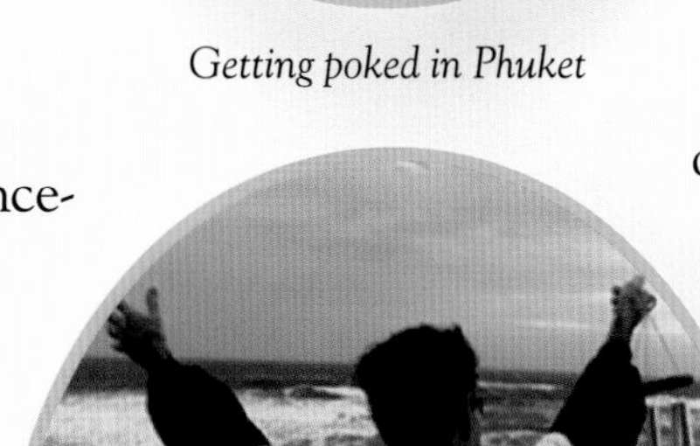

Taking in the silent symphony in New Jersey

History: In the 1820s, when Phuket tin miners and their families were suffering from a malaria epidemic, a traveling opera company from China came to the area. The singers also caught malaria, but for 10 days, they ate nothing but vegetables and performed religious ceremonies. To the surprise of the miners, the performers recovered from the illness much more quickly than the locals did. The opera singers taught the rituals to the townspeople, and within a year the malaria epidemic had ceased. The festival keeps the tradition alive today, though it's unclear how the self-mutilation became part of the festivities.

Don't miss: The ear-plug vendors. In addition to being one of the world's most unusual festivals, it's also one of the loudest. Drums and firecrackers are sounded all week long to scare away evil spirits.

November

Festival: The Quiet Festival, New Jersey

Description: One of the activities at this low-key festival in Ocean City: hearing a pin drop. You can also try your hand at a group whispering session, enter a yawn-off, and take as many naps as you like. It's one of the smallest and most obscure festivals in the world (only a few dozen people usually participate), and also offers silent movies, a sign-language choir, and mimes.

History: "I've been tired for about 40 years now," says Mark Soifer, 72, who organized the first Quiet Festival for stressed-out people in 1989. "I feel uniquely qualified to represent the millions of tired folks in this nation and the world." By day, Soifer works as Ocean City's publicist, but he's also the president of the National Association of Tired People (NAP), which sponsors the event.

Don't miss: The "windchime symphony."

December

Festival: Night of the Radishes, Mexico

Description: Each December 23rd, this pre-Christmas celebration features the most elaborate radish sculptures in the world. Skilled artisans gather in Oaxaca City for La Noche de Rábanos to show off their pink-and-white sculptures of saints, Nativity scenes, conquistadors, and animals. And these are no ordinary radishes, but giant ones, some measuring 1½ feet long and weighing seven pounds. The festival lasts only one night because after that, the artwork starts to rot.

History: Spanish monks brought radishes to Mexico in the 16th century and encouraged the locals to grow them—and also to carve them. The elaborate veggie sculptures have been a tradition ever since. The Night of the Radishes officially began in 1897, thanks to Oaxaca's mayor, Francisco Vasconcelos Flores, who wanted to preserve this unique cultural heritage (and sell more radishes to tourists).

Don't miss: After the judging has ended and a champion radish artist has been named, fireworks light up the sky.

Welcome Home!

Congratulations! Now that you've dodged camel spit in Turkey, splattered your friends with oranges in Italy, devoured fried lamb testicles in New Zealand, danced around the Maypole in Scotland, run around like a chicken with your head cut off in Colorado, wrestled toe to toe in England, frolicked in the mud in South Korea, sailed on a ship through the Nevada desert, performed an alien autopsy in Wisconsin, traversed hot coals in Thailand, made windchime music in New Jersey, and sculpted a radish saint in Mexico, you can take a month or two off.

Or...you could catch a quick flight to Russia and participate in a truly surreal New Year's party: At Lake Baikal, the world's deepest lake, a hole is cut into the ice and divers haul the New Year Tree more than 100 feet below the surface. After you get your picture taken with Russian folk heroes Father Frost and the Ice Maiden, you plunge into the depths where you'll celebrate the night SCUBA-dancing among the sparkling lights of the New Year Tree. Then you can dry off, warm up, up, fly home...and take that well-deserved sabbatical.

Ravishing radishes in Mexico

Vivien Leigh hated kissing Clark Gable while filming *Gone With the Wind*. She said he had bad breath.

Ironic, Isn't It?

More of life's little ironies.

Criminal Irony

- The inmates at the prison in Concord, New Hampshire, spend their days making the state's license plates, which bear the motto LIVE FREE OR DIE.
- Twenty-six-year-old Samuel Worlin Moore was arrested for attempted armed robbery in Long Beach, California. Witnesses were able to ID him because of the distinctive tattoo on his arm. It read "Not Guilty."

Governmental Irony

Katherine Harris

Florida's secretary of state, Katherine Harris, became famous during the 2000 presidential election as the person in charge of the disputed ballot count. In the 2004 local election in her hometown of Longboat Key, Florida, she was informed that her vote would not be counted because she had turned in an invalid ballot. (She forgot to sign it.)

Environmental Irony

In October 2005, Greenpeace's flagship, *Rainbow Warrior II*, was studying the effects of global warming on a fragile underwater coral reef in the Philippines when it accidentally ran aground on the reef, causing it significant damage. The environmental organization was fined 384,000 pesos ($6,800).

Irony Goes "Poof!"

- In 1999 the Mississippi state capitol in Jackson put up an artificial Christmas tree instead of a real one, out of concern for the fire hazard posed by real trees. The artificial tree promptly caught fire, forcing the evacuation of the building.

Irony in the Court

- In 2000 a branch fell off a tree in Nevada City, California, and struck a power line, cutting off power to the town for more than 30 minutes. The outage delayed the courtroom trial of the Pacific Gas & Electric Company, which was charged with "failing to trim vegetation around power lines."
- Love Your Neighbor Corp. of Michigan sued Love Thy Neighbor Fund of Florida for trademark infringement.

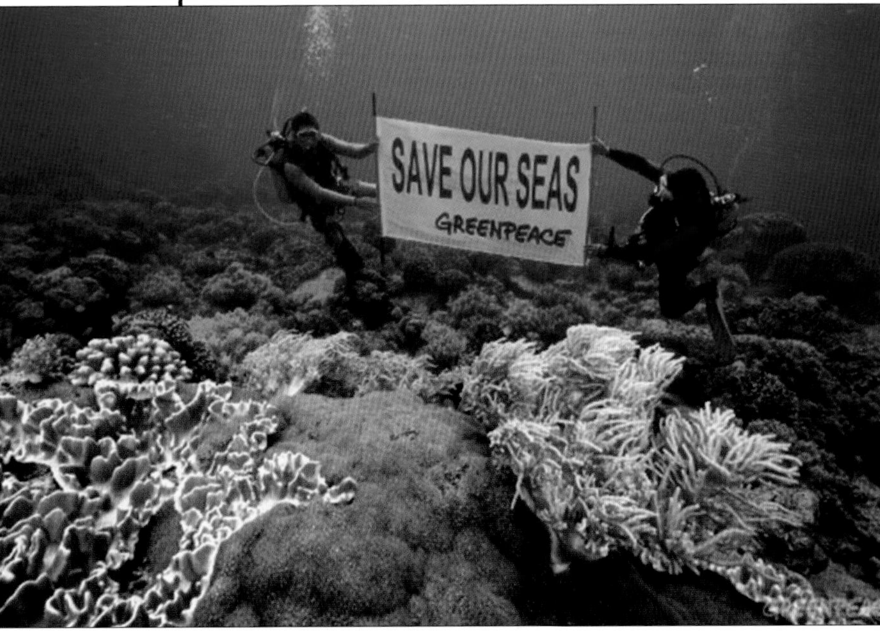

Greenpeace members putting up a sign for the fish

In Iceland, tipping at a restaurant is considered an insult.

Why So Blue, Crater Lake?

Here's the story of an enormous volcano that blew its top, leaving behind one of the most beautiful, other-worldly places on earth: Crater Lake National Park—home of the planet's bluest water.

What Goes Up...

Rising roughly 12,000 feet above sea level, Mount Mazama wasn't the highest of the Cascades volcanoes. Its peak fell slightly short of Mount Shasta (to the south in California) and Mount Ranier (to the north in Washington). But in terms of pure mountainous girth, Mazama was the undisputed heavyweight champion of the Pacific Northwest. For more than 400,000 years, the composite volcano grew layer by layer in spits and spurts over the top of a giant subterranean magma chamber in what is today southern Oregon. Mild eruptions, lava flows, gassy vents, and glaciation created a rugged landscape marked by frequent change. The biggest change occurred just 7,700 years ago (a mere blip on the geologic time scale). Mount Mazama erupted in spectacular fashion. Ten cubic miles of ash and lava shot 30 miles into the sky.

Pyroclastic flows laid waste to entire pine forests. One lava flow carved out 40 miles of what later became the Rogue River. Ash covered the ground as far away as Nebraska. The eruption ranks as a VEI 7, or "super-colossal," on the USGS's Volcanic Explosivity Index. (The scale only goes up to 8.) Put into perspective, Mazama's eruption was 42 times stronger than Mount St. Helens' blowup in 1980. Geologists believe it to be the most violent Cascades eruption of the past million years.

...Must Come Down

Because Mount Mazama was so wide, after all the lava emptied from the chamber, there was nothing left to hold up the mountain. Result: Several million tons of earth, rock, and ash collapsed into the chamber. When the dust cleared, what had been a mountain was now a mountain-sized hole. The volcanic *caldera* formed a nearly perfect circle six miles wide and 4,000 feet deep. Over the next few centuries, the volcanic activity slowly subsided while the caldera steadily filled up with snow and rain. Crater Lake was born.

Eruption of Mount Mazama

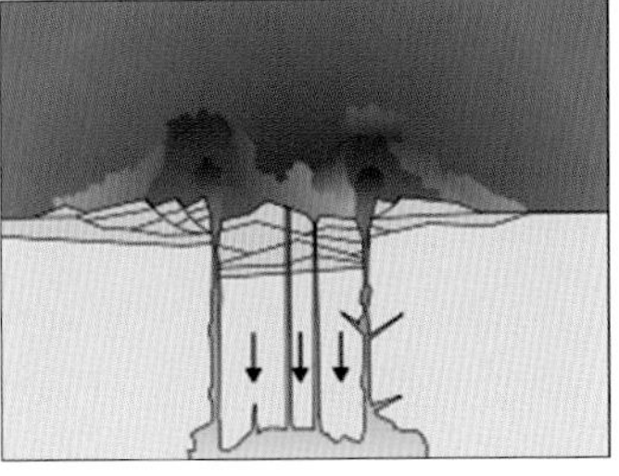

Caldera collapse

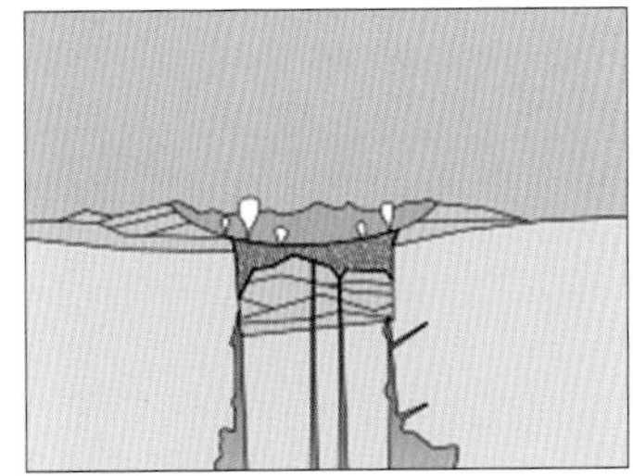

Steam explosions

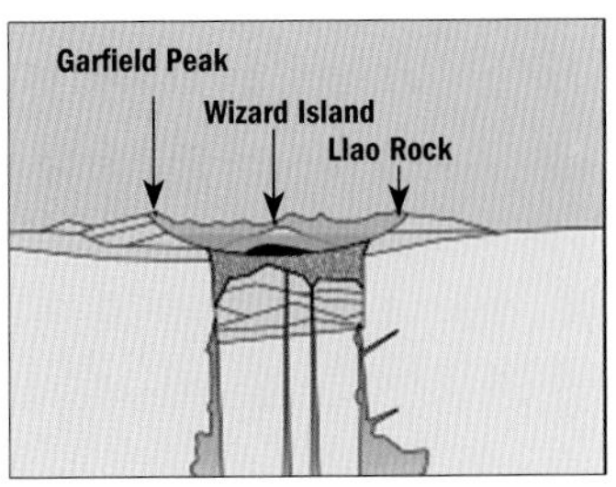

Crater Lake today

Clash of the Titans

Because the eruption occurred so recently (in terms of the earth's history), there were witnesses. The Klamath and Modoc Indians both lived nearby, and the mountain blast shook them to the core. The Klamaths' name for Mazama was *Moy-Yaina* ("Big Mountain"). The Indians, believing the lake to be sacred ground, also kept its existence a secret from white settlers. A group of gold prospectors finally discovered the lake by accident in 1853. Struck by its beauty, they spread the word to others. Before long, curious adventurers made the harsh journey through thick forests, across hardened lava fields, and up the steep terrain to see it for themselves.

The Father of Crater Lake

One such adventurer was William Gladstone Steel, who made it to the southwestern part of the rim (called Discovery Point) in 1885. He was amazed:

> All the ingenuity of nature seems to have been exerted to the fullest capacity to build one grand awe-inspiring temple the likes of which the world has never seen before.

Rising from 1,000 to 2,000 feet above the shore, the rim of Crater Lake offers incredible views. The first sight to strike Steel (and most visitors) was the crystal-clear blue water. It was bluer than the sky. Across the lake, the vertical cliffs of the rim were also colorful, marked by towering castles of orange lava deposits, bright yellow lichen, white speckles of snow, and forests of evergreen trees. On a calm day glassy reflections on the water create abstract patterns of the shore six miles away.

Steel was also taken by Crater Lake's other prominent feature, a conical island that rises more than 700 feet out of the southwestern portion of the lake. It's also covered with volcanic rock and forests of pines, fir, and hemlock. Reminding Steel of a sorcerer's cap, he named it Wizard Island. Over time, Steel named several more of Crater Lake's features, including Llao Rock and Skell Head. And he was the one who called the ex-mountain "Mazama," the name of his mountaineering club.

Crater Lake panorama, with a view of Wizard Island

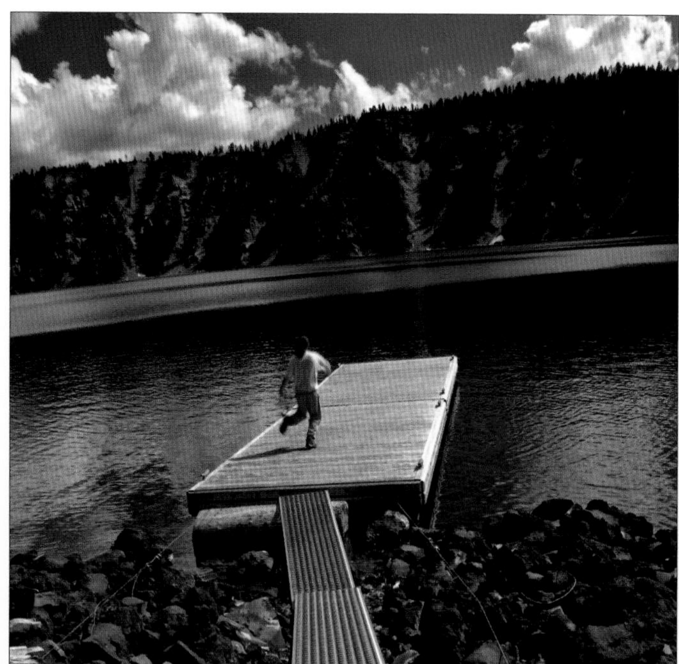

One of Uncle John's writers frolicking on Wizard Island

A Park is Born

Steel became Crater Lake's biggest advocate. He brought in tourists, scientists, surveyors, and developers. In 1886 he hired Clarence Dutton of the United States Geological Survey to measure the lake's depth, who wrote:

> As the visitor reaches the brink of the cliff, he suddenly sees below him an expanse of ultramarine blue of a richness and intensity which he has probably never seen before, and will not be likely to see again.

Steel and Dutton knew the lake was deep, but it wasn't until they lowered a piano wire at various points along the surface that they grasped just how deep: nearly 2,000 feet.

Steel was instrumental in convincing President Theodore Roosevelt to designate the area as the sixth U.S. national park in 1902. However, if Steel had gotten his way, there would have been a lot of development there: He wanted to build an elevator to take visitors from the top of the rim to the shore, and a bridge to Wizard Island. His colleagues at the National Park Service wanted to keep the area pristine, though, and Steel lasted only three years as Crater Lake's superintendent before he was ousted. Today, there is minimal evidence of man's impact at the park.

A Lake Like No Other

Crater Lake wears its geologic past on its sleeves. You can actually look at the inside of a sleeping volcano. Here's some of the science and superlatives of the "Gem of the Cascades."

- **That's deep.** Modern sonar readings show that Dutton was pretty close to the mark. The lowest part of the lake bed is 1,949 feet beneath the surface. That ranks Crater Lake as the deepest lake in the United States, and the ninth deepest on earth. If the Empire State Building were lowered into the lake (not counting for water displacement), by the time the ground floor reached the bottom, the top of the spire would be 500 feet below the surface.
- **A perfect balance.** Most of the world's lakes are fed by streams and rivers, and drain into streams and rivers. Crater Lake does neither. It is filled solely by precipitation. (Average rainfall per year: 66 inches. Average snowfall: 44 feet.) The lake loses its water through evaporation (and to a lesser extent, by seepage into the porous rock). These processes—precipitation and evaporation—balance each other out so well at Crater Lake that the surface rises and falls only by a few feet every century. Plus, because of Crater Lake's great depth, the surface rarely freezes.
- **I can see clearly now.** Crater Lake contains what may be the clearest, purest water known to exist. In most lakes that boast clear water, you can see about 16 feet below the surface in broad daylight. But in Crater Lake, it's possible to see to depths of more than 100 feet. The deepest scientific measurement has been 142 feet, a world record. Several factors contribute to the lake's clarity: Because no rivers run into it, no silt gets deposited. There's little pollution because of Crater Lake's remoteness (the nearest big cities—Portland, San Francisco, and Reno—are each hundreds of miles away). There are also very few organic materials or dissolved minerals in the water, and the human impact around and on the lake is minimal.

It costs the U.S. Treasury 1.73¢ to make and distribute a penny.

- **The blues.** How can the water be so clear—and so blue—at the same time? Actually, it's so blue because it's so clear...and so deep. Here's how it works: As sunlight penetrates the lake, it absorbs all the colors of visible light except for blue, which it reflects back. The deeper and clearer the water, the more blue gets reflected.
- **New growth.** Wizard Island is one of two new volcanoes that have risen out of Mazama's caldera (the other is still underwater). At barely 6,000 years old, the island is very young, yet many of the trees that grow on it are very old, some more than 800 years.
- **Phantom ship.** Mazama's demise unearthed some very old rock formations, including Crater Lake's other island, Phantom Ship. This spire of 400,000-year-old andesite lava was left behind by an ancient eruption. When viewed from the rim, the island looks like an old sailing ship, hence the name. The rocky spires rise 163 feet above the surface; the island itself is about 300 feet long. Clinging to the rocks are an astounding seven species of trees.
- **Going down.** There have been a few scientific expeditions—manned and unmanned—to see what lies at the bottom of Crater Lake. Scientists have learned that the area is still active—steam vents enter the water at great depths. That allows primitive life-forms to exist more than 1,000 feet below the surface, which actually receives faint bits of sunlight on clear days. But perhaps the biggest surprise came at depths of 100 to 460 feet along the lake walls—forests of moss several stories thick.

The Future of Crater Lake

Will the volcano erupt again? Most likely. The constant change that shaped the region is still in flux. What scientists don't know is how much magma—if any—still remains in the chamber, and just how much pressure is building up. Future activity is likely to happen just east of the lake, where the geologic "hot spot" now lies. What's more worrisome is the chance of a large earthquake causing landslides and huge waves on the surface. A cataclysmic seismic event could rupture the rim wall and cause the lake to drain, creating a flood of 4.6 trillion gallons of water. But for now, Mazama remains at rest.

Phantom Ship at Crater Lake

"Paging Mr. Post"

The funeral business (known as "the dismal trade" in the 18th century) necessarily deals with concepts that many people find distasteful. That led to the evolution of a unique set of euphemisms in the death biz.

- **Passed into the arms of God.** Dead. Other euphemisms: *passed away, gone to meet his/her Maker, expired, deceased.*
- **Temporary preservation.** Embalming—the common treatment of dead bodies in which bodily fluids are replaced with preservative fluid. Other euphemisms: *sanitary treatment, hygienic treatment.*
- **Grief therapy.** The "therapeutic" effect of having an expensive funeral "viewing."
- **Burn and scatter.** Slang for services that scatter cremated remains at sea. Also known as *bake and shake.*
- **Casket coach.** Hearse.
- **Consigned to earth.** Buried.
- **Pre-need sales.** Funeral services sold to someone who hasn't died yet.
- **Corpse cooler.** A specialized coffin with a window, once used to preserve the body for viewing. An ice compartment kept the corpse cool.

A cremains container

- **Interment space.** A grave. Used in phrases such as opening the interment space (digging the grave) and closing the interment space (filling the grave).
- **Cremains.** Cremated remains; ashes.
- **Babyland.** The part of a cemetery reserved for small children and infants.
- **Slumber room.** The room in which the loved one's body is displayed.
- **Memorial park.** Cemetery.
- **Lawn-type cemetery.** A cemetery that bans headstones in favor of ground markers, allowing caretakers to simply mow the lawn rather than trim each grave by hand.
- **Funeral director.** Undertaker.
- **O-sign.** A dead body sometimes displays what hospital workers call the "O-sign," meaning the mouth is hanging open, forming an "O."
- The **"Q-sign"** is the same—but with the tongue hanging out.

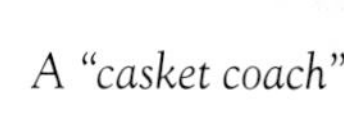

A "casket coach"

Mosquitoes hibernate.

- **Protective caskets.** Coffin sealed with rubber gaskets to keep out bugs and other invaders. Unfortunately, methane gas has been known to build up inside such caskets, causing them to explode and spew out their contents. This prompted the introduction of *burping caskets* that allow gas to escape.
- **Grief counselor.** Mortuary salesperson.
- **Mr. Post.** Morgue attendant. Used by many hospitals to page the morgue when a body has to be removed from a room.
- **Nose squeezer.** Flat-topped coffin.
- **Beautiful memory picture.** An embalmed body displayed in an expensive casket.
- **Body.** This term for a dead person is generally discouraged, along with *corpse*. Preferred: the dead person's name, or *remains*.

The internment space awaits you…

- **Plantings.** Graves.
- **Selection room.** Room in which buyers look at displayed caskets. This term replaces *back room*, *showroom*, *casket room*.
- **Companion space.** An over/under grave set for husband-and-wife couples; one body is placed deep in the ground and the second buried above it.

Close Encounters

Does alien life exist? These people sure think so.

"It was the darnedest thing I've ever seen. It was big, it was very bright, it changed colors, and it was about the size of the moon. We watched it for ten minutes, but none of us could figure out what it was. One thing's for sure, I'll never make fun of people who say they've seen unidentified objects in the sky. If I become president, I'll make every piece of information this country has about UFO sightings available to the public and the scientists."

—Jimmy Carter, 1976, who was elected, but never released the UFO info

"I certainly believe in aliens in space. They may not look like us, but I have very strong feelings that they have advanced beyond our mental capabilities....I think some highly secret government UFO investigations are going on that we don't know about—and probably never will unless the Air Force discloses them."

—Barry Goldwater

"At no time when the astronauts were in space were they alone: There was a constant surveillance by UFOs."

—Scott Carpenter, who photographed a UFO while in orbit in 1962. NASA has not released the photo.

"Since, in the long run, every planetary society will be endangered by impacts from space, every surviving civilization is obliged to become spacefaring—not because of exploratory or romantic zeal, but for the most practical reason imaginable: staying alive."

—Carl Sagan

"My own present opinion, based on two years of careful study, is that UFOs are probably extraterrestrial devices engaged in something that might very tentatively be termed 'surveillance.'"

—Dr. James E. McDonald, 1968, speaking to Congress

"It followed us during half of our orbit. We observed it on the light side, and when we entered the shadow side, it disappeared completely. It was an engineered structure, made from some type of metal, approximately 40 meters long with inner hulls. The object was narrow here and wider here, and inside there were openings. Some places had projections like small wings. The object stayed very close to us. We photographed it, and our photos showed it to be 23 to 28 meters away."

—Cosmonaut Victor Afanasyev, who saw a UFO on his way to the *Solyut* 6 space station in 1979. His photos have never been made public.

Photograph of an alleged UFO in New Jersey, July 31, 1952

The first draft of John Steinbeck's *Of Mice and Men* was eaten by his dog.

"The unidentified craft appeared to take efficient controlled evasive action."

—FBI Memo, describing chase of a UFO over the North Sea, 1947

"I think that we all know that we're not alone in the universe. I can't imagine that we are the only intelligent biological life form out there. I'm a little less sure in my 50s than I was in my late 20s whether we're actually ever going to find out."

—Steven Spielberg

"People ask if there is life out there, but why is it that the only people who get abducted are morons? Why would intelligent life with advanced technology come out to Earth and pick out a drunk idiot that nobody believes in the first place?"

—Michael Stoneman

More of Ol' Jay's Brainteasers

Here we go again. Answers are on page 287.

1. The Runaround

Two-eff Jeff was sitting in a chair in the middle of the room. One-eff Jef walked up and said, "I'll bet you a dollar that before I run around your chair three times, you'll get up. And I promise I won't push you or throw things at you. When you get up, it will be by choice." Two-eff Jeff took the bet, thinking he'd make an easy dollar. But it was soon obvious that One-eff Jef had won. Why?

2. Feeling Flat

Thom drove all the way from Crappo, Maryland, to Flushing, New York, without realizing his car had a flat tire, but arrived safely with four fully inflated tires. How?

3. A Mother's Gift

Brian challenged us with this classic riddle:

Black as night I'll always be,
Until my mother smothers me.
Then clear as ice I will become
In the rough.
Thank you, Mum!

What am I?

4. Coffee Delivery

Trying to figure out the answers to these questions tired us out, but then along came Dr. Dollison with a large pot of freshly brewed coffee. Yay! "I can give you one gallon," he said. "But you'll have to measure it out yourselves." Then he handed us a three-gallon bucket and a five-gallon bucket. As we were sitting there dumbfounded, Kim told us not to worry—she'd do it. How?

Capital-ism

Small towns are flush with pride about their contributions to the world. Here are some places that proudly proclaim themselves "World Capitals."

Sock Capital of the World

Town: Fort Payne, Alabama

Story: There are more than 150 sock mills in the Fort Payne area. Half the local population—6,000 people—produces 12 million pairs of socks each week. It's estimated that one out of every four feet in America is dressed in a Fort Payne sock.

Corn Capital of the World

Town: Olivia, Minnesota

Story: Olivia has more corn seed research facilities and processing plants than any other place on earth, and it celebrated that fact in 1973 by erecting a 50-foot-tall statue of a cornstalk. In 2003 the Minnesota senate passed a resolution making Olivia's claim to the world title official. But don't confuse Olivia with its corny rival, Constantine, Michigan, which grows 20 percent of the nation's seed corn. In 2003 the Michigan legislature proclaimed Constantine the "Seed Corn Capital of the World."

Ear Muff Capital of the World

Town: Farmington, Maine

Story: Chester Greenwood invented earmuffs here in 1873 (he was 15 years old). He subsequently opened a factory in Farmington, and business took off when he won a contract to supply them to World War I soldiers. Farmington celebrates Greenwood with a parade on the first Saturday of every December. Everyone and everything, including pets and police cars, wears earmuffs.

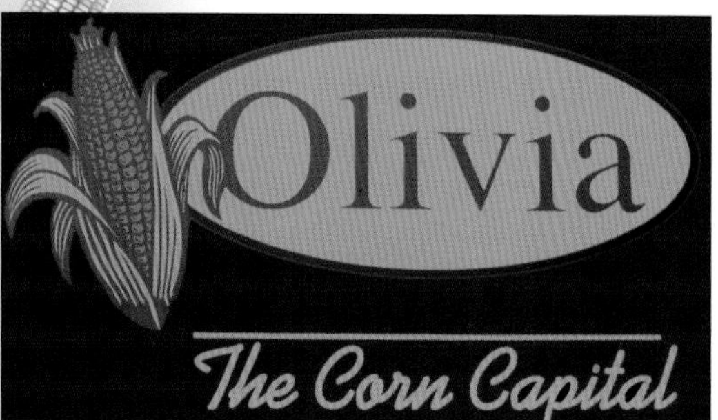

Costume Jewelry Capital of the World

Town: Providence, Rhode Island

Story: In 1794 a Providence resident named Nehemiah Dodge developed a simple, low-cost method of gold-plating. Result: a pirate's booty in expensive-looking jewelry that almost anyone could afford. Today there are more than 1,000 costume jewelry plants in Rhode Island, most of them in Providence.

Three people die annually from using their tongue to check if a battery works.

The pride of Hidalgo

Casket Capital of the World

Town: Batesville, Indiana

Story: Since 1884, the town has been home to Batesville Casket, the country's most prolific coffin manufacturer. (The plant churns out one casket every 53 seconds.) The town built around death has a lot of life, including an annual Raspberry Festival and a Music & Arts Festival…but no Casket Festival.

Killer Bee Capital of the World

Town: Hidalgo, Texas

Story: Killer bees emerged in the 1950s when some African bees escaped from a South American lab and bred with the local bees, creating a volatile spawn that migrated north. In 1990 they crossed into the United States through Hidalgo. Did the town flee in horror? Nope. They used it to promote tourism. Hidalgo spent $20,000 to build the "World's Largest Killer Bee," a 10-foot-tall, full-color bee in the center of town.

Cow Chip Throwing Capital of the World

Town: Beaver, Oklahoma

Story: The World Championship Cow Chip Throw is held here every April. The town's registered trademark: King Cow Chip, a cartoon of a dried pile of cow poop wearing a crown.

Spinach Capital of the World

Town: Alma, Arkansas

Story: The Allen Canning Company, based in Alma, cans 65 percent of all American canned spinach—60 million pounds a year—so in 1987, Alma proclaimed itself the Spinach Capital of the World. Their claim was challenged by Crystal Springs, Texas, which said it already was the Spinach Capital, and had been since 1937, when Del Monte opened a spinach canning plant there. Proof: they have a statue of Popeye in the town square. Not to be outdone, Alma built its own Popeye.

Alternative Energy

A 2006 study found that the average American walks about 900 miles a year. Another study found that Americans drink an average of 22 gallons of beer a year. That means that, on average, Americans get about 41 miles per gallon.

Parasites account for 0.01% of your weight.

Bad Musicals

Plenty of weird concepts make it to the Broadway stage. Some are really successful. Not these.

Musical: *Rockabye Hamlet* (1976)

Total Performances: 7

Story: Adolescent angst and rebellion are major themes in rock music—and in Shakespeare's *Hamlet*. So that would make *Hamlet* the perfect inspiration for a rock musical, right? Wrong. Originally written as a radio play (under the title *Kronberg: 1582*), *Rockabye Hamlet* hit Broadway in 1976 with hundreds of flashing lights and an onstage band. Writers followed Shakespeare's storyline but abandoned his dialogue. They opted instead for lines like the one Laertes sings to Polonius: "Good son, you return to France/Keep your divinity inside your pants."

Notable Song: "The Rosencrantz and Guildenstern Boogie."

2014 poster for the revival of Rockabye Hamlet

Cover art for the audio recording of Bring Back Birdie

Musical: *Carrie* (1988)

Total Performances: 5

Story: Based on Stephen King's gory novel about a telekinetic teenager who wreaks havoc at her high school prom, *Carrie* was full of bad taste and bad ideas. It's regarded by many critics as the biggest flop (it lost $8 million) and worst musical of all time:

- *Newsday* called *Carrie* "stupendously, fabulously terrible. Ineptly conceived, sleazy, irrational from moment to moment, it stretches way beyond bad to mythic lousiness."
- *The Washington Post* likened it to "a reproduction of 'The Last Supper' made entirely out of broken bottles. You can't help marveling at the lengths to which someone went to make it."

Notable Songs: Carrie's mother sings about being sexually molested in "I Remember How Those Boys Could Dance," and Carrie serenades a hairbrush in "I'm Not Alone."

They tried it again: Hilary Cole as Carrie in a 2013 revival of Carrie.

Musical: *Bring Back Birdie* (1981)

Total Performances: 4

Story: A sequel to the 1961 hit *Bye Bye Birdie*. In the original, teen idol Conrad Birdie sings a farewell concert and kisses a lucky girl before joining the

Cold feet? Fewer than 5% of U.S. weddings take place in January.

military (it was inspired by Elvis Presley being drafted in the 1950s). *Bring Back Birdie* takes place 20 years later and couldn't have been further from the real Elvis story—Birdie has settled down as mayor of a small town when somebody talks him into making a comeback. The only problem: Audiences didn't come back.

Notable Moment: One night during the show's brief run, when actor Donald O'Connor forgot the words to a song, he told the band, "You sing it. I hate this song anyway," and walked off stage.

Musical: *Breakfast at Tiffany's* (1966)

Total Performances: 0 (Closed in previews)

Story: It had the highest advance sales of any show in 1966, primarily because of its cast—TV stars Mary Tyler Moore and Richard Chamberlain—but also because audiences expected a light, bouncy stage version of the popular movie. Unfortunately, they got a musical more like Truman Capote's original novella: dark and tragic. After a disastrous trial run, playwright Edward Albee was hired to rewrite the script. He did little to improve it, removing nearly all the jokes and making Moore's character a figment of Chamberlain's imagination. Audiences were so confused that they openly talked to and questioned the actors on stage. The show ran for four preview performances before producer David Merrick announced he was closing it immediately to save theatergoers from "an excruciatingly boring evening."

Musical: *Via Galactica* (1972)

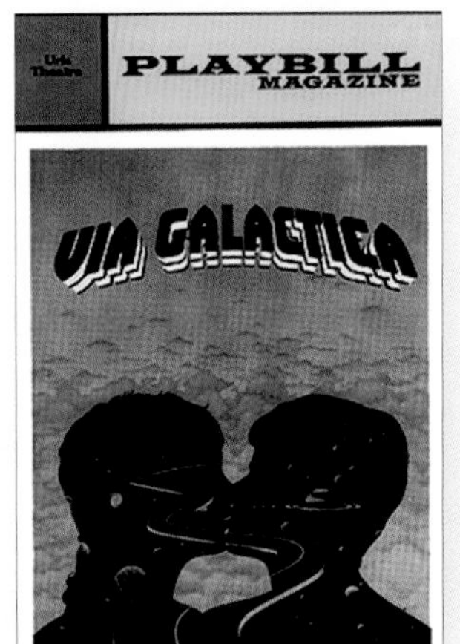

Total Performances: 7

Story: A band of hippies (led by Raul Julia) travel through outer space on an asteroid in the year 2972, searching for an uninhabited planet on which to settle "New Jerusalem." The weightlessness of space was simulated by actors jumping on trampolines for the entire show. A rock score would have suited the 1970s counterculture themes, but for some reason songwriters Christopher Gore and Galt McDermot chose country music.

Notable Name: The original title for the show was *Up!*, but producers changed it because it was being staged at the Uris Theatre and the marquee would have read "*Up!* Uris."

Random Originnnnnnnnnnn

John Wallis, a mathematics professor at Oxford University, was creating a text book called *Arithmetica Infinitorum* in 1655, and needed a symbol to represent a number so high that it could not be counted. He came up with this: ∞ Historians believe that Wallis simply altered the Roman numeral M (1,000), which was sometimes used to mean "many."

On September 11, 2002, New York's winning lottery numbers were 9-1-1.

Let Me Write Sign— I Good Speak English

Here are some actual signs, menu entries, and assorted notices from around the world.

- ***At a religious site in Burma:*** "Foot Wearing Prohibited"
- ***In a Japanese bowling alley:*** "Do you like bowling? Let's play bowling. Breaking down the pins and getting hot communication."
- ***On a tank in a pet shop in China:*** "Letting Them Turtle"
- ***In Saudi Arabia:*** "No slaughtering sheep at the beach"
- ***At a shop in Thailand:*** "Mr. J's Condoms (Homemade). 20 Years Guarantee."
- ***A street sign in Kerala, India:*** "GO SLOW: Accident Porn Area"
- ***At the Great Wall of China:*** "If you have or brain disease, please ascend the Great Wall according to your capability."
- ***Outside a restaurant in Thailand:*** "Our Food is Guaranteed to Not Cause Pregnancy."
- ***In a clothing store in India:*** "The Proceeds gose to women who made all those Stuff."
- ***On a menu in Cairo:*** "Half Gilled Chicken and Herpes"

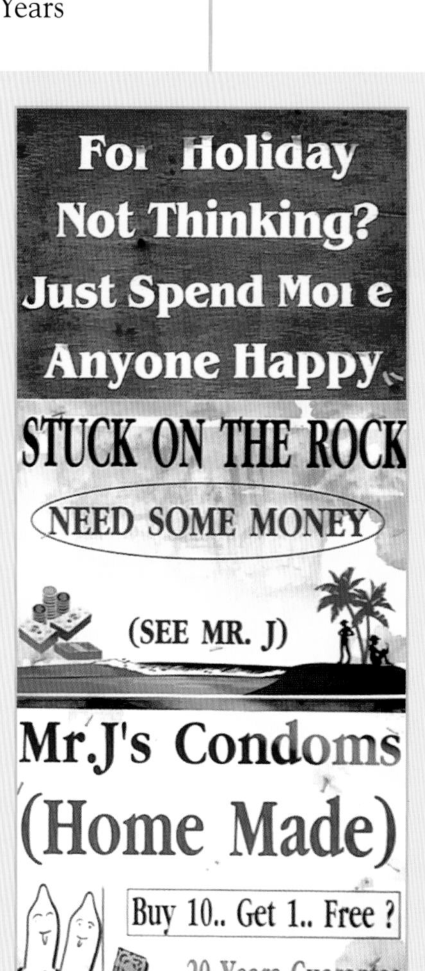

Mr. J takes care of business—and tourists—in Thailand.

- ***On a package of chicken in China:*** "Former chicken"
- ***In an Acapulco hotel:*** "The manager has personally passed all the water served here."
- ***At a Beijing hair salon:*** "ASS Hair Salon"
- ***At an Istanbul souvenir stand:*** "Sorry We're Open"
- ***In a Korean grocery store in Honolulu:*** "Please do not Taste a Food With Your Bear Hand."
- ***On a restaurant menu in Paris:*** "Tomatoes, goat dung on toast, country ham, nuts"
- ***In a hotel in Delhi, India:*** "Our dog is friendly. Please do not touch or pet him."

In Flowery Branch, Georgia, it is illegal to yell "Snake!" within city limits.

It's a Weird, Weird Death

When it's your time to go, try to leave behind a good story.

Eight Arms to Kill You

One of the most popular snacks in South Korea: small octopuses, eaten alive. In 2002 a Seoul man was eating one at home and choked to death on it. Doctors removed the octopus, which was still alive and clinging to the man's throat. Statistics show that as many as six people a year in South Korea die that way.

By the Book

Early-20th-century Ethiopian emperor Menelik II had an unusual habit: When he felt sick or uneasy, he'd eat a few pages out of a Bible. He was feeling especially sick after suffering a stroke in 1913, so he ate the entire Book of Kings. A few days later he died of an intestinal blockage caused by the paper.

Good Luck, Bad Luck

Boonchai Lotharakphong, 43, ran a sportswear factory in Thailand. Facing money problems, he bought a flag from a fortuneteller who foretold good luck if Lotharakphong flew it from the roof of his factory. As Lotharakphong was carrying the flag to the roof, he slipped and fell to his death.

Fishy

In 2003 Lim Vanthan and his family were planting rice near their home in Phnom Penh, Cambodia. Lim went for a swim and caught an eight-inch kantrob fish, a prized delicacy in Cambodia. But the fish jumped out of Lim's hands, into his mouth, and down his throat. The fish's sharp, scaly barbs caused it to lodge in Lim's throat, suffocating him.

Cart-Astrophe

Eighty-year-old Dennis Wiltshire of Neath, South Wales, liked to race grocery carts in his local supermarket. In August 2005, he hopped on a cart and rode it down a loading ramp, yelling "Wheeeee!" The cart spun out of control and Wiltshire fell off, fracturing his skull on the parking lot pavement. According to reports, he died instantly.

Cat milk is 10% protein. Cow's milk is only 3% protein.

Don't Believe Everything You Hear

At the BRI, one of our goals is to make readers look at the world in a new way. After reading this article, you'll also be listening in a new way. Listening to what? To sounds that seem real...but aren't.

What's New Is Old Again

Have you ever heard of a *skeuomorph?* Pronounced SKEW-a-morf, it's a feature that's been added to a new version of a product that, while not functionally necessary, makes consumers more at ease with the new technology. For example, the "PLAY" button on your DVD player has a little arrow on it that points to the right. There's nothing inside a digital player that actually moves to the right, but there was on old VHS tape players. The arrow remains because consumers are used to it.

When it comes to sound, skeuomorphs are a big deal: If a product doesn't sound right, it can be a very tough sell to consumers. Companies employ sound designers—not unlike the sound engineers who work on Hollywood movies—to ensure that every noise a product makes will be pleasing to the ears. Sometimes it's for nostalgia's sake; sometimes for safety...and sometimes for more nefarious reasons.

- **Electric car motors:** To ensure that pedestrians and cyclists hear them coming, silent electric cars come with speakers under the hood that play a recorded engine noise. But not just any random engine noise will do: The designers of the electric Nissan Leaf, for example, hired focus groups to listen to dozens of engine sounds and then vote on the one they found the most satisfying.

- **Digital cameras:** For more than a century, film cameras had mechanical shutters that clicked when the shutter button was pressed. Digital SLR cameras have a similar electro-mechanical shutter that also clicks, although not as loudly. But what about cell phone cameras and small point-and-shoots? They, too, have shutters, but they're so small that the sound they make is barely audible. So manufactures have added fake shutter sounds to let the picture-taker know that a picture has been taken. Many people find this feature annoying, and some camera

Can you hear me now?

models allow you to change the sound to a beep. A few models even allow you to turn off the sound altogether.

However, there's a movement underway to mandate that these fake shutter sounds not only remain, but that they become louder. Reason: to prevent creepy voyeurs from secretly snapping photos in locker rooms and dressing rooms. In 2009 U.S. Rep. Peter King (R-NY) drafted a bill called the "Camera Phone Predator Alert Act" which would "require mobile phones containing digital cameras to make a sound when a photograph is taken." In Japan and South Korea, the governments have urged camera makers to keep the fake shutter noise to deter people from secretly taking pictures up women's skirts (apparently a problem in the Far East). So far, camera makers haven't complied, and King's bill went nowhere, but the shutter-noise issue remains controversial.

- **Segways:** If you've heard a Segway scooter rolling down the sidewalk, you know it makes a very distinctive whir that sounds a bit like the futuristic vehicles from *The Jetsons*. That's no accident. Segway designers tweaked the two-stage transmission until both stages hit notes that are exactly one octave apart. That gives the Segway a modern, musical sound—whereas two random notes could have made it sound clunky and out of tune.

whirrr...whirrr

- **Car doors:** When you close a steel car door, it's loud. In recent years, safety and emissions standards have forced auto makers to use lighter materials, resulting in new doors that sound more like toys. Because most people equate a lower pitch with power, and a higher pitch with weakness, auto engineers have redesigned lighter car doors with dampeners and other materials in order to replace the tinny "tink" with a much more satisfying "thunk."
- **Turn signals:** The "tick-tock" you hear in newer cars doesn't correspond to the actual signal mechanism, which is a silent electrical relay switch. The sound is there mainly to alert the driver that the signal is on, but it's been carefully crafted to be noticeable without being too loud, and to have a pleasing tone. (In fact, nearly every noise you hear in a new car has been labored over by engineers—from the seatbelt click to the sound the seat makes when your butt hits it. If the sound doesn't sound good enough, it will be tweaked until it does.)

potato potato potato

- **Harley-Davidsons:** These motorcycles make a very distinctive "potato-potato" sound, but that wasn't originally by design; it was the result of the cylinders of the V-twin engines firing at an uneven rate (which was necessary to pack more punch into a smaller engine). Over time that noise became so associated with Harleys that other bike makers tried to copy it, leading the company to attempt to trademark the sound in the 1990s. The trademark bid was unsuccessful, but Harley-Davidson claimed they had won "in the court of public opinion."

Ironically, in recent decades Harley engineers have had to perform some trickery to retain that distinctive sound. Because of tighter engine regulations, the cylinders now fire at a more even rate, so the company has set up a "Noise, Vibration & Harshness Department" tasked with meeting regulations, but also meeting riders' expectations of what a Hog should sound like.

- **Ebooks:** There are some aspects of reading a real book that simply can't be captured by reading an ebook…but that hasn't stopped ebook makers from trying. Some ebook readers feature faux paper texture, page-turning animation, and the actual sound of a paper page turning.

- **Football games:** Sports fans have certain auditory expectations when they go to the stadium, so little is left to chance. Even the vendors who walk through the stands are trained to yell "Get yer hot dogs!" and "Cold beer here!" in a certain way. That adds to the nostalgia value of going to a game.

But some things you hear at a sporting venue may be designed to give the home team an advantage. In 2007 the Indianapolis Colts were accused of piping in fake crowd noise during a home game against the New England Patriots—but only when the Patriots had the ball and the snapper needed to hear the quarterback's call. Colts officials denied it, claiming that what fans watching on TV said sounded like a "CD skipping" was actually feedback caused by the CBS Sports broadcast of the game. Nevertheless, the NFL enacted strict rules against this practice, with heavy fines for offenders. Since then, a few other teams have been accused of using fake crowd noise, but nothing's been proven.

- **Slot machines:** As tickets replace coins in slot machines, the familiar "ching-ching" sound is in danger of going away. No problem: Newer slot machines that award tickets play recorded coin sounds. To entice non-gamblers into the room, the same sound is heard whether the player wins 25 cents or 25 dollars. And not just any

Ching! Ching!

Steven Tyler of Aerosmith insists that no one call him Steve.

"ching-ching" will do. As one slot machine designer explained, "We mix several recordings of coins falling on a metal tray and then fatten up the sound." On digital slots that don't have a spinning wheel inside, a simulated spinning sound is played. Same thing if there's no lever. In fact, some slot machines employ up to 40 fake sounds just to keep people gambling.

- **Phones:** You can set your phone's ring tone to whatever you want, but when you make a call— be it on a mobile phone or on a landline—you always hear the familiar "ring-ring" sound. Callers haven't actually heard the sound made by a phone ringing on the other end since the 1950s. It's been simulated ever since.
- **Computer mouses:** The Apple Mighty Mouse makes a clicking sound when the user scrolls, yet there's no actual mechanism that clicks. Instead, a tiny speaker inside the mouse plays a simulated clicking sound. (To see if your mouse has a speaker inside, unplug it and roll the scroll ball. If it's silent, the click is fake.)

click click!

- **The Olympics:** During the 2012 broadcast of the Summer Games in London, NBC admitted to some fakery with the rowing races. Because the motors on the chase boats and the TV helicopters were so loud, it would have been impossible to pick up audio from the actual rowers. So the Games' official sound engineer, Dan Baxter, didn't even try to use the live audio. Result: The viewers watching at home heard a playback of rowers on a calm, quiet river that Baxter had recorded himself. "Some people think it's cheating," he said. "I don't think I'm cheating anybody. The sound is there. It's just not necessarily real time. When you see a rower, your mind thinks you should hear the rower and that's what we deliver."

According to the Latest Research...

...Bears Prefer Hondas

Study: In the mid-1990s, Yosemite National Park spent more than $1 million on "bear safes"—bear-proof food lockers for the park's campsites. The idea was to teach bears that the food in the campgrounds was beyond reach. Instead, campers got the idea that if food was safe in a metal locker, it would be safe in their metal cars, too. Wrong. Cars are much flimsier—bears can easily smash the windows and even peel car doors right out of their frames. After the lockers went in, the number of car "cloutings" went up 600%.

Finding: Park rangers kept statistics on the cars that were broken into, and the bears seem to show a particular preference for certain brands, namely Hondas and Toyotas. In a two-month study of "bear incidents," they broke into 26 Hondas and 21 Toyotas, but only two Buicks and one Lexus. What is it about these cars that makes the bears prefer them over others? No one knows for sure.

Demented Dentists

It takes a special kind of person to take up a profession that involves putting your fingers inside strangers' mouths all day. And while most dentists are really good at what they do, the ones in this article may make you want to switch to false teeth.

Bogus University

A 2004 investigation in Italy discovered that you can't count on your dentist's diploma being real. Officials uncovered a ring of scammers, involving two dental schools in Rome, that sold fake diplomas to dental "students" for as much as $220,000 each. Investigators found evidence of false school-attendance records as well as test answers and term papers provided to students for a fee. Other university staff members were bribed with vacations, gifts, and bonuses to keep them quiet about the scam. Investigators are still trying to locate the dozens of dentists who are practicing without a degree.

Torture Chambers—with Free Sweatshirts

In 2004 twenty dentists in California's Central Valley area were accused of defrauding the state Medi-Cal health system of $4.5 million by performing unnecessary—and cruel—dental work. To lure low-income patients, these dentists went to homeless shelters, shopping malls, and schools and offered gift certificates, sweatshirts, and electric toothbrushes. The patients were then given unnecessary dental work, including root canals. Some dentists were accused of holding crying children down in the dental chair and using straps on elderly patients. Then they charged outlandish amounts of money for the work and sent the bills to Medi-Cal. "In every single one of the 300 files we checked," said an official, "we found fraud." In 2008 the two lead dentists in the scam were sentenced to one year in jail and forced to repay $3 million.

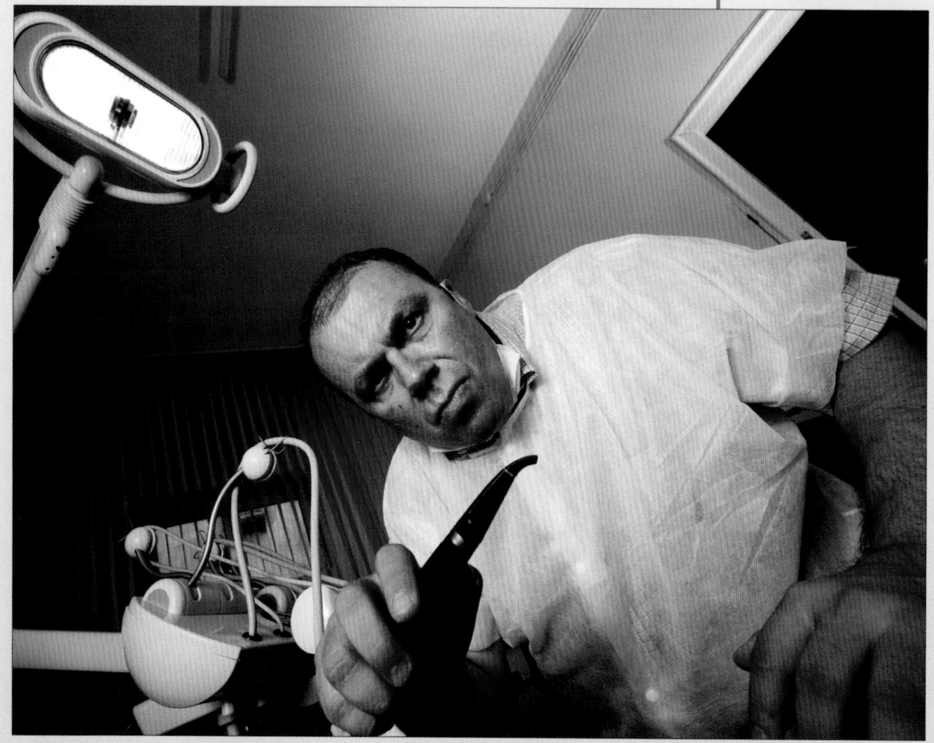

Open wide...

Laughing Matter

On Long Island, New York, a patient (name not released in press reports) showed up for his dentist appointment, but the waiting room was empty. "Is anyone here?" he asked. No one answered, so the man walked into the back, where he found the dentist, Norman Rubin, lying on the

Mark Twain coined the phrase "gossip column" in 1893.

floor. According to police, "He was unresponsive and drooling, and had the gas mask on his face." Rubin was later charged with "inhalation of hazardous inhalants." He blamed the incident on a migraine, but admitted, "It was a mistake." An investigation found that his license had been suspended several times, which he blamed on "six disgruntled patients."

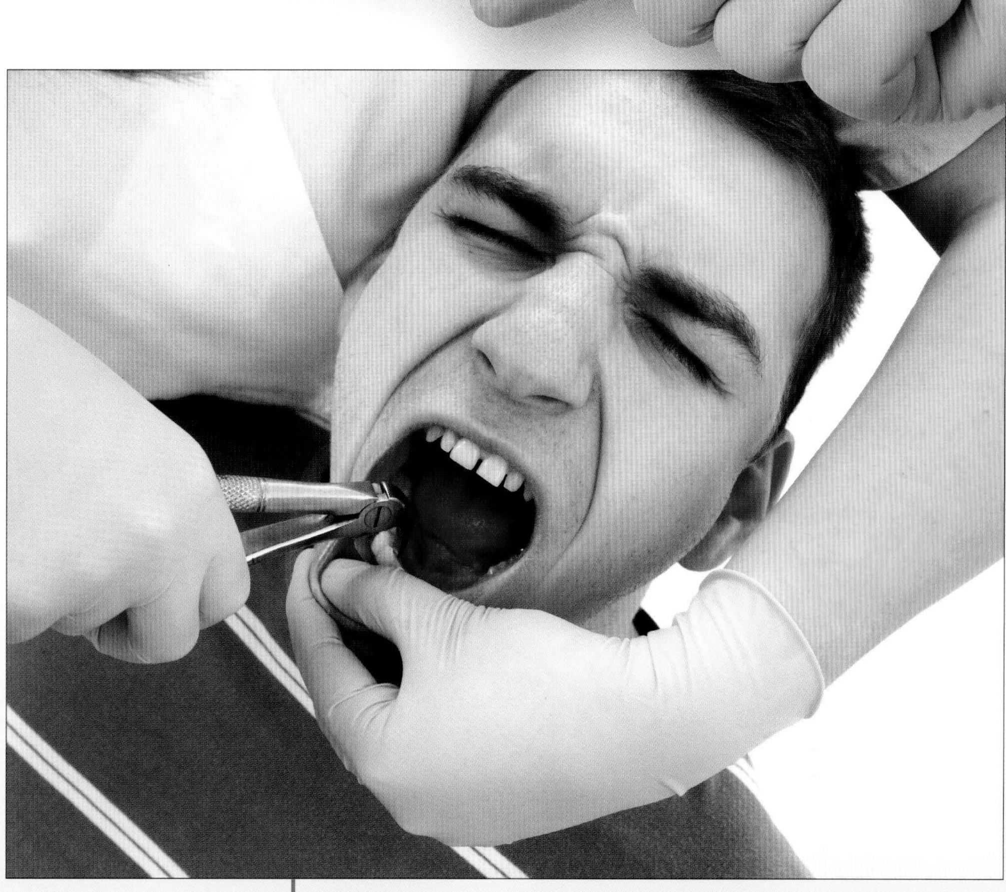

What time is your appointment? Tooth-hurty.

What a Tool

Donna Delgado of Tampa, Florida, had dental surgery in 2008. In the weeks and months afterward, she suffered from frequent nosebleeds and sinus infections. A year later, Delgado was still in pain, so she went to another dentist…who discovered that a one-inch steel dental tool had been left inside her right maxillary sinus. It was removed, and Delgado's symptoms disappeared (although she may have nickel poisoning). A lawsuit is pending.

At Least He's Not a Pilot

In June 2004, Dr. Colin McKay of Halton, England, drank six glasses of wine at lunch and then performed a tooth extraction on Andrea Harrison. It didn't go well. It took McKay two tries to inject the anesthetic into her gums, then he started the procedure before Harrison's mouth became completely numb. "I was in a lot of pain and yelled, but he carried on," she said. "Then he seemed to fall over me. I ended up running out." Another dentist finished the extraction; McKay was found guilty of professional misconduct.

Yank!

"Dr. Allena Burge pulled teeth so hard and fast, the patients' blood would spray," her assistant, Janet Popelier, told investigators. "Sometimes parts of the jawbone or mandible would break." Why did the Florida dentist have to work so fast? "She was trying to make $12,000 a day from Medicaid. I saw many half-conscious, bleeding patients led out the back door soon after their surgeries to make room for new patients." Burge was charged with fraud and malpractice. (She even let her 12-year-old son administer anesthesia.) In just four years, she filed more than 57,000 Medicaid claims totaling $6.6 million. No word on the investigation's outcome, but at last report, Burge was still practicing dentistry.

Invasion of the Frankenfish

We don't want to scare you, but some strange creatures have been showing up on our doorsteps lately. They weren't invited…and they won't go away.

Invading Species: Golden Apple Snail

Background: A native of South America, the golden apple snail became a popular addition to aquariums around the world because it is considered "pretty." In the early 1980s, some private snail farms found a new use for the easy-to-raise, protein-rich snails. They were shipped to snail farmers in Taiwan and the Philippines in the hopes of starting escargot industries.

Here They Come: Unfortunately, the escargot business never took off and prices plummeted, so farmers simply dumped the snails. Bad idea. Golden apple snails are voracious eaters, munching continuously for up to 24 hours a day, and their preferred food is rice seedlings. And what's the primary source of food and employment in Asia? Rice. Laying as many as 500 eggs a week, the renegade snails quickly multiplied. By the mid-1990s they had destroyed an estimated two million acres of rice fields in the Philippines alone, and had spread to nearly every Asian nation, causing billions of dollars in damage. And they're not done yet. The snails were discovered in U.S. waters in the 1990s, probably escapees or throwaways from aquariums. Several states have made owning a golden apple snail a crime.

Golden apple snail

Invading Species: Zebra Mussel

Background: Originally from the Caspian Sea in Russia, by the 1800s, this freshwater mollusk had spread into other waterways in western Europe. In 1988 the zebra mussel showed up on this side of the Atlantic. How? Transatlantic ships probably brought the mussels over in their ballast tanks and unknowingly dumped them into North American ports.

Here They Come: Female zebra mussels produce as many as a million eggs per year, with a very high

Zebra mussel

survival rate. Once they appear, they take over, depleting rivers and lakes of oxygen and killing off native clams, snails, and fish. Not only that, they get into water pipes that feed to power plants and public waterworks, causing massive clogs. It's estimated that they cause $5 billion of damage every year. By 2002 they had spread to the Mississippi, Arkansas, Illinois, Ohio, and Tennessee Rivers…and they're still on the move.

Round goby fish

More Bad News: The zebra mussel brought a friend. The small (10-inch) but super aggressive round goby fish tagged along in the ballast tanks and has found a new home in the Great Lakes. Its long breeding period and ability to feed in complete darkness give it a competitive edge over native fish species…which it eats The fact that it eats baby mussels too—though not enough to control them—means that the goby has an unlimited food source and will likely follow the zebra mussel, wreaking havoc throughout the Mississippi River system and beyond.

Invading Species: Northern Snakehead Fish

Background: This Chinese fish is considered a delicacy in Asia. You can find them in some Asian markets in the United States. In June 2002, a man was fishing a pond in Crofton, Maryland, when he caught a fish he didn't recognize. Biologists later identified the 26-inch specimen as a snakehead. How'd it get there? An unidentified man admitted to dumping his two pet snakeheads after he got tired of feeding them. A subsequent search of the pond turned up more than 100 babies.

Here They Come: The snakehead, dubbed "Frankenfish" by the press, can get up to three feet long and an adult can eat prey as large as itself…including birds and small mammals. Worse: With no natural predators, it can devour everything in sight. Then, if conditions are just right, it can use its long fins as legs to crawl across land to find a new pond or river. It can actually survive on land for up to four days. Officials are hoping that hasn't happened yet and said they'll use a pesticide to kill the snakeheads—and everything else in the pond—just so the Frankenfish doesn't spread. "It's not a dead or alive thing," biologist Bob Lunsford told the *Washington Post*, "we just want it dead."

Northern snakehead fish

Transforming Mars

So what if we ignore all this stuff about saving the environment and go ahead and trash Earth anyway? No problem—we'll just move everybody next door.

Space Oddity

For centuries, humans have looked up at our closest planetary neighbor and wondered if we would ever live there. Today, scientists are working on making this a reality. NASA has even announced a date for the first manned mission to the Red Planet: 2031.

The bad news: It may be closer to the year 3031 before a human can take a stroll around Mars wearing nothing but a pair of shorts and a T-shirt. As it stands right now, Mars's average temperature is –81°F, its atmosphere is extremely thin, and it contains almost no oxygen. To fix all three of these problems would be, by far, the largest and boldest undertaking in human history.

The good news: Mars possesses many of the basic elements necessary for life to develop, the most crucial being water. The planet also has a promising atmospheric makeup: 95.2% carbon dioxide, 2.7% nitrogen, and 0.2% oxygen. While that's far below the 20% oxygen in our atmosphere, it's encouraging because four billion years ago, Earth's atmosphere was nearly the same as Mars's is today. So, to make Mars earthlike—or *terraformed*—it needs heat, more water, a thicker atmosphere, and lots and lots of oxygen. But how do you do it in less than four billion years? Here are two theories.

The Japanese word *koroski* means "death induced by overwork."

Artist's rendition of an asteroid attack

Golden Years

One of the ways that NASA may send humans to Mars is on a ship powered by "solar sails," giant mirrors that harness the sun's energy to propel the ship forward. This same principle could be used to heat Mars by reflecting sunlight to the surface. However, the mirrors would need to be about 150 miles wide to heat enough land to make it worthwhile. Mirrors that large couldn't be assembled on Earth, so the alternative would be to assemble them in orbit out of "space junk"—floating debris from previous space missions, jettisoned fuel tanks, and old satellites (now that's recycling).

Once installed 300,000 miles above the Martian surface, they'd be trained on the frozen polar caps and begin melting the ice. This process would release CO_2 into the atmosphere, theoretically triggering the greenhouse effect: CO_2 absorbs the sun's radiation, and having more of it would warm the planet and thicken the atmosphere.

The moving gases from the melting ice caps would also generate planet-wide dust storms, increasing the temperature even more. Eventually, Mars would be warm enough for liquid water to develop (but not freeze) at the poles. At this point, rockets filled with algae spores would be sent to this new ocean. The new algae would thrive in the water, causing photosynthesis, a byproduct of which is oxygen. Humans would still need to wear air tanks for a few millennia, but the amount of oxygen would increase as the temperature slowly rose.

Ziggy Stardust

A quicker and more violent terraforming method was suggested by aerospace engineer Robert Zubrin in his 1996 book *The Case for Mars*. The plan: Astronauts would attach a nuclear thermal rocket engine to a 10-billion-ton asteroid (kind of like in the movie *Armageddon*). Controlled remotely from Earth, the asteroid would hit Mars with the force of 70 hydrogen bombs. The impact would raise the Martian temperature 3°F, which would melt a trillion tons of ice. This would add CO_2 to the atmosphere, triggering the greenhouse effect and melting the caps even more. One asteroid-bomb per year over 50 years could make up to 25% of the Martian surface habitable (temperaturewise, anyway). And scientists could then send their algae rockets to the planet's new seas.

Sadly, all those nukes would soak Mars in toxic radiation (so we'd better be sure there's no life there), and humans would have to wear air tanks for hundreds of years anyway. But no matter how we get there, Zubrin writes, the time to begin the journey is now. "We need a central overriding purpose to drive our space program forward. At this point in history, that focus can only be the human exploration and settlement of Mars."

This Martian would rather we just stay home.

Human Oil (and other Hoaxes)

These hoaxes are so absurd, it's hard to believe that anybody was fooled...but lots of people were.

What a Hellhole

The Story: In early 1990, the Trinity Broadcasting Network reported that Russian geologists on Siberia's Kola Peninsula had discovered Hell. They were using a giant drill, said TBN, to test how deep into the Earth they could reach. In November 1989, nine miles into the ground, the drill suddenly stopped spinning—it had hit air. The team lowered a thermometer into the hole. The temperature inside was 2,200°F—five times as hot as it should have been at that depth. They lowered a microphone down to record the sounds of shifting plates, and heard human screams. Then a black, spectral figure in the shape of a bat screeched and flew out of the hole.

The Hoax: TBN claimed (on the air) that its source for the story was *Ammennusatia*, "Finland's most respected newspaper." They'd gotten the article from a Texas minister who sent it in, claiming it was from Finland's top scientific journal. Actually, *Ammennusatia* is a paranormal newsletter (it is from Finland). They got the story from a staffer who wrote it from memory after having read it in *Etela Soumen*, another Finnish newspaper, which ran the piece in a section where readers were invited to publish anything they liked—including fiction. Someone had sent the story to *Etela Soumen* after reading it in another weird Finnish newsletter called *Vaeltajat*. That paper got it from an obscure American religious newsletter called *Jewels of Jericho*, which had completely made it up. TBN reported the story without bothering to find out if it was true. A few months later, they announced that because of the story, 3,000 people had converted to Christianity. Ironically, the story is rooted in fact: From 1970 to 1989, Soviet scientists were involved in a project called the Kola Superdeep Borehole. The point was to drill as deep into the Earth as possible. They got about 7.6 miles in, but never encountered any fiery air holes, human screams, or ghostly bats.

The proverbial bat-out-of-Hell

Vivoleum for Everyone

The Story: At the 2007 Gas and Oil Exposition, Canada's largest annual oil-industry convention, a National Petroleum Council representative named Shepard Wolff and an Exxon Mobil executive, Florian Osenberg, unveiled "Vivoleum"—a revolutionary process that turned human flesh into gasoline (very handy, should oil reserves ever dry up). The executives then played a film about a deceased Exxon janitor who had volunteered to be turned into Vivoleum, and passed out candles to be lit in the janitor's memory. That's when they announced that the candles *were* the janitor—transformed by Vivoleum.

The Hoax: After the two men passed out the "human candles," the event's organizers realized "Wolff" and "Osenberg" were phonies. They were really Andy Bichlbaum and Mike Bonanno, two members

Bichlbaum and Bonanno: Fixing the world one hoax at a time

There are at least 33 species of sharks in the Gulf of Mexico.

of the Yes Men, an anti-consumerism group that stages high-profile stunts to embarrass corporations with poor environmental or human rights records. Bichlbaum and Bonanno had set up a fake Exxon website (vivoleum.com), through which they got themselves invited to the Oil Exposition. Convention organizers threw them out and threatened to have them arrested. A few days later, Exxon demanded they shut down the Vivoleum site. They declined, saying it was parody and thus protected under the First Amendment. (The website has since shut down.)

Mostly Cloudy

The Story: On a Sunday morning in June 2007, CT2, a television station in the Czech Republic, was airing a weather update. As weather stats scrolled along the bottom of the screen, the camera panned the country's scenic Krkonose Mountains. Suddenly, off in the distance, a fiery mushroom cloud filled the sky. The screen went black—the Czech Republic had just been nuked.

The Hoax: A Czech performance art group called Initiative Ztohoven had hacked into CT2's feed and replaced it with its own footage—undetectably similar…up until the bomb part. The mushroom cloud was just simple video editing done on a computer. After the initial blackout, CT2 came back on the air to reassure viewers that they weren't under attack. Members of Initiative Ztohoven are under investigation by the Czech government and may face terrorism charges.

Oops! We Stepped in It!

Animal poop has an awful lot of names. Here are the ones we could dig up.

Bodewash

The word, pronounced "BOHD-wash," was used by settlers of both the Canadian and American West as a more "proper" name for dried bison droppings (aka "buffalo chips"), which were regularly used as fuel. Bodewash is a corruption of *bois de vache*, or "wood of the cow," the name given by French explorers in Canada in the 1700s.

Dirt

This isn't used as often as it once was, but you still sometimes hear people refer to dogpoop as "dog dirt." It also refers to flea poop, aka "flea dirt." (If it looks like someone sprinkled a pepper shaker on your pet, that's probably flea dirt, and a sign the pet is infested with fleas.)

Dung

A general name for the feces of animals other than humans, but especially in reference to cattle, the word "dung" has its roots in the Proto-Indo-European prefix *dhengh*, meaning "covering"—referring to the ancient custom of covering thatch-roofed homes with dung for insulation.

Excrement

Derived from the Latin for "discharge," excrement used to refer to discharge from any orifice. It once would have been entirely appropriate to say, "Hey, you've got some excrement coming out of your nose" to someone with the sniffles. Since the 1700s, though, it's been used more specifically to refer to poop.

Watch out below!

With a name like Insect Frass, it's gotta be good.

Warning: Do not lift tail to get closer view.

Feces

From the Latin *faeces*, meaning "sediment" or "dregs," feces refers to the droppings of any kind of animal, including humans, fish, and insects. The singular in Latin: *faex*. The singular in English? There is none—the word is always plural in English.

Frass

This is the poop of plant-eating insects. (Meat-eating insects, such as spiders and mantises, don't have a special name for theirs.) It comes in many forms: Termites leave piles of dry pellets that sort of look like wood shavings; bees poop a thick, yellow liquid that looks like mustard; and if you spend some time watching a beetle feeding on a leaf, you might be lucky enough to see it leaving a little green, tubelike trail behind it. That's beetle frass.

Meconium

This is the fecal discharge of a newborn mammal, which is produced for just a few days after birth. It's the poop produced from the stuff that the newborn "ate" via its umbilical cord while still in its mother's uterus. The name comes from the Latin term for "poppy juice" or "opium." Etymologists say this is because human meconium, which is thick, dark, and tarlike, looks a lot like opium. The same term is also used for the poop of insects whose life cycle includes a pupal stage and refers to a type of poop produced after that stage is completed. A butterfly, for example, upon leaving its chrysalis and first emerging as an adult, will poop a red fluid—that's butterfly meconium.

Muck

Often used today to refer to any "mucky" substance, such as mud, its primary meaning, according to the *Merriam-Webster Dictionary*, is "soft moist farmyard manure." (Manure itself is farmyard poop mixed with decaying organic material, usually straw.)

Guano

The name comes from *huano*, the South American Quechua people's word for the droppings of seabirds. For centuries the Quechua harvested nutrient-rich huano, which accumulates in huge amounts on what is now the Peruvian

A grasshopper answering nature's call

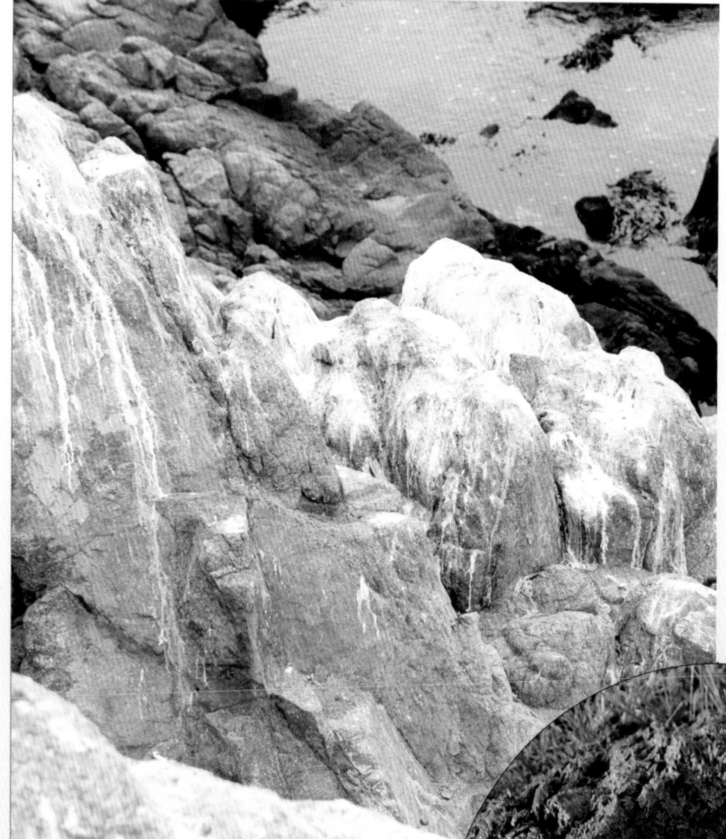

Sea cliff in Chile covered by guano

coastline, for use as a fertilizer. When European and American scientists discovered in the mid-1800s just how good a fertilizer guano is, it became one of the most important trade commodities in the world. The name's meaning grew to include other types of nutrient-rich droppings that tend to accumulate in large amounts, including bat guano (in caves) and seal guano (on rocky islands where seals congregate). Artificial fertilizer brought about the end of the major guano industry, but it is still valued as a fertilizer today, especially by organic farmers.

Spraint

This is used primarily in Great Britain, but it does find its way to North America now and then in literature and film. And what is it? River otter poop. Spraint is an especially odoriferous kind of poop; its powerful smell is variously described as similar to the odor of fish, lavender, and/or freshly cut grass.

Scat

This refers to animal feces, most commonly the poop of wild animals, and is a relatively new word—it's been around only since the 1920s. Its origin is uncertain: Etymologists say it may have come from the word *scatology*, referring to works of art, especially literary, that are deemed obscene…or to the scientific study of feces. (A scatologist is a scientist who studies scat.)

What noise does a cowbell make? DUNG!

Slop

Commonly used to refer to pig feces, this goes back to the Old English word *sloppe*, which literally meant "dung." On a related note: the flower known as the cowslip got its name from *cow sloppe*—or "cow dung"—because it was often seen around pastures.

Bag of bat guano fertilizer

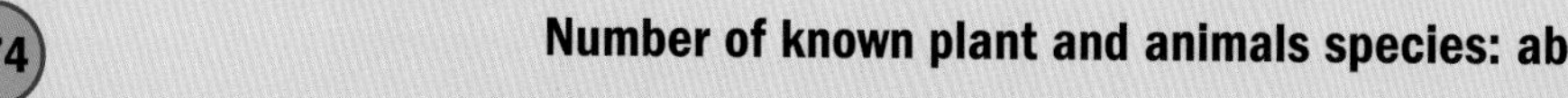

Number of known plant and animals species: about 1.8 million.

Ordure

Another name for feces, first recorded in English in the 14th century, it was derived from the Latin *horridus*, for "dreadful" (also the root of the word "horrid"). It is still used today, especially in literature, for example, "In the madhouse the walls reek with the odors of filth and terminal ills they've soaked up these hundred years. Stains from the rusted plumbing, the ordure slung by irate imbeciles." (From *Sutree*, by Cormac McCarthy.)

Pellets

The feces of many creatures, such as rabbits and deer, are called pellets because of their shape. And why are they pellet-shaped? It has to do with the peristalsis action of these animals' colons, which separates fecal matter into fairly equal-sized chunks as it pushes it along with the animal's anal muscles, which clamp down and cut off pellets of poo as they exit the animal's body.

Pellet-shaped moose droppings

Moments of Candor

These celebrities really do open up.

"The trouble with being me is that at this point, nobody gives a damn what my problem is. I could literally have a tumor on the side of my head and they'd be like, 'Yeah, big deal. I'd eat a tumor every morning for the kind of money you're pulling down.'"

—Jim Carrey

"I have a lust for diamonds, almost like a disease."

—Elizabeth Taylor

"I used to make appearances at cocktail parties in Florida, pretending that I was an old friend of the host."

—Mickey Rooney

With my sunglasses on, I'm Jack Nicholson. Without them, I'm fat and 60.

"It's pretty sad when a person has to lose weight to play Babe Ruth."

—John Goodman

"I could be the poster boy for bad judgement."

—Rob Lowe

"I feel cheated never knowing what it's like to get pregnant, carry a baby, and breast-feed."

—Dustin Hoffman

"Fame can be just so annoying because people are always so critical of you. You can't just say, 'Hi.' You say hi and people whisper, 'Man, did you see the way she said hi? What an attitude.'"

—Juliette Lewis

First record of an organized workers' strike: building of the tomb of Rameses III, in 1150 B.C.

Odes to Nature

Some thoughts on that faraway place known as "outside."

"Nothing is more beautiful than the loveliness of the woods before sunrise."

—George Washington Carver

"A perfect summer day is when the sun is shining, the breeze is blowing, the birds are singing, and the lawn mower is broken."

—James Dent

"You will find something far greater in the woods than you will find in books. Stones and trees will teach you that which you will never learn from masters."

—St. Bernard

"It seems to me that we all look at Nature too much, and live with her too little."

—Oscar Wilde

"For me, another definition of God is 'great outdoors.'"

—Johnny Cash

Oscar Wilde, 1882

"Nature does not hurry, yet everything is accomplished."

—Lao Tzu

"In wilderness I sense the miracle of life, and behind it our scientific accomplishments fade to trivia."

—Charles Lindbergh

"That's the thing about Mother Nature—she really doesn't care what economic bracket you're in."

—Whoopi Goldberg

"I am at two with nature."

—Woody Allen

"When you take a flower in your hand and really look at it, it's your world for the moment."

—Georgia O'Keefe

Wandering Spleen

If you're like Uncle John, when you get an ailment—say, a cold—you ask yourself, "Why is it called a 'cold'?" If you get one of these odd diseases, you probably won't have to ask how it got its name.

Maple Syrup Urine Disease: An inherited metabolic disease that makes the urine and sweat smell like maple syrup.

Kabuki Makeup Syndrome: This birth defect causes facial features to distort, resembling the over-pronounced and elongated made-up faces of Japanese Kabuki actors.

Prune-Belly Syndrome: An absence of abdominal muscles gives the stomach a wrinkled, puckered look and a severe pot belly that stretches out grotesquely.

Jumping Frenchman: An acquired condition first discovered in the 19th century among Canadian lumberjacks. Patients have extreme reactions to sudden noises or surprises: They flail their arms, jump in the air, cry, scream, and hit people.

I have to go oui.

Hairy Tongue: Due to tobacco use or poor oral hygiene, the tiny hairs on the tongue grow to be several inches long and the tongue itself turns black.

Wandering Spleen: The muscles that hold the spleen in position are missing or undeveloped, causing the spleen to "wander" around the lower abdomen and pelvic region.

Foreign Accent Syndrome: After a severe brain injury or stroke, a person begins speaking their native language with a foreign accent. English-speaking Americans might suddenly sound Russian, for example.

Alice in Wonderland Syndrome: Vision is distorted, making objects appear much smaller than they actually are. For example, a house may appear to be the size of a shoebox or a cat may look no bigger than a mouse.

A Killer Recycling Program

The tiger keelback (*Rhabdophis tigrinus*) is a snake native to Asia with an amazing adaptation: The toads upon which it feeds have a gland that dispenses toxic venom to ward off predators. After eating the toad, the snake actually extracts the toxin, stores it in its own special gland…and then releases it to kill other prey (including more toads).

World's largest democracy: India, with over 800 million voters.

Hollywood Duffers

Famous folks and golf—the untold stories.

- **Robert Redford** had a handicap of six at one time, but it had ballooned to a 12 by 2001. His excuse: His game got rusty while he was busy directing *The Legend of Bagger Vance*—a golf movie.
- **O. J. Simpson** used to bet hundreds of dollars on golf games. He often lost, but rarely paid up, invoking his special "off the premises" rule. The rule: The bet was invalid if the loser left the course before the winner could collect. So, after the game, Simpson would tell a long-winded football story to his opponent, who would eventually need to use the restroom. And by the time he returned, Simpson was peeling out of the parking lot.
- **Chevy Chase** and **Bill Murray**, the stars of *Caddyshack*, have high handicaps of 25 and 13, respectively. (**Kevin Costner**, star of *Tin Cup*, has a 12.6.)
- **Dennis Quaid's** father bought him a junior set of clubs when he was nine. He hated golf and he was terrible at it. But his older brother, actor **Randy Quaid**, was a very talented golfer and considered going professional. Dennis didn't take up golf again until his 30s to keep busy after emerging from drug rehab. He quickly caught up with his brother: Both actors now have a six handicap.
- **Samuel L. Jackson** regularly golfs with football legend Jim Brown and former boxer Sugar Ray Leonard. Jackson reportedly enjoys hustling other celebrity golfers out of their money, including Darius Rucker (Hootie and the Blowfish) and Kenny G.
- **Fred Astaire's** 1938 movie *Carefree* included a sequence in which Astaire danced onto a golf course and hit 12 golf balls consecutively—in time to music—while dancing. When the crew went to retrieve the balls after the take, they found that all 12 balls had hit the green—all within eight feet of each other.
- **Donald Trump** showed off his Trump International course by hosting the LPGA's 2001 ADT Championship. Throughout the event, Trump repeatedly pestered golfers, asking them if it was the toughest course they'd ever played. He had a real reason for asking: Prior to the tournament, Trump had ordered the mounds in front of the water hazards be mowed at a slant so that balls would roll into the water. Even more annoying: Inmates from the adjacent Palm Beach County Criminal Justice Complex screamed profanities at the female golfers. (Trump denies this happened, but he later spent $1 million on a barrier of 200 palm trees between the prison and the course.)

Samuel L. Jackson

Missed It by that Mu..

How frustrating is it to work for so long on something only to see it fail right before the payoff?

The Grand Scheme: A group of inmates at Kinross Correctional Facility in Michigan spent three months planning and implementing a daring escape. Because the prison was originally built as an Air Force barracks, the walls weren't fortified the way most modern prison walls are. All the cons had to do was break through eight inches of unreinforced concrete and then dig out about 50 feet of soft dirt. To start, one of the prisoners made a small hole in the back corner of his cell, where guards routinely look but seldom touch. (Authorities believe he may have used a dumbbell from the gym as a hammer.) Then each night he would dig a little more, keeping some of the dirt in the crescent-shaped tunnel and flushing the rest down the cell toilet (which caused clogs in the system that baffled prison administrators). By March 2007, the tunnel extended several feet beyond the outside fence. All they had left to do was dig "up" to freedom.

Foiled! During a routine check of the cell, one of the guards noticed something odd on the wall; he touched it and found the soft spot, prompting an immediate investigation...and the end of the escape plan. Although little information about the case was given to the press, one thing is known: Only one more night of digging and the prisoners would have made it.

The Grand Scheme: For more than two years, John and Penny Adie, organizers of an annual classical music festival in England, had been working tirelessly to raise enough money to buy a grand piano. Valued at £45,000 ($89,000) and made exclusively in Austria, Bösendorfers are the preferred piano of many of the world's greatest players. "They're the Stradivarius of the piano world," said John Adie. By April 2007, they had finally raised all the money they needed and they purchased the piano at a London auction. The only thing left to make their dream a reality was to deliver the Bösendorfer to the concert hall.

Foiled! As the delivery workers were hauling "the Stradivarius of the piano world" up the walkway, 20 feet from their destination they lost control of the dolly...and John and Penny watched in horror as their prized piano fell eight feet off of a ledge and smashed discordantly onto the ground below. "It was a total loss," said John, noting that insurance would probably cover only half of what the piano is worth. "It's more than money that is the issue here," said John. "It was like seeing a priceless painting torn to shreds," Penny added.

The Grand Scheme: Charles McKinley, a 25-year-old shipping clerk from Brooklyn, New York, wanted to fly home to see his parents in DeSoto, Texas, in 2003—but he couldn't afford a plane ticket. So he decided to use one of the big boxes from his workplace and ship himself home (with his employer unknowingly footing the bill). McKinley poked some holes in the box, then packed himself, some clothes, food, and his computer inside. An accomplice sealed the box and marked it "Computer Equipment." McKinley's two-day wild ride in a box took him on a shipping truck from Brooklyn to New Jersey, then on a plane to Buffalo, New York, which then flew him to Fort Wayne, Indiana, then (after changing planes) to Fort Worth, Texas, and finally on a truck to DeSoto, about 14 miles south of Dallas.

Foiled! As the driver was retrieving the "package" from the back of the delivery truck to bring it to McKinley's dad's house, he noticed a little slit in the top, and peeking through the slit was an eye looking up at him. The driver gasped. McKinley kicked open the side of the box, picked up all of his stuff, and calmly walked into the house. The driver called his boss, who then called the Feds, who came and arrested McKinley. He was charged as a stowaway, which is a federal offense. McKinley later revealed that just before the driver went to retrieve the box, he moved a piece of clothing that had been covering him so he could get a peek at the man. If McKinley had only waited one more minute for the driver to leave, he would have been home free.

All the Latest from the News Stream

Musical Notes

Take a minuet and reed these sharp facts...if it's not too much treble.

- There are more than 42,000 playable guitar chords.
- The first modern piano was built in 1700 by Bartolomeo Cristofori in Italy. The instrument's real name: *piano et forte*, which means "soft and loud."
- Since 1955 piano keys have been made of plastic, not ivory.
- In 1987 Missouri named the fiddle its official state instrument.
- In 1990 San Francisco named the accordion its official instrument.
- Purdue University had the first collegiate marching band (1886). They were also the first to play on a sports field and make a formation—they formed a giant "P" (1907).
- Most recognizable piece of Western music: the opening of Beethoven's "Fifth Symphony" (duh-duh duh-duuuh).
- Clarinets are made from the wood of the granadilla tree.
- Most frequently sung songs in English: "Happy Birthday," "For He's a Jolly Good Fellow," and "Auld Lang Syne."
- Written music, as we know it today, originated in the 1200s.
- Mozart wrote the overture to his opera *Don Giovanni* in one sitting. It was first performed the very next day, with no rehearsals.

Strange legacy: Marietta, Ohio, is named after Marie Antoinette.

Credits

Multiple credits per page are listed in a clockwise sequence.

11 Demon | Columbia | Rykodisc | Rhino; George Rose | Getty Images • 12 Jingraham311 | Dreamstime • 13 www.runningtothekitchen.com/2012/04/no-bake-brownie-fudge-balls • 14 Eutoch | Dreamstime • 15 Mike Myers | New Line Cinema | Warner Bros.; Huguette Roe | Dreamstime • 16 Willeecole | Dreamstime; Passigatti | Dreamstime • 17 General Mills | Quaker | General Mills; Ilka-erika Szasz-fabian | Dreamstime • 18 Irina Khomenko | Dreamstime; Telomato | Dreamstime; PD • 19 Subbotina | Dreamstime; www.inspirefusion.com/duck-fashion-show-australia/ • 20 Jack Dean | Dreamstime • 21 Iuliia Kovalova | Dreamstime • 22 PD | International Institute of Social History in Amsterdam, Netherlands; PD | image.toutlecine.com/photos/t/r/e/tresor-de-tarzan-1941-11-g.jpg • 23 PD | Louise Élisabeth Vigée Le Brun; Warner Bros. | Wikimedia Commons; Isselee | Dreamstime; James Kavallines | Library of Congress • 24 unknown; Danny Smythe | Dreamstime; Podius | Dreamstime; L. Adam; Mesatrooper | Wikimedia Commons • 25 Garage de l'Est | Wikimedia Commons | Wikimedia Commons; unknown • 26 betterparts.org/jaguar/jaguar-xj/jaguar-xj40.html MartinHansV | Wikimedia Commons • 27 Mauricio Jordan De Souza Coelho | Dreamstime; TIG Media | Wenn.com • 28 Andreykuzmin | Dreamstime; L. Adam; Grazvydas | Dreamstime • 29 PD | Robert Czarny • 30 PD | H.G. Wells; Robert Czarny • 31 Leonardo Páezonardo Páez | Wikimedia Commons • 32 Androniques | Dreamstime; Sacremist; Daniela Mirner Eberl | Wikimedia Commons • 33 Varsescu | Dreamstime • 34 Chris Doyle | Dreamstime; Isselee | Dreamstime; Richard Lammerts | Dreamstime • 35 Andras Deak | Dreamstime; Isselee | Dreamstime • 36 Brett Lamb | Dreamstime; Susan Law Cain | Dreamstime; Robert Pernell | Dreamstime; L. Adam • 38 Yobidaba | Dreamstime; Paul Fleet | Dreamstime; Chirag Pithadiya | Dreamstime • 39 PD; Sbukley | Dreamstime; Geopappas | Dreamstime • 40 Phil Mcdonald | Dreamstime • 41 PD | Library of Congress; PD| Library of Congress; Swisshippo | Dreamstime • 42 Dmitrii Kiselev | Dreamstime; Swisshippo | Dreamstime; WD-40; Mike_kiev | Dreamstime • 43 PD • 44 www.shockmansion.com/2013/06/14/video-the-most-dangerous-and-spectacular-motorcycle-race-ever-isle-of-man-tt-2013/ • 45 Tomas Svaton | Flickr; Lightcatcher | Dreamstime; Bflorky | Dreamstime • 46 ClubToyotaHilux | Flickr; whenonearth.net/marathon-des-sables-killer-race-sahara/ • 47 www.magraid.it/magraid/news/mauro-prosperi-sfida-olmo-a-magraid-voglio-batterlo.html and others • 48 PD | British Government; PD | Puttnam and Malindine, War Office official photographers • 49 PD; PD • 50 Helene Veilleux | DFA Pictures; Helene Veilleux | DFA Pictures; Matti Paavonen | Wikimedia Commons • 51 Johnfoto | Dreamstime; static.ddmcdn.com/gif/blogs/6a00d8341b67c53ef014e8c558fd0970d-640wi.jpg; www.fishbase.de/Photos/PicturesSummary.php?ID=16829&what=specie • 52 PD | Wikimedia Commons; Sbukley | Dreamstime; Albert Smirnov | Dreamstime • 53 Isselee | Dreamstime • 54 Koya79 | Dreamstime; Radub85 | Dreamstime; Aquariagirl1970 | Dreamstime; Hershey's | Wikimedia Commons; Boobathy | Dreamstime • 55 Sergey Shcherbakov | Dreamstime • 56 Richard

Thomas | Dreamstime; Suljo | Dreamstime • 57 Darkbird77 | Dreamstime; L. Adam • 58 Alexei Poselenov | Dreamstime; Lazar_x | Dreamstime; Alexander Raths | Dreamstime • 59 Vincent Giordano | Dreamstime; Alfonsodetomas | Dreamstime • 60 borderglider | Flickr • 61 Graham White | Flickr; PD | NASA • 62 PD; George Burba | Dreamstime • 63 unknown; PD | White House Press Office | Wikimedia Commons • 64 Photographerlondon | Dreamstime; Christian Lagereek | Dreamstime; Plutonius | Dreamstime • 65 Pictac | Dreamstime; Jerry Coli | Dreamstime; PD | unknown; • 66 Konstantin Iliev | Dreamstime • 67 L. Adam; Anne Helmenstine • 68 Roberto Fiadone and Daniel Schwen | Wikimedia Commons • 69 au.phaidon.com/agenda/design/articles/2011/october/19/everyday-icon-3-the-bic-biro/ ; Peter Emmett | Dreamstime; PD |MGM • 70 Dvmsimages | Dreamstime; PD • 71 Ginasanders | Dreamstime; Ryan Jorgensen | Dreamstime; Lucian Coman | Dreamstime • 72 PD | Wikimedia Commons; Entheta | Wikimedia Commons • 73 Petr Goskov | Dreamstime; Jacoplane | Wikimedia Commons • 74 Anja Wippich; Petr Goskov | Dreamstime; Алексиус2 | Wikimedia Commons • 75 Metro-Goldwyn-Mayer, Inc. | Wikimedia Commons; StampGirl | Dreamstime; yachtsolemates.com • 76 Paul Harvey | harv.com.au; Monkey Business Images | Dreamstime; Kileman | Dreamstime; L. Adam • 77 Paul Harvey | harv.com.au; David Finch | Marvel Comics • 78 www.treknature.com/gallery/photo264610.htm; Mohammed Anwarul Kabir Choudhury | Dreamstime • 79 Bernhard Richter | Dreamstime.co; PD • 80 RKO Radio Pictures Inc; Universal International Pictures • 81 Entheta | Wikimedia Commons; Sci-Fi Channel; Filmgroup • 82 PD | Wikimedia Commons; PD| Wikimedia Commons; PD | Napoleon Sarony; unknown; PD | Henry Robinson | Library of Congress • 83 PD | Nasa; Cafebeanz Company | Dreamstime; Skypixel | Dreamstime; Svetlana Foote | Dreamstime • 84 Jothelibrarian | Creative Commons; AFP • 85 Natursports | Dreamstime • 86 www.india.com/sports/10-weird-sports-you-have-definitely-not-heard-about-161/; Frogtravel | Dreamstime • 87 Matthew Benoit | Dreamstime; Olga Popova | Dreamstime; Clearvista | Dreamstime • 88 PD | Marshall Johnson • 89 PD; PD | Jean Leon Gerome Ferris • 90 PD | Robert_Walter_Weir • 91 Maljalen | Dreamstime; Agoxa | Dreamstime • 92 Anton Starikov | Dreamstime; spamfordpolice.blogspot.com.au/2012/11/pcc-denies-using-election-gimmick.html; Torsak | Dreamstime; L. Adam • 93 PeJo29 | Dreamstime • 94 CBS, NBC; ABC; Sbukley | Dreamstime • 95 NBC | Wikimedia Commons; L. Adam; Dynamite; Albert L. Ortega | PR Photos • 96 Aydindurdu | Dreamstime; Xi Zhang | Dreamstime; Zhang Zhenshi | Wikimedia Commons • 97 Leonardo255 | Dreamstime; Xunbin Pan | Dreamstime; Brad Calkins | Dreamstime; Tomorapan | Dreamstime; Suei Kae Wong | Dreamstime; Konstantin32 | Dreamstime • 98 Albund | Dreamstime; Pa2011 | Dreamstime • 99 www.rottentomatoes.com/celebrity/buddy_hackett/pictures/13705409/; Kaisphoto | Shutterstock • 100 Guinness World Records • 101 Guinness World Records • 102 www.nerdberd.com/2010/10/05/humpback-whale-gives-thanks-after-rescue/; Joshanon1 | Dreamstime • 104 vulkanette | Canstockphoto; Stevegeer/istockphoto • 105 PD • 106 PD • 107 PD | Bruce Bairnsfather; havanaman | Canstockphoto • 108 PD | Bruce Bairnsfather; x Blakeley | canstockphoto • 109 John Brennan | Wikimedia Commons • 110 Department of Energy and Office of Public Affairs | Wikimedia Commons; signalalpha.com • 111 Robert Zehetmayer | Dreamstime • 112 Exploratorium • 113 Exploratorium • 114 Slawek | Wikimedia Commons; unknown; Mirco Vacca | Dreamstime • 115 www.cartoonbrew.com/disney/the-swedish-holiday-obsession-with-donald-duck-19298.html; PD • 116 Rangizzz | Dreamstime; SCPixBit | Dreamstime • 117 Agrino | Dreamstime; PD | Wikimedia Commons; Valery Shanin | Dreamstime • 118 Dedmazay | Dreamstime; Ivonne Wierink | Dreamstime • 119 Steve Allen | Dreamstime; Lisa F. Young | Dreamstime • 119 Akiyoko74 | Dreamstime; Ttatty | Dreamstime • 121 R. Gino Santa Maria / Shutterfree; Llc | Dreamstime; Micahmedia | Wikimedia Commons; Sbukley | Dreamstime • 122 PD | Smithsonian Institution; Suns27 | Dreamstime • 123 Americanspirit | Dreamstime • 124 Suns27; Lewis Hine; Lewis Hine; Lewis Hine; Americanspirit | Dreamstime • 126 Olavs Silis | Dreamstime; Ljupco Smokovski | Dreamstime; Isselee | Dreamstime; L. Adam • 127 PD | Wikimedia Commons; Wangkun Jia | Dreamstime • 128 Azi Paybarah | Flickr • 129 Who's head is it anyway | Flickr; Valentyna Chukhlyebova | Dreamstime; Funky Larma | Flickr • 130 Isselee | Dreamstime • 131 Tdoes1 | Dreamstime; Lcc54613 | Dreamstime • 132 Ig0rzh | Dreamstime • 134 Eastmanphoto | Dreamstime; Victor Zastol`skiy | Dreamstime • 135 Alamy | All Canada Photos • 136 Milkovasa | Dreamstime; Ljupco Smokovski | Dreamstime • 137 Tupungato | Dreamstime • 138 New Line Cinema • 139 Batuque | Dreamstime; Nutshellz® • 140 PD | J. Malcolm Greany; vintagecameraclub.com/polaroid-photography-edwin-land/ • 141 Columbia Pictures; Warner Bros.; Paramount Pictures; Paramount Pictures • 142 Martingraf | Dreamstime; H.C. White Co. | Library of Congress; Guernsey, Lester C. | Library of Congress • 143 PD; Underwood and Underwood | Library of Congress • 144 PD • 145 PD | Wikimedia Commons; Portable Press; William Morrow and Company • 146 Paramount Classics; David Evison | Dreamstime • 147 Angela Ostafichuk | Dreamstime; Michael Zhang| Dreamstime | Wisconsinart | Dreamstime; L. Adam • 148 PD • 150 Paul Harvey | harv.com.au • 151 Paul Harvey | harv.com.au; Ssuaphoto | Dreamstime • 152 Al-capone-36 | Wikimedia Commons • 153 Giò | Wikimedia Commons; Bex | Flickr • 154 PD; blogs.cornell.edu/cuaear225/2011/05/12/the-beltane-fire-festival/ • 155 Steve Nugyen | Flickr; Steve Barnett | Flickr • 156 Maxfx | Dreamstime; Wikimedia Commons; krashco.com/ho-hey-harry-caray-remix/ • 157 Jim Greenhill | Wikimedia Commons; PD • 158 Karen Ocker; Jeff Schwartz | Wikimedia Commons • 159 Gage Skidmore | Wikimedia Commons; Matt Groening | 20th Television • 160 Napoleon Sarony; L. Adam; Gulpen | Wikimedia Commons; Gulpen | Wikimedia Commons • 161 defence.pk/threads/proposed-wwii-uk-aircraft-carrier-made-of-an-iceberg-project-habakkuk.149966 • 162 PD; freernrg.com • 163 William Garver | Modern Drunkard Magazine • 164 Kaspri | Dreamstime; Jeffrey Banke | Dreamstime • 165 Molekuul |

canstockphoto; Steve Allen | Dreamstime • 166 Colorform; PD |Bull-Doser; thegarage-blog.com/garage/actor-ricardo-montalban-passes/ • 167 Sbukley | Dreamstime; Aaron Settipane | Dreamstime • 168 Peter Jurik | Dreamstime; Amit Dave | Reuters | Picture Media • 169 www.howcast.com/videos/421421-How-to-Make-Sugar-Glass; Dpd/cdc.gov | medicalmuseum.mil/index.cfm?p=exhibits.visiblyhuman.page_07 Valarti | Dreamstime • 170 Newlight | Dreamstime; Pterwort | Dreamstime; L. Adam; Yuriy Kirsanov | Dreamstime; Metsafile | Dreamstime • 171 Vladimir Konjushenko | Dreamstime; PD; Gudkova | Dreamstime • 172 PD | PD • 173 PD | PD; • 174 PD | PD; • 175 PD; Aydindurdu | Dreamstime • 176 U-Tube; Fox • 177 web.orange.co.uk/article/quirkies/Soap_actor_dies_five_times_in_a_day; nicijazemlja.net/portal/index.php | Keith Bell | Dreamstime • 178 Vladislav Gajic | Dreamstime; Yuriy Merzlyakov | Dreamstime; Pseudolongino | Dreamstime; Silvertiger | Dreamstime • 179 Linda Bucklin | Dreamstime • 180 PD | PD | Wikimedia Commons • 181 Dave Clements | Dreamstime; Chris Curtis | Dreamstime • Irina Khomenko | Dreamstime • 182 orgemind ArchiMedia • 183 Walter G. Arce | Flickr • 184 Tony Kelley | Flickr • 185 PD; PD; Spark Museum • 186 Daderot | Wikimedia Commons • 187 Feng Yu | Dreamstime; Underwood and Underwood |Corbis • 188 PD | Emile Lassalle; Murmurer | Dreamstime • 189 PD; PD; http://goodandlos.org/2009/11/19/mammoths-and-tigers-and-bears-and-other-dead-american-giants • 190 frontiersofzoology.blogspot.com.au/2012/12/sabertooth-sightings.html; PD • 191Svetlana485 | Dreamstime; Juan Jose Tugores Gaspar | Dreamstime • 192 unsolved.com/ajaxfiles/une_frank_olson.htm | L. Adam; Lculig | Dreamstime; Vasiliy Koval | Dreamstime • 194 Henry Inman | Smithsonian National Portrait Gallery; • 195 www.aboutnorthgeorgia.com/ang/New_Echota_Walking_Tour; | Wikimedia Commons; Robfergusonjr | Wikimedia Commons • 196 Yves Herman | Reuters | Picture Media; Philipp Nicolai | Dreamstime; newslite.tv/2009/03/17/usb-finger-replaces-lost-digit.html • 197 John Black | Dreamstime; Pabkov | Dreamstime; Skypixel | Dreamstime; Senkaya | Dreamstime; L. Adam; Dimasobko | Dreamstime • 198 Bialasiewicz | Dreamstime; Bhutri | Dreamstime; Billyfoto | Dreamstime • 199 Stefaanh | Dreamstime; Andesign101 | Dreamstime • 200 Andrey Pavlov | Dreamstime; Cora Reed | Shutterstock; Isselee | Dreamstime • 201 Elena Moiseeva | Dreamstime; PD | NASA • 202 PD | Tennessee State Library and Archives| L. Adam • 203 PD | Wikimedia Commons; Library of Congress • 204 Valentyna Chukhlyebova | Dreamstime; David Luttrell • 205 Sonja Gehrke | Dreamstime • 206 Drzaribu | Dreamstime; Forensic Anthropology Center and University of Tennessee • 207 Forensic Anthropology Center and University of Tennessee; Pictac | Dreamstime • 208 Unholyvault | Dreamstime; Alanmc | Dreamstime • 209 PD | LBJ Library; flickr.com/photos/71017083@N00/ • 210 Elizabeth Shoumatoff | Wikimedia Commons; www.humanflowerproject.com/index.php/weblog/comments/lady_birds_wild_highways/ • 211 fstockfoto | Dreamstime; Onizuka | Dreamstime • 212 Keith Bell | Dreamstime; Igor Mojzes | Dreamstime • 213 Hengsheng Huang |

Wikimedia Commons; Elmer's; Olaf Speier | Dreamstime • 214 Hxdbzxy | Dreamstime; Libux77 | Dreamstime; Feng Yu | Dreamstime. Picsfive | Dreamstime; L. Adam • 215 StellaAwards.com • 216 Steve Allen | Dreamstime; Toronto Sun; tylerorsburn | flickr • 217 Mohamed Osama | Dreamstime • 218 Featureflash | Dreamstime; PD • 219 Michael Rubin | Dreamstime; PD; Lenice Harms | Dreamstime • 220 PD | Wikimedia Commons; Robert Adrian Hillman | Dreamstime; PD | PD • 221 PD | H. Charles McBarron • PD | unknown; Robert Adrian Hillman | Dreamstime • 223 National Geographic • 224 Photoraidz | Dreamstime; Lightboxx | Dreamstime; Photoeuphoria | Dreamstime; L. Adam • 225 www.lottoleaks.com/michigan-railroad-engineer-claims-337m-powerball-lottery-jackpot/ • 226 Iqoncept | Dreamstime; Thomas Crapper and Co., Ltd. • 227 Verastuchelova | Dreamstime; Robyn Mackenzie | Dreamstime • 228 Bindeshwarpathak | Wikimedia Commons; Sulabh International • 229 Sulabh International; Pee and Poo® • 230 William Perry | Dreamstime; Tony Campbell | Dreamstime; Pancaketom | Dreamstime • 231 Liquidphoto | Dreamstime; Jontimmer | Dreamstime • 232 Cpsphotos | Dreamstime • 233 Stefan Hermans | Dreamstime; Lane Erickson | Dreamstime; Les Cunliffe | Dreamstime • 234 Daboost | Dreamstime; Cathy Keifer | Dreamstime; Anita Potter | Dreamstime; Lane Erickson | Dreamstime • 235 Jha | Dreamstime; Voyagerix | Dreamstime • 236 Elena Schweitzer | Dreamstime; Michael Dykstra | Dreamstime; Marek Kosmal | Dreamstime; Ronalds Stikans | Dreamstime • 237 Rumos | Dreamstime; Teirin | Dreamstime • 238 AP; Reuters; • 239 Reuters; www.amusingplanet.com/2011/05/prison-beauty-contests.html • 240 Slobodan Djajic | Shutterstock; L. Adam; PD | NASA; Mellowbox | Dreamstime • 241 Jiri Hera | Dreamstime • 242 Jay Newman; manitowoc.org • 243 Binder donedat | Phuket Observer | Wikimedia Commons; americanfestivalsproject.net/2008/11/19/the-quiet-festival-ocean-city-nj/comment-page-1/#comment-7104 • 244 drewleavy | Wikimedia Commons • 245 PD; Greenpeace; PD • 246 Americanspirit | Dreamstime • 247 USGS | Wikimedia Commons • 248 Sue and Jay Newman • 249 Jay Newman • 250 3drenderings | Dreamstime; Brent Hathaway | Dreamstime; Chorazin3d | Dreamstime • 251 Paul Maguire | Dreamstime; Stanko07 | Dreamstime; Silviu-florin Salomia | Dreamstime; L. Adam • 252 Troscha | Dreamstime; George Stock | Wikimedia Commons • 253 Dimitar Marinov | Dreamstime • 254 Verkoka | Dreamstime; Danny Smythe | Dreamstime; PD; Youths | Dreamstime • 255 Silverchrome7/Flickr • 256 Ophelia Theatre Group | Wikimedia Commons; Original Cast; Squabbalogic • 257 Uris Theater; Freidman-Abeles | Wikimedia Commons; Sir Godfrey Kneller | Wikimedia Commons • 258 www.waymarking.com/waymarks/WM8KDZ_Ass_Hair_Salon | Narniaexpert • 259 Oleg Blazhyievskyi | Dreamstime; Penywise | Dreamstime • 260 Tribalium | Dreamstime | Rainer Plendl | Dreamstime; Raluca Tudor | Dreamstime • 261 Texelart | Dreamstime; Natursports | Dreamstime • 262 Sergio Vila | Dreamstime; Brad Calkins | Dreamstime • 263 Fritz Saalfeld | Wikimedia Commons; www.byronbear.org/funstuff1.php • 264 Igor Shootov | Dreamstime; Funniefarm5 |

Dreamstime; Chris Brignell | Dreamstime; L. Adam • 265 Andrzej Tokarski | Dreamstime; James Steidl | Dreamstime; Zsolt Bota Finna | Dreamstime • 266 unknown; Photawa | Dreamstime Frans Sluijs | Dreamstime • 267 AP • 268 Vangelis Liolios | Dreamstime; • 269 Denys Kaliuta | Dreamstime • 270 Chatchai Sangsri | Dreamstime; Markus Gann | Dreamstime; www.colorado.edu/cwa/news/2011YesMen.html • 271 Curraheeshutter | Canstockphoto • 272 Isselee | Dreamstime; Organic Nutrients™; Podius | Dreamstime • 273 WorldWide | shutterstock; Orionmystery | Dreamstime • 274 Toniflap | Dreamstime; Elista | Dreamstime; Edward Fielding | Dreamstime; Kewuwu | Dreamstime • 275 Vikas Tiwari | Dreamstime; Sbukley | Dreamstime; • 276 Benis Arapovic | Dreamstime; PD | Napoleon Sarony • 277 Kornilovdream | Dreamstime; unknown • 278 Washington Post • 279 Bösendorfer • 280 Helder Almeida | Dreamstime; Adamsl | Dreamstime

Backgrounds: Peter Jurik | Dreamstime; Clearviewstock | Dreamstime; Mariusz Blach | Dreamstime; Karuppasamy .g | Dreamstime; Elena Schweitzer | Dreamstime; Rumos | Dreamstime; Sebastlan | Dreamstime; Steve Stedman | Dreamstime; Lepas | Dreamstime; Konart | Dreamstime; Prillfoto | Dreamstime; Gualtiero Boffi | Dreamstime; Anthonycz | Dreamstime; Suns27 | Dreamstime; Robert Adrian Hillman | Dreamstime; Elen | Dreamstime; Huguette Roe | Dreamstime; Konart | Dreamstime; Ivan Cholakov | Dreamstime; PixelParticle | Dreamstime; Chatchai Somwat | Dreamstime; David M. Schrader | Dreamstime; Torsak | Dreamstime; Humbak | Dreamstime; Cia Pix | Dreamstime; Huguette Roe | Dreamstime; Eutoch | Dreamstime

Music notes: Viktor Kunz | Dreamstime; Adamsl | Dreamstime; Valeriy Kirsanov | Dreamstime; Dannyphoto80 | Dreamstime

Bats: Markus Gann | Dreamstime; Kruglovorda | Dreamstime

Speech bubbles: Svetlana Shirokova | Dreamstime

Duckies: Andre Adams | Dreamstime; Flynt | Dreamstime; Albund | Dreamstime; Andreblais | Dreamstime; Brightdawn | Dreamstime; Dana Rothstein | Dreamstime

Answers

Pop Music Anagrams (page 37)

1. Mariah Carey, **2.** Loverboy, **3.** Justin Timberlake, **4.** Def Leppard, **5.** Oasis, **6.** Kanye West, **7.** Mariah Carey, **8.** Mary J. Blige, **9.** Snoop Dog, **10.** Kylie Minogue, **11.** Morrissey, **12.** The Beatles, **13.** Foo Fighters, **14.** Elvis Presley, **15.** Dolly Parton

Ol' Jay's Brainteasers (page 135)

1. HUNGRY BOOKWORM. The bookworm only eats through 2½ inches of book. That's because he started at page 1 of the book on the left (which is facing the right side) and only has to eat through the front cover of book 1, the back cover of book 2, all of the pages of book 2, then through the front cover of book 2, then through the back cover of book 3. At that point he will have reached the last page of book 3 and can stop eating.

2. THE 5TH CONDITION. The person must also be elected.

3. SURROUNDED. Trina will just have to wait until the merry-go-round ride ends…and then dismount.

4. BUILDER BLUNDER. The house address numbers were missing. Each number cost $1.00. So 1000 would have cost $4.00, and 50 would have cost $2.00. But since their new neighborhood only had nine houses, their addresses were each a single number, costing them a total of only $3.00.

Ol' Jay's Brainteasers (page 253)

1. THE RUNAROUND. One-eff Jef ran around the chair twice and then said, "I'll be back in a week to run around it a third time," knowing that Two-eff Jeff wouldn't be able to sit there for an entire week.

2. FEELING FLAT. The flat tire was Thom's spare tire—in his trunk the whole time.

3. A MOTHER'S GIFT. Coal. It starts out black, but becomes a diamond in the rough after Mother Earth "smothers" it for a few million years.

4. COFFEE DELIVERY. Kim filled the three-gallon bucket with coffee and then poured it into the five-gallon bucket. Then she filled the three-gallon bucket again and carefully poured it into the five-gallon bucket until it was full, leaving exactly one gallon of coffee in the three-gallon bucket. And then we had coffee!

The Last Page

Fellow Trivia Hounds:

The fight for good bathroom reading should never be taken loosely—
we must do our duty and sit firmly for what we believe in,
even while the rest of the world is taking potshots at us.

We'll be brief. Now that we've proven we're not simply a
flush-in-the-pan, we invite you to take the plunge:

Sit Down and Be Counted! Log on to *www.bathroomreader.com*
and earn a permanent spot on the BRI honor roll!

If you like reading our books...

VISIT THE BRI'S WEBSITE!

www.bathroomreader.com

- Receive our irregular newsletters via e-mail
- Order additional *Bathroom Readers*
- Like us on Facebook
- Tweet us on Twitter
- Blog us on our blog

Go with the Flow...

Well, we're out of space, and when you've gotta go,
you've gotta go. Thanks for all your support.
Hope to hear from you soon.
Meanwhile, remember...

KEEP ON FLUSHIN'!